I0315238

Trajectories in Near Eastern Apocalyptic

Society of Biblical Literature

Resources for Biblical Study

Series Editors
Susan Ackerman
Old Testament/Hebrew Bible

J. Ross Wagner
New Testament

Number 45
TRAJECTORIES IN NEAR EASTERN APOCALYPTIC

Trajectories in Near Eastern Apocalyptic

A Postrabbinic Jewish Apocalypse Reader

John C. Reeves

Society of Biblical Literature
Atlanta

The EEstrangelo, Semitica, and Symbol Greek fonts used in this work are available from Linguist Software (www.linguist software.com), 425-775-1130.

Library of Congress Cataloging-in-Publication Data

Reeves, John C.
Trajectories in Near Eastern apocalyptic : a postrabbinic Jewish apocalypse reader / by John C. Reeves.
p. cm. — (Resources for biblical study ; no. 45)
Includes bibliographical references and index.
ISBN-13: 978-1-58983-102-5 (paper binding : alk. paper)
ISBN-10: 1-58983-102-0 (paper binding : alk. paper)
1. Apocalyptic literature—History and criticism. 2. Eschatology, Jewish. 3. Apocalyptic literature—Translations into English. 4. Judaism—History—Medieval and early modern period, 425-1789—Sources. I. Title. II. Series.

BS1705.R44 2005
296.1'5—dc22

2005015830

13 12 11 10 09 08 07 06 05   5 4 3 2 1
Printed in the United States of America on acid-free, recycled paper conforming to ANSI/NISO Z39.48-1992 (R1997) and ISO 9706:1994 standards for paper permanence.

Contents

PREFACE AND ACKNOWLEDGMENTS vii
ABBREVIATIONS xi
INTRODUCTION 1

A Gallery of Jewish Apocalypses

1. *Sefer Elijah* 29
2. *Sefer Zerubbabel* 40
3. *Pirqe de R. Eliezer* §30 (end) 67
4. R. Šimʿōn b. Yoḥai Complex 76
    The Secrets of R. Šimʿōn b. Yoḥai 76
    The Prayer of R. Šimʿōn b. Yoḥai 89
5. Apocalypses Featuring "Ten Signs" (עשר אותות) 106
    ʾOtot of R. Šimʿōn b. Yoḥai 111
    Ten Signs 116
    ʾOtot Ha-Mašiaḥ (Signs of the Messiah) 121
    Ten Further Things Pertaining to the Days of the Messiah 130
6. Responsum of R. Hai Gaon on Redemption 133
7. *ʾAggadat ha-Mašiaḥ* 144
8. *Pirqe Mašiaḥ* 149
9. *Midrash Wa-Yoshaʿ* (end) 172

Thematic Excursuses

1. Metatron as Apocalyptic Persona 179
2. The Eschatological Appearance of the Staff of Moses 187
3. The "People of Moses" (בני משה) 200

BIBLIOGRAPHY 225
INDICES 245

Preface and Acknowledgments

In contemplating this work my original intent was to assemble an annotated English-language anthology of the influential apocalyptic compositions produced in the Near East by Jews, Christians, certain dualist groups, and Muslims over roughly the second half of the first millennium of the Common Era. This ambitious plan I inevitably but reluctantly had to surrender: the immense quantity of primary source materials—much of it still unpublished or largely inaccessible to many modern scholars—which would require close examination and comparative analysis was far too massive to handle responsibly within a single-volume format. This constrictive circumstance led me to narrow the book's scope to a more cohesive group of works; namely, the fascinating corpus of apocalyptic texts and traditions generated within Near Eastern Jewish scribal circles during late antiquity and the early Middle Ages.

I had initially sounded several of these texts while still a graduate student, nurtured then by a budding interest in what seemed to be the occurrence of verbal and thematic traces of Hellenistic and Roman-era pseudepigrapha like *Jubilees* and *1 Enoch* among postrabbinic midrashic and mystical works. Although I found little in these particular apocalyptic texts to advance that peculiar interest, I did discover that they supplied heretofore unappreciated evidence about the rhetorical uses of a sacred scripture and that category's rise to ideological dominance in a wide variety of late antique Near Eastern religions. These apocalypses provide invaluable testimony for the unpacking of some of the historical and social factors that nourished the notion of a "textual authority," a concept whose illuminative force is best appreciated in the light of the increasingly competitive and eventually combative relationship that emerged among the different "scriptures" of Judaism, Christianity, Manichaeism, Zoroastrianism, and Islam.

There are some regrettable gaps in this volume's presentation of the Jewish apocalyptic tradition. Perhaps the most significant of these is my conscious decision to exclude (at least for the present) two later texts associated with the biblical character Daniel; namely, the works known as *Ḥazon Daniel* and *Maʿaseh Daniel.* Each of these medieval Jewish compositions, largely ignored by contemporary scholarship, requires fresh study in the light of our present understanding of the history of Jewish life in Byzantium and Iran respectively. The canonical book that bears the name of Daniel exerted an enormous influence on the subsequent evolution of both Jewish and Christian eschatological literature during the Roman era. Daniel's reputation as a privileged seer of heavenly mysteries and a trustworthy prognosticator of earthly events made his figure a hugely popular one among the later Jewish, Christian, and Muslim traditionists and pseudepigraphers who were active within the Byzantine and Islamicate cultural orbits. A large number of allegedly Danielic "works" have been identified by bibliographers and manuscript catalogers, but only a small portion of this multilingual and interconfessional corpus has been published to date. To do proper justice to this specific trajectory of apocalyptic thought would entail (it seemed to me) yet another book-length study, a task I must postpone to another time.

Another theme worthy of deeper exploration involves the unpacking of the relationship of the apocalyptic mentality discussed herein to some of the disturbingly analogous formulations found among certain sectarian movements that arose within Islamicate Jewry, including most preeminently Karaism. The "scripturalist" orientation characteristic of both Karaite Judaism and these post-rabbinic apocalypses is simply a single instance of a lengthier series of possible social and conceptual interstices which merit a closer examination. The commentaries, treatises, and apologies produced by the early generations of Karaite ideologues throw the eschatological dimensions of Karaite hermeneutics and praxis into bold relief, and I suspect closer attention to the correspondences between the Karaite and postrabbinic apocalypses would yield significant rewards.

A final theme that warrants a more expansive treatment than I have been able to accomplish here involves a thorough examination of the intellectual and social dimensions of the complex conceptual and literary relationships which recognizably exist between apocalyptic texts like those discussed herein and those works comprising the roughly contemporary corpus of Jewish revelatory texts known as *Hekhalot* or mystical literature. The short excursus on the angelic figure of Metatron makes a feeble attempt to call attention to a few of these issues. Several scholars (e.g., Joseph Dan, Moshe Idel, Ithamar Gruenwald, Martha Himmelfarb) have remarked on and continue to probe various aspects of this general nexus, but it is the tip of a very large iceberg, and there is certainly much more that can be done in this area.

Despite these shortcomings, it is my hope that the present work will still prove useful to scholars and students of the history of Jewish literature in late antiquity and the early Middle Ages. I truly appreciate the patient forbearance displayed by Bob Buller and the editorial staff at the Society of Biblical Literature over the course of their lengthy wait for the completion of this volume. I am profoundly grateful to Mr. Herman Blumenthal (ז"ל) and the Blumenthal Foundation for their generous financial support of the Jewish studies curriculum and my research efforts at the University of North Carolina, Charlotte. Finally, I would also like to acknowledge the following academic institutions which have graciously granted me permission to cite brief passages and/or translations from their unpublished manuscript holdings: the Bodleian Library of the University of Oxford; the Klau Library, Cincinnati of Hebrew-Union College-Jewish Institute of Religion; and the Syndics of the Cambridge University Library at the University of Cambridge.

JOHN C. REEVES
UNIVERSITY OF NORTH CAROLINA, CHARLOTTE

Abbreviations

Primary Sources

ʿAbod. Zar.	*ʿAvodah Zarah*
ʾAbot R. Nat.	*ʾAvot de Rabbi Nathan*
Ant.	Josephus, *Jewish Antiquities*
Apoc. Abr.	*Apocalypse of Abraham*
Apoc. El. (C)	Coptic *Apocalypse of Elijah*
Apoc. Paul	*Apocalypse of Paul*
Apoc. Ps-Ephrem	*Syriac Pseudo-Ephrem Apocalypse*
Apoc. Ps-Meth.	*Syriac Apocalypse of Pseudo-Methodius*
As. Mos.	*Assumption of Moses*
b.	Babylonian Talmud (Bavli)
B. Bat.	*Baba Batra*
B.J.	Josephus, *Bellum judaicum*
B. Meṣiʿa	*Baba Meṣiʿa*
B. Qam.	*Baba Qamma*
2 Bar.	*2 Baruch (Syriac Apocalypse)*
Ber.	*Berakhot*
Cant. Rab.	*Canticles Rabbah*
CD	Cairo *Damascus Document*
CMC	*Cologne Mani Codex*
ʿEd.	*ʿEduyyot*
1 En.	*1 Enoch* (Ethiopic Book of Enoch)
2 En.	*2 Enoch* (Slavonic Book of Enoch)
ʿErub.	*ʿEruvin*
Exod. Rab.	*Exodus Rabbah*
Frg. Tg.	*Fragmentary Targum*
Gen. Rab.	*Genesis Rabbah*
Ḥag.	*Ḥagigah*
HUC	Hebrew Union College
Ḥul.	*Ḥullin*
Jub.	*Jubilees*

Ketub.	*Ketubbot*
L.A.B.	*Liber antiquitatum biblicarum* (Pseudo-Philo)
Lam. Rab.	*Lamentations Rabbah*
Lev. Rab.	*Leviticus Rabbah*
Liv. Pro.	*Lives of the Prophets (Vitae Prophetarum)*
m.	Mishnah
Maᶜaś. Š.	*Maᶜaser Sheni*
Mak.	*Makkot*
Meg.	*Megillah*
Meᶜil.	*Meᶜilah*
Mek.	*Mekhilta*
Menaḥ.	*Menaḥot*
Midr. Tanḥ.	*Midrash Tanḥuma*
Midr. Tanḥ. Buber	*Midrash Tanḥuma* (ed. S. Buber)
Midr. Teh.	*Midrash Tehillim*
Ms.	Manuscript
Naz.	*Nazir*
Ned.	*Nedarim*
Num. Rab.	*Numbers Rabbah*
Pesaḥ.	*Pesaḥim*
Pesiq. Rab.	*Pesiqta Rabbati*
Pesiq. Rab Kah.	*Pesiqta de Rab Kahana*
Pirqe R. El.	*Pirqe de Rabbi Eliezer*
Prot. Jas.	*Protevangelium of James*
Pss. Sol.	*Psalms of Solomon*
Q	Qurʾān
1Qap Gen^{ar}	*Genesis Apocryphon*
Qidd.	*Qiddushin*
1QIsa^{a}	Qumran Isaiah^{a} scroll
1QM	Qumran *War Scroll*
11QMelch	Qumran *Melchizedek*
1QpHab	*Pesher Habakkuk*
Qoh. Rab.	*Qohelet Rabbah*
1QSb	*Rule of the Blessings* (Appendix b to 1QS)
Roš. Haš.	*Rosh HaShanah*
S. Eli. Zut.	*Seder Eliyahu Zuta*
S. ᶜOlam Rab.	*Seder ᶜOlam Rabbah*
Sanh.	*Sanhedrin*
Šabb.	*Shabbat*
Šeb.	*Sheviᶜit*
Šeqal.	*Sheqalim*

Sib. Or.	*Sibylline Oracles*
Sukk.	*Sukkah*
t.	Tosefta
T. Jud.	*Testament of Judah*
T. Levi	*Testament of Levi*
T-S	Taylor-Schechter
Taʿan.	*Taʿanit*
Tg.	Targum
Tg. Ket.	*Targum Ketuvim* (Writings)
Tg. Neb.	*Targum Neviʾim* (Prophets)
Tg. Onk.	*Targum Onkelos*
Tg. Ps.-J.	*Targum Pseudo-Jonathan*
Tg. Tosefta	targumic supplement
y.	Palestinian Talmud (Yerushalmi)
Yal. Šim.	*Yalquṭ Šimoni*
Yebam.	*Yebamot*
Zebaḥ.	*Zebaḥim*

Secondary Sources

AGJU	Arbeiten zur Geschichte des antiken Judentums und des Urchristentums
AJSR	*Association for Jewish Studies Review*
Aug	*Augustinianum*
Beck	Pages 60–71 (lines 1–557) of *Des heiligen Ephraem des Syrers Sermones III*. Edited by Edmund Beck. CSCO 320, scrip. syri 138. Louvain: Secrétariat du Corpus SCO, 1972.
BHM	*Bet ha-Midrasch: Sammlung kleiner Midraschim und vermischter Abhandlungen aus der jüdischen Literatur.* Edited by Adolph Jellinek. 6 vols. Leipzig, 1853–77; repr., Jerusalem: Bamberger & Wahrmann, 1938.
BJS	Brown Judaic Studies
BSOAS	*Bulletin of the School of Oriental and African Studies*
CH	*Church History*
CP	*Classical Philology*
CRINT	Compendia rerum iudaicarum ad Novum Testamentum
CSCO	Corpus scriptorum christianorum orientalium

CSEL	Corpus scriptorum ecclesiasticorum latinorum
DJD	Discoveries in the Judaean Desert
EI[2]	*The Encyclopaedia of Islam.* New edition. 12 vols. Leiden: Brill, 1954–2002.
EncJud	*Encyclopaedia Judaica.* 16 vols. Jerusalem: Keter, 1971.
EncQur	*Encyclopaedia of the Qurʾān.* Edited by Jane Dammen McAuliffe. Leiden: Brill, 2001–.
Finkelstein	*Sifre Devarim.* Edited by Louis Finkelstein. Repr., New York: Jewish Theological Seminary, 1969.
GCS	Die griechische christliche Schriftsteller der ersten [drei] Jahrhunderte
GRBS	*Greek, Roman, and Byzantine Studies*
Hen	*Henoch*
Horovitz	*Sifre de-bey Rav . . . Sifre ʿal Sefer Bemidbar.* Edited by H. S. Horovitz. Repr., Jerusalem: Wahrmann, 1966.
Horovitz-Rabin	*Mekhilta de-Rabbi Yishmael.* Edited by H. S. Horovitz and I. A. Rabin. Repr., Jerusalem: Wahrmann, 1970.
HSM	Harvard Semitic Monographs
HTR	*Harvard Theological Review*
HUCA	*Hebrew Union College Annual*
IOS	*Israel Oriental Studies*
Ish-Shalom (Friedmann)	*Midrash Pesiqta Rabbati.* Edited by Meir Ish-Shalom (Friedmann). Vienna: Joseph Kaiser, 1880.
JAOS	*Journal of the American Oriental Society*
JE	*The Jewish Encyclopedia.* Edited by Isidore Singer. 12 vols. New York and London: Funk & Wagnalls, 1901-06.
JJS	*Journal of Jewish Studies*
JNES	*Journal of Near Eastern Studies*
JQR	*Jewish Quarterly Review*
JSAI	*Jerusalem Studies in Arabic and Islam*
JSJ	*Journal for the Study of Judaism in the Persian, Hellenistic, and Roman Periods*
JSOTSup	Journal for the Study of the Old Testament: Supplement Series
JSQ	*Jewish Studies Quarterly*
JSS	*Journal of Semitic Studies*
JTS	*Journal of Theological Studies*
LCL	Loeb Classical Library

Lieberman	*The Tosefta: According to Codex Vienna, With Variants....* Edited by Saul Lieberman. 2d ed. 4 vols. Repr., New York: Jewish Theological Seminary, 1988-95.
Luria	*Sefer Pirqey Rabbi Eliezer ha-Gadol.* Edited by David Luria. Warsaw, 1852; repr., Jerusalem: [n.p.], 1970.
Mandelbaum	*Pesiqta de Rav Kahana.* Edited by Bernard Mandelbaum. 2d ed. 2 vols. New York: Jewish Theological Seminary, 1987.
Margulies	*Midrash Wayyikra Rabbah.* Edited by Mordecai Margulies. 2 vols. Repr., New York: Jewish Theological Seminary, 1993.
MGWJ	*Monatschrift für Geschichte und Wissenschaft des Judentums*
NHMS	Nag Hammadi and Manichaean Studies
OCP	*Orientalia christiana periodica*
OrChrAn	Orientalia christiana analecta
OTP	*Old Testament Pseudepigrapha.* Edited by James H. Charlesworth. 2 vols. Garden City, N.Y.: Doubleday, 1983–85.
PAAJR	*Proceedings of the American Academy for Jewish Research*
Reinink	*Die syrische Apokalypse des Pseudo-Methodius.* Edited by G. J. Reinink. 2 vols. CSCO 540–541, scrip. syri 220-221. Louvain: E. Peeters, 1993.
REJ	*Revue des études juives*
SAC	Studies in Antiquity and Christianity
SBLEJL	Society of Biblical Literature Early Judaism and Its Literature
SBLTT	Society of Biblical Literature Texts and Translations
Schäfer	*Synopse zur Hekhalot-Literatur.* Edited by Peter Schäfer. TSAJ 2. Tübingen: J. C. B. Mohr, 1981.
Schechter	*Massekhet Avot de-Rabbi Natan.* Edited by Solomon Schechter. Vienna: Ch. D. Lippe, 1887.
ScrHier	Scripta hierosolymitana
Ṭabarī, *Taʾrīkh*	*Taʾrīkh al-rusul waʾl-mulūk.* Edited by M. J. de Goeje et al. 15 vols. Leiden: Brill, 1879–1901.
Theodor-Albeck	*Midrash Bereshit Rabba.* Edited by J. Theodor and Ḥ. Albeck. 3 vols. Repr., Jerusalem: Wahrmann, 1965.
TSAJ	Texte und Studien zum antiken Judentum

Weiss	*Sifra de-bey Rav: hu' sefer Torat Kohanim*. Edited by I. H. Weiss. Repr., New York: Om, 1946.
WUNT	Wissenschaftliche Untersuchungen zum Neuen Testament
ZA	*Zeitschrift für Assyriologie*
ZDMG	*Zeitschrift der deutschen morgenländischen Gesellschaft*
Zuckermandel	*Tosephta, Based on the Erfurt and Vienna Codices.* Edited by M. S. Zuckermandel. New edition. Jerusalem: Wahrmann Books, 1970.

Introduction

THE "APOCALYPTIC IMAGINATION," to lift a useful rubric given currency by John J. Collins,[1] is an incredibly fluid and fertile mentality. Usually but mistakenly confined by modern biblical scholars to marginalized groups of Jewish nationalists and Christian triumphalists resident in or contiguous to Eretz Israel during the two or three centuries surrounding the Roman sack of Jerusalem, it actually operates more or less continuously within the broader ethnic or religious frameworks of the wider Near East, and it surges during those centuries which most historians identify as marking the gradual transition from late antiquity to the early medieval era. During the seventh and following centuries of the Common Era, a number of Jewish, Christian, dualist, and Muslim circles revel in what they perceive to be a deliberately scripted concatenation of natural disasters, military campaigns, historical crises, and oracular utterances. Their collation produced a massive corpus of linguistically diverse yet thematically interlocked narrative emplotments of the episodes and characters whose historical manifestations allegedly signal the triumph of their respective political and religious interests amidst the final days of the present terrestrial order.

Figured as a mentality, the apocalyptic mode of thought is not sterile. It is relentlessly reactive and generative, since by definition it is set in motion by processes whose grounding and authority lie beyond the natural world. The notion of *apokalypsis* signifies an act whereby something previously unknown and which cannot be generated by normal means of research or ratiocination is suddenly uncovered, literally unveiled, for the mind of a percipient. The preeminent characteristic of apocalyptic thought and its concrete realization in discourse—the verbal expression of such thought—is thus its *revelatory* basis, its claim to a certainty or set of truths that are immune from the erosive forces of social domination and corruption, material poverty, and philosophical skepticism. Possessing an unimpeachable authority and intellectual significance, it often forces its conceptual articulation among a wider audience by exploiting those favored vehicles of communication with which a culture expresses its constitutive identity, values,

[1] John J. Collins, *The Apocalyptic Imagination: An Introduction to Jewish Apocalyptic Literature* (2d ed.; Grand Rapids: Eerdmans, 1998).

and aspirations. In the centuries prior to and encompassing the coming of Rome, there were a number of ways in which this task could be and was accomplished; for example, through royal or societal elite proclamation and epigraphic commemoration, behavioral mimesis, oracular pronouncement, figurative illustration, written composition, or oral catechesis of apprentices, students, disciples, or neophytes. For the Abrahamic religious communities of Near Eastern late antiquity, the vehicle par excellence for such dissemination would be the sacred writing or book.

The type of knowledge that is communicated in apocalyptic writings is fundamentally esoteric: its content, character, and essential qualities lie concealed from most members of the social order and rely for their wider dissemination on the willingness of those privileged to receive such knowledge to share it with a broader public. The notion of "privilege" is in fact a key one, since an initial—or what is represented as an exclusive—access to this otherworldly wisdom distinguishes both the producer and the producer's circle of consumers as enjoying the special favor of the deity. Explicit restrictions regarding publication or popular access are occasionally asserted in apocalyptic texts, but this element is certainly a rhetorical ploy that had no practical implementation, for the warnings actually function as a sign to later readers that they, like the author, could be counted among the elect of God.[2] The structures of apocalyptic thought and discourse are thus consonant, as David Frankfurter has insightfully observed, with the conceptual and literary conventions employed in gnostic forms of religiosity.[3] Gnosis might even be arguably viewed as the dominant category for Near Eastern apocalypticism, for it necessarily expands the dimensional field of revealed information to include matters pertaining to cosmology, uranography, angelology, physical science, anthropogony, historiosophy, and eschatology. This is a welcome hermeneutical development inasmuch as apocalyptic thought is often confined by modern scholars to the articulation of speculative or symbolic scenarios about what will supposedly transpire at the end of time. While some or even most of the revealed information might focus on an outline of future events and cosmic woes, it need not do so. The critical criterion is the supernatural mediation of a definitive knowledge—a knowledge, moreover, that permits a properly nuanced evaluation of the larger forces and tensions at work in the contemporary social order. Apocalyptic therefore cannot be simply equated or conflated with literary compositions that discuss the "last days" or the eschaton.

Many students of apocalyptic texts, perhaps even the vast majority, situate their genesis and their perennial appeal within a localized malaise or disillusion

[2] E.g., Dan 12:4, 9–13; *4 Ezra* 12:36–38; 14:44–48.

[3] David Frankfurter, "The Legacy of Jewish Apocalypses in Early Christianity: Regional Trajectories," in *The Jewish Apocalyptic Heritage in Early Christianity* (ed. James C. VanderKam and William Adler; CRINT 3.4; Assen: Van Gorcum; Minneapolis: Fortress, 1996), 150–62.

spawned by the social and historical realities of cultural oppression and subjection. According to this view, social or ethnic persecution and national crisis supply the soil from which apocalyptic springs, and apocalyptic texts are thus reduced to a type of "resistance literature."[4] This regrettable interpretative tendency emerges all too readily from an overly insular reading of early Jewish and Christian apocalypses, which limits their production and appeal to marginalized "sects" or disenfranchised "minority" groups in opposition to the dominant power structures. There is no clear evidence that compels acceptance of apocalyptic as a genre of literary expression that was cultivated exclusively by dissidents, and there is some evidence that speaks against such a simplistic reduction. While some apocalypses admittedly do breathe an atmosphere of factional or cultural hostility,[5] there are others that are designed as vehicles for communicating the material and hence ideological supremacy of the ruling powers. Emperors and caliphs could manipulate and wield the language and imagery of apocalyptic as adroitly as the learned scribe or sage.

Entre écriture et apocalypse?

Gilbert Dagron subtitled his important survey of the tense relations between Jews and Christians in the East during the first half of the seventh century "Entre histoire et apocalypse."[6] His dialectical pairing of the terms "history" and "apocalyptic" illustrates the tyranny of an unexamined premise that underlies almost all modern study of apocalyptic texts; namely, that apocalypses can be read most profitably as a species of historiography. References to battles, the naming of rulers, cities, or nations, cryptic descriptions of the rise and fall of certain figures, and numerical counting formulas are to be read as direct reflections of the author's historical context and concerns, and can thus be utilized as empirical evidence for establishing the putative chronological and geographic provenance of a given work. This largely reflexive type of exegesis is very popular among modern scholars who devote themselves to the study and interpretation of apocalyptic literature, and its results are often used as determinatives for reconstructing the his-

[4] E.g., Averil Cameron and Lawrence I. Conrad, "Introduction," in *The Byzantine and Early Islamic Near East, I: Problems in the Literary Source Material* (ed. Averil Cameron and Lawrence I. Conrad; Princeton: Darwin Press, 1992), 21–22. See the important critique of the influential ideas of Philip Vielhauer (among others) relative to early Christian apocalypticism supplied by William Adler, "Introduction," in *Jewish Apocalyptic Heritage*, 3–8.

[5] Hence John Wansbrough's characterization of apocalyptic as a "type of polemical literature"; see his *The Sectarian Milieu: Content and Composition of Islamic Salvation History* (Oxford: Oxford University Press, 1978), 115–16.

[6] Gilbert Dagron, "Introduction historique: Entre histoire et apocalypse," *Travaux et mémoires* 11 (1991): 17–46.

tory of the transmission of particular texts, smaller constituent units of texts, or even the structural conventions and motifs employed by the texts. On the face of it, as presented, there seems little about this strategy with which one need quarrel. Apocalyptic texts, like all cultural products, are artifacts integrally embedded within their material circumstances, and so one might legitimately expect to discern the reverberations of past and current events within the linguistic coding of the inscribed page. Moreover, the dizzying sequence of political transition and change in the Near East during the first half of the seventh century—the rapid Sasanian conquest and roughly two-decade-long subjection of Christian Syria, Palestine, and Egypt, abetted by the partisan unrest in Constantinople and Asia Minor surrounding the violent accessions of Phokas (602) and Heraclius (610); a suddenly resurgent Byzantine *reconquista* culminating in the triumphant march of Heraclius into Jerusalem (630), but which in turn was almost immediately trumped by the humiliating rout of both Byzantines and Sasanians before the Muslim onslaught beginning around 632; and the swift destruction of the Sasanian empire and the effective expulsion of Byzantine hegemony from the Near East—must have impressed many contemporaries as ominously close to programmed schemes of social and religious turmoil as sketched by scriptural sources like the biblical book of Daniel and its Christian imitators. It would be foolish to deny that historical events play a role in the construction of apocalypses. There are verifiable reasons why Rome bears the moniker of "the evil empire" (המלכות הרשעה) or why a particular Arab ruler might be described as a "friend of Israel" (אוהב ישראל) or as "one who waged war on the descendants of Esau" (עושה מלחמה עם בני עשו). Oppression, hardship, and perseverance under adverse circumstances were the tangible conditions of life for Jews under both Christian and Muslim rule, and being one of the approved cultural expressions of those experiences (among others), apocalyptic literature reflects the emotional peaks and valleys engendered by the seemingly hostile forces of history.

Nevertheless, and in spite of the observations just expressed, it is imperative that greater care to be taken in order to avoid the practice of reading the language of an apocalypse as if it were simply supplying descriptive "facts" about the milieu from which it emerges. The product of the apocalyptic imagination when it is exercised within and for the sake of a literate milieu is a specific type of written narrative that employs a distinctively *formulaic* set of conventions, tropes, and figures. Central to the argument of the present essay, and indeed to the larger work it serves to introduce, is the notion that late antique Near Eastern apocalyptic literature is most properly understood when it is framed as a closed *textual* universe of discourse. Apocalyptic texts of this period, whether produced by Jews, Christians, or Muslims, feature a distinctive phonology, vocabulary, and syntax that, while retaining certain dialectical variations, are still easily recognizable as a discrete *langue*. The basic structural undercarriage of this particular grammar of linguistic markers and signs is not the linear march of time and the fluctuating events that fill it, but rather the relatively stable verbal expression of what was widely perceived within discrete religious communities as a uniquely authoritative revelation of the deity. In other words, sacred scripture (*écriture*) supplies both the raw material and the ultimate rationale for the conceptual elaboration of late antique Near Eastern apocalyptic.

Fluency in this particular mode of discourse would seem to presuppose the notion of a fixed scriptural canon, an authoritative collection of writings codifying the central myths, practices, and values of a religious community. It is probably not coincidental that the growing popularity of apocalyptic books within Near Eastern religions is roughly synchronous with the emerging dominance of written texts among polytheist, dualist, and monotheist forms of religiosity in late antiquity. During the early centuries of the Common Era, the favored means of the authoritative transmission of core teachings or truths gradually but inexorably shifts in Judaism, Christianity, Zoroastrianism, and diverse pagan currents from orality to textuality and from the spoken word to the immutable book. Such books, whether stemming from a Sibylline oracle or the God of Abraham, are the visible and enduring precipitate of an encounter between an inspired seer or prophet and the divine world. One might term this development a "textualizing of authority." The veracity or the trustworthiness of particular teachers or doctrines became tied to "scriptural" registration, preferably one that located the archetype of the scripture in heaven itself. As the authority of written scripture waxed, a spectrum of interpretive readings and exegetical teachings grew up around the sacred text in order to provide guidance regarding communally endorsed meanings—Zand, midrash, commentaries—and those parascriptural expressions that were most widely endorsed also eventually achieved written form.

This seismic shift in the understanding of the cultural locale of authority becomes most readily apparent when one compares the form and structure of the early Jewish apocalypses authored during the Hellenistic and Roman imperial periods to those produced approximately half a millennium later during the turbulent transition from Sasanian and Byzantine to Muslim rule. Works like Daniel, *1 Enoch*, the Qumran *War Scroll*, or *4 Ezra* rarely cite or even refer to the biblical text. Several scholars have made the point that these early apocalypses are largely self-authenticating: the revelatory event itself supplies the necessary validation for the information that is revealed to the seer or prophet.[7] The angel who appears to the seer embodies divine speech, an equation that is glaringly apparent in the proto-apocalyptic visions of Zechariah where the angelic intermediary will eerily and suddenly metamorphose into the deity himself. Neither God nor the angel appeals to scripture to bolster or supplement their cause. By contrast, later Jewish

[7] Adler, "Introduction," 19–21; see also Michael E. Stone, "Apocalyptic Literature," in *Jewish Writings of the Second Temple Period: Apocrypha, Pseudepigrapha, Qumran Sectarian Writings, Philo, Josephus* (ed. Michael E. Stone; CRINT 2.2; Assen: Van Gorcum; Philadelphia: Fortress, 1984), 428–29.

apocalyptic works like *Sefer Zerubbabel* or the *Nistarot* (*Secrets*) *of R. Šimʿōn ben Yoḥai* are thoroughly awash with scriptural diction and citation. The revealing agent, who in both of these instances is identified as the angel Metatron—an entity whose supernal credentials and status in Jewish mystical literature are functionally equivalent to that of God himself—defers to the Bible as the paramount authority to which all external circumstances are subservient. In the Jewish apocalyptic mentality of late antiquity, written scripture becomes the source of revelation. It acts as a surrogate for the Divine Revealer who once spoke and brought the universe into being.[8]

This enhanced role for the Bible in the perception, mapping, and reading of mundane events is not limited to Jewish contexts. It indeed is quite visible within all those religious communities that align themselves among the heirs of the Abrahamic legacy, including most importantly those who eventually coalesce under the banner of the radically monotheist religious movement that became Islam. Biblical characters, narratives, or conceptual complexes figure in almost every page of the Qurʾān, and early traditionists like Kaʿb al-Aḥbār (d. 656) and Wahb b. Munabbih (d. ca. 728) furnished nascent Islam with a rich assemblage of parascriptural interpretative materials. The interest shown by the Prophet and the initial caliphs in Jerusalem and its *sancta* underscores the esteem with which early Islam invested the terrestrial location of the earlier *scriptural* revelations associated with Abraham, Moses, and Jesus. Subsequent textualizing of the Prophet's revelation in scriptural form, whatever the precise historical lineaments of that process, cemented its authority and simultaneously aligned its discourse with and distinguished it from that of the earlier scriptures.

What has been up to now largely unappreciated is the crucial role that the Bible, as opposed to the Qurʾān, plays in the early Muslim appropriation of an apocalyptic discourse. However, according to Uri Rubin, early Muslim collections of hagiographic and didactic sources "seem to indicate that Muslim reliance on the Bible began much earlier than is usually assumed by Islamicists"[9]—and, we might add, "biblicists." Early Jewish and Christian notices of Islam make no mention of a distinctive Muslim scripture,[10] but instead criticize Muslim scholars for

[8] One logical implication of this argument: early Jewish apocalyptic works failed to ground themselves in Bible because there was no canonical entity extant in their eras (roughly 300 BCE to 100 CE) that would have corresponded to modernist notions of the "Bible." For further discussion of this particular point, see James E. Bowley and John C. Reeves, "Rethinking the Concept of 'Bible': Some Theses and Proposals," *Hen* 25 (2003): 3–18.

[9] Uri Rubin, *The Eye of the Beholder: The Life of Muhammad as Viewed by the Early Muslims* (Studies in Late Antiquity and Early Islam 5; Princeton: Darwin Press, 1995), 22.

[10] "It is, however, worth recalling that those sources which may with some assurance be dated before the end of the second/eighth century . . . contain no reference to Muslim scripture" (Wansbrough, *Sectarian Milieu*, 58).

their alleged inability to find biblical warrant for the revelatory claims of Islam. When a number of biblical proof texts are accordingly produced, Jewish and Christian scripturalists attempt to undermine these Muslim readings of the Bible. The Bible thus emerges as the crucial battleground for textual and social authority.

The Messianic Dimensions of Isaiah 21:6–7

A recurrent claim advanced by Muslim exegetes is that the advent of Muhammad and his climactic position as "seal of the prophets" are already presaged in the earlier scriptures revealed to the Jews and the Christians; namely, the *Tawrāt* (Torah) and the *Injīl* (Gospel), the qurʾānic terms for the two major divisions of the Christian Bible. Among the texts typically referenced in such discussions is a particularly intriguing oracle found in the book of Isaiah (21:6–7). That text in its Masoretic recension reads as follows:

כי כה אמר אלי אדני לך העמד המצפה אשר יראה יגיד וראה רכב צמד
פרשים רכב חמור רכב גמל והקשיב קשב רב קשב

> For thus did my Lord say to me: "Go, station the watchman. Let him report what he sees. And should he see chariotry of a team/pair of horses/riders, chariotry of asses, chariotry of camels, he must pay careful attention, a lot of attention."

Insight into the Muslim parsing of this biblical oracle into a prefiguration of the future appearance of Muhammad first emerges from an early tradition relayed by Ibn Isḥāq (d. 767) reporting how the "People of the Book" (a qurʾānic appellation for religions possessing a sacred scripture, usually shorthand for the Bible) anticipated the advent of a prophet "whom Jesus announced would be riding a camel" (*rākib al-jamal*). Suliman Bashear's recent exhaustive analysis of this theme locates another testimony to this same tradition in the collection of prophetic legends ascribed to ʿUmāra b. Wathīma (d. 902), where it is reported that Ibn Isḥāq transmitted a tradition which stated that "Isaiah was the one who entrusted the children of Israel with the matter of Jesus and Muhammad . . . (saying) 'there will come to you the one with the camel, meaning Muhammad (upon whom be peace!).'"[11] The curious confusion in attribution between "Jesus" (*ʿĪsā*) and "Isaiah" (*Šaʿyā*) is one that is easily accomplished in an Arabophone environment;

[11] Suliman Bashear, "Riding Beasts on Divine Missions: An Examination of the Ass and Camel Traditions," *JSS* 37 (1991): 37–75, slightly emended quotation cited from p. 41. For the Arabic text, see Raif Georges Khoury, *Les legends prophétiques dans l'Islam: Depuis le Ier jusqu'au IIIe siècle de l'Hégire = Kitāb bad' al-ḫalq wa-qiṣaṣ al-anbiyāʾ* (Wiesbaden: Otto Harrassowitz, 1978), 300 (text).

and, given the lexical evidence of Isa 21:6–7 versus the silence about "camel-riders" among the huge assortment of logia attributed to Jesus, it is almost certain that "Isaiah" should be the prophetic name correctly associated with this source.[12]

Confirmation of the centrality of the Isaiah oracle for Muslim prophetology can be gleaned from the writings of Ibn Qutayba (d. 889), an important ninth-century Muslim collector of traditions surrounding biblical characters and events. Under the summary entry for the prophet Isaiah in his *Kitāb al-maʿārif*, he tersely states: "Isaiah is the one who annunciated the Prophet (upon whom be peace!) and (provided) his description, and he (also) annunciated Jesus."[13] More pertinent information emerges from his *Dalāʾil al-nubuwwa*, or *Proofs of Prophethood*, wherein after a recognizable paraphrase of Isa 21:6–9 he deciphers the critical images:

> And in Isaiah it is said: "I was told, Stand guard as a watchman and watch, and report what you see. I said, I see two riders approaching, one of them on an ass, and the other on a camel. One of the two said to the other, Fallen is Babylon and its graven idols." The one riding the ass is taken by us and by the Christians to be the Messiah [i.e., Jesus]. Now, if the one on the ass is the Messiah, then why should not the man riding the camel be Muhammad . . . is not the Prophet just as well known for his riding the camel as the Messiah is for riding an ass?[14]

Ibn Qutayba's rendering of Isa 21:6–7 provides a linguistic key for the Muslim parsing of Isaiah's imagery: Hebrew צמד פרשים, "a pair of riders," supplies the "two riders," who are then further qualified as riding an "ass" and a "camel" respectively. Christian exegesis is credited as the source for the messianic identity of the figure riding the ass, an interpretation that indeed garners support from Christian readings of Zech 9:9 and gospel enactments of this same passage. From the perspective of Islam the name "Messiah" denotes Jesus, the final prophet sent to Israel. The remaining rider mounted on a camel, who syntactically and temporally arrives after the ass-rider, can be none other than Muhammad.[15]

[12] The identical confusion of attributions (i.e., ʿĪsā/Išʿiyā) is visible in what was originally a ninth-century Muslim polemical tract against Christians, where Jesus is quoted as saying: "Convert, O Jerusalem, *until the time when the one who rides on an ass comes to you. Then will come after him the one who rides a camel.*" See Jean-Marie Gaudeul, "The Correspondence Between Leo and ʿUmar: ʿUmar's Letter Re-discovered?" *Islamochristiana* 10 (1984): 139.

[13] Ibn Qutayba, *Kitāb al-maʿārif* (ed. Tharwat ʿUkkāsha; 2d ed.; Cairo: Dār al-Maʿārif, 1969), 50. Note also Ṭabarī, *Taʾrīkh*: "Isaiah was the one who annunciated Jesus and Muhammad (upon whom be peace!)"; text cited by Martin Schreiner, "Zur Geschichte der Polemik zwischen Juden und Muhammedanern," *ZDMG* 42 (1888): 627 n. 10.

[14] Translation adapted from that of Camilla Adang, *Muslim Writers on Judaism and the Hebrew Bible: From Ibn Rabban to Ibn Hazm* (Leiden: Brill, 1996), 272.

[15] Note the quotation from Thaʿlabī cited by Martin Schreiner, "Beiträge zur Geschichte der Bibel in der arabischen Literatur," in *Semitic Studies in Memory of Rev. Dr. Alexander-Kohut* (ed. George Alexander Kohut; Berlin: Calvary, 1897), 498 n. 5: "behold, the rider of the ass will come to you, *and*

These essential points recur in a number of contemporary and later Muslim expositions of this passage in Isaiah. They figure in the interreligious disputation literature that begins to flourish near the end of the eighth century CE. The Nestorian patriarch Timothy I attempts to refute the Muslim interpretation of Isa 21:7 in the course of his fictional debate with the ʿAbbāsid caliph al-Mahdī (775–785). In the epistle of Ibn al-Layth, a missionary tract allegedly commissioned by Hārūn al-Rashīd to prompt the conversion of the Byzantine emperor Constantine VI (780–797), Isa 21:6–9 prominently functions as a proof text for the predicted advent of Muhammad. The same Isaiah passage also assumes a visible role in the apocryphal correspondence that reportedly transpired between ʿUmar II (717–720) and the iconoclast emperor Leo III (717–741), where ʿUmar is represented as stating: "the prophet Isaiah gives testimony to our lawgiver as being the equal and the like of Jesus when he speaks in his vision of two riders, the one on an ass and the other on a camel, so why do you not believe in that?"[16] Later Muslim traditionists knowledgeable in the Bible, like the Christian convert ʿAlī Ibn Rabban al-Ṭabarī,[17] the learned polymath Bīrūnī,[18] and the Ismāʿīlī propagandist Kirmānī reiterate the significance of Isaiah's testimony, with the last named scholar visibly bolstering the Muslim argument via a meticulous transliteration into Arabic script of a slightly variant Hebrew version of Isa 21:6–7.[19] In every case where Muslim scholars utilize this proof text, attention is drawn to the "two riders" mentioned in v. 7, the first of whom is mounted upon an ass and the second upon a camel.

Now this is an unusual reading of the Hebrew text of Isa 21:7, for the Masoretic vocalization of the final two occurrences of the Hebrew grapheme רכב as the collective noun *rekhev*, "chariotry," in fact clashes with the Muslim understanding of this form as a singular participle *rōkhev*, "rider," or "one who rides." However, the evidence supplied by the extant Greek, Latin, Syriac, and Aramaic versions of this passage in Isaiah—textual recensions that predate the linguistic labors of the Masoretes upon biblical manuscripts—clearly demonstrates that those who were reading Isaiah in the pre-Masoretic age were pronouncing the consonantal skeleton רכב as *rōkhev*, "rider; one riding" (i.e., as if it were written רוכב), in the latter two of the three occurrences. That this participial reading was in fact the more primitive one for the Hebrew text of Isa 21:7 is confirmed by the graphic evidence

---

afterwards the one associated with the camel." See also the lengthy text quoted by Ignaz Goldziher, "Ueber muhammedanische Polemik gegen Ahl al-kitāb," *ZDMG* 32 (1878): 377.

16 Arthur Jeffery, "Ghevond's Text of the Correspondence Between Umar II and Leo III," *HTR* 37 (1944): 278. Jeffery's study should now be used in tandem with Gaudeul, "Correspondence," 109–57.

17 See Adang, *Muslim Writers;* Theodore Pulcini, *Exegesis as Polemical Discourse: Ibn Ḥazm on Jewish and Christian Scriptures* (Atlanta: Scholars Press, 1998), 23–25.

18 Bīrūnī, *Āthār al-bāqiya ʿan-il-qurūn al-khāliya* (ed. C. E. Sachau; repr., Leipzig: Harrassowitz, 1923), 19.

19 Paul Kraus, "Hebräische und syrische Zitate in ismāʿīlitischen Schriften," *Der Islam* 19 (1930): 246.

supplied by the Qumran Isaiah Scroll (1QIsa[a]), which has רוכב for רכב in both instances.[20]

These considerations suggest that the Muslim reading of the grammar of Isa 21:7 is not unusual at all; rather, it is in line with a normative understanding of the linguistic forms registered there in the centuries prior to the activity of the Masoretes. By contrast, it is the Muslim interpretation of the semantic message of this passage that is truly distinctive. What renders it even more distinctive is the fact that no Jewish or Christian scholar prior to the advent of Islam gives special heed to the possible messianic or eschatological dimensions of Isa 21:6–7: it does not figure among the limited number of texts customarily held by either Judaism or Christianity to be expressive of such matters. Instead, when Jewish and Christian writers do display cognizance of the predictive force of Isa 21:6–7, it is always in reaction to its manipulation by Muslims, as in the aforementioned polemical dialogues between Christian prelates or kings and Muslim caliphs, or in the infamous *Iggeret Teiman* of Maimonides. This circumstance makes it likely that the messianic and prophetological reading of Isa 21:6–7 was an original Muslim reading of this biblical text, primarily directed toward a Christian audience in light of its narratological sequencing of the arrivals of "Christ" (treated as a proper name in Islam) and "Muhammad." Since Jewish messianism by and large looked to the future for its realization, a Muslim argument reliant on an already manifested "messiah" would have been no more impressive or effective than its synonymous Christian analogues. Finally, non-Islamicate biblical scholars, whether Christian or Jewish, betray no knowledge of the apologetic possibilities discovered by Muslim exegetes in this passage.

It is therefore of signal interest to note that there is at least one instance where it appears that this potentially compelling Muslim reading of a biblical text was adopted by a Jewish exegete, reformulated, and semantically subverted in order to generate a new insight into the imminence of the messianic age. A popular post-Muslim Jewish apocalypse introduced as the *Nistarot* or *Secrets of R. Šimᶜōn ben Yoḥai*, a work whose contents span the rise and fall of the Umayyad caliphate, contains in what is arguably its most primitive redaction[21] a surprisingly positive endorsement of the prophetic mission of Muhammad and an intriguing affirmation of the divinely mandated role of Islam in the deliverance of Israel from Byzantine rule:

> R. Šimᶜōn answered and said: "From whence are they ([i.e., Ishmael = Islam] understood as) our deliverance?" He (Metatron) said to him: "Did not Isaiah the prophet speak thusly? 'And should he see chariotry of a pair of riders, one riding an ass,

[20] PAM 7016 is a photograph of the relevant column.

[21] For a brief discussion of the extant manuscript and print editions of the cycle of apocalypses associated with R. Šimᶜōn ben Yoḥai, including their interrelationships, see the introductory remarks to the chapter devoted to the *Nistarot* within the present work.

> (and) one riding a camel' (Isa 21:7)." Why did he (i.e., Isaiah) put the "rider of an ass" before the "rider of a camel"? Should he not instead have said "rider of a camel, rider of an ass"? (No, the textual sequence means that) when the one who rides the camel (Ishmael or Muhammad) emerges, the kingdom ruled by the 'one mounted upon an ass' (Zech 9:9) has manifested (lit. 'sprouted') by his (i.e., Ishmael's or Muhammad's) agency. Another opinion: 'rider of an ass' (means) at the (same) time when he 'rides upon an ass' (Zech 9:9). Consequently they (Ishmael) are a deliverance for Israel like the deliverance (associated with) the 'one mounted upon an ass' (Zech 9:9).[22]

In this extraordinary text, R. Šimᶜōn is represented as being understandably skeptical about the possible redemptive import of the most recent invasion of the Land of Israel by yet another army of foreigners. Questioning Metatron, his angelic interlocutor, about Ishmael's allegedly positive role, the angel responds by quoting Isa 21:7, a favorite passage that Muslim scholars of the Bible invoke as proof of Muhammad's prefigured advent. Interestingly, the author of this Jewish text accepts the Muslim reading of the "camel-rider" as a coded reference to the coming of Islam.[23] Moreover, the "messianic" decipherment of the "ass-rider" is also retained, but it is recalibrated to accord with Jewish expectations.[24] Since the Messiah is associated with events taking place in the future, at the End of Days, and the "camel-rider" has already arrived or is in the process of arriving now, should not Isaiah have reversed the syntactical order of his epithets so as to match their historical sequence? Did the Messiah actually come prior to the advent of Muhammad?

Instead of conceding this exegetical point to Islam (and Christianity), the author(s) of the present midrash ingeniously undermine a segmented understanding of the "riders" by reminding their audience that Isaiah envisioned them as a "pair": they are not diachronic but synchronic figures. The messianic age dawns or, to employ the terminology of the apocalypse, "sprouts" at the same time that Ishmael arrives. The military defeat and expulsion of Edom (Christian Rome) by Ishmael (Islam) in seventh-century Palestine creates the necessary conditions for the triumph of Jacob (Israel). The vicissitudes of history would temper and eventually sour this textually based example of Jewish enthusiasm, generating in turn a series of bitter reassessments and recriminations against what was originally a positive view of Muhammad's prophetic mission and the early Islamic hegemony over Eretz Israel.[25]

[22] Adolph Jellinek, ed., *Bet ha-Midrasch: Sammlung kleiner Midraschim und vermischter Abhandlungen aus der jüdischen Literatur* (6 vols.; Leipzig, 1853–77; repr., Jerusalem: Bamberger & Wahrmann, 1938), 3:78.24–30.

[23] Earlier in this same text the author had acknowledged the prophetic status of Muhammad.

[24] The association of the "ass" (חמור) with the Davidic messiah has an early basis in biblical texts such as Deut 33:17 and Zech 9:9. See, e.g., *Gen. Rab.* 75.6 (Theodor-Albeck, 892–93) and the annotations supplied there.

[25] Note the versions of this portion of *Nistarot* that survive in manuscripts from the Cairo Genizah, as well as the print editions of *ᶜAtidot* and *Prayer*.

Finally, it is clear that the "judaized" interpretation of Isa 21:7 advanced in the *Nistarot*, a work compiled from smaller complexes of apocalyptic traditions emanating from the mid-seventh to the mid-eighth centuries CE, presumes, as do all the extant pre-Masoretic versions of this oracle, a "singular" understanding of the animal riders; namely, one figure riding an ass (ר[ו]כב חמור) and another figure riding a camel (ר[ו]כב גמל). Given the Islamicate cultural context for the bulk of Masoretic textual activity, it is tempting to argue that the inscribed vocalization of the key word רכב in its final two occurrences in Isa 21:7 as *rekhev* in place of the demonstrably older traditional reading *rōkhev* signals a conscious yet subtle polemical move on the part of the Masoretic enterprise. Even less subtle is the roughly contemporary Arabic "translation" (*tafsīr*) of Isa 21:7 by R. Saadya Gaon, where the single "ass-rider" and lone "camel-rider" of the pre-Masoretic versions become "peoples (!) who are riders of asses and camels,"[26] a pluralizing rendition that effectively sabotages its prophetological import. Since Isa 21:6–7 had enjoyed some scholarly recognition even within some Jewish circles as a viable proof text for Islam's divine mandate,[27] it is not difficult to imagine later generations of textual critics seizing this opportunity to counter and subvert a culturally influential yet doctrinally "flawed" textual reading.

Islam and Imperial Eschatology

The synchronic understanding of the relationship between the advent of Islam and the appearance of the Messiah pioneered by this late antique Jewish interpretation of Isa 21:6–7 received powerful scriptural support from another influential exegetical motif that is present already in some of the earliest Jewish apocalyptic compositions. The notion that the world would experience a succession of four world empires followed by the advent of the eschaton, sometimes referred to as the "four-kingdoms" theory,[28] is one with deep roots in the apocalyptic mentalities of the eastern Mediterranean world. Its articulation in the dream visions reported in Daniel 2 (where the kingdoms are signaled by metals) and Daniel 7 and 8 (where the kingdoms are symbolized by animals) forms the textual basis for its subsequent elaboration in both the Jewish and Christian interpretative traditions. As originally conceived, the four kingdoms were correlated with the "uni-

[26] קום רכאב חמיר ורכאב גמאל. Judaeo-Arabic text cited from the edition of Yehuda Ratzaby, *Saadya's Translation and Commentary on Isaiah* (Qiryat Ono: Makhon Mishnat ha-Rambam, 1993), 42.

[27] Moritz Steinschneider, *Polemische und apologetische Literatur in arabischer Sprache zwischen Muslimen, Christen und Juden, nebst Anhängen verwandten Inhalts* (Leipzig, 1877; repr., Hildesheim: Olms, 1966), 329.

[28] See the classic study of J. W. Swain, "The Theory of the Four Monarchies: Opposition History under the Roman Empire," *CP* 35 (1940): 1–21.

versal" empires of Assyria, Babylonia, Persia, and Macedonia (alternatively Babylonia, Media, Persia, and Macedonia), but the social impact of a lengthy Roman domination of the East prompted a conceptual realignment that came to identify Rome as the fourth and final kingdom, which would hold sway over humanity until the coming of the end.[29]

The advent of Islam and its subsequent territorial expansion and administrative hegemony during the seventh and following centuries threatened to disrupt the tidy symmetry of this hermeneutical formula. But time had to pass, and recognition of its dominance had to be grudgingly achieved before the Kingdom of Ishmael could be admitted into an "official" playbill of wicked empires. Early Christian notices considered the Arab invasion to be no more than a temporary irruption of barbarian raiders from beyond the boundaries of Roman civilization, at best God's punishment of Christians for their continual doctrinal and behavioral lapses, and at worst a prolepsis of the looming hordes of Gog and Magog poised to sweep across the steppes from the north as part of the endgame of history.[30] The Syriac *Apocalypse of Pseudo-Methodius*, an extremely influential Christian text dating from the final decades of the seventh century, emphasized that the Muslims were "a fiery trial for all Christians," a crucible for purifying the faithful and exposing sinners, opportunists, and apostates.[31] Even when an imperial value was awarded Islam, it was often the case that Islam's domination was judged to be temporary: Rome would eventually overcome and supplant the Kingdom of Ishmael and thus reassume its scripturally preordained place as the final universal monarchy before God restores Israel at the time of the end.[32]

The incorporation of Islam into Jewish expressions of imperial eschatology[33] first emerges textually in a fascinating compilation of aggadic traditions known as the *Pirqe de Rabbi Eliezer*, a work probably emanating from the Land of Israel during the eighth or early ninth centuries CE (more on the character and structure of this collection is contained in the introduction to the section treating the logion

[29] N. R. M. de Lange, "Jewish Attitudes to the Roman Empire," in *Imperialism in the Ancient World: The Cambridge University Research Seminar in Ancient History* (ed. P. D. A. Garnsey and C. R. Whittaker; Cambridge: Cambridge University Press, 1978), 271.

[30] Note the testimonies cited by Walter Emil Kaegi, "Initial Byzantine Reactions to the Arab Conquest," *CH* 38 (1969): 139–49.

[31] *Apoc. Ps-Meth.* 11.18; 13.4, following the stichometry of *Die syrische Apokalypse des Pseudo-Methodius* (ed. G. J. Reinink; 2 vols.; CSCO 540–541, scrip. syri 220–221; Louvain: E. Peeters, 1993), 1:32, 36.

[32] So *Apoc. Ps-Meth.* 13.6–15. This understanding goes beyond the speculative decodings of Daniel's "four-kingdoms" scheme and relies on relatively straightforward readings of biblical texts like Gen 25:26; Ezek 25:14; and Obad 1:18. Note also *b. Yoma* 10a, where Rav argues that the contemporary Sasanian hegemony must be at least temporarily superseded by Rome before the coming of the messianic age.

[33] Islamicate Christian writers (Sebeos; *Gospel of the Twelve Apostles*) begin identifying Islam with Daniel's fourth kingdom in the late seventh and early eighth centuries.

of R. Ishmael *infra*). Unexpurgated manuscript editions of this work feature several passages that are harshly critical of the historical realities and ideological claims of Islamic rule. There is, however, at least one tradition that takes an intriguingly positive view of the arrival of Ishmael which harmonizes with and even extends the common scriptural warrant explored in the previous discussion. The setting for this last tradition is an eschatological exposition of Abraham's "covenant of the pieces" (Gen 15:7–21), a biblical text whose verbal components had long provided meditative fodder for those exegetes who were convinced, given Abraham's stature as progenitor of Israel, that God must have revealed to him at some point the periods of suffering that his seed would endure at the hands of gentile oppressors.[34] In earlier interpretations of Abraham's vision, Rome concludes the list. But one manuscript version of *Pirqe R. El.* §28 proposes the following scheme:[35]

> R. Eleazar said: The Holy One, blessed be He, showed our ancestor Abraham (during the covenant) between the pieces the four kingdoms who would rule, but then pass away, for scripture says: "He (i.e., God) said to him, Get Me a three-year old heifer, etc." (Gen 15:7). The heifer: this is the kingdom of Edom, for it was like "a trampling heifer" (Jer 50:11; cf. Hos 10:11) as scripture says: "fearsome and terrible and very strong, etc." (Dan 7:7). The goat: this is the kingdom of Greece, as scripture says: "and the he-goat grew very large, etc." (Dan 8:8). The three-year old ram: this is the kingdom of the Medes and Persians, as scripture says: "the ram which I saw" (Dan 8:6); (the reference to) "horns" (ibid.) means the kings of the Medes and the Persians. And the turtledove? These are the Ishmaelites, as scripture states: "not like[36] his posterity and not, etc." (Dan 11:4).[37] It does not express it in the language of the Torah (i.e., Hebrew) but Aramaic, where תור means "bull."[38] Woe to the land when he yokes male and female: they will open up and break up the entire earth, as scripture says: "the fourth beast will be the fourth kingdom . . . it will consume the entire earth, and trample it and crush it" (Dan 7:23). And the young bird: these are Israel, as scripture says: "My dove in the cleft places of the rocks" (Cant 2:14).

Immediately noticeable in this eschatological reading of Abraham's sacrifice is a contemporary recalibration of the standard formulaic sequence of four world empires. Unlike its Hellenistic and Roman prototypes, this new scheme begins with Edom; that is, Rome, whose imperial hegemony is succeeded in turn by

[34] E.g., *Mek.* Yitro, Baḥodesh §9 (Horovitz-Rabin, 236.5–11); *Gen. Rab.* 44.15, 17 (Theodor-Albeck, 437, 439–40).

[35] HUC Ms. 75 fol. 38b lines 11–22. It should be noted that portions of the following exposition of Gen 15:7–21 circulate independently in varying recensions in manuscript and print form under the rubric *ʾAggadat R. Ishmael.* See, e.g., Yehudah Even-Shmuel, *Midreshey Geʾullah* (2d ed.; Jerusalem: Mosad Bialik, 1954), 144–52.

[36] Masoretic text reads לאחריתו instead of manuscript's באחריתו.

[37] See below.

[38] Hebrew תור, "turtledove," does not provide a satisfactory image for the brutal power wielded by the fourth beast!

Greece, Persia, and Ishmael. It is not difficult to discern in this series of biblical labels a tolerably accurate reproduction of the actual historical progression of foreign dominance over Israel during the first eight centuries of the Common Era. The toponym "Edom" apparently encodes the western or Latin principate, whereas "Greece" represents the subsequent eastern or Byzantine suzerainty exercised from Constantinople. The "kingdom of the Medes and Persians" recognizes the Sasanian domination of the eastern Mediterranean provinces during the early decades of the seventh century, and "Ishmael" is of course a cipher for the Arabs or Islam.

An even greater historical precision is supplied by the biblical proof text from Dan 11:4. As is customary in midrash, the entire biblical verse and its surrounding context must be taken into account for an appreciation of its full relevance. According to Dan 11:2, a strong Persian ruler will attempt to wage war against "Greece" (מלכות יון). This Persian aggression will be successfully opposed by a "mighty king," but he will nevertheless be unable to maintain hold upon his domain: it will disintegrate and fall into the hands of those who "are not his posterity," and who "will not rule as he ruled" (11:4). While these verses in Daniel originally pertained to Alexander's victory over the Achaemenid empire and the contentious succession of the Diadochoi after the world conqueror's premature death in Babylon, they also possess a peculiar resonance for the military and cultural upheavals of the first half of the seventh century CE. The Persian ruler can be seen as Khosroes II, the Greek king as Heraclius, and the latter's non-Greek heirs as the Arab conquerors of Syria, Palestine, and Egypt.

More to the point, however, is the continuation of this passage from *Pirqe de R. Eliezer* that forms an intriguing exegetical dovetail with the way that the *Nistarot of R. Šimᶜōn ben Yoḥai* interprets Isa 21:7 to synchronize the advent of Islam with the appearance of the messiah:[39]

> R. Joshua said: Abraham took his sword and sliced every one of them into two (pieces), as scripture states: "he sliced them down the middle" (Gen 15:10). And if he had not sliced them, the world could not have endured. Does it endure on account of their power? Rather, it is because he sliced them that their power was weakened. He offered each piece opposite its corresponding half, as scripture says: "he placed each of its pieces opposite its corresponding half, but the bird he did not divide" (Gen 15:10). And the young bird, the dove (גוזל בן יונה), he left alive, as scripture says: "the bird (הצפר) he did not divide" (Gen 15:10). You learn from this that the only bird present in the scriptural passage is a single dove, all by itself.[40] The raptor came down upon them (the pieces) to scatter them and destroy them, and the raptor is simply the son of David symbolized as a stained raptor (עיט צבוע), as

[39] HUC MS 75 fol. 39a lines 5–17, 22–24.

[40] As was sketched in the preceding exposition, the young bird (גוזל), which should be correlated with the dove (יונה) of Cant 2:14, represents Israel. Hebrew תר of Gen 15:9 ("turtledove") might conceivably be another bird, but the use of the singular צפר in 15:10 "proves" that only one bird is present. Therefore the grapheme תר cannot be Hebrew "turtledove" but must be Aramaic "bull."

> scripture says: "and the raptor came down on the carcasses, but Abram drove them away" (Gen 15:11). (Also) "His inheritance was stained for him;[41] the raptor surrounded it. Come, gather every wild animal; bring them to feed" (Jer 12:9). When the sun rose in the east, Abraham sat down and waved his hand to arrange it so that the raptor would not prevail over them *until the evening had come* (עד שיבא הערב) . . . *it is not before the coming of the evening that Israel's light will emerge* (עד שלא יבוא הערב יצמח אורו לישראל), as scripture states: "it will come to pass that *at the time of evening* (לעת ערב) light will come into being . . ." (Zech 14:7).

It is the concluding assemblage of comments and proof texts that provide a thematic and perhaps temporal connection with the positive reading of the coming of Islam we encountered above in more primitive versions of the *Nistarot*. Therein occur an arresting series of double entendres that textually juxtapose the redemptive arrival of the Messiah (the raptor of Gen 15:11) with the onset of "evening" (ערב). One cannot fail to notice, however, that the Hebrew character string that is read as "evening" (*ʿerev*) is consonantally identical with that for *ʿarav*, "Arabia," and, if supplemented orally with a single vocalic suffix, could be sounded as *ʿaravī*, "Arab." This graphic polyvalence invites us to read the final part of the exposition as follows: "[Abraham] waved his hand to arrange it so that the raptor [= the Messiah] would not prevail over them [i.e., the four kingdoms] until Arabia/the Arab had come"; similarly, "it is not before the coming of Arabia/the Arab that Israel's light [= the Messiah] will emerge," and "as scripture states 'it will come to pass that at the time of Arabia/(the) Arab light will come into being' (Zech 14:7)." As previously in the *Nistarot*, here also the timing of messianic redemption for Israel can be read as being directly dependent on the success of the Muslim conquest.

It is surely the case that the competing vocalizations of *ʿarav(ī)*, "Arabia, Arab" for *ʿerev*, "evening," in the above instances predate an exegetical identification of Daniel's fourth kingdom with Ishmael. There exists otherwise a disturbing tension between the notion of the Arabs as the climactic brutal empire that the Messiah is expected to destroy and that of the Arabs as the longed-for harbingers of the messianic age. The resemblance of this latter evaluation of the eschatological import of the seventh-century Arab invasion to that put forward in early versions of the *Nistarot of R. Šimʿōn ben Yoḥai* suggests their common indebtedness to and perhaps origin among Near Eastern Jewish circles who were inclined to read the emergence of Islam through the lens of Jewish messianism.[42] But, as in the case of the revisionist editions of the *Nistarot*, pessimism overtakes subse-

[41] *Sic*. Masoretic text reads צבוע נחלתי לי.

[42] Fundamentally important in this regard is the impressive series of arguments brought forward by Patricia Crone and Michael Cook, *Hagarism: The Making of the Islamic World* (Cambridge: Cambridge University Press, 1977). See also Uri Rubin, *Between Bible and Qurʾān: The Children of Israel and the Islamic Self-Image* (Studies in Late Antiquity and Early Islam 17; Princeton: Darwin Press, 1999), esp. 11–52 on "Judeo-Muslims."

quent generations who suffer the vicissitudes of Muslim hegemony and generates fresh readings of the scriptural charters that emend and reject the earlier interpretations. The reluctant branding of "Ishmael" as the "fourth kingdom" is undoubtedly the most important of these negative reactions. Perhaps the apex of this development is reached in the attachment of a terse exclamation to the identification of Ishmael as the fourth kingdom found in another later midrashic collection: "they (i.e., the Ishmaelites) were created solely as fuel for stoking Gehinnom(!)."[43]

The Architectonics of Near Eastern Apocalyptic

Near Eastern Jewish, Christian, and Muslim apocalypses of late antiquity and the early medieval era exhibit a series of remarkable structural correspondences that reach across the permeable boundaries of ethnic and religious affiliation. Despite the inevitable individual doctrinal variations, these apocalypses reveal a number of common motifs, dramatis personae, and discursive sequences (see table on following page). One explanation for their relative univocality is undoubtedly the largely shared Abrahamic, that is, "biblical" substrate that undergirds the apocalyptic ideology of this region and epoch. Another influential factor shaping a common scriptural culture involves the phenomenon of textual commerce, whereby the literary products of one culture are appropriated, tweaked, adapted, adjusted, and rebutted by others who are themselves the producers and/or consumers of competing apocalypses. Individual conversions to the dominant religious affiliation provided a vehicle for the parallel movement of writings and teachings from one community to another, thereby augmenting (often via linguistic translation from Hebrew and Syriac into Arabic) the scriptural and parascriptural resources available for apocalyptic reasoning and speculation.

A prominent example underscoring the fundamental importance of textual dynamics for the explication of signal apocalyptic personages and themes can be found among the tangled morass of traditions that surround the clonelike characters of Armilos and the Dajjāl, two dark and sinister figures who mimic the role of the Christian Antichrist within Jewish and Muslim apocalyptic respectively (see table). While the figure of the Antichrist has garnered its share of scholarly attention over the past two centuries of critical scholarship,[44] less attention has been directed by students of apocalyptic to this entity's analogues within Jewish and

[43] *Yal. Šim.* Torah §76.

[44] Wilhelm Bousset, *The Antichrist Legend: A Chapter in Christian and Jewish Folklore* (trans. A. H. Keane; London: Hutchinson, 1896; repr., Atlanta: Scholars Press, 1999); Gregory C. Jenks, *The Origins and Early Development of the Antichrist Myth* (Berlin: Walter de Gruyter, 1991); Bernard McGinn, *Antichrist: Two Thousand Years of the Human Fascination with Evil* (San Francisco: HarperSanFrancisco, 1994; repr., New York: Columbia University Press, 2000).

Structural Comparison of Near Eastern Apocalyptic

Christian	*Jewish*	*Muslim*
1. deterioration of society & nature	1. deterioration of society & nature	1. deterioration of society & nature
a. wars between the "kingdoms"	a. wars between the "kingdoms"	a. wars between the "kingdoms"
b. pestilence, famine, earthquakes, etc.	b. pestilence, famine, earthquakes, etc.	b. pestilence, famine, earthquakes, etc.
2. advent of Gog & Magog	[2. advent of Gog & Magog (although its position varies)]	[2. advent of Yajūj wa-Majūj (although its position varies)]
a. more animal than human		
b. eat corpses, drink blood, etc.		
3. Rome reigns supreme	3. Rome/Ishmael reigns supreme	3. Final clash of Rome/Ishmael
a. necessary for eschaton	a. necessary for eschaton	a. fall of Constantinople
b. Last Emperor abdicates	b. advent of Messiah b. Joseph	b. aided by Jewish "tribes"
c. in Jerusalem	c. comes to Jerusalem	d. recovery of Temple vessels
	d. sometimes restores Temple	
4. advent of Antichrist	4. advent of Armilos	4. advent of Dajjāl
a. conceived of a foul union involving Satan & Jews in Palestine	a. conceived of a foul union involving Satan, gentiles, & a statue in Rome	a. either of human or demonic origin; sometimes termed a "Satan"
b. assumes royal power in or near Jerusalem (sometimes restores Temple)	b. comes to Jerusalem	b. advances on Jerusalem
c. decrees he must be worshiped as God	c. decrees he must be worshiped as God	
d. many are deceived by him, especially the Jews	d. many are deceived by him, especially the gentiles	d. many are deceived by him, especially the Jews*
e. holds sway for 3 ½ years		
5. mission of Enoch & Elijah	5. confrontation with Messiah b. Joseph	5. parousia of ʿĪsā al-Masīḥ
a. refute & denounce the Antichrist	a. refutes & denounces Antichrist	
b. are slain by him	b. is slain by him	b. slays the Dajjāl
6. parousia of Christ	6. advent of Messiah b. David	6. advent of Mahdī
a. accompanied by angels & cross	a. accompanied by angels & Elijah	
b. resurrection of Enoch & Elijah	b. resurrection of Messiah b. Joseph	
c. general resurrection of the faithful	c. general resurrection of faithful plus ingathering of the exiles	
d. slays Antichrist with "breath"	d. slays Armilos with "breath"	
e. all malefactors & Satan dispatched to hell	e. rewards & punishments for faithful and apostates	
f. faithful rewarded with eternal life	f. new heaven, new earth, new Temple, etc.	

* The "misguided" joining of the *beney Mosheh to* Abū ʿĪsā (cf. Maimonides, *Iggeret Teiman*) probably belongs here.

Muslim eschatology. It is nevertheless certain that a distinctively Christian construct—that is, the Antichrist—forms the conceptual fountainhead for the subsequent portrayals of the villainous Jewish Armilos and the deceptive Muslim Dajjāl.

References to the character "Armilos" (ארמילוס) begin to surface in Hebrew liturgical poetry of the late sixth or early seventh century CE. His initial appearance within the narrative stream of a Jewish apocalypse is in *Sefer Zerubbabel*, a Hebrew pseudepigraphon rooted within the bitter wars of the 620s between Heraclius and the final Sasanian rulers for possession of Syria, Palestine, and Egypt. The name of Armilos also recognizably figures in geographically contiguous Christian sources: the roughly contemporary (634?) *Doctrina Jacobi nuper baptizati* calls the maleficent "little horn" of Dan 7:8 "Satan" and "Erēmolaos" (Ἐρημόλαος), a Greek neologism that etymologically connotes "destroyer of a people," while the late-seventh-century Syriac *Apocalypse of Pseudo-Methodius* wields this same name (ܐܪܡܠܐܘܣ) for the "king of Rome" (9:4–5). R. Saadya Gaon in the tenth century dubs the Jewish Armilos legend an "ancestral teaching," phraseology he uses elsewhere when introducing talmudic citations, but here intended probably to refer to *Sefer Zerubbabel*.[45] Physical descriptions of Armilos are plentiful and borrow from the same lexicon of the grotesque that was previously exploited by Christian authors in their vivid depictions of the Antichrist:[46] of monstrous height and girth, he is also bald, leprous, sometimes sporting two heads, but with bloodshot crossed eyes. He is usually deaf in one ear, endowed with misshapen or malformed limbs, and often exhibits the curious attribute of "green" feet. He is the wicked entity usually blamed for the slaying of the Messiah of the lineage of Joseph, an initial redemptive figure who has briefly given Israel hope that the time for national deliverance has dawned, and Armilos superintends a final brutal persecution of Israel prior to the triumphant emergence of the Messiah of the lineage of David, the hero who effortlessly dispatches Armilos with but a single piercing glance or lethal exhalation (cf. Isa 11:4). These peculiar motifs actually mirror similar discursive stages in the plot of contemporary eastern Christian apocalypses, where the Antichrist murders his irritating prophetic critics Enoch and Elijah and engages in a persecution of the faithful prior to a final

[45] Saadya Gaon, *Kitâb al-Amânât wa'l-Iʿtiqâdât von Saʿadja b. Jûsuf al-Fajjûmî* (ed. S. Landauer; Leiden: Brill, 1880), 238.18; Even-Shmuel, *Midreshey Ge'ullah*, 122 n. *s.v.* הקדמונים. Within the present volume, Armilos appears in the following works: *Sefer Zerubbabel*; *Nistarot* and *Prayer of R. Šimʿon ben Yoḥai*; the responsum of R. Hai Gaon; *'Otot of R. Šimʿon ben Yoḥai*; *Ten Signs*; *'Otot ha-Mašiaḥ*; and *Midrash Wa-yoshaʿ*.

[46] See the material cited in Bousset, *Antichrist Legend*, 156–57 and *passim*; also Michael E. Stone and John Strugnell, *The Books of Elijah: Parts 1–2* (SBLTT 18; Missoula, Mont.: Scholars Press, 1979), 28–39.

climactic denouement with Jesus who, like his analogue the Messiah ben David, easily vanquishes his ominous foe.[47]

It is widely accepted among scholars that "Armilos" is simply a Hebrew approximation of Latin "Romulus," the name of the mythical founder of the city of Rome. His prominent role in late antique Jewish apocalyptic is frequently read as an imaginative representation of the final Roman ruler to exert imperial control over the Land of Israel; namely, Heraclius (610–641 CE).[48] Having suffered military setbacks at the hands of the Avars and the Persians and threatened by their combined siege of the capital Constantinople in 626, Heraclius narrowly averted disaster and managed to deal a series of crushing blows to the Sasanian aggressor, thereby reclaiming the eastern provinces lost to Byzantium during the previous two decades. His successful recovery of the holy relic of the True Cross, captured during the Persian looting of Jerusalem in 614, culminated in his personal restoration of it to the city in 630, an event around which highly charged Christian legends would flourish over the following centuries.[49] His infamously personal involvement *à la* his predecessor Constantine with the resolution of ultimately intractable theological issues, including a controversial decree mandating the forced conversion of his Jewish subjects, augments the likelihood that nationalist memory of a seemingly intractable opponent like Heraclius was instrumental in the Jewish construction of the profile of "Armilos the wicked" (ארמילוס רשיעא).

A prominent scriptural image nourishing the murderous figure of Armilos is that of the treacherous Balaam, the pliable gentile prophet hired to pronounce destructive imprecations upon the newly emergent nation of Israel (Numbers 22–24). David Berger has persuasively demonstrated that Greek "Erēmolaos" (Ἐρημόλαος), or "destroyer of a people," is the *philological* (as opposed to the phonetic resemblance with Romulus or the folkloric memory of Heraclius) source for Hebrew "Armilos," a linguistic correlation that is signaled by the Oxford *Yeraḥmeel* manuscript version of *Sefer Zerubbabel* (ויחריב עם) and a stock talmudic wordplay (*b. Sanh.* 105a) on the name "Balaam" (בלע עם).[50] Berger fur-

[47] Similarly it is usually Jesus whom Muslim tradition makes responsible for slaying the Dajjāl. Enoch and Elijah (reading "Ilyās" in place of the text's "Idrīs") also harass the Dajjāl in at least one early Muslim eschatological tradition; see Nuʿaym b. Ḥammād, *Kitāb al-fitan* (ed. S. Zakkār; Beirut: Dār al-Fikr lil-Ṭibāʿah wa-al-Nashr wa-al-Tawzīʿ, 1993), 329–30.

[48] For a summary of the arguments, see Joseph Dan, *Ha-Sippur ha-ʿivri be-yemey ha-beyanim: ʿIyyunim be-toldotav* (Jerusalem: Keter, 1974), 40–43.

[49] See Wolfram Brandes, "Heraclius Between Restoration and Reform: Some Remarks on Recent Research," in *The Reign of Heraclius (610–641): Crisis and Confrontation* (ed. Gerrit J. Reinink and Bernard H. Stolte; Leuven: Peeters, 2002), 35–36; Jan Willem Drijvers, "Heraclius and the *Restitutio Crucis*: Notes on Symbolism and Ideology," in ibid., 175–90.

[50] David Berger, "Three Typological Themes in Early Jewish Messianism: Messiah son of Joseph, Rabbinic Calculations, and the Figure of Armilus," *AJSR* 10 (1985): 155–62. This solution was first proposed in the modern era by Heinrich Graetz ; see Jacob Levy, *Chaldäisches Wörterbuch über die*

ther points out that Balaam is in fact textually assimilated to the city founder Romulus by *Tg.* 1 Chr 1:43, a midrash that identified Belaʿ son of Beʿor (cf. Gen 36:32), the first king of Edom (= Rome), with "the wicked Balaam son of Beʿor . . . who joined with the progeny of Esau in order to destroy Jacob and his descendants. . . .[51] These textual considerations suggest that the apocalyptic character Armilos is essentially the product of an internal exegetical process whereby the originally Christian type of the Antichrist was lifted, scripturally plotted, and conceptualized, and that the prevalent "historical" speculations about the possible origins and significance of Armilos are at root fundamentally misplaced.

Nowhere is this tension more evident than in the recent scholarly theorizing surrounding the peculiar mode by which Armilos is said to originate. According to the Jewish texts, Armilos is the product of a foul sexual congress between a demonic entity (Satan or Belial) and a stone statue of a beautiful maiden, usually said to be located in Rome. When the narrative stage is set for his emergence, the stone bursts open and Armilos steps forth, ready to embark on his mission of mayhem and destruction.[52] It has lately become fashionable to see in this birth prodigy a deliberate polemical distortion of contemporary (i.e., seventh-century) Christian iconic imagery:[53] the stone image is most likely a marble statue of Mary; the stone's unnatural intercourse with Satan is probably a parody of the virgin birth; and the wicked Armilos functions as an antitype of the Christian Son of God as world savior. Aside from the final posited correspondence, there is very little concrete evidence to support these proposals and much that smacks of circular reasoning. The prevailing uncritical assumption that apocalyptic texts *must* parrot historical realities has impelled scholars to sift the Christian literary and archaeological remains of the period in a valiant attempt to demonstrate that the figure of Mary, and especially material representations of the Virgin, *must* have played a special role in the imperial ideology of Heraclian Byzantium.

Targumim und einen grossen Theil des rabbinischen Schrifttums (2 vols.; Leipzig: Baumgärtner, 1867–68), 1:66.

[51] Note also *Tg. Ps.-J.* Gen 36:32 and the commentary of Abraham Ibn Ezra *ad loc.* (see Asher Weiser, ed., *Perushey ha-Torah le-Rabbenu Abraham Ibn Ezra* [3 vols.; Jerusalem: Mosad Harav Kook, 1977], 1:106).

[52] For certain folkloristic aspects of this episode, see already Samuel Krauss, *Das Leben Jesu nach jüdischen Quellen* (Berlin: Calvary, 1902; repr., Hildesheim: Olms, 1994), 216–17.

[53] This idea was in fact first elaborated by Israel Lévi, "L'apocalypse de Zorobabel et le roi de Perse Siroès (3)," *REJ* 71 (1920): 58–61. It has been revived and broadened by Martha Himmelfarb, "Sefer Zerubbabel," in *Rabbinic Fantasies: Imaginative Narratives from Classical Hebrew Literature* (ed. David Stern and Mark Jay Mirsky; Philadelphia: Jewish Publication Society, 1990), 67–90; and further developed by David Biale, "Counter-History and Jewish Polemics Against Christianity: The *Sefer toldot yeshu* and the *Sefer zerubavel*," *Jewish Social Studies* n.s. 6 (1999): 130–45; and Peter Schäfer, *Mirror of His Beauty: Feminine Images of God from the Bible to the Early Kabbalah* (Princeton: Princeton University Press, 2002), 212–16. Of related interest, but which must be used with caution, is the essay by Paul Speck, "The Apocalypse of Zerubbabel and Christian Icons," *JSQ* 4 (1997): 183–90.

If a more balanced recognition is accorded the textual and specifically scriptural dynamics at work in the narrative construction of late Near Eastern apocalypses, a different and potentially more fruitful hermeneutic emerges. Discerning and identifying the biblical and parascriptural substrates governing their formation and shape could plausibly explain the contextual presence of particular motifs, themes, or characters. With regard to the figure of Armilos, the ominous villain born of a stone, a variant recension of a Hebrew apocalypse entitled *ʾOtot R. Šimʿōn b. Yoḥai* (Signs of R. Šimʿōn b. Yoḥai) provides a crucial interpretative key: "Armilos b. Satan will come to the wilderness of Moab: this is the Armilos spawned from a stone *of whom scripture speaks: 'and he produced the wicked one with the stone'* (Zech 4:7)."[54] The highly cryptic scriptural phrase והוציא את האבן הראשה, "and he will bring out the headstone" from Zech 4:7, a clause that has generated a wide diversity of interpretations among the classical Jewish and Christian commentators, seems to be the ultimate source for the mythogenesis of Armilos. By deliberately sounding the word הראשה (*ha-roʾšah*, "the head, chief") as if it were written הרשע (*ha-rašaʿ*, "the wicked one") and by ignoring its immediate context within the original prophecy of Zechariah,[55] probably an oracle exalting the status of the historical Zerubbabel, an alternate reading can be generated along the lines of the one italicized above. With the accusatory figure of Satan lurking in the immediate narrative vicinity (cf. Zech 3:1–2) of the scriptural prophecy, the already ambiguous actor who performs what the biblical verb והוציא possibly signifies can don an appropriately sinister mask.

Similarly, the Muslim *Doppelgänger* of Armilos—the Dajjāl—exhibits clear markers of a heritage that extends back into the Christian depictions of the Antichrist and laterally to invoke connections with the evolving Jewish myth. Unknown to the Qurʾān, this entity's manifestation as the final deceiver or "liar" within history serves as one of the signs of the End of Days. Numerous traditions expound the circumstances surrounding his emergence and nefarious exploits, many of which align him with Jewish interests and concerns.[56] As with Armilos and the Antichrist, the Dajjāl is a physical freak: "the Dajjāl will have pudgy arms, short fingers; (he will be) lacking a neck; lacking an eye; written between his eyes will be *kāfir* ("unbeliever")."[57] Commentators are at odds as to whether he is actu-

[54] Or alternatively, "the wicked one (re)produced with the stone." Text cited from Arthur Marmorstein, "Les signes du Messie," *REJ* 52 (1906): 184; see also Even-Shmuel, *Midreshey Geʾullah*, 313.

[55] It seems significant to note that according to a tradition recounted by the learned convert Kaʿb al-Aḥbār, the Dajjāl "is mentioned in the books of the prophets." See Nuʿaym b. Ḥammād, *K. al-fitan* (ed. Zakkār), 329.

[56] For some representative presentations of these traditions, see Armand Abel, "al-Da<u>dj</u>djāl," *EI*[2] 2:76–77; Neal Robinson, "Antichrist," *EncQur* 1:107–11; and now especially David Cook, *Studies in Muslim Apocalyptic* (Studies in Late Antiquity and Early Islam 21; Princeton: Darwin Press, 2002), 93–120.

[57] Nuʿaym b. Ḥammād, *K. al-fitan* (ed. Zakkār), 328; note also 317: "The Prophet of God said: the

ally a human or demonic creature (*šayṭān*). A particularly interesting complex of traditions holds that he is currently housed in quarantine on a distant island restrained by a set of iron chains: as the doomsday clock relentlessly ticks down, "God breaks a chain every year."[58] This arresting theme of a sequestered Dajjāl is strikingly reminiscent of the legendary episode about the "gates" constructed by Alexander in the far north which effectively confine the barbarous hordes of Gog and Magog (Arabic Yājūj wa-Mājūj) "until my Lord's promise comes to pass" (Q 18:98). Moreover, this distinctive story about an enchained eschatological actor is surely a dark parody of the odd Jewish tradition about an "imprisoned Messiah" who currently bides his time in a secluded chamber within Gan Eden:

> The fifth chamber . . . and there dwell the Messiah of the lineage of David, Elijah, and the Messiah of the lineage of Ephraim . . . Elijah takes hold of his head and allows it to rest on his chest. He encourages him and says to him: "Bear the torment and judgment of your Lord while He punishes you for the sin of Israel, for scripture says 'he is pierced for our rebellions, crushed for our transgressions' (Isa 53:5)—until the time when the End (הקץ) arrives." Every Monday, Thursday, Sabbath, and festival day the ancient patriarchs, Moses, Aaron, David, Solomon, the entire royal line, the prophets, and the pious ones come to greet him and weep together with him. They express gratitude to him and say to him: "Bear the judgment of your Lord, *for the End has almost arrived, and the chains which are on your neck will be snapped off* and you will go forth to freedom!"[59]

When he finally appears, the Dajjāl will purportedly delude and mislead an expanding army of gullible followers by a convincing exhibition of a series of wondrous miracles. Like Armilos and his legions, the Dajjāl and his minions will march against the holy sites (including Mecca and Medina) with the aim of seizing universal dominion, but will finally suffer defeat and extirpation when ʿĪsā (Jesus) descends from heaven and kills him.[60]

The foregoing example must suffice for the present as an instructive illustration of how a close study of this literature in tandem with its scriptural substrates can illuminate the varied interdependencies and thematic echoes that emerge from the apocalyptic texts produced and consumed by Jews, Christians, and Muslims during the second half of the first millennium of the Common Era. It is an important area of research that has been largely uncultivated by modern Western scholars, and hence a comparative study across the religious boundaries of the confessional corpora remains very much in its infancy. One of the more impor-

---

Dajjāl will be blind in his left eye; on his forehead will be written *kāfir*, and above his eye will be a thick claw."

[58] Nuʿaym b. Ḥammād, *K. al-fitan* (ed. Zakkār), 329.

[59] *Midrash Konen*, from Jellinek, *BHM* 2:29.20–33; compare also 2:50.5–9.

[60] Some commentators find an allusion to his *parousia* in the ambiguous opening of Q 43:61: "he (i.e., Jesus) furnishes knowledge of the (final) Hour."

tant tasks awaiting students of Near Eastern apocalyptic involves the systematic identification, collation, and publication of the massive number of late antique and early medieval apocalyptic texts lurking in manuscript collections of libraries and research institutes around the world.[61] While the current renascence in interest in the Cairo Genizah manuscripts bodes well for the continued discovery and recovery of Jewish manuscript resources, no analogous effort governs the cataloging and publication of Syriac- and Arabic-language sources. The recent important publications by Matthias Henze and David Cook exemplify the valuable nature of the textual currency which repays a diligent researcher.[62]

At the same time, a discerning reader cannot fail to recognize the structural role of the Bible in the generation and elaboration of late antique and early medieval Near Eastern apocalyptic scenarios. As has been repeatedly stressed in the foregoing remarks, the external events and actors of mundane existence are mapped upon its textual template, and it is this resultant inscribed pattern that creates meaning in history. For Jews, Christians, and Muslims during Islam's formative period, Bible provides the essential conceptual scheme for locating and reading the signs of the hour.

In order to exemplify these assertions, the next section of the reader presents a gallery of Jewish apocalypses and anthological compilations of end-time events that emanate from around a six-hundred-year period extending from the Sasanian expansion during the initial decades of the seventh century to approximately the twelfth or thirteenth centuries CE. It incorporates what most scholars recognize to be the most important and influential Jewish specimens of the genre. Unlike their forebears from the Hellenistic and Roman periods of Jewish history, these apocalypses explicitly frame their message in a biblical idiom, thus signaling their conceptual affinity with yet another kind of Jewish exegetical and literary expression widely cultivated during this same period—that of the aggadic midrash. The Bible's centrality to the midrashic process is well known and universally acknowledged by students of Jewish literary history. An analogous acknowledgment of its equivalent value for postrabbinic apocalyptic compositions is long overdue.

[61] Two excellent places to start: (1) the various Paris manuscripts of Muslim apocalypses cited by Abel in his *EI*[2] article on the Dajjāl; and (2) the extensive list of manuscript and early print resources, most of which pertain to and expand on the biblical Daniel, cited by Moritz Steinschneider, "Apokalypsen mit polemischer Tendenz," *ZDMG* 28 (1874): 647–59; 29 (1875): 163–66.

[62] Matthias Henze, *The Syriac Apocalypse of Daniel: Introduction, Text, and Commentary* (Studien und Texte zu Antike und Christentum 11; Tübingen: Mohr Siebeck, 2001); Cook, *Studies in Muslim Apocalyptic*; idem, "An Early Muslim Daniel Apocalypse," *Arabica* 49 (2002): 55–96.

A Note on the Translations

Almost all of the annotated translations that comprise the bulk of the present work were prepared from standard printed and hence easily accessible Semitic-language editions of these Jewish apocalypses. The base texts for each rendering are signaled in the introductory remarks to the individual works, and interested readers should consult those editions for continuous versions of the Hebrew or Aramaic text. Occasional variant readings or emendations are included in the translation notes; they stem in large part from suggestions contained in these same editions or from those that are offered in the secondary literature. A limited number of manuscript copies and fragments were consulted by the author during the course of his research, but he has made no systematic attempt to gather all or even most of the extant textual witnesses for any of the compositions featured herein. These translations should therefore not be construed as "critical" or even "canonical" editions of these titles, but they can provide some preliminary guidance regarding whether the preparation of such editions might eventually prove feasible. The titles are arranged in roughly chronological order, ranging from the Sasanian expansion in the Persian incursions into the Roman Near East during the initial decades of the seventh century to the period of the Crusades (approximately the twelfth or thirteenth centuries CE).

Finally, it is surely worth noting that most of the "later" compilations of apocalyptic lore found in the latter half of "A Gallery of Jewish Apocalypses" and advertised under titles like *Pirqey* (or *Pereq*) *Mašiaḥ* or *ʾAggadat ha-Mašiaḥ* are largely derivative anthologies of talmudic and midrashic discussions of eschatological and messianic themes. They do not exhibit the same kind of compositional integrity that is still visible—in spite of recensional variations—in "earlier" works such as *Sefer Zerubbabel* or the *Nistarot of R. Šimʿōn ben Yoḥai.* Medieval manuscripts and early print editions in fact incorporate a fairly hefty number of concise treatises bearing incipits or superscriptions like those listed above, which, apart from their basic outline, exhibit few genetic relationships with one another. The question therefore arises whether it is possible, even intelligible, under such circumstances to make reference (for example) to "the postrabbinic apocalypse entitled *Pirqey Mašiaḥ*." Given the physical situation that there are *many* distinct postrabbinic apocalypses that utilize this name, it seems a wiser course to cite the specific manuscript or print edition of *Pirqey Mašiaḥ* (or an analogous anthology) that one is using. This minimalist procedure is adopted when required in the present work.

A Gallery of
Jewish Apocalypses

1

Sefer Elijah

THE HEBREW TRACTATE KNOWN AS *Sefer Elijah* has lately been characterized as the oldest and the least innovative of the Jewish apocalypses produced during late antiquity. According to Robert L. Wilken,

> There is little in the Book of Elijah that is new. Indeed much of the book is a pastiche of biblical texts strung together in a simple plot: humiliation, hope, conflict, victory, and restoration. Its themes are familiar and traditional and are well documented in Jewish and Christian sources in early centuries, but they indicate that at the time of the Sassanid conquest the ageless hope of deliverance came rushing to the surface with irrepressible force and energy. No event since the destruction of the Second Temple, except Julian's effort to rebuild the Temple, had unleashed such fervor and enthusiasm among the Jews of Palestine.[1]

A closer scrutiny of the work's contents, however, reveals very little that is "simple" or "traditional" with regard to its setting, structure, "plot," or narrative resolution. No explicit instructions or information are provided about the physical production or "accidental" discovery of the work, an unusual omission of what was a standard topos in the late antique representation of the revelatory book.[2] While it purports to be a vision mediated by the angel Michael to the biblical prophet Elijah during the latter's flight to Horeb (1 Kgs 19:1–8), it paradoxically depicts the locus of that same revelation as "Mount Carmel."[3] The vision itself jarringly juxtaposes and intersperses two formally distinct narrative genres. The bulk of *Sefer Elijah* consists of a lengthy third-person discourse by the angel Michael concerning the "mystery" of the End wherein he describes for the prophet a confusing succession of military disasters which would mark that era. Supplementing and framing the angelic discourse is a series of first-person reports put in the mouth of Elijah about a number of marvelous sights he beheld during the course of a cos-

[1] Robert L. Wilken, *The Land Called Holy: Palestine in Christian History and Thought* (New Haven: Yale University Press, 1992), 208.

[2] Compare Dan 12:4; *1 En.* 82:1; *As. Mos.* 1:16–18; *4 Ezra* 12:36–38, 14:45–48; Rev 22:8–10; *Apoc. Paul* 2; *CMC* 49.5–10, 54.11–17; *Massekhet Kelim* (see Jellinek, *BHM* 2:88); end of *Sefer Zerubbabel.*

[3] Also noticed by David Frankfurter, *Elijah in Upper Egypt: The Apocalypse of Elijah and Early Egyptian Christianity* (SAC; Minneapolis: Fortress, 1993), 61. For some medieval Jewish references to a revelatory angelophany at Mount Carmel, see below.

mic tour and again at the time of the eschaton. Curiously, very little direct interaction between the angel and the prophet takes place, a circumstance that hints at the artificial character of the present form of this work. It thus seems likely that *Sefer Elijah* is a conglomerate piece, having been fashioned from at least two separate earlier collections of traditions, only one of which perhaps was originally associated with the figure of the Tishbite prophet. While there are certain broad thematic continuities that link *Sefer Elijah* with earlier Elijah literature (such as the Coptic *Apocalypse of Elijah*), there is no concrete philological evidence that the Hebrew work was dependent upon such sources.[4]

One might outline the narrative progression of the present form of the work in the following manner:

1. Introductory frame narrative
2. [Elijah-discourse 1]: cosmic tour
   a. vision of the south
   b. vision of the east
   c. vision of the west
3. Michael-discourse 1: name of the last emperor
4. [Michael-discourse 2]: conflict between Persia and Rome
   a. defeat of three Roman "mighty warriors"
   b. advent of Gīgīt (the fourth Roman "mighty warrior")
   c. signs of Gīgīt
   d. his oppression of the "faithful people"
5. [Michael-discourse 3]: signs of the End
   a. 20 Marheshvan: earthquakes and tremors
   b. 20 Kislev: heavenly "sword" attacks Gentiles at behest of Israel
   c. 20 Nisan: first group of exiles departs Babylon
   d. 25 Tishri: second group of exiles departs Sambatyon region
   e. 25 Marheshvan: third group of exiles departs from ?
6. [Michael-discourse 4]: signs of the End *redux*
   a. 20 Nisan: king from the west ravages and burns Zion
   b. [ ]: "second battle" waged by Demetrius and Philip (?)
   c. 20 Ellul: advent of Messiah and Gabriel
   d. 20 Tevet: "third battle" waged in Eretz Israel up to Jaffa and Ashkelon
   e. 20 Shevat: advent of Messiah and "angels of destruction"
   f. [ ]: Gentile nations grovel before Israel
   g. 20 Adar: advent of Messiah and "thirty thousand righteous ones"
   h. destruction of besieging armies followed by forty-year period of prosperity
   i. coming of Gog and Magog: their defeat by the Messiah

[4] Note especially the sensible observations of Frankfurter, *Elijah in Upper Egypt*, 44–57.

j. list of devastated cities
7. [Michael-discourse 5]: the final "day"
   a. this "day" lasts for forty days
   b. earthquakes and tremors
   c. earth herself will testify against the wicked
8. Elijah-discourse 2: vision of the resurrection of the dead
9. Elijah-discourse 3: vision of the punishment of apostates and the wicked
10. Elijah-discourse 4: vision of the patriarchs and Land as Eden
11. Elijah-discourse 5: vision of the descent of the heavenly Jerusalem
12. Elijah-discourse 6: vision of the dwellings of the righteous

Sefer Elijah, or the *Book of Elijah*, was first published in an anthology of midrashic texts in Salonika in 1743. This version of the text was subsequently reprinted by Adolph Jellinek in his *Bet ha-Midrasch*.[5] Another edition based on the version of the work found in Munich Ms. Hebr. 222, a manuscript dating from the fifteenth century[6] containing an anthology of brief midrashim, was prepared by Moses Buttenwieser and published in 1897.[7] Even-Shmuel published an eclectic version that combines and harmonizes the editions of Jellinek and Buttenwieser.[8] The same author has also published a later, reworked version that is taken from a Yemenite manuscript of uncertain date.[9] The present translation utilizes Buttenwieser as its base text with frequent reference in the notes to the variant renderings found in the edition published by Jellinek.

Sefer Elijah, May His Memory Be for a Blessing

And he lay down and fell asleep beneath a broom-shrub. Then lo, this angel touched him and said, "Get up, eat!" (1 Kgs 19:5). Michael, "the great prince" of Israel,[10] revealed this mystery to the prophet Elijah at Mount

[5] Adolph Jellinek, ed., *Bet ha-Midrasch: Sammlung kleiner Midraschim und vermischter Abhandlungen aus der jüdischen Literatur* (6 vols.; Leipzig, 1853–77; repr., Jerusalem: Bamberger & Wahrmann, 1938), 3:65–68.

[6] Fol. 65b–68b. Bearing the title ספר המעשים, it also contains versions of *Pirqe Mashiaḥ* (36b–46b) and *Secrets of R. Šimʿōn b. Yoḥai* (107b–111a). See Moses Buttenwieser, *Die hebräische Elias-Apokalypse und ihre Stellung in der apokalyptischen Litteratur des rabbinischen Schrifttums und der Kirche* (Leipzig: Eduard Pfeiffer, 1897), 9.

[7] Buttenwieser, *Elias-Apokalypse*, 15–26.

[8] Yehudah Even-Shmuel, *Midreshey Geʾullah* (2d ed.; Jerusalem: Mosad Bialik, 1954), 41–48.

[9] Ibid., 49–54.

[10] מיכאל שרא רבא דישראל = מיכאל השר הגדול העמד על בני עמך (Dan 12:1).

Carmel;[11] (namely), the eschaton and what was scheduled to transpire at the End of Days at the end of the four empires (and) the things that would take place during the reign of the fourth ruler.[12]

A wind from the Lord lifted me [i.e., Elijah] up and transported me to the southern part of the world, and I saw there a high place burning with fire where no creature was able to enter. Then the wind lifted me up and transported me to the eastern part of the world, and I saw there stars battling one another incessantly. Again the wind lifted me up and transported me to the western part of the world, and I saw there souls undergoing a painful judgment,[13] each one in accordance with its deeds.[14]

Then Michael said to me,[15] "The appointed time for the End of Days will occur during the reign of a king who will be named הרמלת.[16] There are

[11] This clause is in Aramaic: רזא דנא גלא ליה מיכאל שרא רבא דישראל לאליהו הנביא בטורא דכרמל. Interestingly, a Hekhalot adjuration found in Ms. JTS 8128 and published by Peter Schäfer contains a reference to a revelation made to Elijah at Mount Carmel by the angel Malkiel: אילו השמות המפורשות שהם חקוקות בכסא הכבוד שמסר מלכיאל המלאך שהוא עומד תמיד לפני הקב״ה לאליהו בהר הכרמל ובהם נתעלה, "these are the explicit names which are engraved on the Throne of Glory which the angel Malkiel transmitted to Elijah at Mount Carmel, and using them he was raised (to heaven)." Text quoted from Peter Schäfer, ed., *Synopse zur Hekhalot-Literatur* (TSAJ 2; Tübingen: J. C. B. Mohr, 1981), 199 (§505). Note also the Genizah fragment JTSL ENA 3635.17 fol. 17a line 12: ומהם שנגלו לאליהו בהר הכרמל, "and some of them (i.e., powerful angelic and demonic names) were revealed to Elijah on Mount Carmel"; text cited from Peter Schäfer and Shaul Shaked, eds., *Magische Texte aus der Kairoer Geniza*, Band 1 (TSAJ 42; Tübingen: Mohr Siebeck, 1994), 19.

[12] The "four-empires" scheme, a prominent topos in Near Eastern apocalypticism, has its biblical basis in the familiar sequential progression recounted in the dream visions of the book of Daniel. For further discussion of this scheme's background and influence, see especially Oded Irshai, "Dating the Eschaton: Jewish and Christian Apocalyptic Calculations in Late Antiquity," in *Apocalyptic Time* (ed. Albert I. Baumgarten; Studies in the History of Religions 86; Leiden: Brill, 2000), 115 n. 6.

[13] Jellinek: בצער גדול, "in great pain." Frankfurter has pointed out that the association of the western quadrant with the abode of the dead is an Egyptian idea (*Elijah in Upper Egypt*, 45 n. 44).

[14] Buttenwieser suggests that the description of Enoch's journeys through heaven and hell as provided in *1 Enoch* serves as the source for this paragraph (*Elias-Apokalypse*, 15 n. 8). See also idem, *Outline of the Neo-Hebraic Apocalyptic Literature* (Cincinnati: Jennings & Pye, 1901), 31. Cf. *1 En.* 18:6; 21:7; 22:11, none of which, however, displays the close relationship he posits. Nevertheless, Buttenwieser's supposition of an Enochic influence on this section of the apocalypse has been uncritically accepted and extended by Richard Bauckham, "Early Jewish Visions of Hell," *JTS* 41 (1990): 362–65, 375–77. More pertinent parallels are supplied by Michael E. Stone and John Strugnell, *The Books of Elijah: Parts 1–2* (SBLTT 18; Missoula, Mont.: Scholars Press, 1979), 14–24, 25 n.1; note also Frankfurter, *Elijah in Upper Egypt*, 45–46. For Elijah's popularity as a revealer or recipient of visions concerning Gehinnom and its suffering inhabitants, see Martha Himmelfarb, *Tours of Hell: An Apocalyptic Form in Jewish and Christian Literature* (Philadelphia: University of Pennsylvania Press, 1983; repr., Philadelphia: Fortress, 1985), 30–37.

[15] This is the only place in the apocalypse where Michael directly addresses the visionary. It is probably not accidental; see the following note.

[16] A resumptive repetition of much of the final line of the first paragraph, a literary device in Hebrew prose that frequently serves to frame a later insertion within an integral narrative composi-

some that say that תרמילא will be his name."[17] R. Simai says הכשרת will be his name. R. Eleazar says הרתחשסתא (Artaxerxes)[18] will be his name. R. Judah b. Betira says כורש (Cyrus) will be his name.[19] R. Šimʿōn b. Yoḥai says הכסרא (Khusrau) will be his name. The halakhah in this case follows R. Šimʿōn who said "Khusrau" will be his name.[20]

The last king who rules Persia shall come up against the Romans three successive years until he expands (his gains) against them for twelve months. Three mighty warriors will come up to oppose him from the west, but they will be handed over into his control. Then the lowliest of the kings, the son of a slave woman and whose name is Gīgīt, will confront him from the west.[21] These will be his signs, for Daniel has already foreseen him:[22] his face will be long, there will be a bald patch between his eyes,[23] he will be very tall,[24] the soles of his feet will be high [*sic*], and his thighs will be thin.[25] At that time he will attack the faithful people,[26] and he will provoke at that time three agitations. All the constellations will be gathered together and move to one place. They will plunder houses and rob fields and strike the orphan and the widow in the bazaar, but if they perform penitence they will be forgiven.

---

tion. For a brief discussion of this technique, see Shemaryahu Talmon, "The Presentation of Synchroneity and Simultaneity in Biblical Narrative," in *Studies in Hebrew Narrative Art Throughout the Ages* (ed. Joseph Heinemann and Shmuel Werses; ScrHier 28; Jerusalem: Magnes, 1978), 12–17. Note also Michael Fishbane, *Biblical Myth and Rabbinic Mythmaking* (Oxford: Oxford University Press, 2003), 136 n. 8.

[17] Jellinek (*BHM* 3:xviii) suggests that these two designations refer to Armilos, the principal villain found in the roughly contemporary *Sefer Zerubbabel* and its derivative literature; his suggestion is seconded by Samuel Krauss, "Der römisch-persische Krieg in der jüdischen Elia-Apocalypse," *JQR* o.s. 14 (1902): 362. Buttenwieser argues that הרמלת is a corrupt reference to Hurmuz, son of Shāpūr I; see his *Elias-Apokalypse*, 77–78; Even-Shmuel, *Midreshey Geʾullah*, 34 n. 12.

[18] Cf. Ezra 4:7, 8, 11, 23; 6:14; 7:1, 11, 12, 21, 23; 8:1; Neh 2:1; 5:14; 13:6.

[19] See Isa 44:28; 45:1; but contrast *b. Meg.* 12a. Wilken calls attention to the "uncanny correspondence" between the names of the Persian liberators Cyrus and Khusrau; see his *Land Called Holy*, 204.

[20] Either Khusrau Anūširwān (531–79 CE) or Khusrau Aparwīz (591–628 CE), if a historical personage is intended. In Arabic historical literature, the proper name Kisrā (derived from a Syriac rendition of Khusrau) functions as a generic title for all Persian rulers just as Qayṣar (i.e., Caesar) is employed for all rulers of Rome and Byzantium. An analogous usage may be intended here.

[21] Probably to be identified with the Byzantine emperor Phokas (602–610); so Even-Shmuel, *Midreshey Geʾullah*, 37; Michael Avi-Yonah, *The Jews of Palestine: A Political History from the Bar Kokhba War to the Arab Conquest* (New York: Schocken, 1976), 261.

[22] Presumably Dan 7:8; see below.

[23] Read גבחת in place of גבהות; see Buttenwieser, *Elias-Apokalypse*, 16 n. 12.

[24] Cf. *Apoc. El. (C)* 3:15 and Frankfurter, *Elijah in Upper Egypt*, 315 n. 63.

[25] See Stone and Strugnell, *Books of Elijah*, 38; Frankfurter, *Elijah in Upper Egypt*, 121–22.

[26] Cf. Hos 12:1. Wilken (*Land Called Holy*, 322 n. 54) suggests that Heraclius is the intended referent.

On the twentieth (day) of Marheshvan, the world will be shaken "and the heavens and the earth will quake."[27] On the twentieth (day) of Kislev, all Israel will stand in prayer and clamor before their heavenly Father, and a sword will descend and fall upon the nations of the world, in accordance with what scripture says: "The sword kills indiscriminately" (2 Sam 11:25). On the twentieth[28] (day) of Nisan, the first group of exiles will depart from Babylon: they will number eighteen thousand men and women, and not a single one of them will perish. On the twenty-fifth (day) of Tishri, the second group of exiles will depart from the region of the River Sa(m)batyon:[29] they will number seventeen thousand, but twenty men and fifteen women will be slain from among them. On the twenty-fifth (day) of the eighth month [*sic;* i.e., Marheshvan], the third group of exiles will depart. They will weep and cry out on behalf of their brethren who were slain, and they will cry out in the desert for twenty-five days[30] and not taste[31] any (food), living instead "on what issues from the mouth of the Lord" (Deut 8:3). The first group of exiles will not leave Babylon until the second group arrives there, as scripture affirms: "Writhe and push out, O daughter of Zion, like a woman giving birth. For you will now go out of the city and dwell in the countryside, and you shall come to Babylon. There you will be rescued; there will the Lord redeem you from the hand of your enemies" (Mic 4:10).[32]

On the twentieth (day) of Nisan, a king shall come up from the west, ravaging and horrifying the world. He shall encroach upon "the holy beautiful

[27] Cf. Joel 4:16 (see Buttenwieser, *Elias-Apokalypse*, 29 n. 4).

[28] Jellinek: כ"ב, "twenty-second."

[29] שבנהר סבטיון. The legendary river that lies to the east of Eretz Israel and reportedly ceases its flow on the Sabbath; for this same spelling, see *b. Sanh.* 65b. See *Tg. Ps.-J.* Exod 34:10 and *Gen. Rab.* 11.5 (Theodor-Albeck, 92–93). Ramban *ad* Deut 32:26 identifies the Sambatyon with the river Gozan of Media (cf. 2 Kgs 17:6). For a comprehensive listing of sources, see Louis Ginzberg, *The Legends of the Jews* (7 vols.; Philadelphia: Jewish Publication Society, 1909–38), 6:407–9 n. 56; note especially the discussion of Israel Friedlaender, "The Jews of Arabia and the Rechabites," *JQR* n.s. 1 (1910–11): 252–57.

[30] Even-Shmuel's text reads here: וצמים במדבר חמשה וארבעים יום, "and they will fast in the desert for forty-five days," a detail that makes excellent sense but does not figure in the editions of either Buttenwieser or Jellinek.

[31] Jellinek: טוענין, "carry."

[32] This paragraph is dependent on the notion first attested in the Palestinian Talmud that the "ten tribes" (Israel) experienced a threefold exile. See *y. Sanh.* 10.6, 29c; *Lam. Rab.* 2.9(13); *Pesiq. Rab.* §31 (Ish-Shalom, 146b–147a); and the other references cited by Theodor-Albeck in their note to *Gen. Rab.* 73.6 (p. 850). Also presupposed here is the regionally privileged idea that redemption will first take place in Babylon. See *ʾAggadat ha-Mashiaḥ* (Jellinek, *BHM* 3:142); *Midr. Tanḥ.*, Noaḥ §3: ללמדך שמשם מתחלת הגאולה, "this (i.e., Mic 4:10) teaches you that the final redemption will begin there (i.e., Babylonia)."

mountain" (Dan 11:45) and burn it.[33] Most cursed among women is the woman who gave birth to him: that is "the horn" that Daniel foresaw,[34] and that day will be one of torment and battle against Israel.

Demetrius son of Pōryphōs and Anfōlīpōs son of Panfōs will wage a second battle.[35] Accompanying them will be ten myriads of cavalry, ten myriads of foot soldiers, and (another) ten myriads of troops concealed on ships. On the twentieth (day) of Ellul, the Messiah will come: his name is Yinnōn (ינון).[36] On that same day Gabriel will descend (and) from the ninth to the tenth hour will destroy from the world ninety-two thousand people.[37] On the twentieth (day) of Tebet, Mekketz, Qīrtalos, and all the cities allied with them will wage a third battle: a very large nation (extending) from the great plain[38] unto Jaffa and Ashkelon. On the twentieth (day) of Shebat, the Messiah will come: angels of destruction will descend and destroy the whole of that multitude, and they will not leave (alive)[39] a single soul.

(It was) regarding this time that God spoke about to Abraham: "Your

[33] A reference to Jerusalem. Cf. *Otot ha-Mašiaḥ* (*apud* Jellinek, *BHM* 2:61): ויחזור פניו לירושלם להחריבה פעם שניה שנאמר ויטע אהלי אפדנו בין ימים להר צבי קדש . . . (Dan 11:45).

[34] Dan 7:8: ואלו קרן אחרי זעירה . . . . See also Ibn Ezra *ad* Dan 11:44.

[35] These names do not occur in any other source.

[36] Based on an ancient midrash to Ps 72:17. See *b. Pesaḥ.* 54a; *Ned.* 39a; *Sanh.* 98b; *Pirqe R. El.* §32 (Luria, 72b).

[37] According to Theophanes, "some say" (ὡς φασί τινες) ninety thousand inhabitants of Jerusalem were killed "by the Jews" (διὰ χειρὸς τῶν Ἰουδαίων) when Khusrau II captured Jerusalem in 614. See Heinrich Graetz, *Geschichte der Juden von den ältesten Zeiten bis auf die Gegenwart* (3d ed.; 11 vols. in 13; Leipzig: Oskar Leiner, 1890–1908), 5:362; Harry Turtledove, *The Chronicle of Theophanes* (Philadelphia: University of Pennsylvania Press, 1982), 11. Buttenwieser cites two parallel traditions, one Jewish and one Christian. The former is featured in *ʾOtiyyot de-Rabbi ʿAqiva* (Jellinek, *BHM* 3:48): וכיון שבא משיח לישראל יורדין עמו מיכאל וגבריאל שרי צבאות ושרי קדושי׳ ואדירים ועושין מלחמה עם רשעים משלש שעות עד תשע שעות והורגים תשע עשר אלפים רבבות מרשעים שבאומות שנאמ׳ יתמו חטאים מן הארץ וגו׳ "When the messiah comes to Israel, Michael and Gabriel, the princes of the hosts and princes of the holy and noble ones, will descend with him. They will do battle with the wicked from the third to the ninth hours, and will slay nineteen thousand myriads of the wicked among the Gentile nations, as scripture affirms: 'the sinners will be destroyed from the earth, etc.' (Ps 104:35)." Even-Shmuel (*Midreshey Geʾullah*, 300) suggests emending תשע עשר אלפים רבבות, "nineteen thousand myriads," to תשע רבבות, "nine myriads," that is, ninety thousand.

The latter stems from Lactantius, *Div. Inst.* 7.19.5: . . . ducem sanctae militiae descensurum, et descendet comitantibus angelis in medium terrae et antecedet eum flamma inextinguibilis et uirtus angelorum tradet in manus instorum multitudinem illam quae montem circumsederit et concidetur ab hora tertia usque in uesperum. Text cited from Lactantius, *L. Caeli Firmiani Lactanti Opera omnia* (ed. Samuel Brandt; CSEL 19; Prague: Tempsky, 1890), 645; also in Buttenwieser, *Elias-Apokalypse*, 18–19 n. 10.

[38] Buttenwieser (*Elias-Apokalypse*, 30) connects this designation with that used for the Valley of Jezreel in 1 Macc 12:49 (τὸ πεδίον τὸ μέγα).

[39] Jellinek: נותרין.

progeny are destined to sink to the lowest level, as scripture states: 'And you shall be low, and you will speak from the ground' (Isa 29:4), but afterwards they will be exalted higher than all the nations, as scripture affirms: 'and the Lord your God will set you high above all the nations of the earth' (Deut 28:1)." After this all the gentile nations will come and prostrate themselves before every Israelite and lick off the dust from their feet, as scripture says: "kings will serve as your tutors, [while their princesses will be your nursemaids; they will prostrate themselves facedown on the ground to you and lick off the dust from your feet]" (Isa 49:23).[40]

On the twentieth (day) of Adar, the Messiah will come, and with him will be thirty thousand righteous ones, as scripture attests: "Righteousness will be the wrap girdling his loins" (Isa 11:5). When the nations of the world behold this happening, immediately each one of them will putrefy, both it and its cavalry, as scripture says: "and this will be the affliction with which the Lord will strike all the nations,[41] etc." (Zech 14:12, 15). At that time the Holy One, blessed be He, will address the nations of the world: "Woe to you, O wicked ones, who are (alive) at the cessation of the four world empires! All of you are to be expelled from the world, one wherein one *kor* of wheat[42] will yield about nine hundred *kor*s, and there will be analogous (fantastic yields) for wine and oil. Every tree will bear choice produce and fruits, as scripture states: 'and you, O mountains of Israel, will make your branches yield, etc.' (Ezek 36:8)." And Israel will eat (these fruits) and rejoice for forty years.[43]

After this the Holy One, blessed be He, will bring up Gog and Magog "and all their associates" (Ezek 12:14), and then all the peoples of the earth will assemble together and surround Jerusalem in order to make war. The Holy One, blessed be He, will come up and do battle with them. The Messiah will arrive, and with his help the Holy One, blessed be He, will wage war on them, as scripture forecasts: "then the Lord will go forth and fight with those nations as when He did battle on the day of war" (Zech 14:3). On that day mountains will quake and hills will shake and walls and towers will collapse. The Holy One, blessed be He, will gather all the birds of the sky and the beasts of the earth to feast on their flesh and to drink their blood, as scripture says: "the vultures will spend summer upon them, and all the

[40] Wilken points out that this passage was already identified by Jerome as one that the Jewish community of his day applied to the future reconstruction of Jerusalem (*Land Called Holy*, 208).

[41] Buttenwieser's text reads הגוים (cf. 14:18), whereas the biblical text for v. 12 has העמים.

[42] Read with Jellinek חטים in place of Buttenwieser's לטים. One *kor* is equivalent to 395.5 liters; see Avraham Even-Shoshan, *Millon ḥadash* (5 vols.; Jerusalem: Qiryat Sefer, 1964), s.v. כור.

[43] Perhaps an echo of the tradition attributed to both R. Eliezer and R. Aqiba which asserted that the messianic era (ימות המשיח) would last forty years. See *b. Sanh.* 99a; *Midr. Tanḥ.*, ʿEqev §7; *Pesiq. Rab.* §1 (Ish-Shalom, 4a); *Midr. Teh.* 90.17.

beasts of the earth will spend winter upon them" (Isa 18:6). Israel will spend seven years burning their weaponry, as scripture states: "then the inhabitants of the cities of Israel will go out[44] and set fire to the weaponry and burn (it) . . . for seven years" (Ezek 39:9). It (also) says: "The house of Israel will spend seven months burying them in order to purify the land" (Ezek 39:12).

These are the cities that will experience devastation:[45] Jericho, Beʾerot, Beth Hōrōn, Sīserīn,[46] Milkah, Arad, Shallūm,[47] Samaria, Beth Migdōl,[48] Tyre, Beth Ḥalsawet,[49] Lod, Būz, Beth ʿAynam, Hamath, Sefar, Ḥadashah,[50] Antioch, Alexandria, and "Edom." But as for all of the cities of Israel, fire and fiery angels[51] will surround them, as scripture affirms: "and I will be a wall of fire encompassing it—utterance of the Lord" (Zech 2:9). Afterwards the final day will come: its duration will be that of forty days. The mountains and hills will shudder and quake, and the earth will cry out against the wicked, saying: "In such-and-such a place did so-and-so kill so-and-so," as scripture states: "the earth will reveal her blood-guilt, etc." (Isa 26:21).

Elijah said: I beheld the dead taking form[52] and their "dust" being reshaped and made[53] like (the forms they had) when they were formerly alive so that they might render praise to God, as scripture states: "See now that I indeed am He [and there is no deity other than Me; I put to death and I resurrect, I sicken and I heal: none can escape from My power]" (Deut 32:39). Also in Ezekiel it says: "and I looked, and behold, sinews were upon them" (Ezek 37:8). The ministering angels opened their tombs and injected them with their "animating breaths" (cf. Gen 2:7), and they revivified. They (the angels) stood them up on their feet.[54] They shoved everyone who mer-

[44] Read with Buttenwieser ויצאו in place of the scribal error וישבו.

[45] Apparently as a consequence of their largely "pagan" culture?

[46] Jellinek: סוסין. Presumably a corruption of סוסיתא, the Semitic name for the Decapolis town of Hippos, identified in rabbinic sources as having a predominantly gentile population. See Buttenwieser, *Elias-Apokalypse*, 43.

[47] Buttenwieser (*Elias-Apokalypse*, 46) suggests an identification with Χαφαρσαλαμα (1 Macc 7:31), that is, כפר שלם, identified in rabbinic sources as having a predominantly gentile population.

[48] Jellinek: בית מגדיאל.

[49] Jellinek: בית חלפות.

[50] Jellinek: הרשה. Cf. Josh 15:37; 1 Macc 7:40, 45.

[51] Jellinek: מלאכי השרת, "ministering angels."

[52] Jellinek: טבועים בנהר, "sinking in a river," a reading that Buttenwieser rightly notes cannot be correct in this context.

[53] As Buttenwieser notes (*Elias-Apokalypse*, 22–23 n. 11), the language used here echoes that of the description of Adam's initial creation provided in *b. Sanh.* 38b; *Pesiq. Rab Kah.* 23.1 (Mandelbaum, 2:334).

[54] Buttenwieser (*Elias-Apokalypse*, 23 n. 5) calls attention to a parallel episode in the *ʾOtiyyot de-Rabbi ʿAqiva* (*apud* Jellinek, *BHM* 3:31): ועומד הב"ה בעצמו ומחיה אותן ומעמידן על רגליהן, "The Holy

ited punishment into a large hollow place two hundred cubits long and fifty cubits wide. The eyes of the righteous will witness the downfall of all those who did not take pleasure in (observing) the Torah of the Holy One, blessed be He, as scripture states: "they will go out and see the corpses of those people who rebelled against Me . . ." (Isa 66:24).

Elijah said: I beheld fire and brimstone coming down upon the wicked from heaven, as scripture says: "the Lord will rain coals of fire and brimstone upon the wicked" (Ps 11:6). The Holy One, blessed be He, will move the Temple a great distance from the place of eternal torment so that the righteous will not hear the sound of the cry of the wicked (suffering) and seek to obtain mercy for them. "They will be as if they never were."[55]

Elijah said: I saw Abraham, Isaac, Jacob, and all the righteous ones in sitting postures, and the land before them was sown with every sort of delightful vegetation. That tree which the Holy One, blessed be He, had prepared was standing in the middle of the garden, as scripture says: "and there will grow by the stream on its bank on both sides every kind of fruit tree; their foliage will never wither, nor will their fruit ever fail" (Ezek 47:12).[56] Boats will come "from En-gedi as far as" Eglayim[57] bearing wealth and riches[58] for the righteous ones.

Elijah (may his memory be for a blessing) said: I beheld a great city, both beautiful and glorious, descending from heaven wherein it had been built, as scripture states: "The already built Jerusalem, like the city associated to it" (Ps 122:3),[59] perfectly constructed and with its people dwelling within it. It

---

One, blessed be He, will Himself arise and resurrect them, and He will stand them up on their feet." The ministering angels are present also in this latter version of the story, where they are responsible for overseeing the return to the Holy Land of all those who died outside of Eretz Israel.

[55] A quotation of the final clause of Obad 1:16; cf. CD 2:20–21.

[56] Buttenwieser (*Elias-Apokalypse*, 38) calls attention to Rev 22:2; *1 En.* 24:2–25:7.

[57] Both Buttenwieser and Jellinek have אגלים. Cf. Ezek 47:10: מעין גדי ועד עין עגלים.

[58] Jellinek: כבוד.

[59] ירושלם הבנויה כעיר שחברה לה יחדו. A translation along these lines is required, for the verse was read as confirming the existence of a heavenly prototype of the city of Jerusalem. See *4 Ezra* 10:27, where the adjective in the phrase "*established* city" (*aedificabatur*) echoes הבנויה; *2 Bar.* 4:2–6 ("the one already prepared" [4:3]); Heb 11:16; *Tg.* Ps 122:3; *b. Ta'an.* 5a and Rashi *ad loc.*; *Midr. Tanḥ.*, Pequdey §1. Note especially the discussion of the motifs of the "Heavenly Temple" and the "Heavenly Jerusalem" by Avraham Grossman, "Jerusalem in Jewish Apocalyptic Literature," in *The History of Jerusalem: The Early Muslim Period, 638–1099* (ed. Joshua Prawer and Haggai Ben-Shammai; Jerusalem: Yad Izhak Ben-Zvi; New York: New York University Press, 1996), 302–3. For an intriguing argument that the notion of a "heavenly Jerusalem" was of Christian origin, see Rivka Nir, *The Destruction of Jerusalem and the Idea of Redemption in the Syriac Apocalypse of Baruch* (SBLEJL 20; Atlanta: Society of Biblical Literature, 2003), 21–41. The earliest traditions surrounding Q 17:1 and Muhammad's "night journey" (*isrā'*) view it as an ascent to a "heavenly Jerusalem"; see Heribert Busse, "Jerusalem in the Story of Muhammad's Night Journey and Ascension," *JSAI* 14 (1991): 1–40;

is situated by three thousand towers, with 20,000 *ris*[60] separating each tower. Within the span of every *ris* are 25,000 cubits of emeralds, pearls, and (other) jewels, as scripture says: "I will inlay your battlements with gemstones" (Isa 54:12).

Elijah said: I saw the houses and the gates of the righteous with their thresholds and door-frames constructed of precious stones. (I saw) the treasuries of the Temple opened up to their doorways [*sic*], and among them were Torah and peace, as scripture states: "all your children will be instructed by the Lord; [your children will have great peace]" (Isa 54:13), and it says: "those who love Your Torah have great peace" (Ps 119:165), and it says: "How great is Your beneficence which You have stored up for those who revere You" (Ps 31:20).

End of *Sefer Elijah*, may his memory be for a blessing.

Izhak Hasson, "The Muslim View of Jerusalem: The Qur'ān and Ḥadīth," in Prawer and Ben-Shammai, *History of Jerusalem*, 355–59.

[60] According to *m. Yoma* 6.4, one mile consists of seven and one-half *ris* (ריס). For further discussion of this unit of linear measurement, see especially Yigael Yadin, *The Temple Scroll* (3 vols.; Jerusalem: Israel Exploration Society, 1983), 1:317–18.

2

Sefer Zerubbabel

BEFITTING ITS INFLUENCE in the continuing development of Jewish apocalyptic thought, *Sefer Zerubbabel* is extant in a number of manuscript and print recensions.[1] It was first published in Constantinople in 1519 within an anthology entitled *Liqqutim Shonim*, a collection that gathered together a small quantity of similarly revelatory midrashim.[2] This edition of the work was reprinted together with brief annotations in 1807 as ספר זרובבל ונחמת ציון (*Sefer Zerubbabel and the Consolation of Zion*). This annotated edition was reprinted again, together with a so-called *(Sefer) Malkiel*, in Vilna in 1819,[3] and then reprinted once more by S. A. Wertheimer in his *Leqet Midrashim* in 1903 in Jerusalem.[4] Wertheimer had previously uncovered and published two manuscript fragments of the work stemming from the Cairo Genizah and Oxford Ms. Heb. f. 27 (2642) respectively, the latter of which he placed under the artificial rubric "Aggadat yemot ha-mašiaḥ" ("Narrative about the Messianic Age").[5] The revised and enlarged edition of Wertheimer's separate midrash anthologies prepared by his grandson presents a lightly annotated version of the Constantinople *editio princeps* together with five brief fragments culled from the aforementioned "Aggadat yemot ha-mašiaḥ."[6] Another shorter recension of the work based on two manuscripts contained in the municipal library in Leipzig was published by Adolph Jellinek in the mid-nineteenth century.[7] The fullest edition of the work, prepared by Israel Lévi, is based on a

[1] The best discussion of *Sefer Zerubbabel* and its subsequent influence remains that of Joseph Dan, *Ha-Sippur ha-ʿivri be-yemey ha-beyanim: ʿIyyunim be-toldotav* (Jerusalem: Keter, 1974), 35–46.

[2] See also מעשיות (Constantinople: Astruq de Toulon, 1519), 74a-76b.

[3] Hezekiah (Chiskia) ben Abraham, מלכיאל (Vilna and Grodno: [Romm?], 1819), 25a–28a (the latter leaf misprinted as 27), to which are appended the Sabbatian chapters from *Hekhalot Rabbati* (28a–29a) and excerpts from *Pesiqta Rabbati* (29a–29b) and *Yalqut Šimoni* (29b–30b).

[4] For the details of its publication history, see Moses Buttenwieser, *Outline of the Neo-Hebraic Apocalyptic Literature* (Cincinnati: Jennings & Pye, 1901), 33; Israel Lévi, "L'apocalypse de Zorobabel et le roi de Perse Siroès," *REJ* 68 (1914): 130; Leopold Zunz and Ḥanokh Albeck, *Haderashot be-Yisrael* (2d ed.; Jerusalem: Mosad Bialik, 1954), 311 n. 89; Yehudah Even-Shmuel, *Midreshey Geʾullah* (2d ed.; Jerusalem: Mosad Bialik, 1954), 67–70.

[5] S. A. Wertheimer, *Batey Midrashot* (4 vols. in 3; Jerusalem: Lilyanthal, 1893–97), 2:29.

[6] S. A. Wertheimer, *Batey Midrashot* (ed. A. J. Wertheimer; 2 vols.; 2d ed.; Jerusalem, 1948–53; repr., Jerusalem: Ktav wa-Sefer, 1980), 2:497–505.

[7] Adolph Jellinek, ed., *Bet ha-Midrasch: Sammlung kleiner Midraschim und vermischter Abhand-*

lengthy rendition that was incorporated within Oxford Ms. Heb. d. 11 (2797), the *Sefer ha-Zikronot* or the so-called *Chronicles of Yeraḥmeel.*[8] Lévi also drew attention to Oxford Ms. Opp. 236a, a version in an Ashkenazi cursive script that varies from both the *editio princeps* and the briefer recension published by Jellinek,[9] and Paris Ms. 326, a compilation that "contient une paraphrase partielle de notre libelle."[10] Lévi's edition also features a critical apparatus wherein he reproduces a number (although not all) of the variant readings found in the aforementioned manuscript and print editions. Even-Shmuel's *Midreshey Ge'ullah* presents that editor's highly idiosyncratic conflate version of the work. It contains many speculative emendations and questionable reconstructions, but also is accompanied by a comprehensive discussion that includes many valuable annotations. He also separately reproduces the printed editions of Constantinople, Jellinek, and Lévi.[11] Finally, there are some manuscript fragments that have not been employed in the standard printed editions of the work. Oxford Ms. Opp. 603 contains a brief version of *Sefer Zerubbabel* (fols. 32b–34b).[12] Alexander Marx called attention to some further examples of Zerubbabel materials.[13] Simon Hopkins in his published anthology of literary texts has reproduced the photographs of several fragments of *Sefer Zerubbabel* which have been recovered from the Cairo Genizah.[14]

Sefer Zerubbabel, or the *Book of Zerubbabel*, depicts the enigmatic postexilic biblical leader Zerubbabel as the recipient of a revelatory vision outlining the personalities and events associated with the restoration of Israel at the End of Days.

---

lungen aus der jüdischen Literatur (6 vols.; Leipzig, 1853–77; repr., Jerusalem: Bamberger & Wahrmann, 1938), 2:xxi-xxii, 54–57.

8 Lévi, "L'apocalypse," 131–44. That manuscript has recently been transcribed and published by Eli Yassif, ed., *Sefer ha-Zikronot hu' Divrey ha-Yamim le-Yeraḥme'el* (Tel Aviv: Tel Aviv University, 2001); see pp. 427–35 for *Sefer Zerubbabel.*

9 Fols. 13a-15b. Cf. Adolf Neubauer, *Catalogue of the Hebrew Manuscripts in the Bodleian Library* ... (Oxford: Clarendon, 1886), 26–27; also Malachi Beit-Arié, *Catalogue of the Hebrew Manuscripts in the Bodleian Library: Supplement of Addenda and Corrigenda to Volume I (A. Neubauer's Catalogue)* (Oxford: Clarendon, 1994), 22.

10 Lévi, "L'apocalypse," 130. See Alexander Marx, "Studies in Gaonic History and Literature," *JQR* n.s. 1 (1910–11): 61–104, at p. 77, where a lengthy passage from this manuscript is transcribed. Marx dates the manuscript "between 1160 and 1180."

11 Even-Shmuel, *Midreshey Ge'ullah*, 71–88; cf. 379–82 (Constantinople), 383–85 (Jellinek), 385–89 (Lévi).

12 Beit-Arié, *Catalogue*, 440: "with variations from the printed editions and shorter towards the end." This is followed (35a–36b) by a piece entitled מלך המשיח (The King Messiah) and fols. 41b–42a of the same manuscript feature a short presentation entitled ענין נהר סמבטיון ([On] the Subject of the River Sambatyon), a work related to the Eldad ha-Dani legends.

13 See Marx, "Studies," 77–78 n. 35; idem, "Additions et rectifications," *REJ* 71 (1920): 222.

14 T-S A45.5, 45.7, 45.19, and 45.22; published in Simon Hopkins, *A Miscellany of Literary Pieces from the Cambridge Genizah Collections: A Catalogue and Selection of Texts in the Taylor-Schechter Collection, Old Series, Box A45* (Cambridge: Cambridge University Library, 1978).

Literary traditions stemming from the Second Temple period exhibit some confusion regarding the precise period during which Zerubbabel was active, although all invariably identify him as a prominent authority among the initial generations of returnees from the Babylonian exile. Some sources associate Zerubbabel with the time of the Persian ruler Cyrus (prior to 530 BCE): his name appears at the head of the register of families and movable property that emigrated from Babylonia to Eretz Israel as a result of Cyrus's decree permitting their return (Ezra 2:1–2 = Neh 7:6–7 = 1 Esd 5:7–8).[15] Other sources place Zerubbabel later, during the early years of the reign of Darius (521–485 BCE),[16] or even during the reign of Artaxerxes (464–424 BCE).[17] According to the apocryphal narrative of 1 Esd 3:1–4:63, Zerubbabel served as a royal bodyguard in the court of Darius and by virtue of his rhetorical skills won that monarch's support for the return of the Judean exiles and the captured Temple vessels.[18] Complicating matters further is one strand of rabbinic tradition that identifies Zerubbabel with Nehemiah (*b. Sanh.* 38a).[19] All of these variant contextualizations represent him as closely involved in the restoration and regulation of sacrificial worship in Jerusalem (Ezra 3:2, 8; 4:2–3; 5:2; Neh 12:1, 47; Hag 1:14; Zech 4:9; Ben Sira 49:11–12; 1 Esd 6:2). An extremely intriguing testimony contained in the early Muslim historian Yaʿqūbī attributes the postexilic recovery and promulgation of the Jewish scriptures not to Ezra,[20] but to Zerubbabel, who is described as unearthing them from a pit where Nebuchadnezzar had previously attempted to dispose of them:

> Zerubbabel was the one who recovered the Torah and the books of the Prophets from the pit wherein Bukht-Naṣṣar (i.e., Nebuchadnezzar) had buried them. He

[15] See Ezra 3:2, 8; 4:2–5; 1 Esd 5:47–73; Josephus, *Ant.* 11.13–14, 92. According to the Syriac *Cave of Treasures* (oriental recension §42.17; occidental recension §42.11–12), Cyrus marries Zerubbabel's sister and is thus his brother-in-law. See Su-Min Ri, ed., *La Caverne des Trésors: Les deux recensions syriaques* (CSCO 486, scrip. syri 207; Louvain: E. Peeters, 1987), 321–23.

[16] See Ezra 5:2; all the Haggai and Zechariah references; 1 Esd 6:1–2; Josephus, *Ant.* 11.116–19.

[17] Note Clement of Alexandria (*Strom.* 1.21.124), who it states that Zerubbabel and Ezra were contemporaries.

[18] See also Josephus (*Ant.* 11.31–67), who harmonizes the divergent Cyrus and Darius traditions by stating that Zerubbabel was already serving as "governor" of Judah and had returned to Babylon only at the accession of Darius, described as an "old friend."

[19] 2 Macc 1:18–36, which attributes the rebuilding of the Temple and its dedicatory sacrifices to Nehemiah, would appear to vouchsafe the antiquity of this assimilation.

[20] Ezra's reputation as restorer of the Torah after the exile was well known among Muslim scholars thanks to first-century A.H. Judeo-Muslim tradents of *Isrāʾīliyyāt*, or "Jewish scriptural lore," like ʿAbd Allāh b. Salām, Kaʿb al-Aḥbār, and Wahb b. Munabbih. For a convenient translation of Wahb's testimony about Ezra, see Brannon M. Wheeler, *Prophets in the Quran: An Introduction to the Quran and Muslim Exegesis* (London and New York: Continuum, 2002), 287–89. Muslim access to later Christian Arabic translations of the apocryphal book of *4 Ezra* (regarding which see Adriana Drint, ed., *The Mount Sinai Arabic Version of IV Ezra* [2 vols.; CSCO 563–64, scrip. arabici 48–49; Louvain: Peeters, 1997]) would reinforce Ezra's role in the history of Jewish scripturalism.

discovered that they had not burned at all.[21] Hence he restored (and) transcribed (copies of) the Torah, the books of the Prophets, their customary practices (*sunna*), and their religious laws (*šarīʿa*). He was the first to record these scriptures.[22]

Several prophetic oracles dating from the reign of Darius exhort Zerubbabel to maintain confidence and strength in the face of an otherwise unspecified adversity (Hag 1:1; 2:2, 4, 21; Zech 4:6–7; Ezra 5:1–2). As son of Shealtiel[23] and lineal descendant of Jeconiah,[24] Zerubbabel in fact embodies the contemporary link with the preexilic Davidide line of succession, and he thus receives prophetic endorsement as a "messianic" candidate.[25] The prophet Haggai terms him "governor of Judah" (Hag 1:1, 14; 2:2, 21), and it seems possible that the mysterious Sheshbazzar (Ezra 1:8) to whom Cyrus hands over the looted Temple vessels and who bears the epithet "prince of Judah" (הנשיא ליהודה) is none other than Zerubbabel.[26] The historical fate of Zerubbabel, assuming he was such, remains shrouded in mystery. It is unlikely that the imperial authorities would have tolerated the revival of dynastic forms of discourse in the province of Yehud, and it is possible that he was either recalled or simply liquidated. According to the late rabbinic chronographic source *Seder ʿOlam Zuta*, Zerubbabel returned permanently

[21] In his earlier account of the Babylonian sack of Jerusalem, Yaʿqūbī had described how the impious Nebuchadnezzar had taken the Jewish scriptures, dumped them in a hole, tossed flaming torches on top of them, and filled the pit with dirt.

[22] Yaʿqūbī, *Taʾrīkh* (2 vols.; Beirut: Dār Sādir, 1960), 1:66.4–6; cf. M. T. Houtsma, ed., *Ibn Wadih qui dicitur al-Jaʿqubi historiae . . .* (2 vols.; Leiden: Brill, 1883), 1:71.12–15; R. Y. Ebied and L. R. Wickham, "Al-Yaḳūbī's Account of the Israelite Prophets and Kings," *JNES* 29 (1970): 97; Camilla Adang, *Muslim Writers on Judaism and the Hebrew Bible: From Ibn Rabban to Ibn Hazm* (Leiden: Brill, 1996), 226–27.

[23] Zerubbabel is identified as the son of Shealtiel (בן שאלתיאל) in Hag 1:1; 2:23; Ezra 3:2, 8; 5:2; Neh 12:1, and with the slightly variant spelling בן שלתיאל in Hag 1:12, 14; 2:2. Contrast 1 Chr 3:17–19, but note Radaq *ad loc.*, who points out that the naming of Pedaiah as Zerubbabel's father in v. 19 does not necessarily contradict the other sources' ascription of the role of forebear to Shealtiel (see also Ibn Ezra *ad* Exod 2:10)—note however LXX 1 Chr 3:19 for a different resolution of the difficulty. *4 Ezra* 3:1 curiously effects an identification between Shealtiel and Ezra (one Arabic version makes Ezra the "son of Shealtiel"!); for a discussion of the problems this amalgam engenders, see Michael E. Stone, "The Metamorphosis of Ezra: Jewish Apocalypse and Medieval Vision," *JTS* n.s. 33 (1982): 2–3; idem, *Fourth Ezra: A Commentary on the Book of Fourth Ezra* (Hermeneia; Minneapolis: Fortress, 1990), 55–56.

[24] 1 Chr 3:17–19; *b. Sanh.* 37b-38a; *Lev. Rab.* 10.5 (Margulies, 1:208–9).

[25] Cf. Zech 3:8 and the traditional commentaries; also Hag 2:23; 1 Esd 5:5; Josephus, *Ant.* 11.73. According to *Liv. Pro.* 15.3 (see *OTP* 2:394), it was the prophet Zechariah who named Shealtiel's son Zerubbabel.

[26] Ibn Ezra *ad* Ezra 1:8 says of Sheshbazzar that "he is Zerubbabel, but he was called so (i.e., Sheshbazzar) in the language of the Chaldeans." See also Ibn Ezra *ad* Dan 6:29, where he supplies two reasons why Sheshbazzar and Zerubbabel must be the same figure. 1 Esd 6:17 has the Persian monarch transfer the Temple vessels to both Zerubbabel and Sheshbazzar. Other traditional sources identify Sheshbazzar with Daniel.

to Babylonia in order to assume the office of exilarch (Aramaic *resh galuta*; Arabic *ra*ʾ*s al-jālūt*).[27]

The figure of Zerubbabel attracted its share of messianic associations. The fourth-century Christian commentator Ephrem Syrus expounds the infamous imagery of the "star from Jacob" of Num 24:17 as referring to Zerubbabel.[28] Late antique and geonic Jewish traditions occasionally portray Zerubbabel as intimately involved in a series of events coordinated with the advent of the Messiah.[29] The liturgical poet Eleazar ha-Qallir in his popular lament *Be-yamim ha-hem* (In Those Days) depicts Zerubbabel as the one who alerts the angels Michael and Gabriel to begin the final battle against Israel's oppressors.[30] The *ʾOtiyyot de R. Aqiva* (Alphabet of R. Akiva) states that after God expounds the "new Torah" that the Messiah will promulgate, Zerubbabel will arise and recite the *qaddish de-rabbanan*, provoking a response of affirmation from all beings, including even those suffering in Gehenna.[31] An analogous tradition occurs in the pseudo-*Seder Eliyahu Zuta*, where instead of God it is Zerubbabel himself who expounds the Torah "like a *meturgeman*."[32] Yet another closely related tradition is found in

[27] וחזר זרובבל לבבל ומת שם. Text cited from Adolf Neubauer, *Mediaeval Jewish Chronicles and Chronological Notes* (2 vols.; Oxford, 1887–95; repr., Amsterdam: Philo Press, 1970), 2:71.3. Compare Yassif, *Sefer ha-Zikronot*, 372, which envisions two separate journeys by Zerubbabel from Babylon to Jerusalem. After the successful rebuilding of the Temple, he returns to Babylon as above. For Zerubbabel's exilarchate, see Moshe Gil, "The Exilarchate," in *The Jews of Medieval Islam: Community, Society, and Identity* (ed. Daniel Frank; Études sur le judaïsme medieval 16; Leiden: Brill, 1995), 33.

[28] J. S. Assemani, ed., *Sancti patris nostri Ephraem Syri opera omnia* (6 vols.; Rome: Typographia Vaticana, 1737–43), 1:153E; cited by Louis Ginzberg, *The Legends of the Jews* (7 vols.; Philadelphia: Jewish Publication Society of America, 1909–38), 6:133 n. 782.

[29] The following references are taken from Ginzberg, *Legends*, 6:438 n. 25.

[30] בימים ההם ובעת ההיא בחדש הששי הוא חדש אלול בשרו יכריז בן שאלתיאל וירדו מיכאל וגבריאל לערוך מלחמת נקמת אל ולא ישאירו אחד מאיבי אל, "In those days and at that time, in the sixth month which is the month Ellul, *when the son of Shealtiel beholds it* (i.e., the splitting apart of the Mount of Olives and the Messiah's approach) *he will cry out*, and Michael and Gabriel will descend in order to wage the war of God's vengeance. None of God's enemies will remain (alive)." Text cited from the edition of the *piyyut* contained in Even-Shmuel, *Midreshey Geʾullah*, 114.

[31] Jellinek, *BHM* 3:27–28: עתיד הקב״ה להיות יושב בגן עדן ודורש . . . והקב״ה דורש להם טעמי תורה חדשה שעתיד הקב״ה ליתן להם על ידי משיח וכיון שמגיע לאגדה עומד זרובבל בן שאלתיאל על רגליו ואומ׳ יתגדל ויתקדש וקולו הולך מסוף העולם עד סופו וכל באי עולם עונין אמן ואף רשעי ישראל וצדיקי אומות העולם שנשתיירו בגיהנם, "The Holy One, blessed be He, will sit in Paradise and expound . . . and the Holy One, blessed be He, will expound to them the presuppositions of the new Torah which he will reveal to them in the future via the agency of the Messiah. When He reaches (completes?) the exposition, Zerubbabel b. Shealtiel will stand up and recite 'May He be magnified and sanctified, etc.' His voice will reach from one end of the universe to the other. All the inhabitants of the world will answer 'Amen!' Even the wicked ones from Israel and those righteous Gentiles who remain in Gehenna will respond and say 'Amen!'" See also Jellinek, *BHM* 6:63; Even-Shmuel, *Midreshey Geʾullah*, 347; Yassif, *Sefer ha-Zikronot*, 448–49.

[32] Meir Friedmann, *Pseudo-Seder Eliahu Zuta* (Vienna: n.p., 1904), 32: ועולה הקב״ה ויושב בפמליא שלו ועומד זרובבל בן שאלתיאל כמתורגמן והוא מגלה לפניו טעמי תורה. Note also Jellinek, *BHM* 3:75, a text that combines elements of the preceding *ʾOtiyyot de R. Aqiva* tradition with the present one.

Hekhalot Rabbati, wherein Zerubbabel is depicted as the mediator and authoritative interpreter of a divine theophany witnessed by the builders of the Second Temple.[33] In a midrashic fragment preserved in the early geonic code *Halakhot Gedolot*,[34] it is stated that both Elijah and Zerubbabel will be responsible for resolving judicial conundrums at the dawn of the coming age.[35] Finally, a Persian Danielic apocalypse, rendered in medieval Hebrew as *Maᶜaseh Daniel*, states that the Davidic Messiah, Elijah, and Zerubbabel will together ascend the Mount of Olives, whereupon the Messiah will command Elijah to sound the shofar.[36] While Zerubbabel's precise role in these latter eschatological proceedings remains unexplicated by *Maᶜaseh Daniel*, a tradition found in R. Hai Gaon's influential responsum concerning the eschaton avers that "Zerubbabel is the one who blows this shofar."[37]

It should also be noted that Zerubbabel attracted attention from at least one Muslim scholar who was interested in rehearsing or recovering passages from pre-qur'ānic scriptures which in his view prefigured the coming of Muhammad and the religion of Islam. In one manuscript version of the *Kitāb aᶜlām al-nubuwwa* of Māwardī, who was a prominent eleventh-century Iraqi scholar of religious law, there occurs a singular Arabic translation of Zech 4:1–6 wherein the biblical annunciation and mission of "Zerubbabel" are deciphered as a prediction of the advent of Muhammad.[38]

But perhaps the most intriguing messianic reading of the figure of Zerubbabel appears within a garbled summary of obscure prophetological and eschatological

[33] Schäfer §298 (except for Ms. V228 where it is §297); pericope references are to Peter Schäfer, ed., *Synopse zur Hekhalot-Literatur* (TSAJ 2; Tübingen: J. C. B. Mohr, 1981). See Michael D. Swartz, "Hekhalot Rabbati ##297–306: A Ritual for the Cultivation of the Prince of the Torah," in *Ascetic Behavior in Greco-Roman Antiquity: A Sourcebook* (ed. Vincent L. Wimbush; SAC; Minneapolis: Fortress, 1990), 227–34; idem, *Scholastic Magic: Ritual and Revelation in Early Jewish Mysticism* (Princeton: Princeton University Press, 1996), 92–108; Joseph Dan, "The Memory of the Future and the Utopia of the Past," in idem, *Jewish Mysticism* (4 vols.; Northvale, N.J.: Jason Aronson, 1998–99), 1:124.

[34] Compiled in the ninth century by R. Simeon Qayyara. For a recent discussion of this work's provenance, see Robert Brody, *The Geonim of Babylonia and the Shaping of Medieval Jewish Culture* (New Haven and London: Yale University Press, 1998), 223–32.

[35] Ezriel Hildesheimer, ed., *Halakhot Gedolot ᶜal pi ketav yad Romi* (Berlin: Hevrat Meqitze Nirdamim, 1888–92), 223: . . . ולתלות כל תיקו עד שיבא זרובבל ואליהו ויפרשו וידרשו כל סתרי תורה . . . , ". . . and to suspend every insoluble case until the advent of Zerubbabel and Elijah: they will interpret and expound all the mysteries of the Torah. . . ." Text cited from Lévi, "L'apocalypse (3)," *REJ* 71 (1920): 58 n. 1.

[36] Jellinek, *BHM* 5:128: משיח בן דוד אליהו וזרובבל יעלו על ראש הר הזיתים ומשיח יצוה את אליהו לתקוע בשופר. See also Even-Shmuel, *Midreshey Ge'ullah*, 225.

[37] Even-Shmuel, *Midreshey Ge'ullah*, 138: ואומרים כי זרבבל תוקע בשופר הזה.

[38] The Arabic text is transcribed in Martin Schreiner, "Beiträge zur Geschichte der Bibel in der arabischen Literatur," in *Semitic Studies in Memory of Rev. Dr. Alexander-Kohut* (ed. George Alexander Kohut; Berlin: S. Calvary, 1897), 509–10.

lore that was reportedly taught among a Syro-Mesopotamian gnostic sect known as the Ḥewyāyē (i.e., Naassenes).[39] According to Theodore bar Konai, an eighth-century Nestorian bishop whose Syriac treatise the *Scholion* provides us with an invaluable description of a number of pre-Christian and post-Christian religious sects,[40] the Ḥewyāyē promulgate among other things the following set of doctrines:

> With regard to Christ, they claim that his father's name was Nʾwr (ܢܐܘܪ) and that he had a wife named Miriam, and that Christ was born from them. They designate Christ with many names—Abel, Manasseh, Perʿūn,[41] Zerubbabel—and assert that he is associated with the androgyne named Babel.[42] This is why they call him "Zerubbabel," for he sows seed in Babel.[43] They also claim there is a church at the ends of the earth wherein Christ is, along with his father Nʾwr and his mother Miriam, and that he will come after the Antichrist (ܡܫܝܚܐ ܕܓܠܐ) comes and kills the Jews and all of humankind.[44]

Embedded within these lines are a number of tantalizing items that echo the *dramatis personae* as well as the configuring scenes of the Jewish *Sefer Zerubbabel.* First and foremost is their common exploitation and realization of the messianic dimensions of the biblical character Zerubbabel. The gnostic "apocalypse," assuming such a work existed, apparently connected the office and perhaps even

[39] The earlier heresiological compilations of Irenaeus, Hippolytus, and Epiphanius offer no sources or parallels for the information supplied about the Syro-Mesopotamian Ḥewyāyē. See Stephen Gerö, "Ophite Gnosticism According to Theodore bar Koni's Liber Scholiorum," in *IV Symposium Syriacum 1984: Literary Genres in Syriac Literature (Groningen-Oosterhesselen 10–12 September)* (ed. H. J. W. Drijvers et al.; OrChrAn 229; Rome: Pont. Institutum Studiorum Orientalium, 1987), 265–74.

[40] Theodore bar Konai, *Liber Scholiorum* (ed. Addai Scher; 2 vols.; CSCO, scrip. syri series II, t. 65–66; Paris: Carolus Poussielgue, 1910–12). For an excellent introduction to Theodore and his book, see Sidney H. Griffith, "Theodore bar Kônî's *Scholion*: A Nestorian *Summa contra Gentiles* from the First Abbasid Century," in *East of Byzantium: Syria and Armenia in the Formative Period* (ed. Nina G. Garsoïan et al.; Washington, DC: Dumbarton Oaks, 1982), 53–72.

[41] Certainly not the identically spelled "Pharaoh" (ܦܪܥܘܢ), an appellation devoid of messianic significance. As Gerö has perceptively suggested ("Ophite Gnosticism," 271 n. 30), this enigmatic entity should be viewed as a forerunner of the Mandaean *ʿuthra* Pirūn (*pyrwn*). If Lidzbarski is correct in deriving the name from the Syriac stem ܦܪܥ (meaning "to bud, flower, send out shoots"), an appropriately messianic semantic field emerges; namely, that of the "shoot" or "branch" of David (Jer 23:5; 33:15; Zech 3:8; 6:12; cf. Isa 11:1). See Mark Lidzbarski, *Das Johannesbuch der Mandäer* (2 vols.; Giessen: Alfred Töpelmann, 1905–15), 2:7 n. 1.

[42] The "androgyne named Babel" (ܢܡܒܠܬܕܪܬܐ ... ܗܘ ܕܐܡܪܝܢ ܠܗ ܒܒܠ) was previously identified by Theodore as an angelic archon in the shape of a weasel (!) who patrolled the fifth heaven of the Naassene cosmos.

[43] Compare *b. Sanh.* 38a: זרובבל שנזרע בבבל ומה שמו נחמיה בן חכליה שמו "(Why was he called) Zerubbabel? Because *he was sown in Babel.* And what was his (actual) name? Nehemiah ben Hakaliah was his (actual) name." An identical wordplay thus underlies both the amoraic and gnostic "explanations" for this figure's name.

[44] Theodore bar Konai, *Liber Scholiorum* (ed. Scher), 2:336.13–23.

effected the essential identity of its Messiah with several scriptural or angelic worthies, among whom is registered Zerubbabel. The Naassene Christ's sequestration in an unnamed church situated "at the ends of the earth" eerily mirrors *Sefer Zerubbabel*'s analogous incarceration of the Davidic Messiah within a "church" in distant Rome (given the prominence of "Babel" in the gnostic fragment, one must also take into account the possible relevance for both texts of earlier Jewish apocalyptic's common exegetical equation of Rome with Babylon). The redemptive advent of both messianic figures is identically triggered by the murderous depredations of the Antichrist. Interestingly both apocalypses script roles for the "mother" of the Messiah although their respective activities differ: Hephṣibah is at the forefront of the military resistance to the forces of chaos, whereas Miriam remains in seclusion with her son (and husband!) during the period of his occultation. More speculatively, the peculiar name of Christ's father—N'wr (ܢܐܘܪ)—exhibits at least an audible similarity to one of the most common designations for the angelic prince Metatron, who functions as the medium of revelation in the *Sefer Zerubbabel*; namely, "Youth" (נער).[45]

Issues pertaining to the date and provenance of *Sefer Zerubbabel* remain problematic. Although Jellinek termed the work *sehr alt*,[46] a number of nineteenth-century interpreters followed Graetz in placing the work in the eleventh century.[47] Most modern scholars have accepted the persuasive arguments of Lévi for locating the work during the first quarter of the seventh century in Palestine within the context of the fierce struggles of Persia and Rome for control of the Holy Land.[48] Allusions to Islam or the coming of the Arab conquest are minimal at best. The

[45] For the general weakening of the guttural consonants in the various dialects of eastern Aramaic, see J. N. Epstein, *Diqduq Aramit Bavlit* (ed. E. Z. Melamed; Jerusalem: Magnes; Tel Aviv: Devir, 1960), 17–18, and note the responsum of R. Hai Gaon quoted there. It does not seem far-fetched to posit a possible philological connection between these words.

[46] Jellinek, *BHM* 2:xxii.

[47] References supplied by Lévi, "L'apocalypse (2)," *REJ* 69 (1914), 108–11. Graetz also opined that it was composed in Italy and was probably unknown in Palestine, neither of which proposals seems likely now.

[48] See Lévi, "L'apocalypse (2)," *REJ* 69 (1914): 108–15. Note also Dan, *Sippur*, 36–37, 43; Salo W. Baron, *A Social and Religious History of the Jews* (18 vols.; 2d ed.; Philadelphia: Jewish Publication Society; New York: Columbia University Press, 1952–83), 5:354 n. 3; Brannon M. Wheeler, "Imagining the Sasanian Capture of Jerusalem," *OCP* 57 (1991): 73; Walter E. Kaegi, *Byzantium and the Early Islamic Conquests* (Cambridge: Cambridge University Press, 1992), 207; David Biale, "Counter-History and Jewish Polemics Against Christianity: The *Sefer toldot yeshu* and the *Sefer zerubavel*," *Jewish Social Studies* n.s. 6 (1999): 137. Joseph Dan has recently argued against a seventh-century setting, preferring instead to place it indeterminately "within the range of the third to the sixth centuries"; cf. his "Armilus: The Jewish Antichrist and the Origins and Dating of the *Sefer Zerubbavel*," in *Toward the Millennium: Messianic Expectations from the Bible to Waco* (ed. Peter Schäfer and Mark Cohen; Leiden: Brill, 1998), 73–104, at 98. Wheeler departs from a general consensus that the work is Palestinian in provenance by suggesting that *Sefer Zerubbabel* was authored in Edessa after the arrival of Heraclius in Jerusalem in 630.

confusing calculations pertaining to a lapsed number of years or dynastic successions of kings may reflect later attempts to update the book's information in the light of more recent history. Even-Shmuel has suggested that the book's reference to the passage of "990 years" need not begin its count with the destruction of the Temple in 68 CE, but may be keyed to its reconstruction in the sixth century BCE. If so, then by using the rabbinic calculation of the duration of the Second Temple as 420 years and subtracting that sum from 990, the work may aim at 570 + 68 or 638 CE as the anticipated time of the End.[49]

References to or explicit acknowledgment of *Sefer Zerubbabel* among medieval Jewish sources do not clarify these questions to any great extent. The Zohar (3.173b) is cognizant of the legend of Hephṣibah, the mother of the Davidic Messiah: her name and role are unique to *Sefer Zerubbabel* and its derivative literature.[50] R. Eleazar b. Judah of Worms (1165–1230) refers to the book in his *Sefer Roqeaḥ* under the rubric "Baraitha de-Zerubbabel" (ברייתא דזרובבל).[51] In his commentary to Exod 2:22, Abraham Ibn Ezra (1089–1164) criticizes *Sefer Zerubbabel* as "unreliable."[52] Some editions of the commentary to *ʾAbot* contained in *Maḥzor Vitry*, supposedly the work of Rashi (1040–1105), refer to *Sefer Zerubbabel* for the identification of Aaron's rod (*m. ʾAbot* 5.6).[53] It seems likely that both R. Saadya Gaon (882–942) and R. Hai ben Sherira Gaon (939–1038) knew it, although neither refers to it by name.[54] Yet firm evidence for the existence of *Sefer Zerubbabel* prior to the tenth century remains elusive. The partial inclusion and expansion of some sections of *Sefer Zerubbabel* found in the final portion of some editions of *Hekhalot Rabbati* are not indigenous to that work, but stem from the seventeenth-century messianic movement of Shabbatai Ṣevi.[55] Some have pointed to the eschatological poetry of Eleazar ha-Qallir as evidence for the work's existence, especially a *piyyut* known by the title *ʾOto ha-yom* prepared for recitation

[49] Even-Shmuel, *Midreshey Geʾullah*, lix–lx; 61–63.

[50] For some recent discussions of this figure, see Biale, "Counter-History," 139–42; Peter Schäfer, *Mirror of His Beauty: Feminine Images of God from the Bible to the Early Kabbalah* (Princeton: Princeton University Press, 2002), 213–16; Martha Himmelfarb, "The Mother of the Messiah in the Talmud Yerushalmi and Sefer Zerubbabel," in *The Talmud Yerushalmi and Graeco-Roman Culture, III* (ed. Peter Schäfer; TSAJ 93; Tübingen: Mohr Siebeck, 2002), 369–89.

[51] Marx, "Studies," 76.

[52] כל ספר שלא כתבוהו נביאים או חכמים מפי הקבלה אין לסמוך עליו . . . וככה ספר זרובבל . . . ., "any book not authored by a prophet or a Sage reliant upon tradition is unreliable . . . such as *Sefer Zerubbabel*. . . ." Text cited from Asher Weiser, ed., *Perushey ha-Torah le-Rabbenu Abraham Ibn Ezra* (3 vols.; Jerusalem: Mosad Harav Kook, 1977), 2:20. See also Zunz-Albeck, *Haderashot*, 311 n. 88.

[53] Other editions however read "Chronicles of Moses" instead.

[54] Even-Shmuel, *Midreshey Geʾullah*, 66. Jellinek (*BHM* 2:xxii) points out that Saadya already knows the Armilos legend.

[55] See Even-Shmuel, *Midreshey Geʾullah*, 352–70; Gershom Scholem, *Sabbatai Ṣevi: The Mystical Messiah, 1626–1676* (Princeton: Princeton University Press, 1973), 738 n. 135; Ithamar Gruenwald, *Apocalyptic and Merkavah Mysticism* (AGJU 14; Leiden: Brill, 1980), 150 n. 2.

on Tishʿa be-Av, the fast-day commemorating the destruction of the First and Second Temples.[56] J. Yahalom has published a more complete version of this *piyyut* based on at least seven recensions that have been recovered from the Cairo Genizah,[57] all of which (he argues) should be dated prior to the extant "prose versions" of *Sefer Zerubbabel*.[58] It is of course possible that *Sefer Zerubbabel* takes its inspiration from the *payyetan*,[59] whose precise *floruit* at any rate is much disputed. One might cite as an analogy the biblical examples embodied in the Song at the Sea (Exod 15:1–18) and the Song of Deborah (Judg 5:1–31a), each of which is paired with a companion prose rendering of the redemptive events celebrated therein. However, these two biblical songs transmit ancient tribal legends extolling the martial triumphs of ancestral worthies, whereas the *piyyut* points to the future and "plays with eschatological motifs, conjuring up a vision of the march of armies and the proliferation of supernatural events."[60] Further study would seem to be required before more definitive results in their comparative dating can be achieved.

Several targumic passages are reminiscent of the book's distinctive contents. *Tg.* Cant 7:13–8:14 weaves a lengthy eschatological tapestry that intersects at key points with motifs from *Sefer Zerubbabel*.[61] Some manuscripts and printed editions of *Tg.* Isa 11:4 render that messianically charged verse as follows: "he [i.e., the Messiah] will judge the poor fairly and provide reliable evidence for the less fortunate among the people; he will smite the wicked of the earth with the word of his mouth, and with the utterance of his lips he will slay Armilos the evil one (ארמילוס רשיעא)."[62] *Tg. Ps.-J.* Deut 34:1–3 exploits the toponyms found in those verses to depict the following visionary scene:

[56] For an edition of the *piyyut* and bibliographical notices, see Even-Shmuel, *Midreshey Geʾullah*, 154–60. Note also Bernard Lewis, "On That Day: A Jewish Apocalyptic Poem on the Arab Conquests," in *Mélanges d'Islamologie: Volume dédié à la mémoire de Armand Abel* (ed. Pierre Salmon; Leiden: Brill, 1974), 197–200; Robert G. Hoyland, *Seeing Islam As Others Saw It* (Studies in Late Antiquity and Early Islam 13; Princeton: Darwin Press, 1997), 319–20.

[57] Joseph Yahalom, "ʿAl toqpan shel yetsirot sifrut ke-maqor le-berur sheʾelot historiyot," *Cathedra* 11 (1979): 125–33 (Hebrew).

[58] Joseph Yahalom, "The Temple and the City in Liturgical Hebrew Poetry," in *The History of Jerusalem: The Early Muslim Period, 638–1099* (ed. Joshua Prawer and Haggai Ben-Shammai; Jerusalem: Yad Izhak Ben-Zvi; New York: New York University Press, 1996), 278–80.

[59] E.g., Baron, *History*, 5:152.

[60] Hoyland, *Seeing Islam*, 320.

[61] I am indebted to Philip S. Alexander for calling my attention to this passage. One edition of *Tg.* Cant 7:13–8:5 is available in Gustav Dalman, *Aramäische Dialektproben* (2d ed.; Leipzig: J. C. Hinrichs, 1927; repr., Darmstadt: Wissenschaftliche Buchgesellschaft, 1960), 12–14.

[62] Alexander Sperber, ed., *The Bible in Aramaic: Based on Old Manuscripts and Printed Texts* (5 vols.; Leiden, 1959–73; repr., Leiden: Brill, 1992), 3:25 and the critical apparatus. See also Even-Shmuel, *Midreshey Geʾullah*, 92; Heinrich Graetz, *Geschichte der Juden von den ältesten Zeiten bis auf die Gegenwart* (3d ed.; 11 vols. in 13; Leipzig: Oskar Leiner, 1890–1908), 5:413. Many scholars consider this a later addition to the targumic text; see Zunz-Albeck, *Haderashot*, 252 n. 9; 430 n. 31.

Moses went up from the plains of Moab to Mount Nebo, a high peak above Jericho, and the *Memra* of the Lord showed him all the mighty protectors of the Land. (He showed him) the martial feats destined to be performed by Jephthah of Gilead and the victories which would be won by Samson bar Manoah of the tribe of Dan. (He was also shown) the thousand commanders from the tribe of Naphtali who allied themselves with Barak; the kings whom Joshua bar Nun the Ephraimite would slay; the martial exploits of Gideon bar Joash of the tribe of Manasseh; and all the kings of Israel and the kingdom of Judah who would rule in the Land until the final destruction of the Temple. (He was also shown) the king of the south who would ally himself to the king of the north in order to destroy the inhabitants of the Land;[63] the Ammonite and Moabite inhabitants of the plain who would oppress them; that is, Israel; the exile of the disciples of Elijah who would depart from the valley of Jericho along with the exile of the 2,200 disciples of Elisha[64] who would depart from the "City of Palms" (i.e., Jericho) at the hands of their Israelite brethren;[65] the oppression of each and every generation; the punishment of Armalgos [*sic*] the evil one (ארמלגוס רשיעא);[66] the wars fought with Gog; and how Michael would arise with strength to deliver (Israel) at the time of (her) greatest peril.[67]

Finally, *Tg. Tos.* Zech 12:10 expands that biblical verse to read as follows:

I will place a spirit of true prophecy and prayerfulness upon the house of David and the inhabitants of Judah. Afterwards the Messiah of the lineage of Ephraim (משיח בר אפרים) will emerge and fight a battle with Gog, but Gog will slay him in front of the gate of Jerusalem. Then they (i.e., Israel) will look to Me and seek from Me the reason why the nations have stabbed the Messiah of the lineage of Ephraim, and they will mourn him as a father and mother would mourn their only child, and they will grieve for him the way they would grieve for (the death of) a firstborn.[68]

The present translation relies primarily on the text of the Oxford manuscript first published by Lévi and which I have lately compared with the new transcription of Yassif. In addition, I have also consulted the printed editions of Jellinek, Wertheimer, and Even-Shmuel and have made occasional use of the Genizah fragments published in Hopkins. Other manuscript versions of this work that I have consulted include Oxford Ms. Opp. 236a fols. 13a–15b; Oxford Ms. Opp. 603 fols.

63 See Dan 11:5ff.

64 See *b. Ketub.* 106a and Rashi *ad loc.*; also Ginzberg, *Legends*, 6:348 n. 23.

65 Cf. 2 Chr 28:8–15.

66 A marginal note in the manuscript states: "Armilos (ארמילוס) the evil one whom the nations of the world call Antichrist (אנטקריסטו)."

67 Translated from David Rieder, ed., *Targum Yonatan ben ʿUziel on the Pentateuch* (Jerusalem: Salomon, 1974), 308. See also Even-Shmuel, *Midreshey Geʾullah*, 91–92.

68 A marginal note in Codex Reuchlinianus, cited from the critical apparatus of Sperber, *Bible in Aramaic*, 3:495. See also Dalman, *Aramäische Dialektproben*, 12; Even-Shmuel, *Midreshey Geʾullah*, 92 n. 16.

32b–34; and Oxford Ms. Heb. f. 27 (2642) fols. 42–43.[69] Of the extant translations of this work, the best to date is that of Martha Himmelfarb, "Sefer Zerubbabel," in *Rabbinic Fantasies: Imaginative Narratives from Classical Hebrew Literature* (ed. David Stern and Mark Jay Mirsky; Philadelphia: Jewish Publication Society, 1990), 67–90.[70]

THE PROPHETIC VISION OF ZERUBBABEL BEN SHEALTIEL[71]

(This is) the word which came to Zerubbabel the son of Shealtiel, (future) governor of Judah.[72] On the twenty-fourth day of the seventh month,[73] the Lord showed me this spectacle there while I was prostrate in prayer before the Lord my God, experiencing a visionary spectacle which I saw by the river Kebar.[74] And as I was reciting[75] (the passage of the *ʿAmidah* which ends) "Blessed are You, O Lord, the One Who resuscitates the dead!," my heart groaned within me, thinking "[How will][76] the form of the Temple[77] come into existence?" He answered me from the doors of heaven and said to me, "Are you Zerubbabel ben Shealtiel, governor of Judah?" I

[69] With regard to this last manuscript, see Adolf Neubauer and A. E. Cowley, *Catalogue of the Hebrew Manuscripts in the Bodleian Library, Volume Two* (Oxford: Clarendon, 1906), 37.

[70] Another English translation, inexplicably based upon the inferior text found in Jellinek and which appears unaware of Himmelfarb's work, is offered by David C. Mitchell, *The Message of the Psalter: An Eschatological Programme in the Book of Psalms* (JSOTSup 252; Sheffield: Sheffield Academic Press, 1997), 315–20; 340–43 (text).

[71] Oxford Ms. Opp. 236a reads: בעזרת האל אתחיל ספר זרובבל בן שאלתיאל, "With God's help I will begin the Book of Zerubbabel ben Shealtiel."

[72] For this precise prophetic formula (הדבר אשר היה אל . . .), see Jer 7:1; 11:1; 18:1; 21:1; 30:1; 32:1; 34:1, 8; 35:1; 40:1; 44:1. The character Zerubbabel is not simply "prophetized" (so Even-Shmuel); he is a deliberate fusion of the exilic prophets Jeremiah and Ezekiel. The choice of Zerubbabel as agent is probably based on Zech 4:9.

[73] Note Neh 9:1: וביום עשרים וארבעה לחדש הזה נאספו בני ישראל בצום ובשקים ואדמה עליהם, "and on the twenty-fourth day of this month (according to 8:14, the seventh) the children of Israel assembled for a fast wearing sackcloth and dirt." Even-Shmuel emends השביעי to שבט on the basis of Zech 1:7, 16, but there is no textual support for this change.

[74] Following Jellinek (על נהר כבר); the manuscript reads an unintelligible בכברה. The structure of the final clause is indebted to Ezek 43:3; cf. also 3:23 and 10:22.

[75] Manuscript reads ובאומרים; Lévi follows the other recensions and printed editions in emending to ובאומרי.

[76] Supplied from Jellinek.

[77] Literally בית עולמים "eternal House." Early rabbinic sources employ this phrase as a circumlocution for the Temple; see, e.g., *t. Zebaḥ.* 13.6–8; *Mek.* Boʾ, Pisḥa §1 (Horovitz-Rabin, 2.14). Chronologically later sources sometimes use it to refer to Jerusalem; note Rashi to *b. Sanh.* 94a and especially *Ḥul.* 24a (נקראת בית עולמים ירושלים). See also Even-Shmuel, *Midreshey Geʾullah*, 56–57 n. 5.

responded, "I am your servant." He answered me and conversed with me just as a person would speak to their friend.[78] I could hear His voice, but I could not see His appearance. I continued to lie prostrate as before, and I completed my prayer. Then I went to my house.

On the eleventh day of the month ʾAdar He was speaking with me (again) there, and He said to me, "Are you my servant Zerubbabel?" I responded, "I am your servant." He said to me, "Come to me! Ask (anything) and I will tell you!" I answered and said, "What might I ask? That my appointed lifespan be short and my destiny fulfilled?" He said to me: "I will make you live (a long life)." He repeated, "May you live (a long time)!"[79]

A wind lifted me up between heaven and earth[80] and carried me to the great city Nineveh,[81] city of blood,[82] and I thought "Woe is me, for my attitude has been contentious[83] and (now) my life is at great risk!" So I arose in distress in order to pray and entreat the favor of the name[84] of the Lord God of Israel. I confessed all my transgressions and my sins, for my attitude had been contentious, and I said: "Ah Lord! I have acted wrongly, I have transgressed, I have sinned, for my attitude has been contentious. You are the Lord God, the One Who made everything by a command[85] from Your mouth, and (Who) with a word from Your lips will revivify the dead!" He said to me, "Go to the 'house of filth'[86] near the market-district,"[87] and I went just as He had commanded me. He said to me, "Turn this way," and so

[78] Based on Exod 33:11.

[79] Counteracting Zerubbabel's sarcastic wish to die prematurely?

[80] Compare Ezek 8:3.

[81] Jonah 1:2; 3:2; 4:11; and cf. Gen 10:12 through the lens of *b. Yoma* 10a. We learn below that the name Nineveh encodes Rome.

[82] Based on Nah 3:1; cf. Ezek 22:2; 24:6, 9, where this same epithet is applied to Jerusalem.

[83] Both Lévi and Yassif emend to נחלה, but T-S A45.19 (Hopkins, *Miscellany*, 64.3) confirms that נחלק is correct. For the idiom, see Hos 10:2 and its interpretation in early rabbinic sources.

[84] Jellinek's text reads פני in place of שם; cf. Zech 7:2; 8:21–22.

[85] במאמר פיך; T-S A45.19 (Hopkins, *Miscellany*, 64.5) and Jellinek are closer to Ps 33:6 with ברוח פיך.

[86] Jellinek has the correct reading (בית התורף) in place of the manuscript's בית החורף, "winter-palace." As Yassif points out, the former is a term in medieval Jewish literature for a Christian church or cathedral. See also Dan, *Sippur*, 38; Moshe Idel, *Messianic Mystics* (New Haven and London: Yale University Press, 1998), 347 n. 9; Biale, "Counter-History," 139. One might note the comparable disparaging Muslim substitution of *qumāma* ("garbage, refuse") for *qiyāma* ("resurrection") in the Arabic name for the Church of the Holy Sepulchre in Jerusalem; see Oleg Grabar, *The Shape of the Holy: Early Islamic Jerusalem* (Princeton: Princeton University Press, 1996), 53; also F. E. Peters, *Jerusalem: The Holy City in the Eyes of Chroniclers, Visitors, Pilgrims, and Prophets from the Days of Abraham to the Beginnings of Modern Times* (Princeton: Princeton University Press, 1985), 600 n. 9.

[87] There is no need to posit a corruption here as Lévi has suggested. Rome/Constantinople contained more than one Christian sanctuary.

I turned. He touched me, and then I saw a man (who was) despicable, broken down and in pain.[88]

That despicable man said to me: "Zerubbabel!? What business do you have here? Who has brought you here?" I responded and said: "A wind from the Lord lifted me up and carried me to this place." He said to me: "Do not be afraid, for you have been brought here in order that He might show you (and then you in turn might inform the people of Israel about everything which you see)."[89] When I heard his words, I was consoled and regained my self-composure.[90] I asked him, "Sir, what is the name of this place?" He said to me, "This is mighty Rome, wherein I am imprisoned." I said to him, "Who then are you? What is your name? What do you seek here? What are you doing in this place?" He said to me, "I am the Messiah of the Lord, the son of Hezekiah,[91] confined in prison until the time of the End."[92] When I heard this, I was silent, and I hid my face from him. His anger burned within him,[93] and when I looked at him (again), I became frightened.

He said to me, "Come nearer to me," and as he spoke to me my limbs quaked, and he reached out his hand and steadied me. "Don't be frightened," he said, "and let your mind show no fear." He encouraged me, and said: "Why did you become silent and hide your face from me?" I said to him: "Because you said, 'I am the servant of the Lord, His Messiah, and "the

[88] See Isa 53:3; *b. Sanh.* 98a. An exemplary discussion of the motif of the "suffering Messiah" ensconced in Rome is provided by Abraham Berger, "Captive at the Gate of Rome: The Story of a Messianic Motif," *PAAJR* 44 (1977): 1–17. Biale ("Counter-History," 139) suggests that the figure mimics Christian concepts of messianic office.

[89] Ezek 40:4.

[90] T-S A45.19 (Hopkins, *Miscellany*, 64.8) reads instead: וידבר עמי דברים נכונים וכשמעי תמהתי ואש]אל, "and he spoke with me clearly, and when I heard (this) I was astonished and as[ked . . .]." Cf. Lévi, "L'apocalypse," 132 n. 19.

[91] According to Lévi, these words have been erased. They do not occur in any of the other extant manuscripts or printed editions probably because the different name Menahem b. ʿAmiel is provided below for this figure. The effaced "ben Hezekiah" fragment was probably based upon *b. Sanh.* 98b: ויש אומרים מנחם בן חזקיה שמו, "and some say that his name [i.e., the Messiah's] is Menahem ben Hezekiah." See Joseph Klausner, *The Messianic Idea in Israel: From its Beginning to the Completion of the Mishnah* (New York: Macmillan, 1955), 463–65. Himmelfarb plausibly suggests that the patronym ʿAmiel is a cipher for Hezekiah; see her "Mother of the Messiah," 383–87.

[92] For עת קץ as a *terminus technicus* for the eschatological age, see Dan 8:17; 11:25, 40; 12:4, 9. *Midr. Teh.* 21.1 echoes *Sefer Zerubbabel* when it states: זה משיח בן דוד הנחבא עד עת קץ, "this is the Messiah of the lineage of David who has been concealed until the time of the End." Note also *Tg.* Mic 4:8: ואת משיחא דישראל דטמיר מן קדם חובי כנשתא דציון, "and you, O Messiah of Israel, who has been concealed due to the sins of the congregation of Zion. . . ."

[93] Manuscript reads ותבער בי חמתי, "and my anger burned within me." I have followed the reading in T-S A45.19 (Hopkins, *Miscellany*, 64.10), which continues ויאדמו פניו וישתנו ש[, "his face reddened and [his garmen]ts changed [. . .]"; cf. Lévi, "L'apocalypse," 132 n. 26.

light of Israel" (2 Sam 21:17).'" Suddenly he appeared like a strong young man, handsome and adorned.

I asked him: "When will the light of Israel[94] come?" And as I was speaking to him, behold, a man with two wings approached me and said to me, "Zerubbabel! What are you asking the Messiah of the Lord?" I answered him and said, "I asked when the appointed time for deliverance is supposed to come." "Ask me," he replied, "and I will tell you." I said to him, "Sir, who are you?" He answered and said, "I am Michael,[95] the one who delivered good news to Sarah.[96] I am the leader of the host of the Lord God of Israel, the one who battled with Sennacherib and smote 180,000 men.[97] I am the prince of Israel, the one who fought battles against the kings of Canaan. In the time to come, I will fight the battles of the Lord alongside the Messiah of the Lord—he who sits before you—with the king "strong of face" (עז פנים)[98] and with Armilos, the son of Satan, the spawn of the stone statue.[99] The Lord has appointed me to be the commanding officer over his people and over those who love Him in order to do battle against the leaders of the nations."

Michael, who is (also) Metatron, answered me[100] saying: "I am the angel who guided Abraham throughout all the land of Canaan. I blessed him in the name of the Lord. I am the one who redeemed Isaac[101] and [wept][102] for him. I am the one who wrestled with Jacob at the crossing of the Jabbok.[103] I am the one who guided Israel in the wilderness for forty years in the name of the Lord. I am the one who appeared to Joshua at Gilgal,[104] and I am the one who rained down brimstone and fire on Sodom and Gomorrah.[105] He

[94] See Even-Shmuel, *Midreshey Ge᾿ullah*, 56 n. 2 for a brief discussion of the use of this epithet for the Messiah.

[95] T-S A45 19 (Hopkins, *Miscellany*, 64.17): אני מיטטרון מיכאל שר צבא ייי, "I am Metatron Michael, leader of the host of the Lord." For the epithet, see Josh 5:14–15.

[96] Gen 18:10. See *b. B. Meṣiʿa* 86b: מיכאל שבא לבשר את שרה, "Michael (is) the one who delivered good news to Sarah."

[97] Cf. 2 Kgs 19:35–36; Isa 37:36–37; 2 Chr 32:21–22. According to the first two sources, the number of the slain totaled 185,000. *Exod. Rab.* 18.5 identifies the anonymous biblical angel as Michael.

[98] Deut 28:50; Dan 8:23; *Tg. Ket.* Qoh 8:1.

[99] This conjunctive pairing suggests that "the king strong of face" and Armilos are two separate entities, as in, e.g., the later *Secrets of R. Šimʿōn ben Yoḥai*. By contrast, the still later *Midrash Wayoshaʿ* conflates them into one figure.

[100] The manuscript literally reads ויען מיכאל למטטרון ויאמר אלי, "Michael answered Metatron and said to me." I have followed the reading suggested by Lévi, "L'apocalypse," 133 n. 17.

[101] Gen 22:11–13.

[102] Read ובכיתי instead of וביתי. Cf. Lévi, "L'apocalypse," 133 n. 19; now confirmed by T-S A45.19 (Hopkins, *Miscellany*, 64.19): ובכיתי עליו.

[103] Gen 32:25–31.

[104] Josh 5:13–15.

[105] Lévi points out that *b. B. Meṣiʿa* 86b accords this role to Gabriel, not Michael.

placed His name within me:[106] Metatron in *gematria* is the equivalent of Shadday.[107] As for you, Zerubbabel son of Shealtiel, whose name is Jeconiah, ask me and I will tell you what will happen at the End of Days."

Then he said to me: "This is the Messiah of the Lord: (he has) been hidden in this place until the appointed time (for his manifestation). This is the Messiah of the lineage of David, and his name is Menahem ben ʿAmiel.[108] He was born during the reign of David, king of Israel,[109] and a wind bore him up and concealed him in this place, waiting for the time of the end." Then I, Zerubbabel, posed a question to Metatron, the leader of the host of the Lord.[110] He said to me: "The Lord will give a rod (for accomplishing) these salvific acts to Hephṣibah, the mother of Menahem ben ʿAmiel.[111] A great star will shine[112] before her, and all the stars will wander aimlessly from their paths.

Hephṣibah, the mother of Menahem ben ʿAmiel, will go forth and kill two kings, both of whom are determined to do evil. The name(s) of the two rulers (whom she will slay): Noph (נוף), king of Teman, (so named) because he will shake (הניף) his hand toward Jerusalem, (is the first one), and the

[106] Cf. Exod 23:21.

[107] The proper names Metatron (מטטרון) and Shadday (שדי) both have the numerical value 314. For the role of Metatron in eschatological literature, see Idel, *Messianic Mystics*, 46–47 and the excursus later in this volume.

[108] The name Menahem for the Messiah derives from Lam 1:16: כי רחק ממני מנחם משיב נפשי. The numerical value of that name's letters (138) is also equal to that of the letters of the ancient messianic epithet "Branch" (צמח); see Jer 23:5, 33:15; Zech 3:8 and Ibn Ezra *ad loc.*, 6:12; *y. Ber.* 2.4, 5a; *Lam. Rab.* 1.51; *Midr. Tanḥ.* Qoraḥ §12; *Pirqe R. El.* §48 (Luria, 116a). The name Menahem b. ʿAmiel for the future Davidic Messiah is also used in uncensored versions of *Pirqe R. El.* §19 (e.g., HUC Ms. 75 fol. 25b: note too that this manuscript inverts the order of §§18 and 19!), whereas standard printed editions attest an anomalous form Menahem b. ʿAmiel b. Joseph (!) (cf. Luria, 45b). For ʿAmiel see n. 91 above.

[109] According to the text published by Wertheimer, he was born "at the time Nebuchadnezzar entered Jerusalem." Cf. *y. Ber.* 2.4, 5a: דביומא דאיתיליד איחרוב בית מוקדשא, "for on the day he [i.e., the Messiah] was born the Temple was destroyed."

[110] The question is lacking in the manuscript edition. Wertheimer's edition supplies here "What are the signs which this Menahem ben ʿAmiel will realize?" See Yassif, *Sefer ha-Zikronot*, 429 n. 18; also T-S A45.19 (Hopkins, *Miscellany*, 65.5): [מ]ה אותת שעשה מנחם עמיאל, "what are the signs which Menahem ʿAmiel will realize?"

[111] According to 2 Kgs 21:1, this was the name of the mother of Manasseh. The same name is used figuratively for Zion in Isa 62:4. Most scholars view her as a Jewish foil to the Christian image of the Virgin Mary as mother of Jesus; see, e.g., Himmelfarb, "Sefer Zerubbabel," 69; Biale, "Counter-History," 140–41; Schäfer, *Mirror*, 213–15. In an earlier publication, Joseph Dan had suggested that the image of the mother of the Messiah and her prominent role in the messianic drama was almost certainly due to Christian influence; see his *Sippur*, 39; note also Robert L. Wilken, *The Land Called Holy: Palestine in Christian History and Thought* (New Haven and London: Yale University Press, 1992), 210–11. But Dan has lately modified his suggestion; note his "Armilus," 85–86.

[112] Read with T-S A45.19 (Hopkins, *Miscellany*, 65.7) נוגה in place of the base manuscript's יגיח.

name of the second is ʾIsrinan (איסרינן), king of Antioch. This conflict and these signs will take place during the festival of Shavuʿot in the third month.[113]

The word is true.[114] Four hundred and twenty years after the city and Temple have been rebuilt, they will be destroyed a second time.[115] Twenty years after the building of the city of Rome, after seventy kings corresponding to the seventy nations have ruled in it, when ten kings have finished their reigns, the tenth king will come.[116] He will destroy the sanctuary, stop the daily offering, the 'saintly people'[117] will be dispersed, and he will hand them over to destruction, despoiling, and panic. Many of them will perish due to their faithfulness to Torah, but (others) will abandon the Torah of the Lord and worship their (i.e., Rome's) idols. "When they stumble, a little help will provide assistance" (Dan 11:34). From the time that the daily offering ceases and the wicked ones install the one whose name is 'abomination' (שיקוץ) in the Temple, at the end of nine hundred and ninety years, the deliverance of the Lord will take place—"when the power of the holy people is shattered" (Dan 12:7)—to redeem them and to gather them by means of the Lord's Messiah.[118]

The rod which the Lord will give to Hephṣibah, the mother of Menahem [ben] ʿAmiel, is made of almond wood; it is hidden in Raqqat, a city in (the

[113] Manuscript lacks the year. See T-S A45.19 (Hopkins, *Miscellany*, 65.10–11): בשנה הששית בחדש השלישי אשר [...] חג שבועות, "in the sixth year during the third month which [...] the festival of Shavuʿot." Presumably this is the penultimate year of a final sabbatical period of years.

[114] Cf. Dan 10:1; 2 Chr 9:5.

[115] According to rabbinic chronography, 420 years was the duration of the Second Temple. See *b. Yoma* 9a.

[116] Titus.

[117] Literally עם קדושים; based on Dan 8:24, where it signifies Israel. Cf. Deut 7:6; 14:2, 21; Ps 34:10; 1QM 10:10 for analogous locutions referring to Israel. According to Rashi and Ibn Ezra, the ambiguous designation קדישין in Dan 7:18, 21–22, 25, 27 also encodes Israel.

[118] A number of scholars have sought to use this number in order to posit a late date for *Sefer Zerubbabel*. See Lévi, "L'apocalypse (2)," *REJ* 69 (1914), 109 n. 1. Note also Moshe Gil, *A History of Palestine, 634–1099* (trans. Ethel Broido; Cambridge: Cambridge University Press, 1992), 401–2: "It is quite likely that the hardship and stress of these years [the mid-eleventh century] were the major factors contributing to predictions of the imminent end of the world in 1058 ('when 990 years from the destruction of Jerusalem are completed')." The number 990 does possess millenarian and even astronomical/astrological significance within multiple apocalyptic contexts; see Manetho, frag. 64 (W. G. Waddell, *Manetho with an English Translation* [LCL; Cambridge, Mass.: Harvard University Press, 1940], 164–65, with the comments of Ludwig Koenen, "Manichaean Apocalypticism at the Crossroads of Iranian, Egyptian, Jewish and Christian Thought," in *Codex Manichaicus Coloniensis: Atti del Simposio Internazionale (Rende-Amantea 3–7 settembre 1984)* (ed. Luigi Cirillo and Amneris Roselli; Cosenza: Marra Editore, 1986), 315–16 nn. 90–91; and especially Moritz Steinschneider, "Apokalypsen mit polemischer Tendenz," *ZDMG* 28 (1874): 629–34. The "revelation of Akatriel to R. Ishmael" mentioned by the latter scholar (p. 631) refers to the so-called *ʾAggadat R. Ishmael*; see Even-Shmuel, *Midreshey Geʾullah*, 144–52.

territory of) Naphtali.[119] It is the same rod which the Lord previously gave to Adam, Moses, Aaron, Joshua, and King David.[120] It is the same rod which sprouted buds and flowered in the Tent (of Meeting) for the sake of Aaron.[121] Elijah ben Eleazar[122] concealed it in Raqqat, a city of Naphtali, which is Tiberias. Concealed there as well is a man whose name is Nehemiah ben Hushiel ben Ephraim ben Joseph."[123] Zerubbabel spoke up and said to Metatron and to Michael [*sic*] the prince: "My lord, I want you to tell me when the Messiah of the Lord will come and what will happen after all this!" He said to me, "The Lord's Messiah—Nehemiah ben Hushiel —will come five years after[124] Hephṣibah. He will collect all Israel together as one entity and they will remain for <four>[125] years in Jerusalem, (where) the children of Israel will offer sacrifice, and it will be pleasing to the Lord.[126] He will inscribe Israel in the genealogical lists according to their

[119] Josh 19:35. For the identification of Raqqat with Tiberias, see *y. Meg.* 1.1, 70a; *b. Meg.* 5b-6a. For an illuminating discussion of Tiberias as a center of Jewish life during the latter half of the first millennium CE, see Gil, *History of Palestine*, 174–85.

[120] T-S A45.19 (Hopkins, *Miscellany*, 65.14–15) provides an expanded list of worthies: אשר נתן ייי לשת לנח ולאברהם וליצ[חק] . . . וליהודה ולפרץ ולמשה עבד ייי וליהושע ולדויד ולאליהו, "which the Lord gave to Seth, Noah, Abraham, Is[aac ...], Judah, Peretz, Moses the servant of the Lord, Joshua, David, and Elijah." See also Wertheimer, *Batey Midrashot*, 2:499 for a slightly variant roster.

[121] Num 17:16–26. T-S A45.19 (Hopkins, *Miscellany*, 65.16) reads: ויוצא פרח ויצץ ציץ וג׳ ואען ואומר אני זרובבל ואומר למיט[טרון . . .], "'it had budded and flowered and etc. (Num 17:23).' I spoke up and said—I Zerubbabel—to Met[atron ...]."

[122] I.e., Phineas ben Eleazar, grandson of Aaron (cf. Num 25:7). This text attests the popular exegetical assimilation of Phineas with the prophet Elijah; see *L.A.B.* 48.1; *Tg. Ps-J.* Num 25:12; *Pirqe R. El.* §8 and §47; Robert Hayward, "Phineas—the Same is Elijah: The Origins of a Rabbinic Tradition," *JJS* 29 (1978): 22–34. His role here in the concealment of Aaron's rod coheres with his final position in the list of the rod's custodians in some other versions (see above) of the book. The identity of Phineas as the one who conceals the staff is also known to the thirteenth-century Christian *Book of the Bee*; see Ernest A. Wallis Budge, ed., *The Book of the Bee* (Anecdota Oxoniensia Semitic Series 1.2; Oxford: Clarendon Press, 1886), 52.9–10: ܘܛܫܝܗ̇ ܦܝܢܚܣ ܠܚܘܛܪܐ ܗܘ ܒܡܕܒܪܐ ܒܥܦܪܐ ܕܬܪܥܐ ܕܐܘܪܫܠܡ ܘܩܘܝ ܗܘܐ ܬܡܢ ܥܕܡܐ ܕܐܬܝܠܕ ܡܪܢ ܡܫܝܚܐ, "Phineas hid the staff in the desert, beneath the dirt at the gate of Jerusalem, and it remained there until Our Lord the Messiah was born."

[123] The messiah of the lineage of Joseph. For his Galilean association, see also *ʾAggadat ha-Mašiaḥ* (Jellinek, *BHM* 3:141); Even-Shmuel, *Midreshey Geʾullah*, 49.

[124] *Sic* in the base text and Jellinek. Wertheimer and T-S A45.19 (Hopkins, *Miscellany*, 65.18) have לפני, "before," a reading that makes better sense in context.

[125] In spite of the unanimous extant textual evidence, read "four" in place of "forty." See also Lévi, "L'apocalypse," 151 n. 3: "Mais le contexte semble exiger que «quarante» soit ici pour «quatre»."

[126] ויערב לייי. A play on the wording and context of Mal 3:4: וערבה ליהוה מנחת יהודה וירושלם, "the offering of Judah and Jerusalem will be pleasing to the Lord." Some historians read this notice as evidence for the brief restoration of a Jewish sacrificial cultus on the Temple Mount following the Persian capture of Jerusalem in 614. See Peters, *Jerusalem*, 172–73; Gilbert Dagron, "Introduction historique: Entre histoire et apocalypse," *Travaux et mémoires* 11 (1991): 26–28; Wilken, *Land Called Holy*, 212–13; Averil Cameron, "The Jews in Seventh-Century Palestine," *Scripta Classica Israelica* 13 (1994): 80; idem, "Byzantines and Jews: Some Recent Work on Early Byzantium," *Byzantine and Mod-*

families. But in the fifth year of Nehemiah and the gathering together of the 'holy ones,'[127] Šērōy the king of Persia[128] will attack Nehemiah ben Hushiel and Israel,[129] and there will be great suffering in Israel. Hephṣibah—the wife of Nathan the prophet[130] (and) mother of Menahem ben ʿAmiel—will go out with the rod which the Lord God of Israel will give to her, and the Lord will place 'a spirit of dizziness'[131] upon them (i.e., the Persian army), and they will kill one another, each (slaying) his companion or his countryman. There the wicked one (Šērōy) will die."

When I heard (this), I fell upon my face and said, "O Lord! Tell me what Isaiah the prophet (meant) when he said: 'There the calf will graze, and there it will crouch down and finish its branches' (27:10)?" He answered me, "This calf is Nineveh, the city of blood, which represents mighty Rome."

I continued asking there about the prince of the holy covenant. He held me close and they [*sic*] brought me to the "house of filth" [and scorn].[132] There he showed me a marble stone in the shape of a maiden:[133] her features and form were lovely and indeed very beautiful to behold. Then he said to me, "This statue is the [wife][134] of Belial. Satan will come and have

---

ern Greek Studies 20 (1996): 254–55; Hagith Sivan, "From Byzantine to Persian Jerusalem: Jewish Perspectives and Jewish/Christian Polemics," *GRBS* 41 (2000): 291–92. This interpretation is dismissed by Peter Schäfer, *The History of the Jews in Antiquity: The Jews of Palestine from Alexander the Great to the Arab Conquest* (n.p.: Harwood Academic Publishers, 1995), 191.

[127] The "holy ones" or "saints" are Israel; see Deut 33:3 and *Tg. Onk.* to that verse. Sivan suggests that the reference to Nehemiah's "fifth year" represents the end of Jewish-Sasanian collaboration in the conquest and administration of Palestine, roughly 614–619 CE ("From Byzantine to Persian Jerusalem," 302–4).

[128] Šērōy (שירוי), who used the regnal name Kavād II, assumed the Sasanian throne in 628 CE and reigned for less than one year, falling victim to illness rather than military debacle. For a detailed account of his reign, see Theodor Nöldeke, *Geschichte der Perser und Araber zur Zeit der Sasaniden* (Leiden, 1879; repr., Leiden: Brill, 1973), 361–85; *The History of al-Ṭabarī*, Volume 5, *The Sāsānids, the Byzantines, the Lakmids, and Yemen* (trans. C. E. Bosworth; Albany: State University of New York Press, 1999), 381–99.

[129] Oxford Ms. Heb. f. 27 (2642) fols. 42–43 adds at this point: וידקור את נחמיה בירושלים וספדו אותו כל ישראל ויתמרמרו עליו במרירות הבכיות, "and he will kill Nehemiah in Jerusalem, and all Israel will mourn him and complain about this with embittered grief."

[130] A curious designation, since it cannot refer to David's prophet or to David's son. Perhaps it is an interpolation referring to Nathan of Gaza, a major theorist and the prophetic voice announcing the seventeenth-century messianic movement of Shabbatai Ṣevi. The latest study of Nathan of Gaza, although without reference to this passage in *Sefer Zerubbabel*, is Matt Goldish, *The Sabbatean Prophets* (Cambridge, Mass.: Harvard University Press, 2004).

[131] Isa 19:14.

[132] Correcting בית החורף הלאות to בית התורף והלצות in accordance with the varying manuscript evidence assembled by Lévi, "L'apocalypse," 136 n. 4.

[133] A statue of the Virgin Mary? See Lévi, "L'apocalypse (3)," *REJ* 71 (1920): 59–60; Himmelfarb, "Sefer Zerubbabel," 69; Schäfer, *Mirror*, 213.

[134] Read אשת in place of איש; היא in place of הוא. Note Wertheimer, *Batey Midrashot*, 2.500: האבן הזאת היא אשת הבליעל.

intercourse with it, and a son named Armilos will emerge from it, [whose name in Greek means] 'he will destroy a nation.'[135] He will rule over all (peoples), and his dominion will extend from one end of the earth to the other, and ten letters will be in his hand. He will engage in the worship of foreign gods and speak lies. No one will be able to withstand him, and anyone who does not believe in him he will kill with the sword: many among them will he kill. He will come against the holy people of the Most High, and with him there will be ten kings wielding great power and force, and he will do battle with the holy ones. He will prevail over them[136] and will kill the Messiah of the lineage of Joseph, Nehemiah b. Hushiel,[137] and will also kill sixteen righteous ones alongside him. Then they will banish Israel to the desert in three groups.[138]

"But Hephṣibah, the mother of Menahem b. ʿAmiel, will remain stationed at the eastern gate, and that wicked one will not enter there, thereby confirming what was written: 'but the remainder of the people will not be cut off from the city' (Zech 14:2). This battle will take place during the month of Av.[139] Israel will experience distress such as there never was before. They will flee into towers, among mountains, and into caves, but they will be unable to hide from him. All the nations of the earth will go astray after him except for Israel, who will not believe in him. All Israel shall mourn Nehemiah b. Hushiel for forty-one days. His thoroughly crushed[140]

[135] ושמו ארמילוס ויחריב עם ולשון עברית. The phrase is corrupt in all witnesses, but it is clear that an etymology is offered here for the name Armilos, one that is moreover dependent not on Hebrew but on Greek Ἐρημόλαος, "destroyer of a people" (see the use of this same designation for "the little horn, Satan" in *Doctrina Iacobi nuper baptizati* [ed. N. Bonwetsch; Abhandlungen der königlichen Gesellschaft der Wissenschaften zu Göttingen, phil.-hist. klass., n.f., bd. 12, nr. 3; Berlin: Weidmannsche Buchhandlung, 1910], 60, 74, 86; cited by David M. Olster, *Roman Defeat, Christian Response, and the Literary Construction of the Jew* [Philadelphia: University of Pennsylvania Press, 1994], 170–71; 173–74) and which is furthermore consonant with the folk etymology for the name Balaam (בלעם) supplied in *b. Sanh.* 105a (בלע עם, "destroyer of a people"). See Lévi, "L'apocalypse," 152 n. 6, and especially the persuasive arguments of David Berger, "Three Typological Themes in Early Jewish Messianism: Messiah son of Joseph, Rabbinic Calculations, and the Figure of Armilus," *AJSR* 10 (1985): 158–62.

[136] Oxford Ms. Opp. 236a adds: ויפלו לרוב, "and a multitude will fall."

[137] Armilos is the usual slayer of the Messiah of the lineage of Joseph. Note, however, that according to the version of *Sefer Zerubbabel* found in Oxford Ms. Heb. f. 27 (2642) fols. 42–43 (cited above) and an intriguing seventh-century *piyyut* entitled העת לגעור first published by Ezra Fleischer, it is the Persians who are responsible for executing the community leader who temporarily restored the sacrificial service in Jerusalem. See Sivan, "From Byzantine to Persian Jerusalem," 288.

[138] A reference to the expulsion of Jews from Jerusalem by Heraclius upon its recapture from the Persians in 629; see Theophanes, *Chronographia* (ed. Carl de Boor; 2 vols.; Leipzig: B. G. Teubner, 1883–85), 1:328; Harry Turtledove, *The Chronicle of Theophanes* (Philadelphia: University of Pennsylvania Press, 1982), 30; Olster, *Roman Defeat*, 173.

[139] Oxford Ms. Opp. 236a states the war will last "the entire month" (כל החודש).

[140] Read מדוכדכת in place of מודכדכת.

corpse will be thrown down before the gates of Jerusalem, but no animal, bird, or beast will touch it. Because of the intensity of the oppression and the great distress, the children of Israel will then cry out to the Lord, and the Lord will answer them."

As I listened to the content of the prophecy of the Lord to me, I became very agitated and got up and went to the canal. There I cried out to the Lord God of Israel, the God of all flesh, and He sent His angel to me while the prayer was still in my mouth before I had finished (it).[141] The Lord sent His angel to me, and when I saw (him) I knew that he was the angel who had spoken with me regarding all the previous matters. I knelt and bowed before him, and he again touched me as he had the first time. He said to me, "What's the matter with you, O Zerubbabel?" I answered him, "Sir, my spirit remains depressed."[142]

Metatron responded by saying to me: "Ask me (questions) and I will provide you with answers before I depart from you." So I again asked him and said to him, "My lord Metatron, when will the light of Israel come?" He answered and said to me, "By the Lord Who has sent me and Who has appointed me over Israel, I solemnly swear to reveal to you the Lord's doing(s), for the Holy God previously commanded me, 'Go to My servant Zerubbabel, and tell him (the answers to) whatever he may ask of you.'" Then Michael, who is (also) Metatron, said to me, "Come closer and pay careful attention to everything which I shall tell you, for the word which I am speaking to you is true; it was one spoken by the Living God."

He said to me: "Menahem b. ʿAmiel will suddenly come[143] on the fourteenth day of the first month; i.e., of the month Nisan. He will wait by the Valley of ʾArbʾel[144] (at a tract) which belonged to Joshua b. Jehosadaq the priest,[145] and all the surviving sages of Israel—only a few will remain due to the attack and pillage of Gog and Armilos and the plunderers[146] who despoiled them—will come out to him. Menahem b. ʿAmiel will say to the elders and the sages: 'I am the Lord's Messiah: the Lord has sent me to encourage you and to deliver you from the power of these adversaries!' The elders will scrutinize him and will despise him, for they will see that despicable man garbed in rags, and they will despise him just as you previously

[141] Read והפסק לא הפסקתי in place of והספק לא הספקתי.

[142] See Job 32:18.

[143] Compare Mal 3:1.

[144] A locale in Galilee associated with the "dawning" of eschatological redemption. See *y. Ber.* 1.1, 2c; *Yoma* 3.2, 40b; *Cant. Rab.* 6.16 (*ad* Cant 6:10).

[145] Some manuscripts read this name as Joshua b. Saraf (סרף) or Nisraf (נשרף), a priestly figure associated with this locale by *Seder ʿOlam Zuta* and the early roster of "priestly *mishmarot*" published by Samuel Klein; see Even-Shmuel, *Midreshey Geʾullah*, 83 for the relevant citations.

[146] Read השוסים in place of הסוסים.

did. But then his anger will burn within him, 'and he will don garments of vengeance (as his) clothing and will put on[147] a cloak of zealousness' (Isa 59:17b), and he will journey to the gates of Jerusalem. Hephṣibah, the mother of the Messiah, will come and give him the rod by which the signs were performed. All the elders and children of Israel will come and see that Nehemiah (b. Hushiel) is alive and standing unassisted, (and) immediately they will believe in the Messiah." Thus did Metatron, the leader of the host of the Lord, swear to me: "This matter will truly come to pass, for there will be full cooperation between them[148] in accordance with the prophecy of Isaiah, 'Ephraim will not envy Judah, nor will Judah antagonize Ephraim' (Isa 11:13).

"On the twenty-first day of the first month, nine hundred and ninety years after the destruction of the Temple, the deliverance of the Lord will take place for Israel. Menahem b. ʿAmiel, Nehemiah b. Hushiel, and Elijah the prophet will come and stand by the Mediterranean Sea and read the prophecy of the Lord. All the bodies of those Israelites who had thrown themselves into the sea while fleeing from their enemies will emerge: a sea-wave will rise up, spread them out, and deposit them alive within the valley of Jehoshaphat near the Wadi Shittim,[149] for there judgment will transpire upon the nations.

"In the second month, that is, Iyyar, the congregation of Qorah will reemerge[150] upon the plains of Jericho near the Wadi Shittim. They will come to Moses (!),[151] and the cohort of the Qorahites will assemble.

[147] Read ו[י]עט in place of ועט.

[148] See Zech 6:13 and the commentary of Radaq *ad loc.*; note too the commentary of Rashi to Isa 11:13.

[149] See Joel 4:2, 12, 18. According to Radaq *ad* Joel 4:18, Saadya Gaon interpreted the text's Wadi Shittim (נחל השטים) as a reference to the Jordan river.

[150] Cf. Num 16:1–11, 16–24, 26–33, which recount how the refractory congregation of Qorah was swallowed up by the earth "and descended . . . alive to Sheol" (וירדו . . . חיים שאלה). In *m. Sanh.* 10.3, R. Akiva and R. Eliezer disagree as to whether the congregation of Qorah will play a role in the World to Come, with the latter Sage citing 1 Sam 2:6 ("the Lord kills and revitalizes; He sends down to Sheol and brings back up . . .") in support of his opinion that they could potentially "reemerge" at that time. Note also *Midrash Konen* (Jellinek, *BHM* 2:29–30): ואף קרח וכל עדתו מתחננין כל יום רביעי ואומרים לו עד מתי קץ הנפלאות מתי תשוב תחיינו ומתהומות הארץ תשוב תעלנו והוא אומר להם לכו ושאלו לאבות העולם והם מתביישין וחוזרין למקומן, "Moreover Qorah and all his congregation will offer supplications each Wednesday, saying to him (i.e., to the Davidic Messiah sequestered in Paradise, awaiting the time of the eschaton) 'how long until the time of marvels? "When will you restore us to life and raise us up again from the depths of the earth"? (Ps 71:20, according to the *ketiv*).' He will say to them, 'Go and ask the ancestral forefathers,' but they will be too embarrassed (to do so) and will return to their place."

[151] Does this assume an eschatological reappearance of Moses himself (as opposed to the recovery of symbols, such as the staff or the Ark, associated with his authority)? Compare *Frg. Tg.* Exod 12:42; *Pirqe Mašiaḥ* in Jellinek, *BHM* 3:72.6–7; also Socrates, *Hist. eccl.* 7.38, which relates an anecdote about

"On the eighteenth day of it (the second month) the mountains and hills will quake, and the earth and everything on it will shake, as well as the sea and its contents.

"On the first day of the third month those who died in the desert[152] will revive and will come with their families to the Wadi Shittim.[153] On the eighteenth day of the month of Sivan (i.e., the third month), there will be a mighty earthquake in Eretz Israel.[154]

"In Tammuz, the fourth month, the Lord God of Israel will descend upon the Mount of Olives, and the Mount of Olives will split open at His rebuke.[155] He will blow a great trumpet,[156] and every foreign deity and mosque[157] will crumple to the ground, and every wall and steep place will collapse.[158] The Lord will kill all their plunderers,[159] and He will battle those nations 'like a warrior fired with zeal' (Isa 42:13). The Lord's Messiah—Menahem b. ʿAmiel—will come and breathe in the face of Armilos and thereby slay him.[160] The Lord will place each man's sword on the neck of his companion[161] and their dead bodies shall fall there. The 'saintly people' (i.e., Israel; cf. Dan 8:24) will come out to witness the Lord's deliverance: all of Israel will actually see Him (equipped) like a warrior with 'the helmet of deliverance on His head' and clad in armor (cf. Isa 59:17). He will fight the

---

a messianic disturbance in fifth-century Crete occasioned by a charlatan pretending to be Moses. See Naphtali Wieder, *The Judean Scrolls and Karaism* (London: East and West Library, 1962), 8 n.1; Patricia Crone and Michael Cook, *Hagarism: The Making of the Islamic World* (Cambridge: Cambridge University Press, 1977), 177–78 n. 65.

[152] That is, the generation who died during Israel's forty-year wandering in the wilderness prior to the conquest of Canaan (Num 14:35). See again *m. Sanh.* 10.3 for a similar dispute about this group's final fate.

[153] Wertheimer, *Batey Midrashot*, 2.500–501: ובאחד לחדש השלישי יבואו מתי מדבר ויעשו חברות חברות עם אחיהם על נחל השיטים, "On the first day of the third month, those who died in the desert will come and rejoin their brethren at the Wadi Shittim."

[154] Wertheimer, *Batey Midrashot*, 2.501: יהיה רעש בבתים ובחומות ובמגדלים ותרגז הארץ ויושביה ומנחם בן עמיאל ונחמיה בן חושיאל ואליהו הנביא וכל ישראל הקרובים והרחוקים והחיים אשר יחיים ה׳ יעלו לירושלם, "an earthquake will shake the houses, walls, and towers, and the land and its inhabitants will quiver. Menahem b. ʿAmiel, Nehemiah b. Hushiel, Elijah the prophet, all Israel from both near and far, and those revivified ones whom the Lord will resurrect will come up to Jerusalem."

[155] See Zech 14:4.

[156] See Isa 27:13; Zech 9:14.

[157] Literally "decorated shrine" (בית משכית). However, the Hebrew word *masqīt* (משכית) may here serve as an oral pun on Arabic *masjid* "mosque." Compare also *Tg. Onk.* Num 33:52 for another possible paronomasia.

[158] See Ezek 38:20. Yassif (*Sefer ha-Zikronot*, 432 n. 40) suggests that this line refers specifically to the churches built on the Mount of Olives and the mosques installed on the Temple Mount.

[159] As above, read שוסיהם in place of סוסיהם.

[160] See Isa 11:4; *4 Ezra* 13:9–11; 1QSb 5.24–25. There is no need to presume a reliance on Christian sources (e.g., 2 Thess 2:8) for this particular motif (*contra* Biale, "Counter-History," 138).

[161] Cf. Ezek 38:21: חרב איש באחיו תהיה, "the sword of each (warrior) will be on his brother" and the commentary of Rashi *ad loc.*

battle of Gog ha-Magog and against the army of Armilos, and all of them will fall dead in the Valley of ʾArbʾel. All of Israel will then issue forth and '[despoil][162] their despoilers, looting those who previously plundered them' (Ezek 39:10) for seven months.[163] However, some survivors will escape and they will all regroup at Zelaʿ ha-Elef:[164] five hundred men, and (another) one hundred thousand wearing armor. (Opposing them will be) five hundred from Israel with Nehemiah and Elijah, and you, O Zerubbabel, will be their leader. They [*sic*] will kill all of them: one man will pursue a thousand.

"This will be the third battle, for three battles will take place in the land of Israel. One will be waged by Hephṣibah with Šērōy the king of Persia;[165] one will be fought by the Lord God of Israel and Menahem b. ʿAmiel with Armilos, the ten kings who are with him, and Gog and Magog; and the third will be at Zelaʿ ha-Elef, where Nehemiah b. Hushiel and Zerubbabel will see action. The third battle will take place in the month of Av.

"After all this (has taken place), Menahem b. ʿAmiel will come, accompanied by Nehemiah b. Hushiel and all Israel. All of the dead will resurrect, and Elijah the prophet will be with them. They will come up to Jerusalem. In the month of Av, during which they formerly mourned for Nehemiah (and) for the destruction of Jerusalem, Israel will hold a great celebration and bring an offering to the Lord, which the Lord will accept on their behalf. 'The offering of Israel will be pleasing to the Lord as it was formerly during her past history' (cf. Mal 3:4). The Lord will discern the pleasant aroma of His people Israel[166] and greatly rejoice. Then the Lord will lower to earth the celestial Temple which had been previously built,[167] and a column of fire and a cloud of smoke will rise to heaven. The Messiah and all of Israel will follow them to the gates of Jerusalem.[168]

"The holy God will stand on the Mount of Olives. Dread at and reverence for Him will be[169] upon the heavens and the uppermost heavens, the

[162] Read ושללו in place of ושטטו.

[163] See Ezek 39:10–14.

[164] A locale in Benjaminite territory; see Josh 18:28.

[165] Obviously typological, since Šērōy never left Persia after usurping the throne from his father and he died after a reign of only seven months. See Walter E. Kaegi, *Heraclius: Emperor of Byzantium* (Cambridge: Cambridge University Press, 2003), 174–81.

[166] Cf. Ezek 20:41 (בריח ניחח ארצה אתכם) with the commentary of Radaq *ad loc.*

[167] For a parallel descent of a celestial Temple, see *Midrash ʿAseret ha-Dibbarot* (Jellinek, *BHM* 1:64): שאז מוריד הקדוש ברוך הוא בית המקדש שבזבול לירושלים של מטה, "then the Holy One, blessed be He, will lower the Temple which is (located) in (the heaven named) Zevul to the terrestrial Jerusalem." For a conceptually cognate descent of a "celestial Jerusalem" *sans* Temple, see Rev 21:9–27. A new Temple is constructed in Jerusalem by God in *1 En.* 90:29.

[168] See Saadya, *Kitâb al-Amânât waʾl-Iʿtiqâdât von Saʿadja b. Jûsuf al-Fajjûmî* (ed. S. Landauer; Leiden: Brill, 1880), 245.10–17, as well as the responsum of Hai Gaon included within the present work.

[169] Oxford Ms. Opp. 236a: . . . ואימתו יכבד על, "dread at Him will weigh upon. . . ."

entire earth and its deepest levels, and every wall and structure to their foundations. No one will be able to catch their breath when the Lord God reveals Himself before everyone on the Mount of Olives. The Mount of Olives will crack open beneath Him, and the exiles from Jerusalem will come up to the Mount of Olives. Zion and Jerusalem will behold (these things) and ask: '"Who bore these to us? . . . Where have these been?"' (Isa 49:21). Nehemiah and Zerubbabel will then come up to Jerusalem and say to her: 'Behold, (they are) your children whom you bore[170] who went into exile from you. "Rejoice greatly, O daughter of Zion!"' (Zech 9:9)."

Again I started to question Metatron, leader of the host of the Lord: "Sir, show me how far and how wide Jerusalem will extend, along with its architecture." He showed me the walls that surrounded Jerusalem—walls of fire—extending from the Great Desert unto the Mediterranean Sea and unto the Euphrates River.[171] Then he showed me the Temple and the structure. The Temple was built on the peaks of five mountains which the Lord had chosen[172] to support His sanctuary: Lebanon, Mount Moriah, Tabor, Carmel, and Hermon.[173] Michael spoke and said to me, "At the completion of 990 years for the ruins of Jerusalem is the appointed time for the deliverance of Israel." He also continued to interpret for me the message and the vision in accordance with what he had first said to me: "If you wish to know, ask! Keep coming back!" (cf. Isa 21:12).

In the fifth (year) of the week Nehemiah b. Hushiel will come and gather together all Israel. In the sixth (year) of the week Hephṣibah, the wife of Nathan the prophet, she who was born in Hebron, will come[174] and slay the two kings Noph and ʾEsrōgan (אסרוגן).[175] That same year the "shoot of Jesse" (Isa 11:10), Menahem b. ʿAmiel, will spring up. Ten kings from among the nations shall also arise, but they will not supply enough (rulers) to rule for a week (of years) and a half-week (of years), each one (ruling) for a year. These are the ten kings who will arise over the nations for the week of years: these are their names correlated with their cities and their places. The first king is Sīlqōm and the name of his city is Seferad, which is Aspamia, a

[170] Based on Ezek 16:20.

[171] Himmelfarb ("Sefer Zerubbabel," 89 n. 111) suggests that these dimensions echo Deut 11:24; see also Josh 1:4. Note especially the traditions cited in *Sifre* Deut §1 (Finkelstein, 7–8) regarding the eschatological expansion of the boundaries for Jerusalem and for Eretz Israel.

[172] Read בחר in place of בהר.

[173] Based on Isa 2:2 (בראש ההרים) as interpreted in *Midr. Teh.* 68.9, although the latter source names only four peaks (Tabor, Carmel, Sinai, and Zion). Note *Pesiq. Rab Kah.* 21.4 (Mandelbaum, 1:321), and see the further references cited by Ginzberg, *Legends*, 6:31 n. 184; Avraham Grossman, "Jerusalem in Jewish Apocalyptic Literature," in Prawer and Ben-Shammai, *History of Jerusalem*, 299–300 n. 13.

[174] Read with Oxford Ms. Opp. 236a תבוא in place of תביא.

[175] Above this latter king was named ʾIsrinan (איסרינן).

distant country. The second king is Hartōmōs, and the name of his city is Gītanya. The third king is Flēʾvas (Flavius?), and the name of his city is Flōʾyas. The fourth king is Glūʾas (Julius?), and the name of his city is Galya (Gaul?). The fifth king is Ramōshdīs, and the name of his city is Mōdītīka. The sixth king is Mōqlanōs, and the name of his city is Italia. The seventh king is ʾŌktīnōs, and the name of his city is Dōrmīs. The eighth king is ʾAplōstōs from Mesopotamia. The ninth king is Šērōy, the king of Persia.

The tenth king is Armilos, the son of Satan who emerged from the sculpted stone. He will gain sovereignty over all of them. He will come along with the rulers of Qedar and the inhabitants of the East[176] and provoke a battle in the Valley of ʾArbʾel, and they will take possession of the kingdom. He will ascend with his force and subdue the entire world. From there in Riblah, which is Antioch,[177] he will begin to erect all the idols of the nations on the face of the earth and to serve their gods, those whom the Lord hates. During those days "there will be reward for neither human nor beast" (cf. Zech 8:10). He will construct four altars,[178] and he will anger the Lord with his wicked deeds. There will be a very terrible and harsh famine upon the surface of the whole land for forty days—their food will stem from the salt-plant; leaves plucked from shrubbery and broom to sustain them (cf. Job 30:4). On that day "a fountain will flow forth from the Temple of the Lord and fill the Wadi Shittim" (Joel 4:18).[179]

Now this Armilos will take his mother—(the statue) from whom he was spawned—from the "house of filth"[180] of the scornful ones, and from every place and from every nation they will come and worship that stone, burn offerings to her, and pour out libations to her. No one will be able to view her face on account of her beauty. Anyone who refuses to worship her will die in agony (like?) animals.

This is the mark of Armilos: the color of the hair of his head is similar to gold, and (he is) green, even the soles of his feet. His face is one span in width, his eyes are deep-set, and he has two heads. He will arise and rule over ʾĪmīs (?),[181] the province of Satan, the father of Belial.[182] All who see

[176] Literally "the children of Qedem" (בני קדם), a generic term for the nomadic tribes living east of Eretz Israel. See Gen 29:1; Judg 6:3; Job 1:3. "Qedar" and "the children of Qedem" appear together in Jer 49:28.

[177] See *b. Sanh.* 96b.

[178] Oxford Ms. Opp. 236a reads "seven" (ז') instead of "four." Armilos's construction of "seven altars" would establish a parallel with the wicked schemes of Balaam and Balaq (see Num 23:1); see Berger, "Three Typological Themes," 160.

[179] See also Zech 14:8 and Rashi *ad loc.*; Ezek 47:1–12.

[180] As above, reading בית התורף in place of בית החורף.

[181] אימיס. Lévi ("L'apocalypse," 160 n. 1) tentatively suggests the village of Emmaus, but this is unlikely.

[182] An Aramaic phrase: מדינתא דשטן אבי בליעל.

him will tremble before him. Menahem will come up from the Wadi Shittim and breathe in the face of Armilos and thereby slay him, just as it is written: "he will slay the wicked one with the breath of his mouth" (Isa 11:4). Israel will take possession of the kingdom; "the holy ones of the Most High will receive sovereign power" (Dan 7:18).

These were the words which Metatron spoke to Zerubbabel the son of Shealtiel, (future) governor of Judah, while he was still living in exile during the time of the Persian empire. Zechariah ben ʿAnan and Elijah recorded them when the period of exile was completed.[183]

[183] Oxford Ms. Opp. 236a reads: ויכתבם זכריה בן עדוא ואליהו, "Zechariah ben ʿIddo and Elijah wrote them down."

3

Pirqe de-Rabbi Eliezer §30 (end)

THE MEDIEVAL JEWISH TEXT generally known as *Pirqe de-Rabbi Eliezer* is an intriguing aggadic compilation that probably stems from Islamicate Palestine during the eighth or ninth centuries CE.[1] Its extant forms exhibit a division into fifty-four "chapters" (*peraqim*), but it is almost certainly incomplete in its surviving manuscript and printed versions.[2] Following an introductory framing story that attributes the collection and formulation of the traditions transmitted therein to R. Eliezer ben Hyrcanus, a well-known early-second-century sage,[3] the work presents a coherent and almost seamlessly interwoven tapestry of biblical pericopae and interpretative expansions that extend with only minimal digression from the creation of the universe to the story of Esther. Its narrative style is akin to

[1] The most important general discussions of this work are Leopold Zunz and Ḥanokh Albeck, *Haderashot be-Yisrael* (2d ed.; Jerusalem: Mosad Bialik, 1954), 134–40, 417–23; Bern(h)ard Heller, "Agadische Literatur," *Encyclopaedia Judaica* (10 vols.; Berlin: Verlag Eschkol, 1928–34), 1:1030–31; Moshe David Herr, "Pirkei de-Rabbi Eliezer," *EncJud* 13:558–60; H. L. Strack and G. Stemberger, *Introduction to the Talmud and Midrash* (Minneapolis: Fortress, 1992), 356–58.

[2] Three separate structural considerations are suggestive: (1) all extant "complete" versions end abruptly with the divine punishment of Miriam, hardly a propitious topic with which to conclude a book devoted "to expounding what He has accomplished and what He intends to do so that the Name of the Holy One, blessed be He, might be exalted" (*Pirqe R. El.* §3); (2) *Pirqe R. El.* §14 promises to explicate the "ten descents" of the divine presence to earth, but only the first eight are treated in extant versions of the text (§§14, 24, 25, 39, 40, 41, 46, 54); and (3) there is a sustained attempt to "close" chapters in the second half of the work (beginning with §27) with liturgical language connected with the benedictions of the *ʿAmidah*, but only the first eight (out of an expected total of eighteen) survive.

In addition to these formal considerations, medieval commentators occasionally cite passages from *Pirqe de-Rabbi Eliezer* that no longer survive in our extant versions. See, e.g., Ramban *ad* Lev 16:8. For longer lists of such citations, see Zunz-Albeck, *Haderashot*, 417 n. 12, and R. David Luria's "*Mavo*" to his frequently reprinted edition *Pirqe de-Rabbi Eliezer ha-Gadol* (Warsaw: T. Y. Bamberg, 1852), 13a §7.

[3] It should be noted that the opening *petiḥah* of *Pirqe de-Rabbi Eliezer* found in §3 after the framing proem of §§1–2 cites Ps 106:2a (מי ימלל גבורות י״י), a passage that announces the overarching purpose of the larger work and whose value in gematria is also equivalent to that of the name Eliezer ben Hyrcanus (אליעזר בן הורקנוס). This of course attests the artistry of the compiler as well as providing a rationale for the pseudonym. See Zunz-Albeck, *Haderashot*, 420 n. 28; *Pirqe R. El.* §3 (ed. Luria), 5a n. 2.

that found in roughly contemporary works such as the Syriac *Cave of Treasures* or Muslim anthologies of "tales of the prophets" (*qiṣaṣ al-anbiyāʾ*). *Pirqe de-Rabbi Eliezer* enjoyed widespread popularity in Jewish circles and achieved a remarkable geographical and cultural dispersal.[4] This work has also aroused perennial interest on the part of historians and students of medieval Jewish literature because it "utilize[s] narrative techniques similar (if not identical) to the expanded biblical tales of the earlier periods [of Jewish literary activity],"[5] even attesting at times certain distinctive exegetical and legendary details otherwise found only in Second Temple and Roman era pseudepigrapha like *1 Enoch* and *Jubilees*.[6]

Scholars have long noticed that the traditions recounted in *Pirqe de-Rabbi Eliezer* appear to be closely related to those found in the Palestinian targum tradition, particularly those contained in *Targum Pseudo-Jonathan* to the Pentateuch.[7] Both *Pirqe de-Rabbi Eliezer* and *Targum Pseudo-Jonathan* incorporate references, most of which are polemical, to Islamic religious claims and political hegemony.[8]

[4] One of the earliest references to the work appears in the *ʾIggeret* of Pirkoi ben Baboi, an early ninth-century advocate for Babylonian religious hegemony over North African Jewish communities. It subsequently became well known among both Islamicate (Judah ha-Levi; Maimonides) and Ashkenazi (Rashi; Tosafot) learned circles. For other early citations, see especially Zunz-Albeck, *Haderashot*, 420–21 n. 30. The first printed edition appeared in Constantinople in 1514. For the most recent discussion of the manuscripts and printed editions of *Pirqe de-Rabbi Eliezer*, see Lewis Barth, "Is Every Medieval Hebrew Manuscript a New Composition? The Case of *Pirqé Rabbi Eliezer*," in *Agendas for the Study of Midrash in the Twenty-first Century* (ed. Marc Lee Raphael; Williamsburg, Va.: College of William and Mary, 1999), 43–62.

[5] Eli Yassif, *The Hebrew Folktale: History, Genre, Meaning* (Bloomington and Indianapolis: Indiana University Press, 1999), 250.

[6] See Ḥanokh Albeck, "Agadot im Lichte der Pseudepigraphen," *MGWJ* 83 (1939): 162–69, esp. 167–69; Zunz-Albeck, *Haderashot*, 139–40; John C. Reeves, "Exploring the Afterlife of Jewish Pseudepigrapha in Medieval Near Eastern Religious Traditions: Some Initial Soundings," *JSJ* 30 (1999): 148–77. Note also Joseph Dan, *Ha-Sippur ha-ʿivri be-yemey ha-beyanim: ʿIyyunim be-toldotav* (Jerusalem: Keter, 1974), 22.

[7] A roster of correspondences is supplied in Zunz-Albeck, *Haderashot*, 419 n. 20. A convenient example appears in Philip S. Alexander, "Jewish Aramaic Translations of Hebrew Scriptures," in *Mikra: Text, Translation, Reading and Interpretation of the Hebrew Bible in Ancient Judaism and Early Christianity* (ed. Martin Jan Mulder; CRINT 2.1; Assen: Van Gorcum; Philadelphia: Fortress, 1988), 219. The close relationship of *Pirqe de-Rabbi Eliezer* and *Targum Pseudo-Jonathan*, however, has been questioned by Robert Hayward, "The Date of Targum Pseudo-Jonathan: Some Comments," *JJS* 40 (1989): 7–30; idem, "Pirqe de Rabbi Eliezer and Targum Pseudo-Jonathan," *JJS* 42 (1991): 215–46.

[8] See, e.g., *Tg. Ps-J.* Gen 25:14, where the names of three of Ishmael's descendants are parsed as consolatory exhortations for Israel ("Come together, remain silent, and endure!"). Note especially Moritz Steinschneider, *Polemische und apologetische Literatur in arabischer Sprache zwischen Muslimen, Christen und Juden, nebst Anhängen verwandten Inhalts* (Leipzig, 1877; repr., Hildesheim: Georg Olms, 1966), 338–40; Bern(h)ard Heller, "Muhammedanisches und Antimuhammedanisches in den Pirke R. Eliezer," *MGWJ* 69 (1925): 47–54; M. Ohana, "La polémique judéo-islamique d'Ismaël dans Targum Pseudo-Jonathan et dans Pirke de Rabbi Eliezer," *Aug* 15 (1975): 367–87; but contrast Robert Hayward, "Targum Pseudo-Jonathan and Anti-Islamic Polemic," *JSS* 34 (1989): 77–93.

These cluster primarily around biblical passages that are concerned with the biblical character Ishmael, a name commonly read in late antique Jewish literature as a cipher for "the Arabs" or the religion of Islam, just as the character Esau or the locale of Edom functioned as an emblem for the "evil empire" of Rome and triumphalist Christianity.[9] The compilers of *Pirqe de-Rabbi Eliezer* anticipate a future moment when both the Christian and Muslim empires will be annihilated by the power of God: ". . . the Holy One, blessed be He, is going to destroy the descendants of Esau, for they are the adversaries of the children of Israel, and likewise (He will destroy) the Ishmaelites, for they are enemies. Scripture affirms: 'You will raise Your hand against Your adversaries, and all Your enemies will be cut off'" (Mic 5:8).[10]

Among the more interesting of such passages is a lengthy apocalyptic logion attributed to the *tanna* R. Ishmael about the "fifteen things" that the Ishmaelites (i.e., the Muslims) will do in Eretz Israel at the end-time (באחרית הימים). Because of censorship concerns, this passage is often entirely lacking or severely curtailed in most standard printed editions of the work.[11] A truncated periphrastic rendition of the initial lines of this logion is found in the *Secrets of R. Šimʿōn b. Yoḥai*, there introduced by the incipit "moreover R. Šimʿōn reported that he learned from R. Ishmael" (ועוד היה רבי שמעון אומר ששמע מרבי ישמעאל).[12] Based on the roster of items mentioned therein (such as reallocation of lands, changes in legal tender, widespread apostasy, building activities on the Temple Mount, and campaigns against Constantinople), and provided, moreover, that such details were meant to correlate with actual historical events,[13] the Ishmael logion would appear to date from the final decades of the seventh or the initial decades of the eighth century CE.[14]

[9] For this latter equation, see the classic essay by Gerson D. Cohen, "Esau as Symbol in Early Medieval Thought," in *Jewish Medieval and Renaissance Studies* (ed. Alexander Altmann; Cambridge, Mass.: Harvard University Press, 1967), 19–48; also N. R. M. de Lange, "Jewish Attitudes to the Roman Empire," in *Imperialism in the Ancient World: The Cambridge University Research Seminar in Ancient History* (ed. P. D. A. Garnsey and C. R. Whittaker; Cambridge: Cambridge University Press, 1978), 269–71.

[10] *Pirqe R. El.* §48 (HUC Ms. 75 fol. 71a): . . . עתיד הקב״ה להשמיד לבני עשו שהם צריו לבני ישראל וכן לבני ישמעאל שהן אויבין שנאמר תרום ידך על צריך וכל אויביך יכרתו.

[11] This is the case, for example, with the 1852 edition of R. David Luria. The 1514 Constantinople *editio princeps* is missing the folios that would contain this logion.

[12] Adolph Jellinek, ed., *Bet ha-Midrasch: Sammlung kleiner Midraschim und vermischter Abhandlungen aus der jüdischen Literatur* (6 vols.; Leipzig, 1853–77; repr., Jerusalem: Bamberger & Wahrmann, 1938), 3:78.30–79.4. Heinrich Graetz viewed the Ishmael logion in *Pirqe R. El.* §30 as "completely dependent" on the *Secrets* (see his *Geschichte der Juden von den ältesten Zeiten bis auf die Gegenwart* [3d ed.; 11 vols. in 13; Leipzig: Oskar Leiner, 1890–1908], 5:410–11 n. 1), but this is problematic. Aside from the opening lines, there is very little overlap between the two texts.

[13] The *textual* character of apocalyptic discourse does not demand any necessary congruity with the mundane details of contemporary history.

[14] The most important discussions of this logion are Moritz Steinschneider, "Apocalypsen mit

The translation of this passage below is based on a synoptic comparison of the final lines of *Pirqe R. El.* §30 that was prepared from the following four sources: (1) Hebrew Union College Ms. 75 fol. 44a-b, a manuscript of oriental pedigree stemming from the fourteenth or fifteenth century; (2) Hebrew Union College Ms. 2043, a nineteenth-century Yemenite manuscript; (3) the partial transcription of the passage from the 1544 Venice printed edition reproduced in Zunz-Albeck;[15] and (4) the version of *Pirqe R. El.* published by Michael Higger, itself based on an earlier unpublished edition prepared by Ḥ. M. Horowitz that relied on three manuscripts (two Italian and one oriental) dating from the fifteenth or sixteenth centuries.[16]

A Synoptic Version of *Pirqe de-Rabbi Eliezer* §30 (End)

R. Ishmael said: The Ishmaelites will do fifteen things in the Land (of Israel) at the End of Days, to wit: They will measure the Land with ropes,[17] and make cemeteries (places for) the lodging[18] of flocks[19] and[20] (for) trash-heaps,[21] and they will measure from them and by them on the mountains.[22]

polemischer Tendenz," *ZDMG* 28 (1874): 645–46; Graetz, *Geschichte*, 5:186–87; Samuel Krauss, *Studien zur byzantinisch-jüdischen Geschichte* (Leipzig: Buchhandlung Gustav Fock, 1914), 145–46; Robert G. Hoyland, *Seeing Islam As Others Saw It: A Survey and Evaluation of Christian, Jewish and Zoroastrian Writings on Early Islam* (Studies in Late Antiquity and Early Islam 13; Princeton: Darwin Press, 1997), 313–16; Uri Rubin, *Between Bible and Qurʾān: The Children of Israel and the Islamic Self-Image* (Studies in Late Antiquity and Early Islam 17; Princeton: Darwin Press, 1999), 33–34.

15 Zunz-Albeck, *Haderashot*, 420 n. 25.

16 One should also note the translations in *Pirke De Rabbi Eliezer* (trans. Gerald Friedlander; London, 1916; repr., New York: Sepher-Hermon Press, 1981), 221–22; Hoyland, *Seeing Islam*, 313–16; Rubin, *Between Bible and Qurʾān*, 33–34.

17 The *Secrets of R. Šimʿōn b. Yoḥai* cites Dan 11:39 as its proof-text: ואדמה יחלק במחיר, "and he (the king) will apportion the Land for spoil," a verse possessing no lexical overlap with the cited saying. One might compare, however, a Muslim apocalyptic tradition regarding the struggle of Rome and the Muslims for control of Palestine that is attributed to Kaʿb al-Aḥbār, an early Jewish convert to Islam, and which refers to Muslims who will "divide its (Caesarea's) pasture-land with ropes and cubit-measures." Kaʿb's tradition is found in Nuʿaym b. Ḥammād, *Kitāb al-fitan* (ed. S. Zakkār; Beirut: Dār al-Fikr lil-Ṭibāʿah wa-al-Nashr wa-al-Tawzīʿ, 1993), 286.1–4.

18 Instead of מרבץ ("lodging, repose"), the *Secrets of R. Šimʿōn b. Yoḥai* has מרעה, "pasturage."

19 Cf. Ezek 25:5, which promises that the Chaldeans will turn the territory of the Ammonites into a place where "flocks repose" (למרבץ צאן). Note too the similar desecration portrayed in the roughly contemporary *Apoc. Ps-Meth.* 11.18 (Reinink, 1:32): ܘܒܥܝܪܗܘܢ ܒܗܝ̈ܟܠܐ ܕܣܗܕ̈ܐ ܘܒܒܝ̈ܬ ܩܒܘܪ̈ܐ ܕܢܨܝ̈ܚܐ ܐܣܪܝܢ, "they tether their livestock in the shrines of the martyrs and at the mausoleums of the saints."

20 The conjunction is present only in HUC Ms. 75.

21 *Secrets of R. Šimʿōn b. Yoḥai* does not mention "trash-heaps" (אשפתות) but uniquely adds at this point: "and when one of them dies, they will bury him any place they please. They will then turn

Deceit will increase, truth will be hidden,[23] law will be distant from Israel, and transgressions will proliferate in Israel.[24] The ruling kingdom will withdraw coinage.[25] They will confuse scarlet dye and worm,[26] and paper and pen will decay.[27] They will refurbish the destroyed cities[28] and clear the roads.[29] They will plant "gardens and orchards" (Qoh 2:5) and repair the holes in the walls of the Temple.[30] They will build a structure at (the site of

---

around and plow the grave and sow seed on it, as scripture attests: 'Thus the children of Israel will eat their food in a state of impurity' (Ezek 4:13). Why so? Because (the location of) impure field(s) will be unknown."

22 Both Zunz-Albeck and Higger have ראשי ההרים, "peaks of the mountains."

23 Zunz-Albeck has ותגש האמת, "and the truth will be oppressed (?)."

24 These latter two clauses are completely missing from the version of the logion in HUC Ms. 75. The Higger edition reads עונות [*sic!*] ותרבה, whereas HUC Ms. 2043 has the same singular verb with another unfortunately illegible noun.

25 The Hebrew text is ויפסל סלע מלכות. Compare the similar language found in *b. B. Qam.* 97a which speaks of the imperial government's (= מלכות) withdrawal of damaged coins from general circulation. The translation follows the rendering suggested by Krauss, *Studien zur byzantinisch-jüdischen Geschichte*, 145. This clause occurs here in HUC Ms. 75, but appears after the reference to "paper and pen" in the other versions.

26 So HUC Ms. 75 (ויתערבו שני ותולעת). Higger and HUC Ms. 2043 have שני תולעת כצמר ("scarlet-crimson like wool"); Zunz-Albeck has שני תולעת בצמר ("scarlet-crimson with/in wool"), both of which would appear to signal a deterioration in the quality of wool. *Contra* Hoyland (*Seeing Islam*, 315 n. 176), Isa 1:18 does not seem relevant.

27 HUC Ms. 75 reads here: ויקמול חיניר והקומים, whereas HUC Ms. 2043 has: ויקמל הנזר והקלמס. I have followed Zunz-Albeck and Higger's editions in rendering ויקמל הנייר והקולמוס. See Isa 33:9 for the meaning of the verb.

28 Cf. Ezek 36:33–38.

29 HUC Ms. 75 has ויבנו את הדרכים, "and they will rebuild the roads." Milestones bearing the name of ʿAbd al-Malik (685–705) attest this caliph's interest in repairing the roads in Palestine; see Moshe Sharon, "An Arabic Inscription from the Time of the Caliph ʿAbd al-Malik," *BSOAS* 29 (1966): 367–72; Moshe Gil, *A History of Palestine, 634–1099* (trans. Ethel Broido; Cambridge: Cambridge University Press, 1992), 109; Robert Schick, *The Christian Communities of Palestine from Byzantine to Islamic Rule: A Historical and Archaeological Study* (Studies in Late Antiquity and Early Islam 2; Princeton: Darwin Press, 1995), 87. Compare the Syriac *Apoc. Ps-Ephrem*, a text that dates from the latter half of the seventh century CE: ܢܬܩܢܘܢ ܐܘܪܚܬܐ ܒܛܘܪܐ ܘܡܫܒܠܐ ܟܠܗ ܦܩܥܬܐ, "they (the Arabs) will prepare roads in the mountains and highways in the plains." Text cited from Edmund Beck, ed., *Des heiligen Ephraem des Syrers Sermones III* (CSCO 320; Louvain: Secrétariat du Corpus SCO, 1972), 63.153. For the dating of Pseudo-Ephrem, see the remarks of Gerrit J. Reinink, "Pseudo-Ephraems "Rede über das Ende" und die syrische eschatologische Literatur des siebenten Jahrhunderts," *ARAM* 5 (1993): 437–63, esp. 455ff.; idem, "Heraclius, The New Alexander: Apocalyptic Prophecies during the Reign of Heraclius," in *The Reign of Heraclius (610–641): Crisis and Confrontation* (ed. Gerrit J. Reinink and Bernard H. Stolte; Leuven: Peeters, 2002), 90; Hoyland, *Seeing Islam*, 260–63.

30 ויגדרו פרצות חומ[ו]ת בית המקדש. HUC Ms. 75 reads for the object בית המדרש, "house of study." The *Secrets of R. Šimʿōn b. Yoḥai* (Jellinek, *BHM* 3:79.9–11) has this to say about "the second ruler to arise from Ishmael," arguably the second caliph ʿUmar ibn al-Khaṭṭāb (634–644 CE): "[he] will be a friend of Israel. He will repair their breaches (ויגדור פרצותיהם) and (fix) the breaches of the Temple (ופרצו' ההיכל) and shape Mt. Moriah and make the whole of it a level plain. He will build for himself there a place for prayer (השתחויה) upon the site of the foundation stone (אבן שתיה), as scrip-

the) sanctuary.[31] Two brothers will arise over them as leaders.[32] In their days the Branch (צמח), the son of David, will arise,[33] as scripture says: "and in the time of those kings the God of Heaven will establish a kingdom, etc." (Dan 2:44).

---

ture says: 'and set your nest *on the rock*' (Num 24:21)." For Christian readings of Umar's Temple Mount refurbishments as an attempt to rebuild the Jewish Temple, see Sebastian Brock, "Syriac Views of Emergent Islam," in *Studies on the First Century of Islamic Society* (ed. G. H. A. Juynboll; Carbondale, Ill.: Southern Illinois University Press, 1982), 12.

On the other hand, Muʿāwiya b. Abī Sufyān (661–680), the founder of the Umayyad caliphate, enjoyed some renown as a builder and patron of construction projects during his reign. A Genizah fragment of a Judeo-Arabic apocalypse originally published by Israel Lévi ("Une apocalypse judéo-arabe," *REJ* 67 [1914]: 178–82) explicitly mentions Muʿāwiya and states that "he will restore the walls of the Temple." According to Maqdisī, Muʿāwiya was in fact the builder of the al-Aqṣā mosque. See Hoyland, *Seeing Islam*, 316–17; Amikam Elad, *Medieval Jerusalem and Islamic Worship: Holy Places, Ceremonies, Pilgrimages* (2d ed.; Leiden: Brill, 1999), 23–24, 33–35.

[31] ויבנו בנין בהיכל. A reference to the construction of the Dome of the Rock by ʿAbd al-Malik in 691–692 CE? So Josef van Ess, "ʿAbd al-Malik and the Dome of the Rock: An Analysis of Some Texts," in *Bayt al-Maqdis: ʿAbd al-Malik's Jerusalem* (ed. Julian Raby and Jeremy Johns; 2 vols.; Oxford: Oxford University Press, 1992), 1:97; Hoyland, *Seeing Islam*, 316; Gordon D. Newby, "Text and Territory: Jewish-Muslim Relations 632–750 CE," in *Judaism and Islam: Boundaries, Communication and Interaction: Essays in Honor of William M. Brinner* (ed. Benjamin H. Hary, John L. Hayes, and Fred Astren; Leiden: Brill, 2000), 89.

[32] ושני[ם] אחים יעמדו עליהם [ל]נשיאים. The Zunz-Albeck version appends the word בסוף, "at the End"; Higger instead adds a final word בגופן, "with/in their body" (?). The latter probably is a corruption of the former.

Abba Hillel Silver (*A History of Messianic Speculation in Israel* [New York, 1927; repr., Boston: Beacon, 1959], 40–41) argues that the two brothers are Muʿāwiyah (661–680 CE) and Ziyād b. Abī Sufyān (665–673). Hoyland (*Seeing Islam*, 316) nominates ʿAbd al-Malik (685–705 CE) and ʿAbd al-ʿAzīz, the latter of whom was governor of Egypt during his brother's reign as caliph. Newby offers "the Umayyad caliphs Yazīd III, who died in 744 CE and his brother Ibrāhīm, who succeeded him and ruled for only four months" ("Jewish-Muslim Relations," 89). Yet another attractive possibility is that the early ʿAbbāsid caliphs Saffāḥ and Manṣūr are intended. It is well attested that the twenty-one-year reign of Manṣūr (754–775 CE) was a time of great messianic upheaval among Jews, Muslims, and other Islamicate religious communities. See Bernard Lewis, "An Apocalyptic Vision of Islamic History," *BSOAS* 13 (1949–51): 330–31, and especially Steven M. Wasserstrom, *Between Muslim and Jew: The Problem of Symbiosis Under Early Islam* (Princeton: Princeton University Press, 1995), 27–33.

One might also compare a synonymous "sign" found in the Latin Pseudo-Ephrem's sermon *On the Last Times, the Antichrist, and the End of the World*: "In those days [i.e., the End] *two brothers* (*duo fratres*) will come to the Roman empire who will rule with one mind; but because one will surpass the other, there will be a schism between them." This passage is not attested in the Syriac version of this pseudepigraphic *mēmrā*. Quotation cited from Bernard McGinn, *Visions of the End: Apocalyptic Traditions in the Middle Ages* (rev. ed.; New York: Columbia University Press, 1998), 61. For discussion of this passage and the difficulties it presents for dating purposes, see especially Wilhelm Bousset, *The Antichrist Legend: A Chapter in Christian and Jewish Folklore* (trans. A. H. Keane; London: Hutchinson, 1896; repr., Atlanta: Scholars Press, 1999), 33–41; Paul J. Alexander, *The Byzantine Apocalyptic Tradition* (ed. Dorothy deF. Abrahamse; Berkeley: University of California Press, 1985), 144–47.

[33] Both Zunz-Albeck and Higger attest the phraseology יעמוד צמח בן דוד. HUC Ms. 2043 reads בא בן דוד, "the son of David comes." HUC Ms. 75 has בני דוד יצמח, "My son David will sprout."

R. Ishmael also said: The Ishmaelites will fight three great battles[34] on the earth[35] at the End of Days, as scripture affirms: "for they fled from swords" (Isa 21:15); the expression "swords" refers to "battles."[36] One (will be) in the forest[37]—"from the drawn sword" (ibid.); one (will be) on the sea—"from the drawn bow" (ibid.); and one (will be) at the great city of Rome,[38] which (will be) more fierce than the (preceding) two, as scripture states: "from the ferocity of battle" (ibid.).[39] From there [i.e., Rome] the son of David will sprout up,[40] and he will come to the Land of Israel and behold the destruction of both these and those,[41] as scripture states: "Who is this *who comes from Edom*, red of garment from Bosra, this one majestic in his clothing etc." (Isa 63:1).[42]

[34] So HUC Ms. 75 (מלחמות גדולות). Higger's version reads מלחמות של מהומה, "wars of confusion." For an identification of these battles in line with his suggested historical profile, see Silver, *History*, 41–42.

[35] This phrase (בארץ) is lacking in HUC Ms. 75.

[36] This particular oracle is introduced in Isa 21:13 as pertaining to Arabia (משא בערב), and the number 3 is derived from the three separate scenarios envisioned in v. 15b.

[37] Higger's version adds "of Arabia" (בערב).

[38] Translating HUC Ms. 2043: בכרך גדול שלרומי. HUC Ms. 75 has: בכרך הגדול שברומי, "at the great city which is in Rome (i.e., Byzantium)."

[39] HUC Ms. 75: מפני כבוד מלחמה, which would be "from the glory (!) of battle." The consonantal text of Isa 21:15 however reads כבד מלחמה, "ferocity of battle."

[40] For the occultation of the Messiah in Rome, see *Sefer Zerubbabel* and the various sources collected by Abraham Berger, "Captive at the Gate of Rome: The Story of a Messianic Motif," *PAAJR* 44 (1977): 1–17.

[41] That is, the destruction of both the Edomites (= Christians) and the Ishmaelites (= Muslims). The above translation follows the rendering in HUC Ms. 75, which views the final destruction of Rome and Arab rule as taking place in Palestine. HUC Ms. 2043 and Higger's edition reverse the order of these two clauses: the Messiah of the lineage of David will witness the mutual destruction of the evil empires *at Constantinople*, and only then will make his triumphal journey to Eretz Israel.

[42] See Ibn Ezra and Radaq *ad loc.*, as well as the remarks of Radaq about Edom and the necessity for its destruction *ad* Isa 34:1–17. Note too the abstract published by Jacob Mann, "Proceedings of the American Oriental Society at the Meeting in Cincinnati, Ohio, 1927," *JAOS* 47 (1927): 364. Newby ("Jewish-Muslim Relations," 90–91) argues that this messianic figure is Abū ʿĪsā al-Iṣfahānī, but this historical identification does not correlate with the biblical text's assumption that this "messiah" hails from Edom, that is, Rome, presumably Constantinople, and not the East. For an identification of Isaiah's "Bosra" with Constantinople, see the letter from the Genizah first published by Adolf Neubauer ("Egyptian Fragments, C," *JQR* o.s. 9 [1897]: 29–36) and excerpted by Joshua Starr, *The Jews in the Byzantine Empire, 641–1204* (Athens: Verlag der byzantinisch-neugriechischen Jahrbücher, 1939), 214.

Zunz-Albeck, *Haderashot*	Higger (§29 end)
ר׳ ישמעאל אומר חמשה עשר דברים	ר׳ ישמעאל אומ׳ חמשה עשר דברים
עתידין בני ישמעאל לעשות בארץ	עתידין בני ישראל (!)* לעשות בארץ
באחרית הימים ואלו הן	באחרית הימים ואלו הן
ימדדו את הארץ בחבלים	ימודו הארץ בחבלים
ויעשו בית הקברות למרבץ צאן אשפתות	ויעשו בית הקברות למרבץ צאן אשפתות
וימדדו בהם ומהם על ראשי ההרים	ומדדו בהן ומהן על ראשי ההרים
וירבה השקר	וירבה השקר
ותגש האמת	ויגנז האמת
וירחק חק מישראל	וירחק חק מישראל
וירבו עונות בישראל	ותרבה עונות בישראל
שני תולעת בצמר	שני תולעת כצמר
ויקמל הנייר והקולמוס	ויקמל הנייר והקולמוס
ויפסל סלע מלכות	ויפסל סלע מלכות
ויבנו את הערים החרבות	ויבנו {ההרים} הערים החרבות
ויפנו הדרכים	ויפנו הדרכים
ויטעו גנות ופרדסים	ויטעו גנות ופרדסים
ויגדרו פרצות חומות בית המקדש	ויגדרו פרוצות חומות בית המקדש
ויבנו בנין בהיכל	ויבנו בניין בהיכל
ושני אחים יעמדו עליהם נשיאים בסוף	ושני אחים יעמדו אליהם נשיאים בגופן
ובימיהם יעמוד צמח בן דוד.	ובימיהן יעמד צמח בן דוד שנ׳ ביומיהון
	דמלכא אינון
	ועוד היה ר׳ ישמעאל אומ׳
	שלשה מלחמות של מהומה עתידין
	בני ישמעאל לעשות בארץ באחרית
	הימים שנ׳ כי מפני חרבות נדדו
	ואין חרבות אלא מלחמות
	אחת ביער בערב מפני חרב נטושה
	ואחת בים מפני קשת דרוכה
	ואחת בכרך גדול... שהוא כבד משניהם
	שנ׳ כי מפני כובד מלחמה
	ומשם בן דוד יצמח ויראה באבדן של
	אלו ואלו ומשם יבא לארץ ישראל
	שנ׳ מי זה בא מאדום.

*Read ישמעאל in place of ישראל in accordance with the parallel versions and Moritz Steinschneider, "Apokalypsen mit polemischer Tendenz," *ZDMG* 28 (1874): 645 n. 38.

HUC Ms. 75

ר׳ ישמעאל אומ׳ חמשה עשר דבר
עתידין בני ישמעאל לעשות בארץ
באחרית הימים ואלו הן
ומדדו את הארץ בחבלים
ויעשו בית הקברות מרבץ צאן ואשפתות
וימדדו מהם ובהם על ההרים
וירבה השקר
ויגנז האמת

ויתערבו שני ותולעת
ויקמול חיניר והקומים
ויפסל סלע מלכות
ויבנו את הערים החרבות
ויבנו את הדרכים
ויטעו גנות ופרדסים
ויגדרו פרצות חומות בית המדרש
ויבנו בנין בהיכל
ושנים אחים יעמדו עליהם לנשיאים
ובימיהם בני דוד יצמח שנ׳ וביומיהון
דמלכיא יקום וג׳
ר׳ ישמעאל אומ׳
שלש מלחמות גדולות עתידין
בני ישמעאל לעשות באחרית
היומים שנ׳ מפני [חרבות]
ואין חרבות אלא מלחמות
אחת ביער מפני חרב נ[טושה]
ואחת על הים מפני קשת דרוכה
ואחת {ב}בכרך הגדול שברומי מפני
שהוא כבוד משניהום שנ׳ מפני כבוד
מלחמה
ומשם בן דוד יצמח
ויבוא אל ארץ ישראל ויראה באבדן
של אלו ואלו שנ׳
מי זה בא מאדום חמוץ בגדים
מבצרה זה הדור בלבושו וגו׳
סליק פירקא

HUC Ms. 2043

אמר ר׳ ישמעאל חמש עשרה דברים
עתידין בני ישמעאל לעשות בארץ
באחרית הימים ואלו הן
ימדדו את הארץ בחבלים
ויעשו בבית הקברות מרבץ צאן אשפתות
ומדדו בהן ומהן על ההרים
וירבה השקר
ויגנז האמת
וירחק חוק מישראל
ותרבה ע..לת בישראל
[שני] תולעת כצמר
ויקמל הנזר והקלמס
ויפסל סלע [מלכות]
[ויבנו א]ת הערים החרבות
ויפנו הדרכים
ויטעו גנות ופר[דסים]
ויגדרו פרצות חומת בית המקדש
ויבנו בנין בהיכל
ושני א[חים יעמדו] עליהם נשיאים
ובימיהם בא בן דוד בא.. דכת׳ ובימיהון די
[מלכיא אנון] יקים אלה שמיא מלכו
ועוד היה ר׳ ישמעאל או׳
שלש מלחמ[ות ???] [עתידין
ב]ני ישמעאל לעשות בארץ באחרית
הימים שנ׳ כי מפ[ני חרבות] נדדו
ואין חרבות אלא מלחמות
אחת ביער שנ׳ כי מפני חרב נטו[שה
ואחת] בים שנ׳ מפני קשת דרוכה
ואחת בכרך גדול שלרומי
ומפני כבד מל[חמה] מלחמה
ומשם בן דוד יצמח ויראה באבדן
שאלו ואלו ומשם יבוא לארץ י[שראל
שנ׳] מי זה בא מאדום חמוץ בגדים
מבצרה זה הדור בלבושו צעה ברב כוח
[אני מדבר] בצדקה רב להושיע
סליק פרקא

4

R. Šimᶜōn b. Yoḥai Complex

THE *SECRETS OF R. ŠIMᶜŌN BEN YOḤAI*

The eminent nineteenth-century historian Heinrich Graetz enthusiastically endorsed the *Secrets* (נסתרות) *of R. Šimᶜōn ben Yoḥai* as "das älteste Schriftdenkmal aus der gaonäischen Zeit und die älteste mystische Schrift."[1] While Graetz's temporal evaluation of this apocalypse's significance is no longer a tenable one, his perceptive recognition of its fundamental importance for the history of Jewish apocalyptic thought continues to stand the test of time.

Rabbi Šimᶜōn ben Yoḥai, a prominent rabbinic Sage whose *floruit* was in the generation following the disastrous Second Jewish Revolt (132–135 CE), is characterized by Daniel Boyarin as "the most radical rejector of Rome, its culture, its legitimacy, and its value among the Tannaitic figures."[2] His strident opposition to foreign imperial hegemony made him an ideal figure around which to cluster literary expressions of nationalist hopes for ultimate vindication and deliverance. Rabbinic literature also represents R. Šimᶜōn as especially prone to consultations with representatives of the celestial world and as an adept in magical lore, thereby fostering a profile that is mimicked in these apocalypses by his successful performance of an efficacious ascetical regimen that invokes Metatron, angelic Prince of the Divine Presence, for the purpose of conveying "the secrets" (הנסתרות) pertaining to the last days. Emblematic of the popular estimation of R. Šimᶜōn's occultist talents will be the later pseudepigraphic ascription to him of the Zohar, undoubtedly the most important and influential collection of esoteric teachings that comprise Jewish Kabbalah.[3]

[1] Heinrich Graetz, *Geschichte der Juden von den ältesten Zeiten bis auf die Gegenwart* (3d ed.; 11 vols. in 13; Leipzig: Oskar Leiner, 1890–1908), 5:412. Graetz dates *Secrets* to between August and October 750 CE, and *Prayer* several centuries later to the time of the last Crusades.

[2] Daniel Boyarin, *Dying for God: Martyrdom and the Making of Christianity and Judaism* (Stanford: Stanford University Press, 1999), 64.

[3] The primary rabbinic traditions about R. Šimᶜōn have been thoroughly explored in B.-Z. Rosenfeld, "R. Simeon b. Yohai: Wonder Worker and Magician Scholar, *Saddiq* and *Hasid*," *REJ* 158 (1999): 349–84. For a stimulating presentation of the "messianic" dimensions of his persona, see Yehuda

Given his reputation, it is not surprising to find the name of R. Šimᶜōn attached to a small number of apocalypses stemming from the postrabbinic era. The oldest of these works is undoubtedly the *Secrets*, a narrative compilation of traditions that achieved an initial written form sometime not long after the mid-eighth century. The historical section of *Secrets* is notable for its thinly veiled allusions to the prophetic mission of Muhammad and the Arab conquest of Jerusalem and Eretz Israel during the fourth decade of the seventh century and its selectively truncated sequencing of seventh- and eighth-century Umayyad rulers up until the ᶜAbbāsid revolution. Based on the originally positive appraisals of the advent of Muhammad and the early years of the Muslim conquest detectable in this section, it is possible that core portions of the *Secrets* rely on sources that date from the mid-seventh century.[4] On the other hand, its immediate inclusion of the beginning of a popular eschatological logion attributed to R. Ishmael[5] alongside a second negatively colored interpretation of Num 24:21 vituperating the "kingdom of Ishmael" as simply another oppressive empire that would enslave and mistreat Israel drastically tempers what must have once been a qualified endorsement of nascent Islam as a type of Jewish messianic movement. Other apocalypses belonging to this same cycle—the so-called *ᶜAtidot* (עתידות) *of R. Šimᶜōn ben Yoḥai* and the *Prayer of R. Šimᶜōn ben Yoḥai*—accentuate the invective against Islam and extend the historical narrative of the apocalypse well into the ᶜAbbāsid period and into the era of the Crusades.

The *Secrets of R. Šimᶜōn ben Yoḥai* were first published in Salonika in 1743 within the same anthology of midrashic texts that contains *Sefer Elijah*. This version of the text was reprinted by Adolph Jellinek in his *Bet ha-Midrasch*.[6] Jellinek's text was subsequently reproduced by Yehudah Even-Shmuel;[7] using the various extant versions of this midrash, the same scholar also generated a suggested *Vorlage* for the *Secrets*[8] and also reproduced the variant recension (עתידות ר' שמעון בן יוחאי) contained within a larger eschatological work concerning the "Ten Kings" which was first published by H. M. Horowitz in 1891. A. Z. Aescoly pro-

Liebes, "The Messiah of the Zohar: On R. Simeon bar Yohai as a Messianic Figure," in idem, *Studies in the Zohar* (Albany: State University of New York Press, 1993), 1–84.

[4] See Salo M. Baron, *A Social and Religious History of the Jews* (18 vols.; 2d ed.; New York: Columbia University Press; Philadelphia: Jewish Publication Society, 1952–83), 3:93, 274 n. 27; Gilbert Dagron, "Introduction historique: Entre histoire et apocalypse," *Travaux et mémoires* 11 (1991): 43. A valuable discussion of the *Secrets* and its possible historical context is provided by Graetz, *Geschichte*, 5:406–13.

[5] See the translation of and commentary to the end of *Pirqe R. El.* §30 in the present volume.

[6] Adolph Jellinek, ed., *Bet ha-Midrasch: Sammlung kleiner Midraschim und vermischter Abhandlungen aus der jüdischen Literatur* (6 vols.; Leipzig, 1853–77; repr., Jerusalem: Bamberger & Wahrmann, 1938), 3:78–82.

[7] Yehudah Even-Shmuel, *Midreshey Geᵓullah* (2d ed.; Jerusalem: Mosad Bialik, 1954), 401–3.

[8] Ibid., 187–98.

vides an abridged version of Jellinek's text along with a brief commentary in his important anthology of Jewish messianic literature.[9] A Cairo Genizah fragment of the opening section of the *Secrets* was published by S. A. Wertheimer.[10] A fifteenth-century manuscript version of *Secrets* is available in Munich Ms. Hebr. 222, a work that also features important editions of *Pirqe Mašiaḥ* and *Sefer Elijah*.[11] Unpublished manuscript fragments include Oxford Ms. Heb. f. 27 (2642) fols. 42–43 and Oxford Ms. Heb. d. 46 (2643) fols. 72–73.[12] The present translation is based on the text reproduced by Jellinek.[13]

The *Secrets* of Rabbi Šimᶜōn b. Yoḥai

These are the secrets that were revealed to R. Šimᶜōn b. Yoḥai when he was hiding in a cave on account of (the persecutions of) Caesar king of Edom (i.e., Rome).[14] He stood in prayer forty days and forty nights, and began thusly: "Lord God, how long will you spurn the prayer of your servant?" [15] Immediately there were revealed to him the secrets of the eschaton and (various) hidden things.

He began to sit and expound (the passage) "and he beheld the Kenite" (Num 24:21).[16] When he perceived that the kingdom of Ishmael would

[9] Aaron Ze'ev Aescoly, *Messianic Movements in Israel,* Volume 1, *From the Bar-Kokhba Revolt until the Expulsion of the Jews from Spain* (ed. Yehudah Even-Shmuel; 2d ed.; Jerusalem: Mosad Bialik, 1987), 133–38.

[10] S. A. Wertheimer, *Batey Midrashot* (2 vols.; repr., Jerusalem: Ktav wa-Sefer, 1980), 2:25–26; see also 2:506–7.

[11] Moses Buttenwieser, *Outline of the Neo-Hebraic Apocalyptic Literature* (Cincinnati: Jennings & Pye, 1901), 39. *Secrets* occupies fols. 107b–111a of this manuscript, where it "contains better readings in some places" according to Buttenwieser; whereas Moritz Steinschneider opined that "die Varianten sind sehr unbedeutend" ("Apokalypsen mit polemischer Tendenz," *ZDMG* 28 [1874]: 637).

[12] See Adolf Neubauer and A. E. Cowley, *Catalogue of the Hebrew Manuscripts in the Bodleian Library Volume Two* (Oxford: Clarendon, 1906), 37 §9.

[13] Another English translation of the Jellinek edition is in David C. Mitchell, *The Message of the Psalter: An Eschatological Programme in the Book of Psalms* (JSOTSup 252; Sheffield: Sheffield Academic Press, 1997), 329–34, 347–50 (text).

[14] The talmudic legend of R. Šimᶜōn's thirteen-year sequestration in a cave can be found in *b. Šabb.* 33b–34a; see also *y. Šeb.* 9.1, 38d; *Gen. Rab.* 79.6; *Pesiq. Rab Kah.* 11.16 (Mandelbaum, 1:191–93); *Qoh. Rab.* 10.8. A comprehensive analysis of the rabbinic legend is provided by Jeffrey L. Rubenstein, *Talmudic Stories: Narrative Art, Composition, and Culture* (Baltimore and London: Johns Hopkins University Press, 1999), 105–38.

[15] Cf. Ps 80:5. A suitably penitent and supplicatory prayer is supplied in the closely allied apocalypse entitled *Prayer of R. Šimᶜōn ben Yoḥai.*

[16] The identity of the "Kenite" in the *Secrets*, as opposed to the fuller *Prayer*, is allegedly problematic in that it seems to encode the same group as the phrase "kingdom of Ishmael." See the arguments of Patricia Crone and Michael Cook, *Hagarism: The Making of the Islamic World* (Cambridge: Cam-

come (and exercise dominion over Israel), he exclaimed: "Is it not sufficient what the wicked kingdom of Edom has done to us that we should also (suffer the dominion of) the kingdom of Ishmael!?"[17] Immediately Metatron the prince of the Presence answered him and said:[18] "Do not be afraid, mortal, for the Holy One, blessed be He, is bringing about the kingdom of Ishmael only for the purpose of delivering you from that wicked one (i.e., Edom).[19] He shall raise up over them a prophet in accordance with His will,[20] and He will subdue the land for them; and they shall come and

---

bridge University Press, 1977), 35–37; Moshe Gil, *A History of Palestine, 634–1099* (trans. Ethel Broido; Cambridge: Cambridge University Press, 1992), 62 n. 65. The responsum of R. Hai Gaon (translated later in this volume) explicitly declares the "Kenite" to be Midian or Ishmael.

[17] Genizah fragment reads: לא דיינו מה שעשת בנו מלכות הרשעה, "is it not sufficient what the wicked kingdom has done to us?"

[18] Genizah fragment reads: אמר ר׳ שמעון כך נענה לי מטטרון שר הפנים.

[19] Genizah fragment reads: אל תירא בני שאין הקדוש ברוך הוא עתיד להוציא את ישראל אלא שגלוי וידוע לפניו בלחץ שישראל לחוצים בו הקדוש ברוך הוא מוציא מלכות ישמעאל עליהם כדי להושיעם מיד מלכות הרשעה.

[20] Genizah fragment reads: נביא שוטה ואיש הרוח, "a demented prophet possessed by a spirit," clearly a revision of the older positive evaluation of Muhammad found in our text above. Munich Ms. Heb. 222 similarly reads: שוטה נביא ומשוגע, "a demented and crazed prophet." See the corresponding portion of *Prayer*; also Steinschneider, "Apokalypsen," 635 n. 18; Bernard Lewis, "An Apocalyptic Vision of Islamic History," *BSOAS* 13 (1949–51): 323 n. 4. For further evidence that Levantine Jews initially welcomed the mission of Muhammad, see the early-seventh-century *Doctrina Iacobi nuper baptizati* (ed. N. Bonwetsch; Abhandlungen der königlichen Gesellschaft der Wissenschaften zu Göttingen, phil.-hist. klass., n.f., bd. 12, nr. 3; Berlin: Weidmannsche Buchhandlung, 1910), 86, cited by David M. Olster, *Roman Defeat, Christian Response, and the Literary Construction of the Jew* (Philadelphia: University of Pennsylvania Press, 1994), 171; see also Robert G. Hoyland, *Seeing Islam As Others Saw It: A Survey and Evaluation of Christian, Jewish and Zoroastrian Writings on Early Islam* (Studies in Late Antiquity and Early Islam 13; Princeton: Darwin Press, 1997), 55–61. It has been plausibly suggested that the original text's recognition of the prophetic status of Muhammad reflects a close relationship with the eighth-century Jewish ʿĪsāwiyya sect, a messianic movement sparked by Abū ʿĪsā al-Iṣfahānī, who accorded prophetic status to a number of Gentile figures as well as Jesus and Muhammad. Note S. D. Goitein, *Jews and Arabs: Their Contacts Through the Ages* (rev. ed.; New York: Schocken, 1974), 170; Steven M. Wasserstrom, "The ʿĪsāwiyya Revisited," *Studia Islamica* 75 (1992): 62, 65–70; Yoram Erder, "The Doctrine of Abū ʿĪsā al-Iṣfahānī and its Sources," *JSAI* 20 (1996): 168. Maqrīzī reports that ʿĀnān likewise acknowledged the prophetic status of Muhammad: "He (ʿĀnān) affirmed the prophetic standing of Muhammad, God bless him and grant him salvation, and stated that he was a prophet sent (by God) to the Arabs." Text cited from A. I. Silvestre de Sacy, *Chrestomathie arabe* (3 vols.; Paris: Imprimerie impériale, 1806), 1:162.9–10. On the more general possibility that Muhammad was initially viewed with favor by segments of the Jewish community, see Chaim Rabin, *Qumran Studies* (Oxford: Oxford University Press, 1957; repr., New York: Schocken, 1975), 123–28; Crone and Cook, *Hagarism*, 4–9; Gil, *History of Palestine*, 63 n. 65; Uri Rubin, *Between Bible and Qurʾān: The Children of Israel and the Islamic Self-Image* (Studies in Late Antiquity and Early Islam 17; Princeton: Darwin Press, 1999), 32–33.

restore it with grandeur.[21] Great enmity[22] will exist between them and the children of Esau."

R. Šimʿōn answered and said: "From whence are they (understood as) our deliverance?"[23] He said to him: "Did not Isaiah the prophet speak thusly? 'And should[24] he see chariotry of a pair of riders, one riding an ass, (and) one riding a camel' (Isa 21:7)."[25] Why did he put the "rider of an ass" before the "rider of a camel"? Should he not instead have said "rider of a camel, rider of an ass"? (No, the textual sequence means that) when the one who rides the camel (Ishmael or Muhammad) emerges, the kingdom ruled by the 'one mounted upon an ass' (Zech 9:9)[26] has manifested (lit. 'sprouted') by his (i.e., Ishmael's or Muhammad's) agency.[27] Another opinion: 'rider of an ass' (means) at the (same) time when he 'rides upon an ass' (Zech 9:9). Consequently they (Ishmael) are a deliverance for Israel like the deliverance (associated with) the 'one mounted upon an ass' (Zech 9:9).[28]

[21] Genizah fragment reads: והם באים ומחזיקים המלכות בגדולה, "and they shall come and seize the kingdom with might."

[22] Read with the Genizah fragment ואיבה here instead of ואימה as in Jellinek's edition; see Graetz, *Geschichte*, 5:407; Lewis, "Apocalyptic Vision," 309 n. 2; 312 n. 3.

[23] Genizah fragment reads: וכי ישועה הם בני ישמעאל, "are the Ishmaelites a deliverance?!?"

[24] See the remarks of Ibn Ezra on this verse.

[25] There is no need to posit a reliance on the targumic rendering of this verse, as suggested by Crone and Cook (*Hagarism*, 153 n. 13), since consonantal רכב can just as easily be read רוכב in the pre-Masoretic age. Note, e.g., the 1QIsa[a] scroll, where the received text's רכב חמור רכב גמל becomes רוכב חמור רוכב גמל. The רכב צמד פרשים in this specific interpretative context is almost certainly an allusion to the return of Elijah; cf. 2 Kgs 2:12. Contrast the interpretation of this verse contained in the *Prayer of R. Šimʿōn b. Yoḥai* (Jellinek, *BHM* 4:119.23–28).

For the various uses of this proof text by Jews, Christians, and Muslims alike, see Gustave E. von Grunebaum, *Medieval Islam: A Study in Cultural Orientation* (2d ed.; Chicago: University of Chicago Press, 1953), 17–18. According to Q 7:157, both the Jewish and Christian scriptures contain prophetic predictions of the advent of Muhammad.

[26] See the medieval commentaries *ad loc.* The *Prayer* inserts a quotation from Zech 9:9 at this point in order to cement the identification between the "ass-rider" and the Messiah.

[27] Compare the language of *Prayer* (Jellinek, *BHM* 4:119.26–27: שבימיו תצמח מלכות משיח, "for in his (Ishmael"s) days the messianic kingdom will sprout."

This argument may reflect the author's cognizance of a popular Muslim reading of this proof text. See, e.g., Kirmānī, *Kitāb al-maṣābīḥ:* "the rider of the ass is Jesus, upon whom be peace, and the rider of the camel is Muhammad, may God bless and exalt him." Text cited from the edition provided by Paul Kraus, "Hebräische und syrische Zitate in ismāʿīlitischen Schriften," *Der Islam* 19 (1930): 246; and see Kraus's remarks on p. 250. Note also Bīrūnī, *al-Āthār al-bāqiya ʿan-il-qurūn al-khāliya* (ed. C. E. Sachau; repr., Leipzig: Otto Harrassowitz, 1923), 19, cited in English translation by Gil, *History of Palestine*, 63; and also the broader discussion of Suliman Bashear, "Riding Beasts on Divine Missions: An Examination of the Ass and Camel Traditions," *JSS* 37 (1991): 37–75.

[28] There are some intriguing messianic dimensions, including the riding of an ass, to the traditions surrounding the advent and activities in Jerusalem of the second caliph ʿUmar ibn al-Khaṭṭāb. See Crone and Cook, *Hagarism*, 5; Heribert Busse, "ʿOmar b. al-Ḫaṭṭāb in Jerusalem," *JSAI* 5 (1984):

Moreover, R. Šimʿōn reported that he learned from R. Ishmael[29] at the time when the latter learned that the kingdom of Ishmael was coming that (the kingdom of Ishmael) will measure the land with ropes,[30] as scripture says: "and the land will be apportioned for wages" (cf. Dan 11:39; also Joel 4:2). They will make cemeteries pastureland for (grazing) flocks,[31] and when one of them dies, they will bury him any place they please. They will then turn around and plow the grave and sow seed on it, as scripture attests: "Thus the children of Israel will eat their food in a state of impurity" (Ezek 4:13). Why so? Because (the location of) impure field(s) will be unknown.

Again "he beheld the Kenite" (Num 24:21). What was the parable that wicked one (Balaam) pronounced? When he foresaw that his (i.e., the Kenite's) descendants[32] were destined to arise and enslave Israel, he began rejoicing and said: "'Ethan (איתן) is your place of dwelling' (Num 24:21)—I see human beings who are occupied only with the commandments of 'Ethan (איתן) the Ezrahite' (1 Kgs 5:11; Ps 89:1)."[33]

The second king who will arise from Ishmael[34] will be a friend of Israel.

73–119; idem, "'Omar's Image as the Conqueror of Jerusalem," *JSAI* 8 (1986): 149–68; Suliman Bashear, "The Title «*Fārūq*» and its Association with ʿUmar I," *Studia Islamica* 72 (1990): 47–70.

[29] Regarding the source of these traditions, see the following two notes.

[30] Some versions of *Pirqe R. El.* §30 conclude with a statement attributed to R. Ishmael outlining the "fifteen things" that the Ishmaelites will do in the land of Israel at the "End of Days." There too the list begins with ומדדו את הארץ בחבלים, "they will measure the land with ropes." Text cited from HUC Ms. 75 fol. 44a.

[31] *Pirqe R. El.* §30 (HUC Ms. 75 fol. 44a): ויעשו בית הקברות מרבץ צאן ואשפתות. For a possible correlation of this surveying activity with the reign of al-Ma'mūn (813–833 CE), see D. Chwolsohn, *Die Ssabier und der Ssabismus* (2 vols.; St. Petersburg: Kaiserlichen Akademie der Wissenschaften, 1856), 1:98 n. 4; Gil, *History of Palestine*, 295.

[32] The Arab tribes. See Judg 4:11; Num 10:29; 1 Chr 2:55. *Tg. Onk.* Num 24:21 translates "Kenite" as "Shalmaite" (שלמאה), the name of an Arab tribe; see also Crone and Cook, *Hagarism*, 35–36; Moshe Gil, *Jews in Islamic Countries in the Middle Ages* (trans. David Strassler; Leiden: Brill, 2004), 16. Graetz (*Geschichte*, 5:407 n. 1) appeals to a parallel passage from a manuscript copy of the *Sefer haʿOsher* of the eleventh-century Karaite commentator Jacob ben Reuben: וירא את הקני זו מלכות ישמעאל, "he beheld the Kenite (Num 24:21)—this is the kingdom of Ishmael."

[33] Lewis ("Apocalyptic Vision," 313 n. 1) notes the frequent midrashic assimilation between Ethan and Abraham; see, e.g., *b. B. Bat.* 15a; *Lev. Rab.* 9.1 (Margulies, 1:174); *Tg.* Ps 89:1 and Rashi *ad loc.*; Rashi and Radaq *ad* 1 Kgs 5:11. Since the Qur'ān expressly equates the religion of Islam with the "religion of your ancestor Abraham" (Q 22:78) and repeatedly invokes Abraham as a precursor of Muhammad, this peculiar exegesis reflects a Jewish accommodation to these rhetorical claims. For a suggestive association of one or more "commandments" with Abraham, see Q 2:124; 43:28. Note also the important discussion of Crone and Cook, *Hagarism*, 10–15.

[34] Apparently the second caliph ʿUmar ibn al-Khaṭṭāb (634–644 CE); see Graetz, *Geschichte*, 5:407; Aescoly, *Messianic Movements*, 137 n. 2. Contrary to what is often reported, ʿUmar apparently relaxed the Hadrianic ban against Jewish residence in Jerusalem. See the numerous primary sources cited and discussed by Gil, *History of Palestine*, 68–74; idem, "The Jewish Community," in *The History of Jerusalem: The Early Muslim Period, 638–1099* (ed. Joshua Prawer and Haggai Ben-Shammai;

He will repair their breaches[35] and (fix) the breaches of the Temple and shape Mt. Moriah[36] and make the whole of it a level plain. He will build for himself there a place for prayer (השתחויה) upon the site of the "foundation stone" (אבן שתיה),[37] as scripture says: "and set your nest *on the rock*" (Num 24:21).[38] He will wage war with the children of Esau and slaughter their troops and capture a large number of them, and (eventually) he will die in peace and with great honor.[39]

And there shall arise a great king from Ḥaṣarmawet (cf. Gen 10:26), but he will exercise rule only for a few years. Warriors of the children of Qedar[40] shall rise up against him and kill him,[41] and bring to power another king

---

Jerusalem: Yad Izhak Ben-Zvi; New York: New York University Press, 1996), 163–71. ʿUmar, however, did not "die in peace," as the end of the notice states, but was murdered. See Hoyland, *Seeing Islam*, 311–12.

[35] Cf. Amos 9:11.

[36] That is, Zion or the Temple Mount. Cf. 2 Chr 3:1; *y. Ber.* 4.5, 8c; *Sifre* Deut §62 (Finkelstein, 128).

[37] According to Jewish tradition, this rock marked the site where the Ark of the Presence resided in Solomon's Temple and was reportedly part of the raw material from which God formed the universe; see *m. Yoma* 5.2 and especially *t. Yoma* 2.14 (Lieberman). It is this same rock that serves as a launching pad for Muhammad's tour of the heavens. The author apparently viewed this caliph's construction activity as tantamount to rebuilding the Temple.

[38] Given the proof text, there is here a possible confusion with the later construction (692 CE) by ʿAbd al-Malik of the shrine known as the Dome of the Rock (*qubbat al-ṣakhra*); see Gil, *History of Palestine*, 91–92. Despite numerous assertions, it is very unclear what ʿUmar might have erected on the Temple Mount. The earliest unambiguous reference to a structure is in the report of the Christian pilgrim Arculfus (from between 679 and 682 CE) that speaks of a "quadrangular house of prayer" (*quadrangulam orationis domum*) constructed of wooden beams and boards that could reportedly hold three thousand worshipers; for his testimony, see F. E. Peters, *Jerusalem: The Holy City in the Eyes of Chroniclers, Visitors, Pilgrims, and Prophets from the Days of Abraham to the Beginnings of Modern Times* (Princeton: Princeton University Press, 1985), 195–96; Gil, *History of Palestine*, 91; Hoyland, *Seeing Islam*, 221. An elegant summation of possibilities is provided by Heribert Busse, review of Andreas Kaplony, *The Ḥaram of Jerusalem 324–1099, JSAI 29* (2004): 435-36. For thorough discussions of ʿUmar's reputed activities on the Temple Mount, including legends involving the "foundation stone," see Busse, "ʿOmar b. al-Ḫaṭṭāb in Jerusalem," 73–119, esp. 86–94; Amikam Elad, *Medieval Jerusalem and Islamic Worship: Holy Places, Ceremonies, Pilgrimage* (2d ed.; Leiden: Brill, 1999), 29–33.

[39] Some of this material that purportedly pertains to the caliphate of ʿUmar probably should be correlated with Muʿāwiya b. Abī Sufyān (661–680 CE), the first Umayyad caliph, who also took an interest in Jerusalem and its holy sites. Note Lewis, "Apocalyptic Vision," 328; Peters, *Jerusalem*, 200; Averil Cameron, "The Jews in Seventh-Century Palestine," *Scripta Classica Israelica* 13 (1994): 81–82; Hoyland, *Seeing Islam*, 312; Elad, *Medieval Jerusalem*, 23–24.

[40] The patronymic Qedar (קדר) functions as a code for "Arabs"; see *Tg.* Isa 21:17; *Tg.* Jer 2:10; *Tg. Ps.-J.* Gen 25:13; and Radaq *ad* Isa 21:13: נבואה זו נאמרה על ערב והם בני קדר. See Moritz Steinschneider, *Polemische und apologetische Literatur in arabischer Sprache zwischen Muslimen, Christen und Juden, nebst Anhängen verwandten Inhalts* (Leipzig, 1877; repr., Hildesheim: Georg Olms, 1966), 254. For an extended discussion of the mythopoeic dimensions of this name, see Jaroslav Stetkevych, *Muhammad and the Golden Bough: Reconstructing Arabian Myth* (Bloomington and Indianapolis: Indiana University Press, 1996), 69–77.

[41] A reference to the rebellion against (*fitna*) and murder of the third caliph ʿUthmān (644–656 CE)? So Graetz, *Geschichte*, 5:407; more hesitantly, Aescoly, *Messianic Movements*, 137 n. 3. A better

whose name is מריאו.[42] They shall take him from following flocks and mule-herds and elevate him to the kingship. There shall arise from him "four arms"[43] who will make repairs on the Temple.

At the end of the reign of the "four arms" there shall come to power another king.[44] He will diminish measures for quantity, length, and weight, and enjoy three years of tranquility. A dispute will erupt in the world during his reign, and he will send out mighty forces against the Edomites. There (Byzantium?) they[45] will die of hunger, even though they will have abundant provisions—he will refuse (sustenance) from them, (and) none will be given him. The children of Edom will prevail over the children of Ishmael and slaughter them. Then the children of Ishmael will arise and burn the provisions, and those who are left will flee and depart.[46]

After this a great king will come to power and rule for nineteen years.[47] These are his distinguishing marks (lit. "signs"): reddish-hued, squinty-eyed (?),[48] and he will have three moles: one on his forehead, one on his right hand, and one on his left arm. He will plant saplings and rebuild ruined cities and tap subterranean waters to bring up water to irrigate his plantings so that his future descendants will have plenty to eat. All who arise to oppose him will submit to his power, and the land will remain undisturbed during his reign, and he will die peacefully.

Then another king will arise who will seek to cut off the waters of the Jordan.[49] He will bring faraway peoples from alien lands to excavate and

---

candidate is probably the ill-fated ᶜAlī (656–661); see Steinschneider, "Apokalypsen," 637; Lewis, "Apocalyptic Vision," 328; Crone and Cook, *Hagarism*, 178 n. 68.

42 Graetz (*Geschichte*, 5:407–8) suggests that this is corrupt for Muᶜāwiya (מעויאו or מעאויה). His emendation is accepted by Aescoly, *Messianic Movements*, 137 n. 4. However, as Steinschneider observes, the same supposedly "corrupt" reading (i.e., מריאו) is also present in Munich Ms. Heb. 222. The corresponding passage in *Prayer* has מרוון; i.e., Marwān. Lewis ("Apocalyptic Vision," 325 n. 4) suggests that it is Marwān I (684–685 CE), father of ᶜAbd al-Malik.

43 זרועות ארבע. Lewis identifies this group as the four sons of ᶜAbd al-Malik (685–705 CE) who became caliphs ("Apocalyptic Vision," 327). For a similar vocabulary, see Dan 11:31.

44 Sulaymān (715–717 CE)?

45 Read with Lewis's emendation ("Apocalyptic Vision," 325 n. 5).

46 A reference to Sulaymān's expedition against and siege of Constantinople. See Graetz, *Geschichte*, 5:408–9; Lewis, "Apocalyptic Vision," 327; Harry Turtledove, *The Chronicle of Theophanes* (Philadelphia: University of Pennsylvania Press, 1982), 88–90.

47 Hishām (724–743 CE), rather than ᶜAbd al-Malik (Gil, *History of Palestine*, 109). Regarding the construction projects of Hishām, see especially the references cited by Garth Fowden, *Quṣayr ᶜAmra: Art and the Umayyad Elite in Late Antique Syria* (Berkeley: University of California Press, 2004), 169 n. 144; also 280.

48 So Aescoly, *Messianic Movements*, 137 n. 8. The Hebrew is שיפן העין, which Steinschneider ("Apokalypsen," 638 n. 25) translates "cross-eyed." Cf. Lewis, "Apocalyptic Vision," 325 n. 7 for further discussion of this difficult text.

49 Walīd II (743–744 CE). Walīd's involvement in the Jordan canal project and his assassination by Yazīd are confirmed by Ṭabarī; see Gil, *History of Palestine*, 108–9. See also Fowden, *Quṣayr ᶜAmra*, 156–57, 254.

build a canal to bring up the waters of the Jordan to irrigate the land. The excavated portion of the land will collapse upon them and kill them. Their leaders will hear (about this), and then rebel against the king and kill him.

Another king will then arise—a strong (king) and warrior.[50] A dispute will erupt in the world during his reign. This will be the sign for you: when you see that the western גירון has fallen[51]—(the one) at the western side of (the place of) prayer of the children of Ishmael in Damascus—his dominion will have "fallen." They will be assembled and marched out to do forced labor, and indeed the kingdom of Ishmael will collapse. Scripture affirms concerning them: "The Lord has broken the rod of the wicked" (Isa 14:5), where (the word) "rod" (מטה) signifies Ishmael.[52] And who is this? It is Marwān.[53] Warriors from the sons of Qedar will still remain with him, but the northeastern corner (of his kingdom) will rebel and come up against him.[54] There shall fall from among his forces three great armies at the Tigris and at the Euphrates,[55] and he himself will flee from them, but he will be captured and put to death. His sons will be hung upon wooden scaffolding.

[50] Marwān II (744–750 CE), the last Umayyad ruler. See below.

[51] גירון is the *eastern* wall or gate of the Damascus mosque; it is identified correctly at the end of the present composition in a passage which probably derives from a version of *Prayer*. See especially Steinschneider, "Apokalypsen," 638–45; note also Naphtali Wieder, *The Judean Scrolls and Karaism* (London: East and West Library, 1962), 19–20.

According to an eschatological prophecy attributed to Arṭāt b. al-Mundhir (d. 779–780), an ascetic visionary of Syria, the so-called Sufyānī, the legendary adversary of the ʿAlid Mahdī, would be slain by the Mahdī "at the gate of Jayrūn" in Damascus. Another prophecy associates the advent of the Sufyānī with the time when "a portion of the west (front) of her mosque will fall down"; cf. Wilferd Madelung, "The Sufyānī Between Tradition and History," *Studia Islamica* 63 (1986): 5–48, at 25–28. Compare the intriguing tradition found in *Midr. Tanḥ*. Buber, Wayishlaḥ §8: ילמדנו רבינו מה סימן נתן ר׳ יוסי בן קיסמא לתלמידיו שהיו מטיילין בטבריא אמרו לו לר׳ יוסי רבי אימתי בן דוד בא אמר להם ר׳ יוסי אם אני אומר לכם אתם תבקשו ממנו אות אמרו לו לאו אמר להם הרי השער הזה יבנה ויפול יבנה ויפול ואין מספיקין לבנותו עד שבן דוד בא; note its occurrence also in *b. Sanh*. 98a, where Rashi identifies the collapsing gate as not in Tiberias but in Rome. Note Jacob Mann, *The Bible as Read and Preached in the Old Synagogue*, Volume 1, *The Palestinian Triennial Cycle: Genesis and Exodus* (Cincinnati, 1940; repr., New York: Ktav, 1971), 262–64.

[52] Read with Munich Ms. Heb. 222 (cited by Steinschneider, "Apokalypsen," 638 n. 27). The equation with "Ishmael" is effected via aural wordplay with the last part of Isa 14:5 (שבר י״י מטה רשעים שבט משלים), where "the scepter of rulers (*moshlim*)" is read as "the scepter of the Muslims (*musl[em]im*)."

[53] Marwān II was termed al-Ḥimār, the "wild ass of Mesopotamia" in Muslim sources. For the corrupt Hebrew מרואן שער, read instead מרואן שעד or, as in *Prayer*, שעדיין. See Graetz, *Geschichte*, 5:410; Steinschneider, "Apokalypsen," 638 n. 27; Lewis, "Apocalyptic Vision," 326.

[54] That is, Khurāsān, the province where the ʿAbbāsid movement originated.

[55] Read ובפרת in place of ובפרס. See the parallel passage in *Prayer*; also Graetz, *Geschichte*, 5:410; Even-Shmuel, *Midreshey Ge'ullah*, 194.

And after this a king "strong of face" (עז פנים)[56] will arise for three months,[57] and then the wicked kingdom (i.e., Rome) will rule over Israel for nine months, as scripture says: "Therefore He will give them until the time the one laboring in childbirth has borne" (Mic 5:2). And there shall sprout up for them the Messiah of the lineage of Joseph, and he will bring them up to Jerusalem. He will rebuild the Temple and offer sacrifices;[58] fire shall descend from heaven and consume their sacrifices, as scripture promises: "and the violent ones among your people will arise" (Dan 11:14). If they are not worthy, the Messiah of the lineage of Ephraim comes; but if they are worthy, the Messiah of the lineage of David will come.[59]

A wicked king will arise whose name is Armilos:[60] bald, with small eyes and a leprous forehead; his right ear closed up and his left ear open. If a good person should speak to him, he will turn his closed ear toward him, and if a wicked person should speak to him, he will turn his open ear to him.[61] He is the offspring of Satan and a stone (statue),[62] and he will come up to Jerusalem and incite war with the Messiah of the lineage of Ephraim at the eastern gate, as scripture states: "and and they shall look to Me about the one whom they pierced" (Zech 12:10).[63] Israel will go into exile into the uncleared wilderness to forage among the salt-plants and broom-sage roots for forty-five days, and then they will be tested and refined, as scripture says: "I shall bring a third (of them) through the fire, etc." (Zech 13:9). The Messiah of the lineage of Ephraim shall die there, and Israel shall mourn for

[56] See Deut 28:50; Dan 8:23; *Tg. Ket.* Qoh 8:1.

[57] Graetz identified this ruler as al-Saffāḥ (*Geschichte*, 5:411–12).

[58] This reputed activity is presumably dependent on the cultic tasks ascribed to this figure in *Sefer Zerubbabel*.

[59] This is apparently an application of the interpretation of Isa 60:22 (אחישנה בעתה) found in *b. Sanh.* 98a: זכו אחישנה לא זכו בעתה, "(if) they are worthy, 'I will speed it (i.e., redemption) up'; (if) they are not worthy, '(it will unfold) at its predetermined pace.'"

[60] Hebrew ארמילאוס. As pointed out in the introduction, Armilos is the Jewish equivalent of the Christian Antichrist and the Muslim Dajjāl. This particular designation is first attested in both Jewish and Christian literature stemming from the first half of the seventh century CE. See Leopold Zunz and Ḥanokh Albeck, *Haderashot be-Yisrael* (2d ed.; Jerusalem: Mosad Bialik, 1954), 429–30 n. 31. Note also the remarks of Saadya, *Kitâb al-Amânât wa'l-Iᶜtiqâdât von Saᶜadja b. Jûsuf al-Fajjûmî* (ed. S. Landauer; Leiden: Brill, 1880), 239.4–6; 241.11–13; English translation, *The Book of Beliefs and Opinions* (trans. Samuel Rosenblatt; New Haven: Yale University Press, 1948), 301–2, 304.

[61] Compare the end of *Midrash Wa-yoshaᶜ* (Jellinek, *BHM* 1:56): ואזנו הימנית סתומה ואחת פתוחה וכשיבא אדם לדבר לו טובות מטה לו אזנו הסתומה ואם ירצה אדם לדבר לו רעה מטה לו אזנו הפתוחה, "and his right ear will be closed up and the (other) one open. Whenever a person comes to tell him good things, he turns his closed up ear toward him, but if a person wants to speak wickedly, he turns his open ear toward him."

[62] This clause is Aramaic: והוא בריה דסטנא ודאבנא. I reject Buttenwieser's suggested emendation; cf. his *Outline*, 34.

[63] See *b. Sukkah* 52a; Ibn Ezra *ad* Zech 12:10.

him. After this the Holy One blessed be He will reveal to them the Messiah of the lineage of David, but Israel will wish to stone him, and they will say to him: "You speak a lie, for the Messiah has already been slain, and there is no other Messiah destined to arise." They will scorn him, as scripture says: "despised and abandoned (by) men" (Isa 53:3). He shall withdraw and be hidden from them, as scripture continues: "like one hiding faces from us" (ibid.). But in Israel's great distress, they will turn and cry out from (their) hunger and thirst, and the Holy One, blessed be He, will be revealed to them in His glory, as scripture promises: "together all flesh will see" (Isa 40:5). And the King Messiah will sprout up there, as scripture says: "and behold with the clouds of heaven etc." (Dan 7:13), and it is written after it "and authority was given to him" (Dan 7:14). He shall blow (his breath) at that wicked Armilos and kill him, as scripture forecasts: "he will slay the wicked one with the breath of his lips" (Isa 11:4).

The Holy One, blessed be He, will signal for and gather together all Israel and bring them up to Jerusalem, as Scripture says: "Let me signal for them and I will gather them" (Zech 10:8). Fire will come down from heaven and consume Jerusalem up to three cubits, and uncircumcised foreigners and the impure will be removed from its midst. Then a rebuilt and decorated Jerusalem will descend from heaven; in it seventy-two precious stones will shine from one end of the world to the other. And all the nations will come to (bask in) her splendor, as scripture affirms: "and the nations will come to your light" (Isa 60:3). A rebuilt Temple will descend from the heavens—the one which was folded within Zebul,[64] for thus Moses perceived under prophetic inspiration, as scripture says: "You will bring it and You will plant it" (Exod 15:17).[65]

Israel will dwell in peace for two thousand years.[66] They will feast upon Behemoth, Leviathan, and Ziz.[67] They will slaughter Behemoth; Ziz shall rend Leviathan with its ankles; and Moses will come and slaughter the "wild Ziz" (Ps 50:11; 80:14). At the end of two thousand years, the Holy One, blessed be He, will sit upon a throne of judgment in the valley of Jehoshaphat.[68] Immediately the heavens and the earth will wear out and fade away: the sun will be ashamed and the moon embarrassed;[69] the mountains

[64] See *b. Ḥag.* 12b.

[65] Both a new Jerusalem and a new Temple descend from the heavens, a fusion of what were originally two separate motifs. See Avraham Grossman, "Jerusalem in Jewish Apocalyptic Literature," in Prawer and Ben-Shammai, *History of Jerusalem*, 302–4.

[66] "Our apocalyptic writer accepted the old aggadic scheme [see *b. ʿAbod. Zar.* 9b and Rashi *ad loc.*—Reeves] wherein the world would exist for only six thousand years, of which the last two thousand would constitute the days of the Messiah" (quoted from Baron, *History*, 5:148).

[67] For the Ziz, a fabulous bird, see *b. B. Bat.* 73b.

[68] Cf. Joel 4:2, 12. Note also the corresponding passage in *Midrash Wa-yoshaʿ*.

[69] Cf. Isa 24:23.

will shake and the hills will quake (cf. Isa 54:10), so that Israel will no longer have her sins recounted (by them) to her. The gates of Gehinnom will be opened in the Wadi Joshua, and on the third day the gates of Eden (will be opened) in the east, as scripture attests: "He will revitalize us for *two days*; [on the *third day* he will raise us up and we will live before Him"] (Hos 6:2)—this (verse) refers to the days of the Messiah, which are *two thousand years* (cf. Ps 90:4). And this "third day" is the Day of Judgment, and alas for the one who is among all those who perish during it! The Holy One, blessed be He, shall cause to pass before Him every nation, and He shall say to them: "You who worshipped gods of silver and gold—see now if they are able to deliver you!" Immediately they shall pass by and be immolated, as scripture states: "the wicked will return to Sheol" (Ps 9:18). Israel shall come after them, and the Holy One, blessed be he, shall say to them: "Whom have you worshipped?" They shall respond: "indeed You are our Father etc." (Isa 63:16). And the nations of the world will gripe from the midst of Gehinnom: "Let us see whether He will judge His people Israel like He judged us!" Immediately the Holy One, blessed be He, will pass with Israel[70] through the midst of Gehinnom, and it will be made like cool water before them, as scripture attests: "and their king shall pass through before them" (Mic 2:13), and it says: "when you walk through fire you will not be burned" (Isa 43:2). At that time the transgressors among Israel will be dumped into Gehinnom for twelve months,[71] but after that (period) the Holy One, blessed be He, will bring them up and settle them in Eden, and they will enjoy its fruits, as scripture says: "and your people will *all* be righteous" (Isa 60:21).[72]

R. Šimʿōn said: The Holy One, blessed be He, will signal to the bee who is at the end of the rivers of Egypt, and they shall come and wage war in the midst of Egypt. The first king who leads them and brings them forth is a slave who has rebelled against his master, as scripture says: "Thus says the Lord . . . to the despised one, to the one loathed by the nation" (Isa 49:7)—that is the one held abominable among the nations; namely, the Canaanites—"to the slave of kings" (ibid.). He shall rebel against his overlord, and others who have rebelled against their masters will be gathered to him, and they shall gradually go out and seize the kingdom by force. They will make war with the Ishmaelites, kill their warriors, and take possession of their

[70] The proof text would seem to demand this translation.

[71] See *m. ʿEd.* 2.10; *t. Sanh.* 13.4 (Zuckermandel, 434); *y. Sanh.* 10.3, 29b; *b. Roš. Haš.* 17a; *S. ʿOlam Rab.* 3.

[72] Most scholars hold that the *Secrets* originally ends here (Graetz, *Geschichte*, 5:413; Buttenwieser, *Outline*, 39). The remainder of Jellinek's text is essentially a garbled abridgment of the *Prayer of R. Šimʿōn bar Yoḥai.*

wealth and property. They are repulsive men, dressed in black and coming from the East, and they are quick[73] and impetuous, as scripture says: "the nation cruel and impetuous" (Hab 1:6). They will ascend the mountain of the height of Israel intending to tear down the Temple and to uproot the doors, but will (instead) weep bitterly (?).

Four kings shall arise over them: two of them will be princes and two of them chieftains. The first . . . (?) and the king who rules after them [*sic!*] will conduct himself humbly: his eyes will be attractive and his hair lovely, and he will die in peace, with no one in the world collecting tribute from him. After him there shall arise a king accompanied by strife. He will station armies by the Euphrates River, but all of them will fall in a single day. He will flee, but will be captured, and all the time he is held captive there will be peace in the world. His brothers will rule over all lands.

The fourth king who shall arise over them will be a lover of silver and gold. He will be a dark man and tall, old and shriveled (?).[74] He will kill those whom they bring to him, and they will install him as king. He will build boats of bronze and fill them (with) silver and gold, and store them beneath the waters of the Euphrates in order to reserve them for his sons.[75] But they are destined for Israel, as scripture says: "I will give you treasures (concealed in) darkness and secret hidden things" (Isa 45:3). During his reign the western quadrant will rebel, and he will dispatch there many troops, but he (the leader of the rebellion) will kill the easterners. Again he (the fourth king) will send out many troops, and they will come and slay the westerners, and take up residence in their land.

And this will be the sign for you—when you see that at the beginning of one week there is rain, and in the second (week) the loosing of the "arrows of hunger," and in the third a severe famine, and in the fourth no hunger but (also) no satisfaction, and in the fifth there is great satiety. A star shall appear from the east with a rod on top of it—this is the star of Israel, as

[73] *Sic.* Read מרים, as in *Prayer* (Jellinek, *BHM* 4:120) in place of the present text's מהרים.

[74] Lewis emends גרגר to גרגרן, "gluttonous" ("Apocalyptic Vision," 330 n. 1).

[75] Compare the analogous pronouncement found in the apocalypse attributed to "John the Lesser" in the Syriac *Gospel of the Twelve Apostles*: ܘܬܗܘܐ ܒܝܘܡܐ ܗܘ ܬܘܟܠܢܗܘܢ ܥܠ ܩܢܝܢܐ ܕܢܟܠܘ ܘܐܣܢܘ ܘܛܠܘܡܘ ܒܕܘܟܬܐ ܕܕܓܠܬ ܫܡܐ, "on that day their trust will be in the wealth which they acquired by deceit and despoliation and which they stored in a place by the name of Diglat (i.e., the Tigris River)." Syriac text cited from J. Rendel Harris, ed., *The Gospel of the Twelve Apostles: Together with the Apocalypses of Each One of Them* (Cambridge: Cambridge University Press, 1900), 21.10–11 (text), and note especially the remarks of Harris, *Gospel*, 22. For further discussion, see Han J. W. Drijvers, "The Gospel of the Twelve Apostles: A Syriac Apocalypse from the Early Islamic Period," in *The Byzantine and Early Islamic Near East, I: Problems in the Literary Source Material* (ed. Averil Cameron and Lawrence I. Conrad; Studies in Late Antiquity and Early Islam 1; Princeton: Darwin Press, 1992), 208.

scripture says: "a star shall step forth from Jacob etc." (Num 24:17). If it shines, it is for the benefit of Israel. Then the Messiah of the lineage of David shall emerge.[76]

And this will be the sign for you—when you see that the eastern גירון in Damascus has fallen, the kingdom of those in the East has fallen.[77] Then deliverance will sprout for Israel. The Messiah of the lineage of David will come, and they [*sic!*] will go up to Jerusalem and rejoice over her, as scripture says: "the lowly will take possession of the land and delight in an abundance of peace" (Ps 37:11). May God in His mercy send to us the deliverer quickly in our era, Amen!

The Prayer of Rabbi Šimᶜōn b. Yoḥai

The *Prayer of R. Šimᶜōn ben Yoḥai* (תפלת ר' שמעון בן יוחאי) poses as an expanded and updated version of the influential *Secrets of R. Šimᶜōn ben Yoḥai*.[78] Its distinctive title stems from a superscription accompanying the text which refers in turn to a plaintive plea directed by the tannaitic Sage to God requesting revelatory answers concerning the time and manner of Israel's redemption.[79] The work was first published in the nineteenth century by Adolph Jellinek from a privately owned manuscript in Mantua.[80] Jellinek's text was in turn reproduced, emended, and supplemented by Yehudah Even-Shmuel in his comprehensive anthology of Jewish messianic literature.[81] The present translation is based on the version of the text published by Jellinek.[82]

[76] See the notes to this section in *Prayer*.

[77] Note the remarks above regarding this particular sign.

[78] Whereas *Secrets* appears to emerge from the turbulent period marking the transition from Umayyad to ᶜAbbāsid suzerainty over Islamicate Jewry, *Prayer* contains clear references to events associated with the era of the Crusades. See Adolph Jellinek, ed., *Bet ha-Midrasch: Sammlung kleiner Midraschim und vermischter Abhandlungen aus der jüdischen Literatur* (6 vols.; Leipzig, 1853–77; repr., Jerusalem: Bamberger & Wahrmann, 1938), 4:viii–ix; Heinrich Graetz, *Geschichte der Juden von den ältesten Zeiten bis auf die Gegenwart* (3d ed.; 11 vols. in 13; Leipzig: Oskar Leiner, 1890–1908), 5:413.

[79] It seems doubtful that this is the genuine title. Note the opening words of the text below ("secrets and revelations"); also Moritz Steinschneider, "Apokalypsen mit polemischer Tendenz," *ZDMG* 28 (1874): 635.

[80] Jellinek, *BHM* 4:117–26.

[81] Yehudah Even-Shmuel, *Midreshey Geʾullah* (2d ed.; Jerusalem: Mosad Bialik, 1954), 268–86.

[82] For discussion of this work, see Moses Buttenwieser, *Outline of the Neo-Hebraic Apocalyptic Literature* (Cincinnati: Jennings & Pye, 1901), 41. An important translation and study were prepared by Bernard Lewis, "An Apocalyptic Vision of Islamic History," *BSOAS* 13 (1949–51): 308–38; its main arguments are accepted by Salo M. Baron, *A Social and Religious History of the Jews* (18 vols.; 2d ed.; New York: Columbia University Press; New York: Jewish Publication Society, 1952–83), 3:93, 274 n. 27.

These are the secrets and revelations (הנסתרות והנגלות) divulged to R. Šimʿōn. This is R. Šimʿōn ben Yoḥai whom they dispatched from Jerusalem to Rome to (entreat) Caesar. While he was (still voyaging) on the ship, Ašmedai, ruler of the demons, appeared to him (in) a dream. He [Ašmedai] addressed him, "Ask what I might do for you!" R. Šimʿōn responded, "Who are you?" He answered: "I am Ašmedai, the one whom the Holy One, blessed be He, has sent to perform a miracle for you." He exclaimed: "Master of the Universe! For Hagar, the serving-maid of Sarai, You summoned an angel, but for me You have sent the ruler of the demons?!?" Ašmedai said to him, "Does the source from which the miracle comes matter—whether from I or from an angel—as long as your wishes are accomplished?" Ašmedai continued: "I am going now to enter into (and take possession of) the body of the daughter of Caesar. I will weaken her and have her cry out your name ('R. Šimʿōn! R. Šimʿōn!'). Then, when you arrive and they ask you to expel me so that I might leave from this household, I will say 'I shall not leave it until they satisfy the wishes of R. Šimʿōn and what he desires!'"[83]

Ašmedai departed and went to the palace of Caesar and did everything that he told R. Šimʿōn (he would do). The daughter of Caesar arose (from her bed?) and he entered into her. As soon as he had entered into her, she shattered all the crockery in the palace of her father, and was crying out "R. Šimʿōn! Šimʿōn ben Yoḥai!" After a few days a ship arrived, and R. Šimʿōn was on board. They went and announced (this news) to Caesar. Caesar sent for him and said to him, "What is your wish?" He replied, "The Jews of Jerusalem have sent a gift for you." He [Caesar] said, "I will accept nothing from you, nor do I wish anything (from you) except that you expel this demon from my daughter. I have no one to succeed me in rule save for her, for there is no other offspring." R. Šimʿōn went and addressed him: "Ašmedai! Come out from this maiden!" He [Ašmedai] replied, "I will not leave until they do everything which you want (them to do)!" He repeated this a number of times—"I will not leave (the girl) until they satisfy your wishes!"

The ruler then went and sent for all his elders, princes, and servants. He asked them: "What do you advise (me) to do about my daughter? This demon has lately taken possession of her, but we have already decreed against the Jews that they will not circumcise their sons, observe the Sabbath, or permit their wives to observe (the rules of) menstrual impurity. The custom of our kingdom is that those who issue a decree can never

[83] This story is based on an older tale found in *b. Meʿil.* 17a–b. See also the discussion of Eli Yassif, *The Hebrew Folktale: History, Genre, Meaning* (Bloomington and Indianapolis: Indiana University Press, 1999), 154–55.

revoke (it); should a ruler revoke it, they must remove him from his royal station in accordance with the law of the Medes and Persians!" One of his counselors arose and said to him, "My lord king, allow me to say something to you by which your daughter will be healed and which will permit you to revoke all of your decrees, for this decree against the Jews is bad both for us and for you." He [Caesar] replied to him, "Speak on!" He [the counselor] continued, "If one has an enemy, would one rather that he [the enemy] be poor or rich?" The king answered him, "Poor." The counselor said to him, "It is the Jews' universal custom to labor all week long during which they accumulate wealth. On the sixth day they spend it all for the sake of honoring the Sabbath. But now, if you discontinue their Sabbath observance, the resources spent on Sabbath will (instead) be left (unspent) by them, and they will continue collecting wealth and (eventually) rebel against you. However, if you restore the Sabbath to them, they will expend many resources on it and remain poor." The king replied, "Restore the Sabbath to them!"

The same counselor again said to him, "If a man has enemies, which would he prefer them to be? To be many or few?" The ruler replied, "Few!" He [the counselor] continued, "My lord king, the Jews perform circumcision upon their sons when they are (only) eight days old. Even should one of them survive (the operation), a hundred (others) will die!" The ruler declared, "Also restore (the practice of) circumcision to them!"

Once more he [the counselor] said to him, "My lord king, (the rules of) menstrual impurity operate thusly: when Israelite women are assumed to be in a state of menstrual impurity, they engage in little sexual activity, for they must observe seven days (as) 'days of bloodflow' and seven (further) days as days of purification." The ruler declared, "Permit their law regarding menstrual impurity as before!"

The ruler (then) said to R. Šimᶜōn, "I grant your condition. Go, inform the demon that he should leave my daughter!" R. Šimᶜōn ordered Ašmedai (to come forth), and he [the demon] departed from the ruler's daughter. The ruler returned to R. Šimᶜōn the gift which he had brought to him (from Jerusalem), gave him numerous additional presents, and wrote for him letters of endorsement for his official who was in Jerusalem. And R. Šimᶜōn returned to Jerusalem rejoicing and in good spirits, and the decrees were annulled.[84]

[84] For another version of this proem, see Jellinek, *BHM* 6:128–30. An extended discussion with further references can be found in Richard Kalmin, "Rabbinic Traditions about Roman Persecutions of the Jews: A Reconsideration," *JJS* 54 (2003): 33–38. One might compare the account in the eleventh-century *Megillat Aḥimaᶜaṣ* of an analogous exorcism performed by R. Shephatiah upon the daughter of the Byzantine emperor Basil I within a similar context of anti-Jewish legislation: see Adolf

This was the R. Šimʿōn who was incarcerated[85] in a cave before this (adventure) on account of (the persecutions of) Caesar. He fasted for forty days and nights[86] and prayed before the Lord, and this is what he said in his prayer: "Blessed are You, O Lord our God and God of our ancestors, God of Abraham, Isaac, and Jacob, the great, mighty, and awesome God Who out of His mercies created heaven and earth, alive and enduring forever and forever! May You be glorified, praised, coroneted, adorned, and professed as One, for You are King of kings and Lord of lords! (A perfect) Unity, for You are equivalent to Your name: You are hidden from the sight of all living things, and (so too) Your name is hidden; You are marvelous and Your name is marvelous; You are unique and Your name is unique! You are the One who chose Abram and brought him forth from Ur of the Chaldeans and revealed to him the suffering caused by the oppression of the empires who would place his descendants in subjection.[87] I ask You now, O Lord God, to open the gates of prayer for me and to send to me an angel to instruct me (regarding) when the Messiah of the lineage of David will come, how he will gather together the exiled of Israel from all the various places where they have been dispersed, and how many wars they must endure after their ingathering? May he explain to me the topic by the pleasure of the Lord God! How long (is it) until the time of marvels?"

R. Šimʿōn said: "Immediately the gates of heaven were opened to me and I beheld visions of God.[88] I fell upon my face and behold, a voice was addressing me, 'Šimʿōn! Šimʿōn!' I answered and said to the one addressing me, 'What are you saying?' My Lord said to me, 'Rise up from your place (on the ground).' As he spoke to me, I stood up trembling and said to him,

---

Neubauer, *Medieval Jewish Chronicles and Chronological Notes* (2 vols.; Oxford: Clarendon, 1887–95; repr., Amsterdam: Philo Press, 1970), 2:116–17; Samuel Krauss, *Studien zur byzantinisch-jüdischen Geschichte* (Leipzig: Buchhandlung Gustav Fock, 1914), 44 n. 3; Joshua Starr, *The Jews in the Byzantine Empire, 641–1204* (Athens: Verlag der byzantinisch-neugriechischen Jahrbücher, 1939), 129; Andrew Sharf, *Byzantine Jewry from Justinian to the Fourth Crusade* (New York: Schocken, 1971), 88–89; J. H. Chajes, *Between Worlds: Dybbuks, Exorcists, and Early Modern Judaism* (Philadelphia: University of Pennsylvania Press, 2003), 182 n. 12.

[85] Even-Shmuel emends חבוש to חבוי on the basis of the text of *Secrets*; I have retained and translated Jellinek's text.

[86] *Secrets* states only that "he stood in prayer forty days and forty nights," with no explicit indication of fasting. See, however, Deut 9:18.

[87] This revelation took place during the "covenant of the pieces" narrated in Gen 15:7–21. See *4 Ezra* 3:14; *Mek.* Yitro, Baḥodesh §9 (Horovitz-Rabin, 236.5–11); *Pirqe R. El.* §28 according to HUC Ms. 75 fols. 38b–39b (this passage is severely truncated in most printed editions owing to censorship), a passage preserved in the so-called *ʾAggadat R. Ishmael* and *Yal. Šim.* Torah §76; discussed in John C. Reeves, "Scriptural Authority in Early Judaism," in *Living Traditions of the Bible: Scripture in Jewish, Christian, and Muslim Practice* (ed. James E. Bowley; St. Louis: Chalice Press, 1999), 79–80.

[88] A paraphrase of Ezek 1:1b: נפתחו השמים ואראה מראות אלהים.

'What is your name?' He responded to me, 'Why this (need) to ask for my name? It is incomprehensible!'[89]

"I said to him, 'When will the deliverer of Israel come?' He answered me (quoting), 'And He [God][90] beheld the children of Israel, and God knew' (Exod 2:25). Immediately he caused the Kenites to pass before me. I asked him, 'Who are these?' He said to me, 'These are the Kenites.'[91] He moreover showed me the kingdom of Ishmael which would come into existence after (that) of the Kenites. I immediately wept an intense shower of tears and said to him, 'My lord! Will he (also) have horns and hooves with which he will crush Israel?' He answered me, 'Yes.'[92]

"I was still speaking with him when, behold, an angel whose name was Metatron touched me 'and roused me like a man who is roused from his sleep.'[93] When I saw him, I stood trembling and 'my pains racked me, and I could retain no strength'[94] and 'was seized with pains like those of a woman giving birth.'[95] He said to me, 'Šimᶜōn!' I responded, 'Here I am.' He said to me, 'Know that the Holy One, blessed be He, has sent me to you in order to inform you with regard to your question which you asked Him. Now, when you saw the Kenite and the kingdom of Ishmael, you wept, but you should confine your weeping to the matter of the kingdom of Ishmael alone. For during the final period of its rule, it will effect a great slaughter beyond measure among Israel and decree harsh edicts against Israel and announce (that) "anyone who reads Torah will be pierced by the sword." A portion of Israel will turn to their (i.e., Ishmael's) laws. At that time the kingdom of the Kenites will come to Jerusalem, subdue it, and kill more than thirty thousand within it.[96] Due to the pressure with which they constrain Israel, the

[89] A quotation of the anonymous angel's response to Manoah in Judg 13:18.

[90] The subject is expressed (אלהים) in the biblical text.

[91] As the immediately following sentence makes clear, the Kenites are here interpreted (unlike in *Secrets*) as an imperial oppressor who precedes the advent of Islam. See Patricia Crone and Michael Cook, *Hagarism: The Making of the Islamic World* (Cambridge: Cambridge University Press, 1977), 35. Should the later Kenite siege and sack of Jerusalem refer to the First Crusade, then the term "Kenites" encrypts Byzantine hegemony, an identification facilitated by reading Num 24:21 through the lens of Obad 1:3–4. Even-Shmuel (*Midreshey Geʾullah*, 270–71) suggests that the equation was cemented by gematria: עץ, that is, "cross" = קין, "Kenite," both words having a numerical value of 160.

[92] The "kingdom of Ishmael" is here recognized as a full-fledged "empire" (מלכות) in accordance with the prescriptive fourfold "imperial eschatology" of the biblical visions of Daniel. See also *Pirqe R. El.* §28 according to HUC Ms. 75 fols. 38b–39a; Abraham ibn Ezra *ad* Dan 2:39. The term "imperial eschatology" (*Reichseschatologie*) is borrowed from Paul Magdalino, "The History of the Future and its Uses: Prophecy, Policy and Propaganda," in *The Making of Byzantine History: Studies Dedicated to Donald M. Nicol* (ed. Roderick Beaton and Charlotte Roueché; Aldershot: Variorum, 1993), 3–34.

[93] A quotation from Zech 4:1.

[94] A quotation from Dan 10:16. See also 1 Sam 4:19: כי נהפכו עליה צריה.

[95] Cf. Isa 21:3: צירים אחזוני כצירי יולדה.

[96] A reference to the crusader capture of Jerusalem in 1099. See Lewis, "Apocalyptic Vision,"

Holy One, blessed be He, will send (more) Ishmaelites against them, and they will make war with them in order to deliver Israel from their grasp. A demented, demon-possessed man[97]—one who speaks lies about the Holy One, blessed be He—will arise and subdue the land, and there will be enmity between them (the Ishmaelites) and the children of Esau.'

"I turned to Metatron and said to him, 'Are the Ishmaelites a deliverance for Israel?' He said to me, 'Did not Isaiah the prophet speak thusly? "And should he see chariotry of a pair of riders, one riding an ass, (and) one riding a camel" (Isa 21:7).' 'Chariotry'—this (word) refers to the Achaemenid empire. 'Pair'—this (word) refers to the Greek empire(s). 'Riders'—this (word) refers to the Roman empire. 'One riding an ass'—this (phrase) refers to the Messiah, as scripture attests: 'humble and mounted upon an ass' (Zech 9:9). 'One riding a camel'—this (phrase) refers to the kingdom of Ishmael, during whose rule the messianic kingdom will sprout.[98] This is why (the phrase) 'one riding an ass' precedes (the phrase) 'one riding a camel' (in the verse from Isaiah).[99] The 'one riding a camel' will rejoice at the advent of the Messiah; nevertheless, the sages perish and the power of the riff-raff (בני בליעל) grows stronger."[100]

Again "and he beheld the Kenite" (Num 24:21). What was the symbolic message which Balaam the wicked saw? When Balaam foresaw that the tribe of Kenites would in the future arise and place Israel under subjection, he began (and)[101] said: "'Ethan is your dwelling' (ibid.)—I see that you will occupy yourselves only with the bell (?)[102] of Ethan the easterner."[103]

The second king who will arise from the Ishmaelites will love Israel. He will repair the breaches of the Temple, make war with the descendants of

---

322–23. For a description of this event and the slaughter associated with it, see Steven Runciman, *A History of the Crusades* (3 vols.; Cambridge: Cambridge University Press, 1951–54), 1:279–88; Moshe Gil, *A History of Palestine, 634–1099* (trans. Ethel Broido; Cambridge: Cambridge University Press, 1992), 826–29. Gil, however, denies that this *Prayer* passage reflects the First Crusade (62 n. 65).

[97] Probably derived from Hos 9:6–7; see the "unidentified polemical and apocalyptic piyyut" T-S A45.3 verso 15–17 published by Simon Hopkins, *A Miscellany of Literary Pieces from the Cambridge Genizah Collections: A Catalogue and Selection of Texts in the Taylor-Schechter Collection, Old Series, Box A45* (Cambridge: Cambridge University Library, 1978), 7. Muhammad's contemporaries employ a similar rhetoric: see Q 15:6; 17:47; 38:4. Note that the originally positive evaluation of Muhammad expressed in *Secrets* has undergone considerable polemical revision owing to its possible ʿĪsāwiyya origin as well as the historical experience of Muslim rule.

[98] Note that this originally *Muslim* proof text has now been adapted and fitted by Islamicate *Jewish* exegetes into the "four-kingdom" eschatological schemes favored by earlier Jewish interpreters.

[99] Compare the lengthier explanation of *Secrets*.

[100] A pessimistic note on contemporary conditions?

[101] *Secrets*: התחיל שמח ואמר "he began *rejoicing* and said."

[102] So the text. *Secrets* reads here ממצוות, "with the commandments."

[103] איתן המזרחי. A scribal conflation of Ps 89:1, 1 Chr 2:6, and Isa 41:2?

Esau, and slaughter their armies. There shall arise a king whose name is Marwān (מרוון). He will be a herder of asses, and they will take him from following the asses and coronate him as ruler. The Edomites shall arise against him and kill him, and another will succeed him, and he (this latter one) shall have peace from all who transgress against him. He will be a friend of Zion[104] and die in peace.[105]

Another king will arise in his place and strengthen his hold upon the kingdom with his sword and his bow. Strife will occur during his reign: occasionally in the east, occasionally in the west, occasionally in the north, and occasionally in the south, and he will wage war with all (of them). At the time when the *gyrdwn*[106] in the west collapses upon the Ishmaelites in Damascus, the kingdom of Ishmael will fall, for regarding this time (scripture) said: "the Lord has broken the rod of the wicked" (Isa 14:5).[107] Warriors from the sons of Qedar will still remain with him. The northeastern quadrant will rebel against him and defeat many of his armies:[108] the first by the Tigris, the second by the Euphrates, and the third in Mesopotamia. He will flee from them, but they will capture his sons, kill (them), and hang (them) upon wooden scaffolding.

"On that day the Lord will signal for the fly" (Isa 7:18). The Holy One, blessed be He, will signal "for the bees who are in the region of Assyria" (ibid.) and they shall wage war with the Ashkenazim. The first king who leads them and brings (them) forth is one who rebelled against their masters,[109] as scripture attests: "Thus says the Lord . . . to the despised one, to the one loathed by the nation, to the slave of kings" (Isa 49:7). And (the phrase) "slave of kings" (עבד מושלים)[110] indicates whom? He said, "This (phrase) refers to the Canaanites who are the most despised of all the nations."[111]

104 Read ציון in place of the text's צאן, "sheep." See Even-Shmuel, *Midreshey Geʾullah*, 272; Lewis, "Apocalyptic Vision," 313 n. 4.

105 This ruler has been identified as ᶜAbd al-Malik; see Lewis, "Apocalyptic Vision," 329; Josef van Ess, "ʿAbd al-Malik and the Dome of the Rock: An Analysis of Some Texts," in *Bayt al-Maqdis: ᶜAbd al-Malik's Jerusalem* (ed. Julian Raby and Jeremy Johns; 2 vols.; Oxford: Oxford University Press, 1992), 1:101.

106 Read גירון (so *Secrets*) in place of the text's גירדון. This term refers to an architectural feature of the Damascus mosque. See the extended discussion in *Secrets*; also Steinschneider, "Apokalypsen," 638–45.

107 For the identification of "the wicked" in Isa 14:5 with "Ishmael," see the parallel passage in *Secrets*.

108 Read חיילים (so *Secrets*) in place of the text's חללים, "corpses."

109 *Sic*. The corresponding text at the end of *Secrets* reads: הוא עבד שמרד על אדונו.

110 A Hebrew wordplay on the name of Abū Muslim, fomenter of the ᶜAbbāsid Revolution in Khurāsān. See Lewis, "Apocalyptic Vision," 329.

111 The explanation does not correlate with the expression "slave of kings," which is treated in the following sentence, but instead explicates the preceding phrase, "the one loathed by the nation." According to Lewis ("Apocalyptic Vision,"329), this is a reference to Khurāsān.

Regarding (the phrase) "slave of kings": there will be a slave of rulers who will rebel against his masters,[112] and (other) men who have rebelled against their masters will be gathered to him and assemble themselves with them. They will make war with the Ishmaelites, kill their warriors, and take possession of their wealth and property. They are very repulsive men, dressed in black, and coming forth from the east. They are cruel and impetuous, as scripture attests: "Lo, I shall raise up against (על) the Chaldeans the nation cruel and impetuous" (Hab 1:6).[113] All of them are horsemen, as scripture attests: "horsemen charging up" (Nah 3:3). They come from a distant land to take possession of dwellings that do not belong to them, and they will ascend onto the height of the mountains—this refers to "the mountain-height of Israel"[114]—and demolish the sanctuary, extinguish the lamps, and split the doors.[115]

Moreover four other kings will arise—two of them have been revealed—and two others will arise against them. During their reigns the son of David will appear, as scripture says: "and in the days of those kings" (Dan 2:44).[116] The form of the first king: an aged man, but not exceedingly old. The king is modest, his eyes attractive, and his hair lovely (and) black. But they will be led astray by him. After him another (ruler) will arise amidst dissensions, and he will station large armies by the Euphrates River. Yet his armies will fall in a single day, those in the north and those in the south, and he will flee, but will be captured and imprisoned, and all the time he is held captive there will be peace in the land. The fourth king is a lover of silver and gold: he is elderly and tall and has a mole upon the big toe of his right foot. He will mint bronze coins and hide them and store them beneath the Euphrates with (his) silver and gold, but these (treasures) are (actually) held in storage for the King Messiah,[117] as scripture attests: "I will give you treasures (concealed in) darkness and secret hidden things" (Isa 45:3). During his reign the western quadrant will rebel, and he will dispatch two squadrons of

[112] Some traditions impute such a pedigree to Abū Muslim. See Sabatino Moscati, "Abū Muslim," *EI*[2] 1:141.

[113] The Masoretic Text of Hab 1:6 reads: הנני מקים <u>את</u> הכשדים, where the Chaldeans are identified as "the cruel and impetuous nation." By subtly altering the text, *Prayer* constructs two "national" entities in this verse and effects an exegetical equation between "Chaldeans" and the Umayyad dynasty.

[114] Ezek 17:23; 20:40; cf. 34:14. Targumic and traditional commentaries interpret this phrase as a reference to Jerusalem.

[115] Compare the text in *Secrets*: ועל הר מרום ישראל יעלו ויסבר לפרוץ בהיכל ודלתים יעקירו ומרות יבכו (Jellinek, *BHM* 3:81).

[116] Even-Shmuel (*Midreshey Ge'ullah*, 274) suggests that this clause may stem from one who recognized the messianic candidacy of Abū ʿĪsā al-Iṣfahānī.

[117] Compare the text in *Secrets* (Jellinek, *BHM* 3:81): ... ויעשה ספינות מנחשת וימלא אותם כסף וזהב וטומן אותם תחת מימי פרת להצניעם לבניו והם עתידים לישראל שנ׳. Note that the identity of the "servant" of Isaiah 45 is decoded differently by the two recensions of this apocalypse.

troops, and they (those in the west) will kill some of the easterners, consequently (necessitating) the dispatch of still others (to the west).

And at the beginning of week one there is no rain, and in the second (week) "arrows of hunger,"[118] and in the third will be a severe famine accompanied by drought, and in the fourth an average (climatic state), and in the fifth there will be great satiety.[119] And during the sixth a star shall appear from the east and on top of it a rod of fire like a spear. The Gentile nations will claim "this star is ours,"[120] but it is not so; rather, it pertains to Israel, as scripture forecasts: "a star shall step forth from Jacob, etc." (Num 24:17). The time of its shining will be during the first watch of the night for two hours. It will set (for) fifteen days in the east, and then revolve to the west and act (similarly?) for fifteen days. If it should be more (its period of shining), this is good for Israel.[121]

Again I returned to my prayer and also my fasting (for) forty days until this angel appeared to me. He said to me, "Ask!" I answered him, "Lord, what will be the end of these (things)?" The angel said to me, "After all these (things) the westerners[122] will become overpowering, with mighty armies, and they will come mingled [*sic*] and make war with the easterners who are in their land. They [the westerners] will kill them, and those who survive will flee before them and enter Alexandria. Some of the westerners will pursue after them and arrive (at the city), and a great battle will take place there. The easterners shall flee from there and come into Egypt. They shall capture it, take spoil, and make it a desolate place in order to affirm what scripture says: 'Egypt will become a desolate place' (Joel 4:19). They will advance over into 'the glorious land' (Eretz Israel) and (the land will suffer) complete destruction at their hand.[123] Anyone whom they capture will not return (to Eretz Israel) until the Messiah comes."

[118] See Ezek 5:16.

[119] This periodization is modeled on a *baraita* found in *b. Sanh.* 97a which recounts events associated with the שבוע שבן דוד בא בו. For a translation and discussion paired with *2 Baruch* 26–29, see Ephraim E. Urbach, *The Sages: Their Concepts and Beliefs* (2 vols.; Jerusalem: Magnes, 1979), 1:676–77.

[120] Not contained in the talmudic *baraita*, but seems to reflect the Christian prophecies associated with the "star of the Magi" found in Syriac sources like the *Cave of Treasures*.

[121] Compare ᵓ*Aggadat ha-Mašiaḥ* (Jellinek, *BHM* 3:141): ויצמח כוכב ממזרח והוא כוכבו של משיח והוא עושה במזרח ט״ו יום ואם האריך הוא לטובתן של ישראל, "A star will emerge in the east. This is the star of the Messiah, and it will be visible in the east for fifteen days. Should it linger, it will be to Israel's benefit."

[122] I accept the argument of Lewis ("Apocalyptic Vision," 331–32) that this sequence of events refers to the Fāṭimid invasion of Egypt in 969 CE and its immediate aftermath.

[123] An adapted paraphrase of Dan 11:16: ויעמד בארץ הצבי וכלה בידו.

When I heard this discourse, I wept very much. The angel said to me, "Šimʿōn, why do you weep?" I answered him, "Will there be no escape for the descendants of Abraham, Isaac, and Jacob during his [*sic*] days?" He said to me, "The situation will be very difficult: if you leave meat over the fire, you cannot escape its savor; so too Israel cannot escape. But everyone who enters into a chamber and flees and hides will escape, as scripture says: 'Go, my people, enter your chambers!' (Isa 26:20). 'All who are discovered will be stabbed, and all who are captured shall fall by the sword' (Isa 13:15). They will pass through 'the glorious land' and pillage, as scripture notes: 'and he shall enter the lands, sweeping and passing through' (Dan 11:40). They come into 'the ravines of the precipices,'[124] and they will be in the middle,[125] and a great battle will take place there concerning which all the prophets have prophesied, and the streams and waters of the Euphrates will turn to blood. Those who remain will be unable to drink from it, and (it is) from there that the kingdom of the east will be destroyed.

"And after all these things a king 'strong of face' (עז פנים)[126] will arise and be active for three and one-half years.[127] At the beginning of his rule when he arises, he will receive those who are rich, remove their money, and kill them: hence wealth will not deliver its owner, as scripture attests: 'their silver and their gold will be unable to save them' (Ezek 7:19), nor will his counsel and planning stand up against him. He will kill whoever recites the *Šemaʿ*, and he will kill whoever says 'God of Abraham.' And they will say: 'Let us all return (and become) one nation, and let us abolish the Sabbaths, festivals, and new moons from Israel,' as scripture attests: 'and he will plan to change times and law' (Dan 7:25). 'Times' (זמנין) refers to festivals and 'law' (דת) refers to the Torah, as scripture proves: 'a fiery law (דת) to them' (Deut 33:2). During his reign there will be great distress for Israel. (Nevertheless), all whom he exiles will escape to Upper Galilee, as it is written: 'for on Mount Zion and in Jerusalem there will be escape' (Joel 3:5) until he reaches Meron.[128] He will kill some from among Israel until he comes (to Damascus), and when he arrives at Damascus, the Holy One, blessed be He,

[124] See Isa 7:19.

[125] This clause is Aramaic: והם באמצעיתא.

[126] Deut 28:50; Dan 8:23; *Tg. Ket.* Qoh 8:1.

[127] According to Lewis ("Apocalyptic Vision," 332, and cf. 335 n. 4), this figure symbolizes the Qarmaṭī campaigns in south Syria and Palestine in 971–974 CE. See Wilferd Madelung, "Ḳarmaṭī," *EI*[2] 4:660–65; Gil, *History*, 335–44; idem, "The Political History of Jerusalem during the Early Muslim Period," in *The History of Jerusalem: The Early Muslim Period, 638–1099* (ed. Joshua Prawer and Haggai Ben-Shammai; New York: New York University Press, 1996), 18–20.

[128] An Aramaic phrase (עד דמטי מרון) that Even-Shmuel groundlessly emends to "until our Lord [i.e., Messiah] arrives." Meron is the site of the tomb of R. Šimʿōn ben Yoḥai, a circumstance that seems hardly unimportant in the present context.

will provide assistance and relief to Israel.[129] During his reign there will be strife and war in the world: a town will battle with its neighbor, and a city with (another) city, and a people with (another) people, and a nation with (another) nation. There will be no peace for those who go and come, as scripture says: 'I will press humanity hard, and they shall walk about like the blind' (Zeph 1:17). The people of the Lord shall suffer dislocation and experience distress for three years, and they will be subject to his power until the end of the three years, as scripture says: 'they will be delivered into his hand for a time, times, and half a time' (Dan 7:25). 'A time' signifies one year; 'times' signifies two years, (and) 'half a time' signifies half of a year: consequently (after) three [and a half][130] years the decree and foolishness will be annulled, as scripture predicts: 'and from the time of the suspension of the daily offering and installment of the abomination of desolation—one thousand two hundred and ninety days' (Dan 12:11). These are the three and a half years. There shall arise a king who will turn them to apostasy, as scripture states: 'and they will install the abomination of desolation' (Dan 11:31). He will rule for three months.[131]

"After that, the Ishmaelites will do battle with the Edomites on the plain of Acco,[132] and immediately the Assyrians[133] will come upon them and capture them, as scripture says: 'until Assyria takes you prisoner' (Num 24:22). (And as for) 'ships from the coast of Kittim' (ibid.), these are the Edomites who are destined to arise in the last days. When they (eventually) emerge, they will come forth like robbers, as scripture predicts: 'when robbers come against you' (Obad 1:5; cf. also Jer 49:9). They will do battle with the Ishmaelites and kill many of them and assemble themselves at the camp at Acco. Iron shall crumble clay, and its leg(s) will break down to the toes, and they will flee naked without horses.[134] (New) legions from Edom will unite with them, and they will come and do battle on the plain of Acco until a horse sinks to its flank in blood. The children of Israel will flee to the plain

[129] Naphtali Wieder has argued that the toponym Damascus functions in midrash and allied interpretive traditions as a cipher for the locale of national and religious redemption. See his *The Judean Scrolls and Karaism* (London: East and West Library, 1962), 1–30.

[130] The context requires this restoration.

[131] Lewis ("Apocalyptic Vision," 336) opines that this refers to the Fāṭimid Muᶜizz. Note that in the *Secrets of R. Šimᶜōn ben Yoḥai*, it is "the king strong of face" who rules for three months, as opposed to the three and one-half year period granted him here and in *ᵓAggadat ha-Mašiaḥ*.

[132] According to Lewis ("Apocalyptic Vision," 333–37), this section refers to the Byzantine campaigns in Syria and Palestine under John Tzimisces in 974–976 CE.

[133] Alptakin and his Turkish forces? So Lewis, "Apocalyptic Vision," 336–37.

[134] An Aramaic passage with allusions to Dan 2:31–45. I follow Jellinek's suggested readings here; compare Lewis, "Apocalyptic Vision," 316.

of Jericho, and there they will pause and ask one another, 'To where can we flee? Let us leave (here) our wives (and) our children.' They will return and wage another battle on the plain of Megiddo, and the Edomites will flee and board ships, and a wind shall come forth and bring them to Assyria. They will oppress the Assyrians and (the region of) upper Mesopotamia, but at the end of nine months the Assyrians shall come forth and destroy the children of Israel [*sic*][135] and the Romans, as scripture states: 'until Assyria takes you prisoner' (Num 24:22). When you see Syrians (?)[136] coming forth and traveling about the land of Israel, they will establish peace, and Elijah will come forth and proclaim news of peace to them, as scripture says: 'and this will be peace: when Assyria comes into our land' (Mic 5:4). The Italians will seek to wage war with them, and the kingdom will revert to the Ishmaelites for a short while, but they will not have sufficient time to evacuate their wives before Assyria captures them.

Suddenly a heavenly voice[137] will come forth and proclaim in all the places where the Israelites are:[138] 'Issue forth and enact the vengeance of God against Edom!' For scripture says: 'I will enact my vengeance against Edom by the agency of my people Israel' (Ezek 25:14). Immediately the young men of the Israelites will band together and obey, and they will recognize as king over them a Davidide ruler. (However), dissension will break out among them, and the inhabitants of the land of Israel will rebel against the descendant of David, (a reaction) that will confirm what scripture says: 'and Israel has rebelled against the house of David until this day' (2 Chr 10:19): '*until* this day' signifies the day *when* the royal Messiah comes. The contending parties will come and take hold of one another, and a heavenly voice will come forth and whistle: '"what has been is what will be" (Qoh 1:9)—the Holy One, blessed be He, existed before the creation of the universe, and He will continue to exist after the destruction of the universe; "what He has already done is what He will do"' (ibid.). It [the heavenly voice] will continue: 'Just as Joshua did to Jericho and its ruler, so do to the nations of the world!' They shall respond: 'The ark of the covenant is not with us as it was with Joshua!' It [the heavenly voice] will answer them, 'There was nothing in the ark except the two stone tablets[139] (of the Law) and their seal "*Shemaʿ Israel*"!' Immediately they will burst out with a great shout and say, 'Hear, O Israel! The Lord is our God; the Lord is One!' (Deut 6:4). They will encircle Jericho, and the wall will collapse at once. They will

[135] Lewis ("Apocalyptic Vision," 317 n.1) suggests emending "Israel" to "Ishmael."
[136] Jellinek's text reads שוורים; he suggests emending to אשורים.
[137] Literally a בת קול, the talmudic expression for a revelatory audition.
[138] See Lewis, "Apocalyptic Vision," 317 n. 3.
[139] A paraphrase of 1 Kgs 8:9.

enter within her and find young men dead in her squares so as to affirm what scripture states: 'truly her young men will fall in her squares, and all her warriors will perish' (Jer 50:30). They will engage in slaughter for three days and three nights, and afterwards they will collect all her spoil in the midst of her square. But (then) news will come to them from the Land of Israel, and they will be very fearful."

Again I returned to my prayer before the Lord while fasting and (garbed in) sackcloth and ashes until I had seen (a vision?). Behold, a hand touched me and stood me up on my feet, and he said to me, "Ask, O righteous one, what you would ask!" So I asked him (and) said to him, "At the end of these things, how will all Israel be gathered together from the four corners of the earth? How will their escape from the control of the kingdoms take place? When they depart, to where will they go? How will their journey transpire? What will they be able to do? I want you to tell me about these things and others like them until the conclusion of the matter."[140]

He responded to me from the doors of heaven, saying to me: "At the end of the kingdom of the Ishmaelites, the Romans will go forth against Jerusalem and make war with the Ishmaelites. The land will be subdued by them.[141] They will enter it [i.e., Jerusalem] and slaughter many Ishmaelites and cast down numerous corpses in it. They will capture a great many Ishmaelite women and dash out the brains of the children. Each day they will sacrifice children to Jesus.[142] At that time Israel (too) will suffer much distress, and at that moment the Lord will arouse the tribes of Israel and they will come to Jerusalem, the holy city.[143] They will discover that it is written in the Torah: 'the Lord was traveling before them daily in a column of cloud(s)' (Exod 13:21), and it is also written 'for the Lord will travel before you, and the God of Israel will guard your rear' (Isa 52:12). They will journey in the company of thick clouds,[144] engage the Edomites in battle, and kill a large number of them. News about them—'the tribes have come!'—will spread throughout the world. At that time the verse pertaining to Israel will be fulfilled: 'There will be a time of trouble the like of which has not occurred since you became a nation, and at that time all of your people who(se names) are found inscribed in the book will be delivered' (Dan

140 Hebrew עד סוף כל הדבר is the equivalent of Aramaic עד כה סופא די מלתא (Dan 7:28).

141 A description of the First Crusade and the capture of Jerusalem in 1099.

142 This curious charge is probably a reflection of the blood libel which accused Jews of engaging in the ritual murder of Christian youth. See Israel J. Yuval, "Jewish Messianic Expectations Towards 1240 and Christian Reactions," in *Toward the Millennium: Messianic Expectations from the Bible to Waco* (ed. Peter Schäfer and Martin Cohen; Leiden: Brill, 1998), 113.

143 See Isa 52:1; Neh 11:1.

144 For a stimulating survey of the prominence of the motif of the "divine cloud" in Jewish eschatology, see Wieder, *Judean Scrolls and Karaism*, 35–48.

12:1). The nations will rise up against Israel and effect a great massacre among them, and many of the unlearned[145] will apostatize. They will torture with chains many of the pious so as to (make them) abandon the Torah of the Lord.

"And after they have endured this distress for a short time, the Lord will bring a great and strong wind, a mighty earthquake, and a cloud so dark that its equal has never appeared before in the world, and from the midst of that wind the Holy One, blessed be He, will disperse the tribes in each and every city.[146] With regard to them it has been said, 'Who are these who fly about like a cloud?' (Isa 60:8). A few persons from Israel will gather together in Jerusalem, but they will find no food, and the Holy One, blessed be He, will transform the sand into fine flour for Israel, and with regard to this time it has been said: 'Let there be an abundance of grain in the land on the top(s) of mountains' (Ps 72:16).[147] Nehemiah ben Hushiel will arise and perform miracles in accordance with the word of the Lord.[148] A ruler will arise and become a religious heretic: he will make himself appear to be a servant of the Lord, but his heart will not be truly with Him. A mighty thundering[149] will go forth throughout the world, and the whole world will fear it. Israel will gather themselves to Nehemiah ben Hushiel. The ruler of Egypt will make a pact with him, and he (Nehemiah?) will effect a slaughter in all the cities surrounding Jerusalem, such as Tiberias, Damascus, and Ashkelon. The nations of the world will hear (about this), and terror and panic will fall upon them.[150]

145 עם הארץ, literally "people of the land."

146 Even-Shmuel detects in this section a reference to the messianic activities of David Alroy. Lewis ("Apocalyptic Vision," 338) suggests instead that it reflects general messianic excitement surrounding the period of the First Crusade. The most important Jewish testimonies to Alroy are collected and discussed in Aaron Ze'ev Aescoly, *Messianic Movements in Israel,* Volume 1, *From the Bar-Kokhba Revolt until the Expulsion of the Jews from Spain* (ed. Yehudah Even-Shmuel; 2d ed.; Jerusalem: Mosad Bialik, 1987), 186–200.

147 Rashi *ad* Ps 72:16 notes that the entire psalm is traditionally interpreted as referring to the days of the messiah. The phrase בראש הרים is here being read as the "*best* . . ." or "*choicest* of mountains," namely, Zion. Jellinek (*BHM* 4:124) directs attention to *Qoh. Rab.* 1.28, a passage that correlates the miraculous provision of manna during the exodus with this future miracle. The paralleling of the "first" and "final" redemptions is exegetically generated from Mic 7:15: כימי צאתך מארץ מצרים אראנו נפלאות "I will display to him marvels corresponding to (those during) the time of your emergence from Egypt." For further discussion of this motif along with further references, see Louis Ginzberg, *An Unknown Jewish Sect* (New York: Jewish Theological Seminary of America, 1976), 234–38; Crone and Cook, *Hagarism*, 158–59 nn. 44–46; Oded Irshai, "Dating the Eschaton: Jewish and Christian Apocalyptic Calculations in Late Antiquity," in *Apocalyptic Time* (ed. Albert I. Baumgarten; Leiden: Brill, 2000), 124–29.

148 The Messiah of the lineage of Joseph; cf. Ibn Ezra *ad* Cant 7:11 and *Midr. Teh.* 60.3.

149 Even-Shmuel has "great anger" (זעם גדול) in place of Jellinek's רעם גדול.

150 Compare the *Ten Signs of the Messiah* (translated later in this volume) for a parallel with these

"The sign which will occur at that time (is) that the stars will appear in blood, and about that time it has been said, 'The sun will be changed into darkness, and the moon to blood' (Joel 3:4). The Holy One, blessed be He, will send ten plagues against the nations of the world, just like the ones He sent against Egypt so as to affirm what scripture has said: 'On that day the Lord will again manifest His power—for a second time—in order to acquire the remnant of His people' (Isa 11:11).

"They say that in Rome there is a marble statue in the shape of a beautiful maiden (which) was made during the six days of the creation week. Worthless scoundrels from the nations of the world will come and have intercourse with it, it will become pregnant, and at the end of nine months it will split open and a male in the form of a human being will emerge. He will be twelve cubits long and two cubits wide, his eyes will be red (and) crooked, the hair of his head will be red like gold, and the soles of his feet will be green. He will have two heads, and they will call him Armilos. He will come to Edom and announce to them, 'I am your messiah; I am your god!'[151] Although he is misleading them,[152] they will instantly believe him and they will install him as king, and all the descendants of Esau[153] will join together and come to him. He will travel about and announce in all the cities and say to the descendants of Esau, 'Bring me my scripture[154] which I have given to you,' and again the nations of the world will come and bring a book . . .[155] and he will say to them, 'This is (indeed) what I have given to you,' and he will reiterate to them, 'I am your god' and 'I am your messiah and your god!'

"At that time he will send for Nehemiah and all Israel, and he will say to them: 'Bring me your Torah and testify to me that I am God!' Immediately all Israel will be astonished and intimidated, and at that time Nehemiah will arise, along with three men from the tribe of Ephraim, and they will come bearing a *sefer Torah* with them. They will read aloud before him: 'I am (the Lord your God . . .)' and 'You shall not have (any other gods before Me).'[156]

---

final two sentences. Even-Shmuel (*Midreshey Geʾullah*, 297) suggests that this betrays the dependence of *Ten Signs* upon this section of the *Prayer*.

[151] This scene and the ensuing dialogue with representatives of the Jewish community are closely related to Byzantine Christian apocalyptic legends surrounding the advent of the "Son of Destruction" or "Lawless One" (2 Thess 2:1–12), an eschatological figure frequently conflated with the Antichrist. See especially *Apoc. Ps-Ephrem* (ed. Beck), 68.359–404.

[152] This clause is missing in Even-Shmuel's edition.

[153] That is, the Christians.

[154] Literally, "my Torah" (תורתי), but here presumably the Christian scriptures.

[155] According to Jellinek, the word has been erased from the manuscript. Based on a parallel passage contained in the work entitled *ʾOtot ha-Mašiaḥ* (Jellinek, *BHM* 2:58–63), Steinschneider suggested restoring the word תפלות, "frivolity"; see his "Apokalypsen," 635 n. 17.

[156] A mnemonic reference to Exod 20:2–3.

He will retort, 'None of this can be in your Torah! I will give you no rest until you believe that I am God in the same way that the nations of the world believe in me!' Immediately Nehemiah will arise to confront him, and he will say to him, 'You are not God, but Satan!'[157] He (Armilos) will say to them, 'Why do you lie about me? I could give the order to execute you,' and then will command his servants, 'Seize Nehemiah!' Immediately he [Nehemiah] will arise along with 30,000 warriors from Israel and do battle with him, and he will slay 200,000 from the camp of Armilos. Enraged, Armilos will gather all the forces of the nations of the world and make war on the Israelite people and kill 1,000,000 Israelites, and he will even kill Nehemiah at midday. Concerning this time it has been said: 'And it will come to pass on that day—so says the Lord God—that I shall make the sun set at midday, and I shall darken the earth on a bright day' (Amos 8:9). Those Israelites who remain alive will flee into the 'desert of the peoples'[158] and remain there for forty-five days without food or water, with only wild grass to serve as their sustenance. After forty-five days have passed,[159] Armilos will invade and make war against Egypt and capture it, as scripture attests: 'even the land of Egypt will not be a refuge' (Dan 11:42). Then he will turn back and set his face toward Jerusalem in order to devastate it a second time, as scripture states: 'he will pitch the canopies of his pavilion between the seas at the splendid mountain of holiness; however, he will have reached his limit, and no one will aid him' (Dan 11:45).

"At that time Michael the great prince will stand and blow three blasts on the shofar, as scripture attests: 'and it will come to pass on that day that he will blow a great trumpet (*shofar*)' (Isa 27:13). That shofar is (actually made from) the right horn of the ram of Isaac,[160] which the Holy One, blessed be

[157] According to *Sefer Zerubbabel* and *Secrets*, Armilos is the *son* of Satan. In *ʾOtot ha-Mashiaḥ* (see also Even-Shmuel, *Midreshey Geʾullah*, 318–23), the author states: "his name is Armilos Satan; this is the one whom the nations term Antichrist (אנטיקרישטו)" (ibid., 320).

[158] Cf. Ezek 20:35; 1QM 1.3 for the peculiar syntagm. Note also Hos 2:16 and the medieval commentators on both biblical passages, as well as *Pss. Sol.* 17:17, where the devout inhabitants of Jerusalem are portrayed as fleeing to the wilderness in order to escape the reign of the "lawless one" (17:11). It is clear from these passages that the locale invokes the "original wilderness" trials of Israel as a means of purgation and presages a successful "reconquest" of the Land.

[159] The cipher "forty-five" is derived from the numerical difference between the 1290 and 1335 "days" of Dan 12:11–12.

[160] That is, the ram substituted for Isaac as sacrificial victim in Gen 22:13. Even-Shmuel calls attention to *Pirqe R. El.* §31 (Luria, 72a): וקרן של ימין הוא גדול מן השמאל ועתיד לתקוע בו לעתיד לבא בקבוץ של גליות שנאמר והיה ביום ההוא יתקע בשופר גדול, "and its right horn is larger than its left, and it will be blown in the future as part of what is destined to occur at the ingathering of the exiles, as scripture says: 'and it will come to pass on that day that he will blow a great trumpet' (Isa 27:13)" (*Midreshey Geʾullah*, 285). See also Isaak Heinemann, *Darkey ha-Aggadah* (2d ed.; Jerusalem: Magnes; Ramat Gan: Masadah, 1954), 31.

He, will lengthen until it is one thousand cubits long. He will blow a strong blast, and the Messiah of the lineage of David[161] and Elijah will be revealed. Both of them will journey to where Israel is in the 'desert of the peoples.' To them Elijah will announce, 'Here is the Messiah,' and he will restore their hearts and strengthen their hands, as scripture states: 'Strengthen (your) wavering hands and fortify (your) faltering knees! Say to the anxious ones, "Be strong and unafraid!"' (Isa 35:3–4). All of the Israelite people will hear the sound of the shofar blowing, and they will know[162] that He has redeemed Israel, as scripture says: 'for the Lord has ransomed Jacob (and redeemed him from the power of one stronger than he)' (Jer 31:11). 'Those who were lost in the land of Assyria will come (as well as those who were wandering in the land of Egypt)' (Isa 27:13). Fear of the Lord will instantly fall upon the peoples and upon all the nations. Israel will come back with the Messiah until they reach the wilderness of Judea, and they will rendezvous there with all of Israel and enter Jerusalem together. They will climb the steps of the House of David—those that remain from the destruction—and the Messiah will sit down there. Armilos will hear that a king has appeared in Israel, and he will collect the forces of all the nations of the earth, and they will advance against the King Messiah and Israel.

"The Holy One, blessed be He, will fight on behalf of Israel. He will say to the Messiah, 'Sit at My right hand' (Ps 110:1), and the Messiah will say to Israel, 'Assemble yourselves and "stand aside and witness the Lord's deliverance"!' (Exod 14:13). Immediately the Holy One, blessed be He, will go forth and do battle with them, as scripture promises: 'The Lord will go forth and do battle with those nations' (Zech 14:3), and it is recorded in scripture: 'At that time I will bring you, and at that time I will gather you; for I will make you famous and an object of praise for all the peoples of the earth' (Zeph 3:20)."

Amen! May that time and that occasion be soon!

[161] משיח בן דוד.

[162] Read with Even-Shmuel וידעו instead of Jellinek's וישמעו.

5

Apocalypses Featuring "Ten Signs" (עשר אותות)

ONE POPULAR FEATURE of the Near Eastern apocalyptic lexicon involved the enumeration of a series of "signs" or "portents" that were held to signal the imminent approach of the End. These signs range freely through a broad variety of natural disruptions and cataclysms, social upheavals, political disturbances, and ominous preternatural occurrences. Many of these are shaped by and explicitly tied to scriptural passages that allegedly presage one or more of these events, whereas others belong to the more nebulous realm of traditional lore. Unlike the crucial references to identifiable personages or events (*vaticinia ex eventu*) in the so-called historical apocalypses of early Judaism or Christianity, these *mythologoumena* rarely shed light on determining the precise period when the work that employs such a list was composed, apart from the production of vague analytical generalities such as "Byzantine" or "post-Islamic." Nevertheless, the frequent and prominent exploitation of this sort of roster by Jews, Christians, and Muslims over the course of at least a millennium of their intertwined literary activity suggests that a comparative examination of a representative sampling of the phenomenon might aid our understanding of the interrelationships linking discrete forms of Near Eastern apocalypticism.[1]

Lists of eschatological portents or "signs" in Jewish apocalypses are sometimes catalogued under the rubrics of the "footprints of the Messiah" (עקבות משיחא), a syntagm based on an enigmatic phrase in Ps 89:52[2] and more fully developed in *m. Soṭah* 9.15,[3] or the "agony of the Messiah" (חבלו של משיח),[4] a locution whose

[1] Important methodological observations whose utility extend well beyond their immediate context can be found in David Frankfurter, *Elijah in Upper Egypt: The Apocalypse of Elijah and Early Egyptian Christianity* (SAC; Minneapolis: Fortress, 1993), 106–27, 195–200.

[2] אשר חרפו עקבות משיחך, "who scorn the footsteps of Your Messiah," rendered by the Targum as די חסידו איחור בושמת רגלי משיחך ײ.

[3] It is likely that this mishnah represents a later supplemental addition to the tractate drawn from two *baraitot* contained in *b. Sanh.* 97a. See Ḥanokh Albeck, ed., *Shishah sidrei Mishnah* (6 vols.; Jerusalem: Mosad Bialik; Tel Aviv: Devir, 1957–59), 3:394; Ephraim E. Urbach, *The Sages: Their Concepts and Beliefs* (2 vols.; 2d ed.; Jerusalem: Magnes, 1979), 2:1000 n. 92; Rivka Nir, *The Destruction of*

graphic birth imagery underscores the emergence of the novel order to which the world's inhabitants must adapt at the advent of the messianic era. Some scholars have suggested that the notion of a progressive series of worsening end-time sufferings and woes was dictated by the Jewish adoption of a foreign conceptual model of universal history that likened the expected duration of the universe to that of the life span of an organic entity. Characterized by good health and vigor during its early stages of life, the world falls victim to increasing weakness, structural breakdown, and physical decline as old age ensues.[5] The analogous exploitation by the author of Daniel 2 of an originally Indo-European scheme correlating the successive stages of world history with a sequential series of metals or other mineral substances of decreasing value demonstrates the cross-cultural attraction of this type of conceptual structure for those engaged in the construction of apocalyptic models.[6]

A cursory examination of the earlier Hellenistic and Roman-era apocalypses uncovers a rich treasury of signs and occurrences that supposedly mark the end of the present world order.[7] They are usually assembled together as catalogues or lists, exhibiting little semantic or logical connection among their components, and are most frequently addressed as a response to a seer's query about a timetable for the end. Occasionally variant lists of signs are provided within the same apocalypse.[8] These lists can vary widely with regard to their editorial arrangement. Generally speaking, the later apocalypses tend to adopt one (or more) numerical schemes that pattern the "signs" in accordance with certain symbolic numbers; for example, seven (based on the number of planets, the number of days in a week, or the positioning of the Sabbath in the creation week), ten (based on the number of plagues leveled against Egypt, or the expected number of world empires), or twelve (based on the number of months of a year, the number of signs of the zodiac, or the number of the sons of Jacob). *B. Sanh.* 97a, for example, arranges its list in accordance with a sabbatical scheme:[9]

Jerusalem and the Idea of Redemption in the Syriac Apocalypse of Baruch (SBLEJL 20; Atlanta: Society of Biblical Literature, 2003), 128 n. 23.

[4] For the phrase, see *Mek.* Beshalaḥ, Va-yassaʿ §4 (Horovitz-Rabin, 169.10–12), §5 (Horovitz-Rabin, 170.13–15); *b. Šabb.* 118a; *Pesaḥ.* 118a; *Sanh.* 98b. Compare Matt 24:8; Mark 13:8 (ὠδίνων).

[5] Note *4 Ezra* 5:48–56, where Ezra's angelic informant compares the present time to an aging woman at the end of her childbearing years. See also 14:10 ("for the world has lost its youth, and the times draw closer to old age" [Syriac]); *2 Bar.* 85:10.

[6] See John J. Collins, *The Apocalyptic Vision of the Book of Daniel* (HSM 16; Missoula, Mont.: Scholars Press, 1977), 40–43; Arnaldo Momigliano, "The Origins of Universal History," in his *On Pagans, Jews, and Christians* (Middletown, Conn.: Wesleyan University Press, 1987), 31–57.

[7] Note *1 En.* 93:1–10 + 91:12–17; *Jub.* 23:11–25; Matt 24:3–44; Mark 13:3–36; *Sib. Or.* 2.154–213; 3.796–808; *4 Ezra* 4:52–5:13; 6:20–24; 8:63–9:6; *2 Bar.* 24:3–30:5; 48:30–41; 70:1–71:2; *Apoc. Abr.* 29:15–30:8. For a convenient narrative review of these end-time signs, see D. S. Russell, *The Method & Message of Jewish Apocalyptic: 200 BC — AD 100* (Philadelphia: Westminster, 1964), 271–76.

[8] Compare the passages from *4 Ezra* and *2 Baruch* cited in the preceding note.

[9] For a slightly variant text, see also *Pesiq. Rab Kah.* 5.9 (Mandelbaum, 1:97–98).

> Our Sages have taught (that) the septennial cycle (שבוע) wherein the Son of David comes (will transpire as follows): the first year this verse will be fulfilled—"I will make it rain on one city, but on another city I will not allow it to rain" (Am 4:7); the second (year), the "arrows of famine" (cf. Ezek 5:16) will be unleashed; the third (year will have) a severe famine in which men, women, children, pious ones, and miracle-workers will die, (and) Torah will be forgotten by those who learned it; in the fourth (year) will be an alternation between plenty and poverty; in the fifth (year there will be) great plenty, and they will eat, drink, and celebrate, and the Torah will return to those who learned it; in the sixth (year) noises;[10] in the seventh (year) battles. At the end of the septennial cycle will come the Son of David."

Islamic eschatology also schematizes a number of catastrophic events that mark the advent of what the Qur᾽ān terms the "Hour" (*al-sāʿa*), the cataclysmic moment that ushers in the Day of Judgment (*yawm al-qiyāma*).[11] These occurrences are usually designated, on the basis of Q 47:18, as the "signs of the Hour" (*ashrāṭ al-sāʿa*). Most of these signs are signaled at various places in the Qur᾽ān: earthquakes,[12] smoke (Q 44:10), the darkening of the luminaries (Q 75:8),[13] the rolling up or splitting apart of the heavens,[14] the opening of tombs (Q 82:4; 100:9), and trumpet blasts or shouts (Q 18:99; 39:68; 50:20, 41–42). A mysterious "beast" (*dābba*) will emerge from the earth (Q 27:82; cf. Rev 13:11), and Yājūj and Mājūj (i.e., Gog and Magog) will break loose from their place of imprisonment (Q 18:93–99; 21:96). The Qur᾽ān, however, does not prescribe a fixed order for these occurrences, nor does it specify in most cases who or what produces them, nor does it provide a timetable for gauging the period of their occurrence. When the people press Muhammad as to when the "Hour" will come, he stresses that only God is privy to this information: "They ask you about the Hour, when it will strike. Say: 'The knowledge thereof is with my Lord; none but He will disclose it at the right time. It will be fateful in the heavens and on earth, and will not come upon you except suddenly'" (Q 7:187).[15]

10 קולות. Either shouts or blasts of the *shofar*.

11 For initial guidance regarding the topic of qur᾽ānic and Islamic eschatology, see the discussions and references supplied by L. Gardet, "Ḳiyāma," *EI²* 5:235–38; Uri Rubin, "Sāʿa," *EI²* 8:655–57; Frederik Leemhuis, "Apocalypse," *EncQur* 1:111–14; Jane I. Smith, "Eschatology," *EncQur* 2:44–54; Isaac Hasson, "Last Judgment," *EncQur* 3:136–45.

12 Q 73:14; 81:3; 99:1–3. For earthquake as an accompaniment to the biblical Day of the Lord, see Isa 13:13; 24:18–20; Jer 4:24; Ezek 38:19–20; Joel 2:10; Zech 14:4–5; and cf. Ps 29:6; 46:3–4, 7.

13 The biblical Day of the Lord is marked also by a darkening of sun, moon, and stars; see Isa 13:10; Jer 4:23, 28; Joel 2:10.

14 For the folding or rolling up of the heavens, see Q 21:104. For the splitting or parting of the heavens, see Q 25:25; 55:37; 69:16; 73:18; 82:1; 84:1.

15 See also Q 33:63; 79:42–46. Unless otherwise indicated, all quotations from the Qur᾽ān are cited from *An Interpretation of the Qur᾽an: English Translation of the Meanings, A Bilingual Edition* (trans. Majid Fakhry; New York: New York University Press, 2002).

In order to retrieve a more comprehensive presentation of Muslim apocalyptic traditions and of the "signs of the Hour," it is necessary to consult the post-qurʾānic commentators and tradents of *ḥadīth* who were active during the first three Islamic centuries.[16] Despite the qurʾānic warnings, these *ḥadīth* often contain traditions that attempt to predict the timing of the Hour, or at least emphasize its imminence. Traditions regarding the signs were often assembled in collections of *malāḥim* ("wars")[17] and *fitan* ("strife, disorders"),[18] which attempted to correlate the qurʾānic data with other parascriptural elements drawn from a variety of written and oral sources, both native and foreign. One noteworthy example of such a nonqurʾānic element is the legend surrounding the manifestation of a sinister adversary known as the Dajjāl, a figure who clearly corresponds both in type and function to the character of Armilos in the medieval Jewish apocalypses and to that of the Antichrist in Byzantine and oriental Christian compositions.[19] According to some of these traditions, the Dajjāl (like his Jewish and Christian analogues) will march on Jerusalem, but he will be confronted and slain by ʿĪsā (i.e., Jesus), who will descend from heaven in order to accomplish this feat. There are also persistent traditions predicting the recovery or reappearance of ancient artifacts like the staff of Moses or the Israelite Ark of the Covenant. The sheer quantity and diversity of these speculations bear witness to the fructifying effect of contemporary Jewish and Christian apocalyptic legends upon the development of Islamic eschatology. It is surely not coincidental that a large number of these apocalyptic prophecies derive ultimately from Kaʿb al-Aḥbār (d. 654), a learned Yemeni Jewish convert to Islam.[20]

[16] See now the important observations and bibliographical references supplied by David Cook, *Studies in Muslim Apocalyptic* (Studies in Late Antiquity and Early Islam 21; Princeton: Darwin Press, 2002), 1–33.

[17] This term is often used in Arabic literature of battles associated with eschatological events. For its possible connection with Jewish apocalyptic vocabulary, see the remarks of Chaim Rabin, *Qumran Studies* (Oxford: Oxford University Press, 1957; repr., New York: Schocken, 1975), 118–19. Note also Moritz Steinschneider, "Apokalypsen mit polemischer Tendenz," *ZDMG* 28 (1874): 628–29 n. 3.

[18] Arabic *fitna* (the singular of *fitan*) refers to the process of refining impurities from metals and is thus conceptually cognate with Hebrew apocalyptic formulas featuring the stem צרף. For an excellent exposition, see Cook, *Studies in Muslim Apocalyptic*, 20–21.

[19] The Arabic term *al-dajjāl* in fact is derived from the Syriac designation for the Antichrist or "pseudo-Messiah" (ܡܫܝܚܐ ܕܓܠܐ); cf. 1 John 2:22.

[20] See Wilferd Madelung, "Apocalyptic Prophecies in Ḥimṣ in the Umayyad Age," *JSS* 31 (1986): 143; for examples of Kaʿb's important role as a conduit of Jewish eschatology to early Islam, see Uri Rubin, *Between Bible and Qurʾān: The Children of Israel and the Islamic Self-Image* (Studies in Late Antiquity and Early Islam 17; Princeton: Darwin Press, 1999), 13–35. The figure of Kaʿb was also known among Christian polemicists: see Ms. Sachau 10 fol. 5a-b as published by Richard Gottheil, "A Christian Bahira Legend," *ZA* 13 (1898): 212–13: ܘܗܝܕܝܢ ܡܢ ܒܬܪ ܕܡܝܬ ܛܒܐ، ܣܪܓܝܣ ܩܡ ܓܒܪܐ ܡܢ ܝܗܘ̈ܕܝܐ ܕܫܡܗ ܟܥܒ ܣܦܪܐ ܘܗܘܐ ܠܗܘܢ ܡܠܦܢܐ ܘܒܥܝܐ ܘܫܠܡ ܠܡܠܦܢܘܬܗ ܕܣܪܓܝܣ ܠܗ ܐܡܪ ܗܘܐ ܠܗܘܢ ܕܗܘ ܕܐܡܪ ܠܟܠܗܘܢ، ܡܫܝܚܐ ܕܗܘܐ ܐܬܐ ܠܬܗܘܢ ܒܬܪ ܦܪܩܠܛܐ ܗܘ ܗܘܐ ܡܚܡܕ. "then after the death of the blessed Sergius, a man arose among the Jews whose name was Kaʿf the scribe who

Collections of *fitan* commonly list a numerical series of signs that mark the advent of the Hour.[21] These vary widely in number and content, and little scholarly effort has been expended to date in attempting to analyze and clarify their interrelationships.[22] In addition to the material noted above, events commonly mentioned include military disasters; wars (*malāḥim*) with ancient and contemporary enemies such as the Jews, Byzantines, or the Turks; civil strife; devastating plagues; and the manifestation of individual "sectarian" actors like the Qaḥṭānī, the "Pure Soul" (al-Nafs al-Zakiyya), or the Mahdī. One such example of an early catalogue of signs is attributed to Wahb ibn Munabbih (d. 728?), yet another prominent tradent of biblical and Jewish lore in early Islam:[23] "He (i.e., Wahb) said: First are portents associated with (the fall of) Rome (i.e., Constantinople); second, the Dajjāl; third, Yājūj and Mājūj; fourth, ʿĪsā b. Maryam; fifth, smoke; and sixth, the *dābba*."[24]

Of interest in the present context are lists that enumerate ten signs. The constituent elements most often cited in such lists include (1) smoke; (2) the rising of the sun in the west;[25] (3) the appearance of the *dābba*; (4) the appearance of the Dajjāl; (5) fire emanating from Yemen; (6) Yājūj and Mājūj; i.e., Gog and Magog; (7) the descent of ʿĪsā from heaven; (8) an avalanche in the east; (9) an avalanche in the west; and (10) an avalanche in the Arabian peninsula.[26] Uri Rubin refers to another ten-sign scheme found in the *Jāmiʿ* of Maʿmar b. Rāshid (d. A.H. 154). There we read: (1–3) three separate instances where people are swallowed up by the earth; (4) the appearance of the Dajjāl; (5) the descent of ʿĪsā from heaven; (6) the appearance of the *dābba*; (7) smoke; (8) Gog and Magog; (9) a cold wind that draws out the souls of the believers; and (10) the rising of the sun in the west.[27]

was a scholar and prophet among them. He perverted the teaching of Sergius, for he said to them: 'the one about whom Christ spoke (saying) «he will come to them after the Paraclete» is Muhammad.'" For further important discussion of the role of Kaʿb in early Islam, see Mark Lidzbarski, *De propheticis, quae dicuntur, legendis arabicis: Prolegomena* (Lipsiae: Guilelmi Drugulini, 1893), 31–40; also Reuven Firestone, "Jewish Culture in the Formative Period of Islam," in *Cultures of the Jews: A New History* (ed. David Biale; New York: Schocken, 2002), 291–98.

[21] Three early collections are those of Yaḥyā b. ʿAbd al-Hamid al-Hamani (d. 228/842); Nuʿaym b. Ḥammād (d. 229/844); and Ḥanbal b. Isḥāq (d. 273/886). See now Nuʿaym b. Ḥammād, *Kitāb al-fitan* (ed. S. Zakkār; Beirut: Dār al-Fikr lil-Ṭibāʿah wa-al-Nashr wa-al-Tawzīʿ, 1993), and the important bibliographic remarks supplied by Cook, *Studies in Muslim Apocalyptic*, 24–29.

[22] For now, see Saïd Amir Arjomand, "Islamic Apocalypticism in the Classical Period," in *The Encyclopedia of Apocalypticism* (3 vols.; ed. Bernard McGinn et al.; New York/London: Continuum, 1998), 2:238–83, esp. 248–65; Cook, *Studies in Muslim Apocalyptic*, a ground-breaking study that inaugurates a new era in the comparative understanding of this material.

[23] See the important article by R. G. Khoury, "Wahb b. Munabbih, Abū ʿAbd Allāh," *EI*² 11:34–36.

[24] Nuʿaym b. Ḥammād, *K. al-fitan* (ed. Zakkār), 402.

[25] According to *b. Sanh.* 108b, this same sign signaled the imminent advent of the Deluge. Note also Moritz Steinschneider, "Apokalypsen mit polemischer Tendenz: Nachträge zu Bd. XXVIII S. 627ff.," *ZDMG* 29 (1875): 163.

[26] Neal Robinson, "Antichrist," *EncQur* 1:110.

[27] Rubin, *EI*² 8:656.

ʾ*Otot of* R. Šimʿōn b. Yoḥai[28]

Ten signs were revealed to R. Šimʿōn b. Yoḥai (may his memory be for a blessing!) which will transpire in the world when the Messiah's advent is near—may he be revealed soon!

The first sign. Three fiery columns will descend from heaven, and they will remain upright extending from the earth up to the sky for three days and three nights. Because of the mighty power that they are beholding, all of the gentile nations will arise and grasp hold of Israel, saying to them: "Make fringe on the edge of our garments for us!"[29] Israel will make fringe for them, as scripture attests: "for ten individuals from every gentile group will grasp and take strong hold of the shirttail of every Jew, saying 'Let us come with you, for we have heard that God is with you!'" (Zech 8:23). The Holy One, blessed be He, will place portents in the sky and on the earth, as scripture states: "I will place portents in the heavens and on earth: blood, fire, and columns of smoke" (Joel 3:3).[30] And why does the (portent of) blood precede that of the fire? Because the same sequence was followed in Egypt.[31]

The second sign. Three individuals will come forth. One of them will stand on the grave and resurrect the dead; one will restore sight to the eyes of the blind; and one will cure the lame by using incantations. Eighty thousand Israelites will go astray by following them, but they are in fact not authentic Israelites; rather, they are the descendants of the Gibeonites[32] and the assorted riff-raff (האספסוף)[33] who mixed themselves with Israel (in the past). The Holy One, blessed be He, will purge them all (from Israel), as scripture states: "I will purge them (of dross) as one purges silver" (Zech 13:9).[34]

[28] From a Genizah manuscript published by Arthur Marmorstein, "Les signes du Messie," *REJ* 52 (1906): 176–86; another Genizah manuscript published by Michael Higger, *Halakhot va-aggadot* (New York: Jewish Theological Seminary, 1933), 115–23; Yehudah Even-Shmuel, *Midreshey Geʾullah* (2d ed.; Jerusalem: Mosad Bialik, 1954), 311–14, and his textual notes on pp. 422–24.

[29] See Num 15:37–41.

[30] See Ibn Ezra and Radaq *ad loc.*, both of whom emphasize that the blood is a terrestrial sign as opposed to the "heavenly" signs of fire and smoke.

[31] For the notion that Israel's "historical" deliverance from Egyptian bondage functions as a model for her eschatological redemption, see *Pesiq. Rab Kah.* 7.11 (Mandelbaum, 1:132–33); *Pesiq. Rab.* §17 (Ish-Shalom, 90a-b); *Midr. Tanḥ.*, Boʾ §4.

[32] See Josh 9:3–27; 2 Sam 21:2.

[33] See Exod 12:38; Num 11:4 and Rashi *ad loc.*

[34] Compare the Christian *Apoc. Ps-Meth.* 13.4 (ed. Reinink): "the faithful will appear and the unfaithful will become manifest, the wheat separated from the chaff; for this time is a fire of trial." David M. Olster points out that the "apocalyptic genre" facilitates the transformation of what looks

The third sign. The Holy One, blessed be He, will cause three rainbows to appear in the sky, and they will remain (visible) in the sky for three days and three nights. Their lengths will span the entire world. All of the gentile peoples will be overcome with great fear, and they will say: "Is the Holy One, blessed be He, intending to bring a flood upon the world?" But He has already sworn an oath not to bring a flood upon the world, as scripture confirms: "for this is (like) the waters of Noah to Me, which I swore I would never bring again . . ." (Isa 54:9). In the same way that He swore that He would not bring a flood, He also swore that He would not express anger, as scripture states: "thus I have sworn not to be angry with you or to rebuke you" (Isa 54:9). The Holy One, blessed be He, will wrap Israel in strength on that day, as scripture says: "the bows of the mighty ones are broken; those who stumble are wrapped in strength" (1 Sam 2:4). And who are "those who stumble"? They are Israel, for thus scripture says: "You have wrapped me in strength to do battle" (2 Sam 22:40).

The fourth sign. A rain will fall from the sky for three days and three nights, a rain consisting not of water but of blood. The eighty thousand who had previously gone astray after the apostles of the Lie[35] will drink from that fluid and die. Every man and woman who has followed them will drink and die.

The fifth sign. The Holy One, blessed be He, will cause a dew to fall from the sky for three days and three nights, and it will nullify the deadly effects of that blood which had previously fallen upon the earth. It will make the grain sprout. All the gentile peoples and nations will think that it is rain, but actually it will be only dew, as scripture promises: "I will be like dew for Israel: he will bloom like a lily and extend his roots like Lebanon. His shoots will spread, and his beauty will be like that of an olive tree, and his fragrance like Lebanon. Those who dwell in his shade will return and sprout (like) grain" (Hos 14:6–8).

The sixth sign. All the gentile peoples will experience darkness for three days and three nights, but Israel will have light, as scripture states: "for behold, darkness will cover the earth and thick darkness (will cover) the nations, but the Lord will shine upon you" (Isa 60:2). All of the gentile peoples will be overcome with great fear, and they will come and bow down

like a defeat into a crucial component of the divine scheme for achieving final victory; see his *Roman Defeat, Christian Response, and the Literary Construction of the Jew* (Philadelphia: University of Pennsylvania Press, 1994), 7; idem, "Byzantine Apocalypses," in McGinn et al., eds., *Encyclopedia of Apocalypticism*, 2:61.

35 שליחי השקר.

before Israel, saying: "'Let us come with you, for we have heard that God is with you!'" (Zech 8:23).

The seventh sign. The king of Edom [i.e., Rome] will come forth and enter Jerusalem. All of the Ishmaelites[36] will flee from him and go to Tēman. They will assemble a mighty army, and there shall go forth with them a man whose name is Ḥōṭer (חטר).[37] He will become king, and all of them will go to Boṣra. The king of Edom will hear (about this) and come after them. These two will fight a battle, as is said in scripture: "for the Lord will have a sacrifice in Boṣra, a great slaughter in the land of Edom" (Isa 34:6).[38] Scripture also states: "those who eat the flesh of swine and the detestable thing and mice will perish together—utterance of the Lord" (Isa 66:17). Ḥōṭer will kill many of the Edomites, and the king of Edom will flee from him. But Ḥōṭer will die, and the king of Edom will return to Jerusalem a second time. He will enter the sanctuary, take the golden crown off his head, and place it on the foundation stone.[39] He will then say: "Master of the Universe! I have now returned what my ancestors removed. . . ."[40] There will be trouble during his time.

The eighth sign. The Holy One, blessed be He, will "suddenly" bring forth Nehemiah b. Hushiel, who is the Messiah of the lineage of Joseph. "Suddenly" accords with what scripture says: "suddenly the Lord whom you

[36] Marmorstein conjectures that the name Ishmael is used in this apocalypse to connote the Sasanian Empire ("Les signes," 178–79). There is of course no exegetical justification for this equation.

[37] The Genizah recension published by Marmorstein gives his name as Manṣūr (מנצור). Interestingly both designations bear a "messianic" significance: for Ḥōṭer, see Isa 11:1; *y. Ber.* 2.4, 5a; for Manṣūr, see Cook, *Studies in Muslim Apocalyptic*, 76, 144–47.

[38] Perhaps a reference to the fall of Bostra in 634 to the invading Arab armies, which according to Muslim legend was the first Byzantine stronghold to fall to Islam. See Armand Abel, "Boṣrā," *EI²* 1:1275–77; Fred M. Donner, *The Early Islamic Conquests* (Princeton: Princeton University Press, 1981), 129, 140, 145; Moshe Gil, *A History of Palestine, 634–1099* (trans. Ethel Broido; Cambridge: Cambridge University Press, 1992), 40; Walter E. Kaegi, *Byzantium and the Early Islamic Conquests* (Cambridge: Cambridge University Press, 1992), 83.

[39] The אבן שתיה. See *m. Yoma* 5.2. According to *t. Yoma* 2.14 (ed. Lieberman), the ark of the covenant once occupied this space. For the mythological traditions associated with this numinous locale, see especially Michael Fishbane, *Biblical Myth and Rabbinic Mythmaking* (Oxford: Oxford University Press, 2003), 126–29.

[40] See Even-Shmuel, *Midreshey Geʾullah*, 296 n. 39. This act of surrender represents a Jewish adaptation of the popular Christian legend of the "Last Roman Emperor" found in many Byzantine apocalypses; note also Olster, *Roman Defeat*, 174; Cook, *Studies in Muslim Apocalyptic*, 76. For an extensive discussion of this legend, see Paul J. Alexander, *The Byzantine Apocalyptic Tradition* (ed. Dorothy deF. Abrahamse; Berkeley: University of California Press, 1985), 151–84; idem, "The Medieval Legend of the Last Roman Emperor and Its Messianic Origin," *Journal of the Warburg and Courtauld Institutes* 41 (1978): 1–15.

seek will enter His Temple" (Mal 3:1).[41] He will do battle with the king of Edom and kill him, and will then put on the crown which the king of Edom had returned to Jerusalem.[42] The fame of Nehemiah will become widespread in the world.

The ninth sign. A man will come forth from the city of Rome whose name is Armilos b. Satan, spawned from a stone statue located in Rome. The statue is that of a woman, and Satan will come and have sexual intercourse with it, and it will give birth to this man. On the day when he is spawned he will be as if he is one hundred years old. He will come and wage war at Alexandria and destroy the entire seacoast. Woe to the one (unlucky enough) to be seized by his hand! He will come to Gaza by himself and establish his throne there.[43] [These are his signs]: he will be ten cubits tall. . . . He will sit there upon his throne and utter profanities and blasphemies. He will say to the gentile nations: "I am God! Bring me my Torah which I gave to you!" They will bring him the images of their idols, and he will respond: "this is indeed the Torah which I gave you!" He will then say to the children of Israel: "Bring your Torah!" Thirty people from the leadership of Israel will enter along with Nehemiah b. Hushiel, and they will bring him a Torah scroll. He will say: "I do not believe in this Torah!" They will answer (him): "If you do not believe in this Torah, then you are not God but Satan! 'May the Lord rebuke you, O Satan!'"[44] At that time he will seize those thirty Israelites who came with Nehemiah, and he will burn them together with the Torah. Then he will say to Nehemiah, "Now do you not believe in me?" He will answer him: "I put my faith in no one but the God of Israel, the God of heaven who gave His Torah through the agency of Moses our teacher! He is the One in Whom I believe!" He [Armilos] will issue an order to execute him [Nehemiah] in the Temple of his God, for he had immediately set his foot within the sanctuary.[45] So they will kill Nehemiah in Jerusalem, and his corpse will be discarded in Jerusalem. Israel will mourn for him, as scripture states: "and the land will mourn, every family separately" (Zech 12:12). At

[41] See Ibn Ezra *ad loc.*

[42] According to the Christian legend, the crown which the Last Emperor surrenders is miraculously transported to heaven atop an ascending cross. Nehemiah's deliberate expropriation of this potent symbol is an ingenious polemical twist.

[43] Another recension reads here: "He will come to the city of ʿAmwās (Emmaus?), the city of his father. He will establish his throne upon it. And these are his signs. . . ." Emmaus was a principal mustering place for the Arab armies during the seventh-century conquest of Eretz Israel; see Gil, *History of Palestine*, 60 n. 63.

[44] Quoting Zech 3:2.

[45] See above in the eighth sign.

that time Israel will experience great distress:* some will hide themselves in pits, and some of them will flee into the wilderness, where they will remain for forty days. Others will follow after them, and they will (all) cry out due to their distress. "At that time Michael, the great prince who watches over the sons of Your people, will arise"[46] and say before Him: "Master of the Universe! Remember the oath which You swore to their ancestors, as well as what You promised them; (namely), 'I will pardon those whom I let remain'" (Jer 50:20)! And He will hearken to the prayer of Michael, the prince of all Israel.

The tenth sign. The Holy One, blessed be He, will bring forth the Messiah of the lineage of David, the one who has been incarcerated in prison, and by his actions all Israel will be delivered.

*Another recension expands these final two signs as follows:

Israel will experience great distress. They will hide themselves in caves and pits, and the rest of them will flee into the wilderness of ʿAmmon and Moab, as scripture states: "Let my dispersed ones sojourn among you, O Moab" (Isa 16:4). They will wander about there for forty days, nourishing themselves with broom and salt-plant, for scripture says: "they pluck salt-plant (and) leaves of shrubbery and the root(s) of broom for their food" (Job 30:4). Armilos b. Satan will come to the wilderness of Moab: this is the Armilos spawned from a stone of whom scripture speaks: "*and he produced the wicked one with the stone*" (Zech 4:7).[47] At that time the children of Israel will piteously cry out unto heaven, and Michael, the prince of the Throne of Glory, will be filled with mercy for them. He will stand in prayer before the Holy One, blessed be He, as it is written: "At that time Michael, the great prince who watches over the sons of Your people, will arise" (Dan 12:1)—the expression "standing" (עמידה) explicitly signifies that it will be a "prayer"—and he will say before Him, "Master of All Existence! Remember what You swore to their ancestors and to them, and what You said to Your servant Moses; (namely), 'I will pardon in accordance with your words'

[46] Dan 12:1.

[47] The text needs to be translated along these lines in order to yield the target sense. The Masoretic Text of Zech 4:7 reads: והוציא את האבן הראשה, "and he [Zerubbabel] will produce the headstone (of the new Temple)," but by sounding הראשה (*ha-roʾšah,* "the head, chief") as הרשע (*ha-rašaʿ*, "the wicked one"), the new reading can be generated. A similar oral pun lies behind the epithet for the Qumran villain known as "the Wicked Priest" (הכהן הרשע; see 1QpHab *passim*), which plays on one of the Second Temple era designations for high priest (כהן הראש; see Ezra 7:5 and Chronicles *passim*).

(Num 14:20), and also 'I will pardon those whom I let remain' (Jer 50:20)! Moreover, You Yourself called them 'saints,' as scripture attests: 'You are My saints' (Lev 20:26), and You have set them apart for the sake of Your Name!" The Holy One, blessed be He, hearkened to the prayer of Michael regarding Israel at that time.

Tenth sign. He will produce Menahem b. ʿAmiel, the Messiah of the lineage of David,[48] from the place of imprisonment, as scripture states: "for one came out of prison in order to reign" (Qoh 4:14), and He will transport him upon a cloud, as scripture says: "and behold (one resembling a human being came) accompanied by the clouds of the sky" (Dan 7:13). The distinguishing mark(s) of the royal Messiah: of high stature and his neck is thick; his face (shining) like the solar disk; his eyes flashing; the soles of his feet are thick . . . and he will exercise authority over all lands, and sovereignty, honor, and high rank will be granted him.[49] Armilos will arise, and together with him will be assembled the seventy language groups [i.e., gentile nations], as scripture states: "the rulers of the earth stand together" (Ps 2:2), and all who stand before him will join him. But the Messiah of the lineage of David will put them to death, as scripture says: "he will slay the wicked with the breath of his mouth" (Isa 11:4),[50] and he will kill Armilos, the spawn of the stone, and he will deliver Israel. Then his fame will spread from one end of the world to the other.

So the All-Merciful promises. May He bring that hour near and that appointed time to pass during our lifetime and the lifetime of all Israel, Amen and Amen!

TEN SIGNS[51]

Ten signs will transpire in the world prior to the End.

The first sign. The Holy One, blessed be He, will send three <angels>[52] out in three directions in the world, and they will promulgate atheism. They

[48] See *Sefer Zerubbabel* for a discussion of this name.

[49] A Hebrew paraphrase of Dan 7:14.

[50] See also 1QSb 5.24–25; cf. *Pss. Sol.* 17:24.

[51] Originally published by Higger, *Halakhot va-aggadot*, 125–30; reprinted by Even-Shmuel, *Midreshey Ge'ullah*, 315–17 and his textual notes on p. 425. A variant version of this work is attested in T-S A45.8 fol. 1, a photograph of which is published by Simon Hopkins, *A Miscellany of Literary Pieces from the Cambridge Genizah Collections: A Catalogue and Selection of Texts in the Taylor-Schechter Collection, Old Series, Box A45* (Cambridge: Cambridge University Library, 1978), 16. This fragment is translated separately below. Note also the text entitled "Ten Signs" (עשר אותות) found in the anthology מעשיות (Constantinople: Astruq de Toulon, 1519), 34a–35a.

[52] Read מלאכים in place of מלכים?

will make themselves appear to human beings (as if) they serve Him, (but in fact they do not) and they will subjugate all creatures. But at the End of Days all the gentile nations will renounce their native religions, as it is written: "and the idols will be completely destroyed,"[53] and scripture states: "and the idols will totally vanish" (Isa 2:18). (This will happen) because the Holy One, blessed be He, will manifest troubles in the world, each one different from the other.

The second sign. The Holy One, blessed be He, will make the sun emerge from its sheath.[54] Every day He will scorch with it one million (people) from among the nations until all the nations begin weeping and saying: "Woe is us! Where will we go? To where might we flee?" They will dig down (in) all the caverns in the earth in order to find a cool breeze for themselves, as scripture states: "they will enter rocky caves" (Isa 2:19), and one will say to the other: "Go inside the rock! Hide yourself in the dirt!" Malachi prophesied about that sun: "Behold, the day comes burning like an oven" (Mal 3:19), but that sun will be medicinal for Israel, as it is said: "O those who revere My name, a sun of righteousness will rise for you, and it will heal (you) with its wings" (Mal 3:20). Balaam the wicked (also) prophesied about those troubles and said: "Woe to whoever is alive when God brings it about!" (Num 24:23).

The third sign. The Holy One, blessed be He, will rain a dew of blood for three days, but it will appear to the nations of the world to be a dew of water. They will drink of it and die. Moreover, (some) wicked ones among Israel will also drink of it and die, whereas others who are wavering (in their faith) will fall ill. The world will experience great distress during those three days, as scripture says: "I will place portents in the heavens and on earth: blood, fire, and columns of smoke" (Joel 3:3).

The fourth sign. The Holy One, blessed be He, will rain a dew of healing for three days and three nights—in order to counteract the effects of the blood—and all those who were wavering will drink of it, and those who had become ill will be cured, as scripture states: "I will be like dew for Israel; he will bloom like the lily" (Hos 14:6).

[53] From the synagogal prayer *ʿAlēnu*; see *Seder Rav ʿAmram* and also *Maḥzor Vitry* §99.

[54] See *Gen. Rab.* 6.6 (Theodor-Albeck, 46) and the notes of Theodor *ad loc.* According to this tradition, the notion of a celestial "screen" or "sheath" for the sun derives from Ps 19:5 (לשמש שם אהל בהם, "among them *He placed a tent for the sun*"). This "tent" (i.e., sheath) serves to temper the sun's heat on earth under normal circumstances, but here also the future loss of this sheath is envisioned: "in the time to come, the Holy One, blessed be He, will strip off its sheath from it and burn it (the world). What is the proof text? 'That coming day will burn them'" (Mal 3:19). Note also *Midr. Tanḥ.*, Teṣawweh §8.

The fifth sign. A ruler shall arise in Rome, and he will devastate large areas. He will capture Egypt, as scripture affirms: "he will stretch his hand out against the north" (Zeph 2:13). He will turn his anger upon Israel, laying a heavy tax upon them, and he will seek to make them perish from the world, as scripture states: "he will turn his face(s) toward the strongholds of his land" (Dan 11:19): (the term "strongholds" [מעוזי]) signifies those among Israel who are strong among the nations, and "his face(s)" (פניו) signifies his anger and his wrath which he will direct against them.

The sixth sign. The Holy One, blessed be He, will produce at that time the Messiah of the lineage of Joseph, whose name is Nehemiah ben Hushiel. He will be accompanied by warriors "from the descendants of Zerah the son of Judah" (cf. Neh 11:24). He will come with all the forces of Israel who are in those places and fight a battle with the king of Edom and those rulers allied with him. He will kill the king of Edom and the remainder (of the latter's army) will flee. He will approach Jerusalem and capture it, and all Israel will hear (of this) and gather themselves to him. The king of Egypt will conclude a peace treaty with him. He will kill all the nations who are in the environment of Jerusalem:[55] all the (remaining) nations will hear (of this), and a great fear will overcome them.

The seventh sign. Armilos will emerge from that stone statue of a woman which is in Rome. They say about him that the stone will give birth to him. He will be twelve cubits tall [literally "long"] and two cubits wide, and there will be between his eyes a space equaling one span. He is the Messiah of the descendants of Esau. He will gather all the nations, and then say to the descendants of Esau: "Bring to me the Torah which I gave you . . . ." All Israel will suddenly be confused, but Nehemiah b. Hushiel will arise, he and thirty warriors with weapons (concealed) beneath their garments, and they will take a Torah scroll and bring it to him [i.e., to Armilos]. They will read out before him: "You shall have no other gods before Me!" (Exod 20:3). He will say to them: "This is not (my Torah) at all!" Nehemiah will say to him: "You are no deity, only Satan!" He will quickly flee, but he [Armilos] will command his servants, (saying), "Seize him and hang him!" (Nevertheless he will effect his escape) and fight a battle with him and kill a large number of them. Then the wrath of Armilos will intensify, and he will assemble all the nations and come to do battle with Israel "between the seas and the beautiful holy mountain" (Dan 11:45). Israel will effect a great slaughter among them, but he [Armilos] will kill the Messiah, and when Israel perceives that the Messiah has been slain, their courage will melt away and they

[55] See Ezek 44:9; Joel 4:17; *Pss. Sol.* 17:28.

will flee. The world will experience great trouble. They will hide themselves for twenty-five days in caves and in pits, and the rest will lock themselves within Jerusalem. He [Armilos] will turn toward her [Jerusalem] to wage war and destroy it for the second time, but he will not succeed (in doing so).

The eighth sign. "At that time the great (angelic) leader Michael will arise" (Dan 12:1), and at that time Elijah will come along with the Messiah of the lineage of David in order to fulfill what scripture has said: "he shall turn the heart of the fathers to the sons, and the heart of the sons to the fathers" (Mal 3:24). The Messiah will not need to wage battle: he will only have to fix his eyes on Armilos in order to exterminate him from the world, as scripture states: "he will slay the wicked (one) with the breath of his mouth" (Isa 11:4).

The ninth sign. The Messiah will request of the Holy One, blessed be He, that He resurrect the dead. The Messiah of the lineage of Joseph will be the first of all those who are brought back to life, and he will become the emissary of the Messiah of the lineage of David. He will send him into all the lands wherein Israel dwells, and they will be gathered together from every corner of the earth. Then he will send him beyond the rivers of Cush, and he will lead forth the (lost) ten tribes. He will also bring out the Temple vessels from Rome. (In) every place where the Messiah of the lineage of Joseph goes which contains Israelite dead, he will resurrect them and bring all of them with him, as scripture says: "behold, these will come from afar, [and behold, these from the north and from the west, and these from the land of Syene]" (Isa 49:12).

The tenth sign. The coming of Gog and Magog, just as is described in the book of Ezekiel.[56]

May the Holy One, blessed be He, grant us the privilege of seeing it! Amen, may it happen quickly during our lifetime! May His will be done! Amen!

*The following somewhat variant lines render T-S A45.8 fol. 1 based on the present author's transcription of the photograph published by Hopkins, *Miscellany*, 16. The fragment commences toward the end of the sixth sign, beginning with the word יברחו.

. . . they will flee before him (i.e., Nehemiah b. Hushiel). He will enter Egypt and capture it, and he will kill all the (gentile) nations in the vicinity

[56] See chaps. 38–39.

of Jerusalem. All the nations will hear (about this), and fear and dread will fall upon them.

The seventh sign. Armilos the Satan[57] will emerge from the stone statue that is in Rome. They say with regard to him that the stone will give birth to him. He will be twelve cubits long, and between his two eyes is (the distance of) a span. He is the Messiah of the party of Esau. He will assemble all the nations and say to them: "I am God," and all the nations will believe him. He will say to the party of Esau: "Bring me the Torah which I gave to you!" Then they will bring him their book of lies,[58] and he will assent, saying: "Truly this is what I gave to you!" Israel will suddenly be confused, but Nehemiah b. Hushiel will come, he and thirty warriors accompanying him with weapons (concealed) beneath their garments, and they will take a Torah scroll and come to him and read aloud before him: "You shall have no other gods before Me!" (Exod 20:3). He will say to them: "This is not (my Torah) at all!" Nehemiah will say to him: "You are no deity, only Satan!" Immediately he [Armilos] will cry out against him and say to his servants: "Seize him and hang him!" He will do battle with them and kill many of them. Then the anger of Armilos will intensify, and he will gather all the nations and advance to make war on Israel "between the seas and the beautiful holy mountain" (Dan 11:45). He will strike a great blow against Israel and will kill the Messiah. At that time the Holy One, blessed be He, will issue a command to the sun and it will at that time remain underground, and the world will be dark. Israel will experience great distress. When Israel sees that the Messiah is dead, their courage will fail and they will run away, and the world will experience extremely great distress. Israel will conceal themselves in caves for forty-five days, sustaining themselves (during that time) on weeds. Why was Armilos given the power to kill the Messiah of the lineage of Ephraim? It was done so as to break the hearts of those dissidents among Israel who said: "The Messiah for whom we were waiting has come and been killed. There is no longer any redemption for us in the wilderness."[59] Many of these will immediately commit apostasy and become joined with the gentile nations. But the gentile nations will slay them nevertheless, as scripture foresees: "they will kill with the sword all of those among My people who commit sin" (Amos 9:10).

The eighth sign. "At that time the great (angelic) leader Michael will arise" (Dan 12:1), and at that time Elijah will come along with the Messiah of the lineage of David in order to fulfill what scripture has said: "he shall

[57] ארמילוס השטן.
[58] כתב שקריהם.
[59] For the final clause, the manuscript appears to read ואין לנו עוד ישועה ב׳מ׳ד׳.

turn the heart of the fathers to the sons, and the heart of the sons to the fathers" (Mal 3:24). The Messiah will not need to wage battle: he will only have to fix his eyes on Armilos in order to exterminate him from the world, as scripture states: "he will slay the wicked (one) with the breath of his mouth" (Isa 11:4).

The ninth sign. The Messiah will request of the Holy One, blessed be He, that He resurrect the dead, and the Messiah of the lineage of Joseph will be resurrected first. (*End of fragment*)

ʾ*Otot ha-Mašiaḥ* (Signs of the Messiah)[60]

The first sign. The Holy One, blessed be He, will cause three kings to arise who are apostates from their religion.[61] They will behave deceptively, for they will make themselves appear to people (as if) they serve the Holy One, blessed be He, but they (in fact) do not serve (Him). They will lead astray and confuse the entire created order,[62] and all the nations of the world will become apostates by following their laws. Moreover, (certain) wicked ones of Israel who have given up hope in (Israel's) eventual redemption will commit apostasy against the Holy One, blessed be He, and abandon His veneration. Regarding this generation, scripture states: "truth will be driven away" (Isa 59:15). What does "driven away" (נעדרת) mean?[63] It means that those in possession of the truth will become like herds of animals (עדרים עדרים) and they will depart and flee and hide themselves among caves and underground burrows.[64] All the mighty ones of that generation will perish, faithful ones will cease to exist, the "gates of wisdom"

[60] Jellinek, *BHM* 2:58–63, who took it in turn from R. Makhir, ספר אבקת רוכל (Amsterdam: Nehemiah b. Abraham, 1716), 2b-5b. This edition reprints the Rimini imprint of 1526 (see 2b-4a), which is apparently the first printed edition. See M[oritz] Steinschneider, *Catalogus librorum hebraeorum in bibliotheca Bodleiana* (Berlin: Ad. Friedlaender, 1852–60), 1638–40. A variant version of this apocalypse appears in Oxford Ms. Heb. d. 11 (2797), the *Sefer ha-Zikronot* or the so-called *Chronicles of Yeraḥmeel*; see Eli Yassif, ed., *Sefer ha-Zikronot huʾ Divrey ha-Yamim le-Yeraḥmeʾel* (Tel Aviv: Tel Aviv University, 2001), 436–42. Another edition is supplied by Even-Shmuel, *Midreshey Geʾullah*, 318–23; see his textual notes on pp. 425–26. The translation and annotations found in David C. Mitchell, *The Message of the Psalter: An Eschatological Programme in the Book of Psalms* (JSOTSup 252; Sheffield: Sheffield Academic Press, 1997), 308–14; 336–40 (text) must be used with caution.

[61] Read בדיניהם (Yassif, 436) in place of Jellinek's בדעתם.

[62] Yassif: ומקלקלין את כל הבריות, "they will corrupt the entire created order."

[63] Instead of this question, Yassif has simply כלומר, "that is to say . . . ."

[64] See *m. Soṭah* 9.15; *b. Sanh.* 97a; and especially *Cant. Rab.* 2.4: להיכן הולכת דבי ר׳ ינא׳ אומר הולכת ויושבת לה עדרים עדרים במדבר, "where does it (truth) go? The school of R. Yannai taught: It goes and takes up residence like flocks of animals in the wilderness." See also *Pesiq. Rab Kah.* 5.9 (Mandelbaum, 1:98); *Pesiq. Rab.* §15 (Ish-Shalom, 75b).

will be hidden,[65] and the world will become different.[66] At that time there will be neither king nor prince in Israel, as scripture says: "Israel will dwell for many days without a king or a leader" (Hos 3:4). Jacob will have no academy heads, no gaon, no faithful shepherds, no pious ones, and no wonder workers.[67] The celestial doors will be locked, and the gates of support and sustenance will be closed.

At the time that the Messiah is revealed by His power,[68] a generation will depart and collapse into its grave while still alive[69] because of the harsh, fickle, and disturbing things that those three kings decree. And while they are decreeing that one should commit apostasy against the Temple, the Lord, and the Torah, the Holy One, blessed be He, will decree that the evil empire[70] will enjoy world sovereignty for no longer than nine months, as scripture states: "therefore He will give them until the time when she who is pregnant [has given birth]" (Mic 5:2), and the word "therefore" (לכן) signifies here an oath, as where it is said: "therefore (לכן) I have sworn an oath to the family of Eli" (1 Sam 3:14). They shall issue harsh decrees, and they shall increase the tax on Israel tenfold. Whoever formerly paid ten now pays one hundred, and everyone who formerly paid eight now pays eighty, and they will cut off the head of all those who do not have it. During all these nine months they will issue one new decree after another, each one harsher than its predecessor.

Then some extremely ugly people from the end of the earth will appear, and everyone who sees them will die on account of the terror evoked by them. They will not need to wage war, for they kill everyone by fear of them alone. Each one of them has two heads and seven eyes; they will glow like fire and be as swift in their movement as deer. At that time Israel will cry out and say, "Woe! Alas!" Children from Israel will become frightened, and each of them will come and hide themselves beneath their father and mother, saying, "Woe, my father! Alas, my mother! What shall we do?!?" Their parents will respond to them (saying): "Now we must rely on the (promised) redemption of Israel!"

[65] Cf. *b. Soṭah* 13b, where the expression "gates of wisdom" refers to the heavenly source of the Mosaic Torah. Yassif has instead כל אנשי החוכמה, "all the wise men."

[66] Yassif: והעולם עומד ושומם, "and the world will become desolate."

[67] Yassif: ולא חסידים לבטל אשמ[ה], "and no pious ones to annul [its] guilt."

[68] ובזמן שמשיח יתגלה בגבורתו. Yassif has והשבוע שמשיח נגלה בו, "in the week in which the Messiah is revealed"; cf. *b. Sanh.* 97a.

[69] The latter part of the preceding paragraph and the initial part of the present paragraph are loosely paraphrased in §33 of *Hekhalot Rabbati*, part of a late expansion of *Sefer Zerubbabel* that emanates from the seventeenth-century Sabbatian sect. I have followed the reading ונופל בקבר בחייו contained therein; see Even-Shmuel, *Midreshey Ge'ullah*, 425.

[70] Yassif: אדום, "Edom," i.e., Christian Rome.

The second sign. The Holy One, blessed be He, will introduce heat into the world from the heat of the sun, along with consumption and fever, many terrible diseases, plague, and pestilence. Every day there will die among the gentile nations one million people, and all the wicked ones among Israel will perish. (This will continue) until the nations of the world weep and cry out: "Woe to us! Where can we go and to where shall we flee?" Everyone will dig their own grave while they still retain strength, and then they will wish for death. They will conceal themselves in arid places and among towers and crevices in order to cool themselves, and they will go into caves and earthen caverns. And if you should ask how the righteous will be delivered from the heat of the sun, (the answer is that) the Holy One, blessed be He, will render that heat medicinal (for them), as scripture says: "O those who revere My name, a sun of righteousness will rise for you, and it will heal (you) with its wings" (Mal 3:20). Balaam the wicked prophesied about these troubles[71] (when he said), "Woe to whoever is alive when God brings it about!" (Num 24:23).

The third sign. The Holy One, blessed be He, will cause a dew of blood to fall, but it will appear to be water to the gentile nations. They will drink of it and die. Moreover the wicked of Israel—those who have abandoned all hope of redemption—will drink of it and die. However, the righteous—those who have maintained faith in the Holy One, blessed be He—will suffer no harm at all, as scripture states: "the wise will shine like the brightness of the sky" (Dan 12:3). The whole world will become blood for three entire days, as Hosea [*sic*][72] has said: "I will place portents in the heavens and on earth: blood, fire, and columns of smoke" (Joel 3:3).

The fourth sign. The Holy One, blessed be He, will cause a dew of healing to fall in order to counteract the blood, and those who were wavering will drink of it and be healed of their illness, as scripture states: "I will be like dew for Israel: he will bloom like a lily and extend his roots like Lebanon" (Hos 14:6).

The fifth sign. The Holy One, blessed be He, will turn the sun to darkness for thirty days, as scripture says: "The sun will be changed into darkness, and the moon to blood" (Joel 3:4). After thirty days the Holy One, blessed be He, will return it to its former state, as scripture says: "they will be gathered together like a group of prisoners in a pit and locked away in prison, and after many days they will be recalled" (Isa 24:22). The gentile nations will feel fear and shame, for they will realize that it is on account of

[71] Read ועל אותן צרות in place of Jellinek's ועל אותו עדות.
[72] This mistaken attribution presumably belongs with the proof text for the fourth sign.

Israel that all these signs are occurring, and many of them will secretly become Jewish, as scripture has envisioned: "those who observe (a religion devoted to) worthless vanities will abandon their faith" (Jonah 2:9).

The sixth sign. As we stated above, the Holy One, blessed be He, will grant the wicked Edom sovereignty over the entire world.[73] A final king[74] will arise in Rome, and he will rule the entire world for nine months and bring about the destruction of many regions. His wrath will increase against Israel, and he will burden them with a heavy tax. At that time Israel will experience great distress on account of the multitude of restrictive edicts and disturbances affecting them which will recur every day. Israel will undergo decline and be subject to annihilation at that time, and there will be no one to help Israel. Isaiah prophesied about this time when he said: "he saw that there was no person; he was astonished that there was no one to interpose" (Isa 59:16).

When the nine months are completed, the Messiah of the lineage of Joseph—whose name is Nehemiah b. Hushiel—will appear accompanied by the tribes of Ephraim, Manasseh, Benjamin, and some of the tribe of Gad. Israelites who dwell in every region will hear that the Lord's Messiah has come, and a small number from every region and every city will assemble around him to fulfill what is said in Jeremiah: "Come back, O apostate children—utterance of the Lord! For I have been your Lord, and I will take one of you from the city and two of you from a family and bring you to Zion" (Jer 3:14).

The Messiah of the lineage of Joseph will come and fight a battle with the ruler of Edom. He will win a victory against Edom, kill great heaps of them,[75] and also kill the king of Edom. He will devastate the province of Rome. He will recover some of the Temple vessels that had been deposited in the palace of Julianos Caesar[76] and come to Jerusalem. Israel will hear (about this) and gather themselves to him. The ruler of Egypt will make a peace treaty with him.[77] He [Nehemiah] will slay all the people of the

[73] See the description of the first sign.

[74] Or מלך אחר, "another king"; Even-Shmuel (*Midreshey Ge'ullah*, 320) has מלך אחד, "a king." I have translated this text as above because of the explicit presence of the motif of the "Last (Roman) King" in the preceding apocalypse.

[75] ויהרוג מהם תילי תילים. The meaning of this expression derives from an exegesis of the word תלתלים in Cant 5:16; cf. *b. ʿErub.* 21b and Rashi's commentary to the biblical verse.

[76] יולייי"נוס קיסר. Samuel Krauss suggests emending this reading to יוסטינוס, "Justinos"; see his *Studien zur byzantinisch-jüdischen Geschichte* (Leipzig: Buchhandlung Gustav Fock, 1914), 106 n. 3. For a list of the Temple vessels that were carried off as spoil and deposited in Rome, see *'Abot R. Nat.* A §41 (Schechter, 67a). Note also *b. Meʿil.* 17b; *b. Yoma* 57a and Rashi's commentary *ad loc.*

[77] This same event is also signaled in the *Prayer of R. Šimʿōn b. Yoḥai*; see Even-Shmuel, *Midreshey Ge'ullah*, 297.

regions surrounding Jerusalem up to Damascus and Ashkelon, and all the people of the world will hear (about this), and a great fear will fall upon them.

The seventh sign. The Holy One, blessed be He, who is the Master of Marvels, will effect a miracle in the world. They say that in Rome there is a marble statue (in) the likeness of a beautiful maiden: she was not fashioned by a human hand; rather, the Holy One, blessed be He, created her so by His power. Certain wicked ones belonging to the gentile nations will come—utterly worthless fellows—and excite "her" and have sexual relations with her, and the Holy One, blessed be He, will preserve their seminal emissions within the statue. He will make a creature with it and form with it an offspring: she will (suddenly) split open and a human form will emerge from her. His name is Armilos the Satan; this is the one whom the gentile nations term "Antichristo(s)."[78] He is twelve cubits long and twelve[79] cubits wide, and the distance between his two eyes is a span's length, and they are deep-set[80] (and) bloodshot. The hair on his head is like the color of gold, the soles of his feet are green, and he has two heads.

He will come to the wicked Edomites and say to them: "I am the Messiah! I am your god!" They will immediately believe him and elevate him over themselves as ruler, and all the descendants of Esau will join forces with him and come to him. He will march forth and subdue all the regions. He will say to the descendants of Esau: "Bring before me my revelation[81] which I gave to you!" They will bring him their "frivolity,"[82] and he will respond to them: "This is indeed what I gave to you!" He will address the nations of the world (saying), "Believe in me, for I am your Messiah!" They will immediately put their trust in him.

At that time he will send for Nehemiah b. Hushiel and for all Israel, saying to them: "Bring to me your Torah and bear witness to me that I am God!" Suddenly they will grow fearful and be perplexed. But at that time Nehemiah b. Hushiel will arise with thirty thousand warriors from among the forces of the tribe of Ephraim, and they will bring a Torah scroll and read aloud before him: "I am the Lord your God! You shall have no other gods before Me!" (Exod 20:2–3). He [Armilos] will say to them: "There is nothing like this at all in your Torah! Come and bear witness to me that I am God just as all the gentile nations have done!" Immediately Nehemiah will rise up to oppose him. He [Armilos] will command his attendants (say-

[78] אנטיקרי״שטו.

[79] Even-Shmuel: "two."

[80] So Jellinek (עמוקות); Even-Shmuel reads עקמות, "crooked."

[81] Literally, "my Torah which I gave to you" (תורתי שנתתי לכם).

[82] תפלותם. For gauging the semantic range of this term, see *m. Soṭah* 3.4.

ing), "Seize him and bind him!" But Nehemiah b. Hushiel will arise, along with the thirty thousand who are with him, and do battle with him, and they will kill two hundred thousand of his (troops).

The anger of Armilos the wicked will increase in intensity, and he will assemble all the forces of the nations of the world in "the Valley of Decision" (Joel 4:14). They will do battle with Israel, and they [Israel] will slay great heaps of them, whereas they will fatally strike only a small number of Israelites, but the Lord's Messiah will be killed. The ministering angels will come, take him, and conceal him among the ancestors of the world. The courage of Israel will immediately fail, and their strength will dissipate. Armilos the wicked will not know that the Messiah is dead, for if he knew (that were the case), he would not allow Israel to have a single survivor or fugitive. At that time all the nations of the world will expel Israel from their territories and will not permit them to dwell alongside them in their countries. They will say: "You see this despicable and lowly people who rebelled against us; can they possibly raise up a king?" Israel will experience trouble the like of which has never happened to her before during the days of the world up to that time.

At that time Michael will arise to purge the wicked from Israel, as scripture states: "At that time Michael, the great prince who watches over the sons of Your people, will arise, and there will be a time of trouble such as has not taken place from the time (Israel) became a nation until that time, and at that time all of your people who are found inscribed in the book will escape" (Dan 12:1). All of Israel will immediately flee into the deserts, whereas everyone who is entertaining doubts about their religion will turn to the nations of the world and state: "This is the redemption for which we have been waiting, for the Messiah is dead!" All those who are no longer anticipating the redemption will be embarrassed by it (i.e., the Messiah's demise) and they will turn to the gentile nations. At that time the Holy One, blessed be He, will test Israel and refine them like silver and gold, as it is said in Zechariah: "I will bring the third part through the fire, and I will purge them (of dross) as one purges silver" (Zech 13:9), and as it is written in Ezekiel: "I will purge from among you those who rebelled and disobeyed Me" (Ezek 20:38), and as it is written in Daniel: "They will be purged and made white: many will be refined and they will convict the wicked. None of the wicked will understand, but the wise will understand" (Dan 12:10).

The entire remnant of Israel—the sanctified and purified ones—will remain in the desert of Judah for forty-five days. They will forage and feed on salt-plant and pluck leaves of shrubbery (cf. Job 30:4), and by them will be fulfilled what is said in Hosea: "Therefore, behold, I will entice her and lead her out to the desert, and I will console her" (Hos 2:16).[83] What is the

[83] See the targum to this verse and the commentary of Radaq *ad loc.*

scriptural basis of the forty-five days? Scripture states: "from the time of the removal of the daily offering and of the installation of the desolating abomination will be 1,290 days" (Dan 12:11), and it is (also) written: "happy is the one who waits and attains 1,335 days" (Dan 12:12). Consequently one learns that the difference between these two figures is forty-five days. At that time all the wicked of Israel will perish, for they are unworthy of experiencing redemption. Armilos will come and do battle with Egypt and capture it, as scripture states: "and the land of Egypt will no longer escape" (Dan 11:42). Then he will turn his face toward Jerusalem in order to destroy it a second time, as scripture says: "he will pitch the tents of his pavilion between the seas and the beautiful holy mountain. Yet he approaches his end, and no one will help him" (Dan 11:45).

The eighth sign. Michael will arise and blow three blasts on the shofar, as scripture attests: "and it shall come to pass on that day that a great shofar will be blown, and those who are lost in Assyria will come [along with those cast out in Egypt, and they will worship the Lord on the holy mountain in Jerusalem]" (Isa 27:13), and as it is written: "and the Lord God will blow the shofar and travel with the storm winds of the south" (Zech 9:14). At the first blast, the Messiah of the lineage of David and Elijah the prophet will be revealed to those proven righteous ones of Israel, the ones who had fled into the desert of Judah, at the end of the forty-five days. They will restore their hearts, invigorate their weakened hands, and strengthen their tottering knees. All Israel—those who remain throughout the whole world—will hear the sound of the shofar and realize that God has remembered them and that complete redemption has arrived. They will gather together and come (to Jerusalem), as scripture says: "those who are lost in Assyria will come [along with those cast out in Egypt, and they will worship the Lord on the holy mountain in Jerusalem]" (Isa 27:13). Fear and trembling will fall upon the nations of the world on account of that sound, and terrible diseases will afflict them. Israel will gird themselves for departure, and the Messiah of the lineage of David will come, together with Elijah the prophet and those righteous ones who returned from the desert of Judah and with all those who have assembled from Israel. He will enter Jerusalem, climb the steps of the Temple ruins,[84] and take his seat there.

Armilos will hear that a king has arisen for Israel, and he will say: "How long will this despicable and contemptible nation behave this way?" He will immediately muster all the forces of the nations of the world and come to do battle with the Lord's Messiah. Then the Holy One, blessed be He, will deem it unnecessary for him (i.e., the Messiah) to engage in battle. Instead, He will say to him: "Remain by My right hand!" (Ps 110:1), and He will

[84] 'ויעלה במעלות בית הנשאר'.

inform Israel: "Stand still and behold the Lord's deliverance which He effects for you today!" (Exod 14:13). Then the Holy One, blessed be He, will wage war with them, as scripture says: "and the Lord will go forth and wage war against those nations as at the time He fought on the day of battle" (Zech 14:3). The Holy One, blessed be He, will rain down fire and brimstone from heaven, as scripture states: "I will contend with him using plague and blood; and I will rain down flooding rains, hailstones, fire, and brimstone upon him, his troops, and the many peoples allied with him" (Ezek 38:22). Armilos the wicked will immediately die, both he and all his army, and so too (will perish) the wicked Edom who destroyed the Temple of our God and exiled us from our land. At that time Israel will exact much vengeance against them, as scripture foretells: "the house of Jacob will become fire, and the house of Joseph will be a flame, and the house of Esau will serve as dry chaff: [they will burn them up and consume them, and no survivor will remain for the house of Esau, for the Lord has spoken]" (Obad 1:18).

The ninth sign. Michael will blow a loud blast (on the shofar), and the graves of the dead will split open in Jerusalem, and the Holy One, blessed be He, will resurrect them. The Messiah of the lineage of David and Elijah the prophet will then come and resurrect the Messiah of the lineage of Joseph, the one who expired by the gates of Jerusalem. They will send out the Messiah of the lineage of David[85] for the sake of the remnant of Israel that remains scattered among all the lands. Immediately all the rulers of the nations of the world will lift them up on their shoulders and bring them to the Lord (cf. Isa 49:22).

The tenth sign. Michael will blow a loud blast (on the shofar), and the Holy One, blessed be He, will lead forth all the tribes located beyond the river of Gozan and from Halah and from Habor and from the cities of Media (cf. 2 Kgs 17:6).[86] They will come together with the "people of Moses" (בני משה),[87] (a large group) impossible to number or to measure.

[85] So Jellinek. Even-Shmuel amends to: "the Messiah of the lineage of David will dispatch him (the Messiah of the lineage of Joseph)." This correction is based on the description provided about the mission of the revivified Messiah of the lineage of Joseph in the "Ten Signs Apocalypse" rendered above.

[86] The eventual return of the "ten lost tribes" from their Assyrian deportation was widely anticipated in biblical and postbiblical eschatological lore. See 1 Chr 5:26; Isa 11:11; Jer 31:8; Ezek 37:19–24; *4 Ezra* 13:34–45. The distinction assumed here between this distinct group of tribes and the "people of Moses" who will supposedly join them at the time of their return betrays a dependence on the medieval Eldad ha-Dani legends.

[87] This is the designation employed by the legendary medieval itinerant Eldad ha-Dani for the pious levitical community inhabiting the region beyond the "river of sand" or Sambatyon river. See

"The land before them will be like the garden of Eden, and behind them a flame will burn" (cf. Joel 2:3; note Ezek 36:35), and nothing will remain alive among the nations of the world.[88] At the time that the tribes depart, clouds of glory will encompass them,[89] and the Holy One, blessed be He, will march before them, as scripture states: "the breaker will go up before them" (Mic 2:13).[90] The Holy One, blessed be He, will open for them springs connected with the Tree of Life in order to supply them with water on the way, as it says in Isaiah: "I will open rivers on the high places and fountains in the midst of the plains; I will turn the wilderness into a pool of water and the dry land into springs of water" (Isa 41:18), and it is written: "they will not be hungry or thirsty; heat and sun will not afflict them, [for the One showing them mercy will lead them and He will guide them by springs of water]" (Isa 49:10).

May the Holy One, blessed be He, grant us the merit to witness the redemption soon! May He grant us the merit to see the (rebuilt) Temple![91] May He fulfill for us the verse in which it is written: "Behold I will bring back the captives of the tents of Jacob and show mercy to his places of dwelling; the city (i.e., Jerusalem) will be rebuilt on its mound and the palace will reoccupy its proper place" (Jer 30:18), and may He confirm for us all of His redemptive deeds and assurances which have been spoken through His prophets! For it is written: "at that time I will bring you, and at that time I will assemble you so that I might make you a name and (an object of) praise" (Zeph 3:20).

The *Signs of the Messiah* are concluded.

Sefer Eldad ha-Dani (*BHM* 2:xxviii-ix, 102–13; 3:6–11; 5:17–21) 2:103ff.; Elkan Nathan Adler, ed., *Jewish Travellers in the Middle Ages: 19 Firsthand Accounts* (London: Routledge, 1930; repr., New York: Dover, 1987), 12–15; Micha Joseph bin Gorion, *Mimekor Israel: Selected Classical Jewish Folktales* (ed. Emanuel bin Gorion; trans. I. M. Lask; Bloomington/Indianapolis: Indiana University Press, 1990), 126–28. The twelfth-century Muslim heresiologist Shahrastānī relates that the eighth-century Jewish messianic pretender Abū ʿĪsā al-Iṣfahānī "traveled to the Banū Mūsā b. ʿImrān, the ones who are beyond the sand (river), in order to have them hear the word of God" (William Cureton, ed., *Kitāb al-milal wa-al-niḥal: Book of Religious and Philosophical Sects, by Muhammad al-Shahrastáni* [London, 1846; repr., Leipzig: O. Harrassowitz, 1923], 168.8–9). See further Israel Friedlaender, "The Jews of Arabia and the Rechabites," *JQR* n.s. 1 (1910–11): 252–57, as well as the excursus on the "people of Moses" in the present volume.

[88] Note the final clause of Joel 2:3 (ואחריו מדבר שממה וגם פליטה לא היתה לו).

[89] Cf. Isa 60:8. For a stimulating survey of the prominence of the motif of the "divine cloud" in Jewish eschatology, see Naphtali Wieder, *The Judean Scrolls and Karaism* (London: East and West Library, 1962), 35–48.

[90] Compare *Midr. Tanḥ*. Buber, Wayeṣe §24 (end); *Pesiq. Rab.* §35 (Ish-Shalom, 161a); and the commentary of Radaq *ad loc.*

[91] Hebrew בית הבחירה. This is a common rabbinic designation for the Temple based on Deut 12:5 and its parallels. See *m. Maʿaś. Š.* 5.12; *t. Peʾah* 4.7; *t. Sanh.* 4.5; *t. Menaḥ.* 7.8; *b. Naz.* 25a–b; etc.

Ten Further Things Pertaining to the Days of the Messiah[92]

Corresponding to these ten signs, the Holy One, blessed be He, will refurbish Jerusalem with ten kinds of precious stones. These will be ruby, topaz, emerald, turquoise, sapphire, diamond, beryl, onyx, jasper, and gold—ten types of stones.[93] And for the reconstruction of the Temple He (the Holy One, blessed be He) will supplement[94] them with two more; namely, porphyry and carbuncle, as scripture states: "I will inlay your walls with porphyry, and your gates with carbuncle" (Isa 54:12).[95] Similarly, the Holy One, blessed be He, is planning to restore to Israel ten things that had disappeared from among them,[96] as scripture says: "I will be pleased with it and glorify it" (Hag 1:8). Five of these things were missing from the Second Temple; namely, the Ark and the cherubim, the ointment for anointing, the proper arrangement of the woods on the altar, the Urim and Thummim, and the Holy Spirit,[97] along with five other things. The Holy One, blessed be He, is going to intensify the illumination of the sun 343 times more than its current brightness, as scripture states: "the light of the moon will be like the light of the sun, and the light of the sun will be sevenfold (stronger); it will be like the light of seven days on the day when the Lord bandages the fractured state of His people and heals the severity of its wound" (Isa 30:26). And from whence do we learn that the factor will be 343? Because it is interpreted thus by Jonathan b. ʿUzziel: "the brightness [of the moon] will be like the brightness of the sun, [and the brightness of the sun] will become 343 times brighter, like the brightness of seven days."[98] For when you multiply seven by seven the product is forty-nine; (then) multiplying them (again) by seven—as scripture says: "like the light of seven days" (ibid.)—consequently the total is 343.

[92] Oxford Ms. Heb. d. 11 (2797) as transcribed and published by Yassif, 442–43. See also Jellinek, *BHM* 6:118–20; Even-Shmuel, *Midreshey Geʾullah*, 345–46, where this piece is entitled נחמות מלך המשיח.

[93] Jellinek: הרי עשר.

[94] Jellinek: והקב״ה מוסיף.

[95] Compare Rev 21:18–20.

[96] Jellinek: עשרה דברים שאבדן הקב״ה מהם וחסרן בבנין בית שני.

[97] See *b. Yoma* 21b and Rashi *ad* Hag 1:8. Since the *ketiv* verb ואכבד in Hag 1:8 is missing a final ה, the Sages interpreted this spelling to signify that the Second Temple would be lacking "five" (ה = 5) attributes that the First Temple possessed.

[98] Jellinek: ויהא זיהור סיהרא כזיהור שמשא וזיהור שמשא עתיד לזוהרא כזוהר על חד תלת מאה וארבעין ותלתא כזוהר שבעת יומיא. As the witness indicates, this is a rendition of *Tg. Neb.* to Isa 30:26.

So too the Holy One, blessed be He, will cause the righteous to shine with an intensity equal to this same number, for scripture says: "and His friends (will be) like the emergence of the sun at its peak intensity" (Judg 5:31). We have it translated (into Aramaic as): "His servants, the righteous ones, are destined to shine like the brightness of His glory, (shining) 343 times brighter like the brightness of the sun at its peak intensity."[99] Now those are seven things that the Holy One, blessed be He, is planning to restore to them. The crowns that they lost at Sinai,[100] the blessing of the grain, and the plumpness of the fruit[101]—the total sum (of things He will restore) is ten.[102]

And mirroring these (ten things), the Holy One, blessed be He, is planning to restore and produce ten great redemptive acts (הנחמות) along with the rest of their associated marvels. First will be the advent of the redeemer, as scripture says: "behold, your king will come to you, etc." (Zech 9:9). Second will be the ingathering of the exiles, as scripture states: "behold, I will bring them from a northern land, and I will gather them in from the ends of the earth, among them those who are blind and crippled" (Jer 31:7). Why "those who are blind and crippled"? This teaches that each and every righteous person will return just as they were when (they were) removed from the world. Whoever was blind will return blind at the time of their resurrection, whoever was crippled will return crippled at the time of their resurrection, and so too with regard to all the rest of the nation, so that each person might recognize his friend (and) so that others might not say that they were (actually) these (people).[103] After this, the Holy One, blessed be He, will heal them, as scripture promises: "then the crippled one will leap like a deer, etc." (Isa 35:6). Third will be the resurrection of the dead, as scripture states: "and many of those asleep in the soil of the ground will awaken, etc." (Dan 12:2). Fourth will be the rebuilding of the Temple in accordance with the vision of the structure that Ezekiel saw in his prophecy. Fifth: Israel will

[99] ועבדוהי צדיקיא עתידין לזהרא כזיהור יקריה על חד תלת מאה וארבעין ותלתין כזיהור שמשא בגבורתיה. Jellinek reads as follows: ועבדוהי צדיקיא עתידין לזיהרא כזיהור יקרא על חד תלת מאה וארבעין ותלתא כזיהור שמשא בתוקפיה.

[100] See *b. Šabb.* 88a.

[101] See *m. Soṭah* 9.12.

[102] Jellinek: והכתרים שנאבדו בסיני שכולם זכה בהם משה ונטלם שנאמר ומשה יקח את האהל ועתיד הקב"ה להחזירן דכתיב ושמחת עולם על ראשם עוד תעדי תפיך ויצאת במחול משחקים וברכת הדגן לשויין הפירות, "and the crowns which they lost at Sinai which Moses had won for all of them, and (then) he removed them, as scripture states: 'and Moses would take the Tent' (Exod 33:7), the Holy One, blessed be He, is planning to restore them, as it is written in scripture: 'and eternal joy upon their heads' (Isa 35:10; 51:11); 'You will again outfit yourself with your timbrels and go forth dancing with those enjoying themselves' (Jer 31:3). Also the blessing on grain which will be equal to that of the fruits."

[103] See the concurring explanations of Saadya and R. Hai Gaon.

implement the sovereignty of the jurisdiction of the Holy One, blessed be He, and His Torah throughout the entire world, as scripture says: "then *He* will revert to the nations a pure speech so that all of them can call *together* on the name of the Lord, etc." (Zeph 3:9).[104] Sixth: the Holy One, blessed be He, will destroy all the enemies of His people and exact vengeance on them, as scripture says: "I will take my vengeance out <on Edom>[105] by the hand of My people Israel" (Ezek 25:14). Seventh: the Holy One, blessed be He, will remove every pestilence and illness from Israel,[106] as scripture says: "and no one who dwells there will say 'I am ill'; the people inhabiting it will have (their) transgression forgiven" (Isa 33:24). Eighth: the Holy One, blessed be He, will prolong the days of Israel to be like those of a tree, as scripture states: "like the days of a tree will the days of my people be" (Isa 65:22), and it is written: "for one who dies at the age of one hundred will be considered a youth, and [the sinner] (who dies) when one hundred will be thought cursed" (Isa 65:20), and it is written: "He will destroy death forever, and the Lord will wipe away the tear(s) from every face, and He will remove the disgrace of His people, etc." (Isa 25:8). Ninth: the Holy One, blessed be He, will reveal Himself visibly to Israel, as scripture says: "the glory of the Lord will be revealed, and all flesh will behold (it) together, for the mouth of the Lord has spoken" (Isa 40:5). He will make all Israel to be prophets, as scripture states: "it shall come to pass after this that I will pour out My spirit upon all flesh, and your sons and your daughters will prophesy, etc." (Joel 3:1). Tenth: the Holy One, blessed be He, will remove the evil impulse (יצר הרע) from Israel, as scripture affirms: "and I shall give you a new heart, and I shall place a new spirit inside of you, and I shall extract the heart of stone from your flesh, and I shall give you a heart of flesh" (Ezek 36:26).

Happy is he who patiently awaits the day of redemption! He hopes that he will prove worthy of the reward (dispensed on that) delayed day! But if perchance their heart is overcome when "wars break out" (Exod 1:10), or when "he cries out, but He does not answer" (Prov 21:13), let me say (that) this is the consummation!

[104] The wording of the proof text in the Oxford manuscript varies slightly from that of the Masoretic Text; the variants are italicized. See Radaq *ad loc.* for further comments on the eschatological significance of this verse.

[105] The Oxford manuscript proof text lacks the word באדם, "on Edom," i.e., Christian Rome.

[106] Jellinek: שהקב״ה יסיר כל מחלה וכל נגע מישראל.

6

Responsum of R. Hai Gaon on the Topic of Redemption

HAI BEN SHERIRA GAON (939–1038 CE), head of the academy in Pumbedita, was one of the most influential Jewish thinkers of his era. The Andalusian Jewish chronicler Abraham Ibn Daud termed him the "last of the geonim" (סוף הגאונים), a tribute to the intellectual leadership he wielded among Mediterranean Jewry during the final decades of the tenth and initial half of the eleventh century.[1] In addition to his mastery of talmudic and halakhic lore, he was an accomplished poet and a disciplined philologist, well versed in Arabic and perhaps even Persian belles-lettres.[2] The surviving responsa of R. Hai, that is, his authoritative answers to questions posed to him from diaspora communities, are more numerous than from any other Babylonian gaon.

The present responsum, focusing on aspects of Jewish eschatological hopes and predictions, is heavily indebted to the earlier presentation of these themes in the seventh and eighth chapters of R. Saadya Gaon's *Kitāb al-Amānāt wa*ʾ*l-I*ʿ*tiqādāt*, or "Book of Beliefs and Opinions."[3] This is particularly noticeable from R. Hai's recurrent attempt to link almost every facet of the anticipated end-time events with a biblical proof text, a tactic ultimately grounded in R. Saadya's fierce ideological controversies with the Karaites, a Mesopotamian Jewish sect that cate-

[1] Adolf Neubauer, *Mediaeval Jewish Chronicles and Chronological Notes* (2 vols.; Oxford, 1887–95; repr., Amsterdam: Philo Press, 1970), 1:66. See also Gerson D. Cohen, *A Critical Edition with a Translation and Notes of the Book of Tradition (Sefer Ha-Qabbalah) by Abraham ibn Daud* (Philadelphia: Jewish Publication Society, 1967), 43–45 (text), 58–62 (translation). Note also the fragment of *Seder* ʿ*Olam Zuta* found in Eli Yassif, ed., *Sefer ha-Zikronot hu*ʾ *Divrey ha-Yamim le-Yeraḥme*ʾ*el* (Tel Aviv: Tel Aviv University, 2001), 368: ואחרי רב האיי לא נתמנה ראש ישיבה בבבל, "and after R. Hai no one was appointed to lead the Yeshiva in Babylon."

[2] For recent wide-ranging discussions of his scholastic attainments and literary output, see Robert Brody, *The Geonim of Babylonia and the Shaping of Medieval Jewish Culture* (New Haven and London: Yale University Press, 1998), 379 *s.v.* Hayya b. Sherira Gaon; Moshe Gil, *Jews in Islamic Countries in the Middle Ages* (trans. David Strassler; Leiden: Brill, 2004), 381–404.

[3] S. Landauer, ed., *Kitâb al-Amânât wa*ʾ*l-I*ʿ*tiqâdât von Sa*ʿ*adja b. Jûsuf al-Fajjûmî* (Leiden: Brill, 1880), 211.6–254.19; Saadia Gaon, *The Book of Beliefs and Opinions* (trans. Samuel Rosenblatt; Yale Judaica Series 1; New Haven: Yale University Press, 1948), 264–322.

gorically rejected rabbinic tradition and literature in favor of a close exegesis of the biblical text.[4]

This responsum was first published in R. Eliezer Ashkenazi, טעם זקנים (Frankfurt am Main: I. Kauffman, 1854), 59–61. Additional versions with some textual variation can be found in *ʾOṣar ha-Geonim: Tractate Sukkah* (ed. B. M. Lewin; Jerusalem: [s.n.], 1934), 72–75, and Abraham ben Azriel, *Sefer ʿArugat ha-Bosem* (ed. Ephraim E. Urbach; 4 vols.; Jerusalem: Mekitze Nirdamim, 1939), 1:256–63. The present translation renders the text published by Yehudah Even-Shmuel, *Midreshey Geʾullah* (2d ed.; Jerusalem: Mosad Bialik, 1954), 135–41.

Regarding what you asked to have explained to you; namely, how the redemption will transpire from its start to its end, and (regarding) the resurrection of the dead, and (regarding) the renewal of the heavens, were I to expound each and every matter in all its particulars, the appointed time would expire (before I could finish), but I will indicate some general points about each matter, and so I speak (as follows):

When seven years remain of the years comprising the "appointed time" (הקץ), these will be the years when redemption commences, for the Sages provided an identifying sign for them when they said: "the week (שבוע) when the son of David comes . . . ."[5] During that week Edom will rule over Israel for a period not less than nine months[6] and no more than three years. This is because Israel can only take sovereignty away from Edom, as scripture affirms: "Edom will have possession; Seʿir, their enemies, will have possession, but Israel will powerfully prevail. One from Jacob will rule, and he will destroy what remains of the city" (Num 24:18–19),[7] after Edom has taken sovereignty away from Asshur, as scripture states: "ships will come from the place of the Kittim, and they will afflict Asshur and ʿEver, and even he will be destroyed forever" (Num 24:24), after Asshur has taken sovereignty away from the Kenites, who are the Midianites, who are the Ishmaelites,[8] as scripture says: "however Qayin [i.e., the Kenite] will be consumed until the time when Asshur takes you captive" (Num 24:22). Therefore when we see that Edom has attained ruling authority over the

[4] See Avraham Grossman, "Jerusalem in Jewish Apocalyptic Literature," in *The History of Jerusalem: The Early Muslim Period, 638–1099* (ed. Joshua Prawer and Haggai Ben-Shammai; Jerusalem: Yad Izhak Ben-Zvi; New York: New York University Press, 1996), 305–9.

[5] *B. Sanh.* 97a; *Cant. Rab.* 2.4; *Pesiq. Rab Kah.* 5.9 (Mandelbaum, 1:97–98); Jellinek, *BHM* 3:141–43.

[6] See *b. Yoma* 10a; *Sanh.* 98b; *Yal. Šim.* Micah §552.

[7] Note the Targumim to these verses.

[8] This symbolic value correlates with that advanced in the *Secrets of R. Šimʿōn b. Yoḥai*. See Moritz Steinschneider, "Apokalypsen mit polemischer Tendenz," *ZDMG* 28 (1874): 636 n. 20.

land of Israel, we can affirm that our redemption is beginning, for scripture declares: "deliverers will ascend Mount Zion in order to judge the mountain of Esau, and sovereignty will belong to the Lord" (Obad 1:21).[9]

At that time [at God's instigation] there shall arise from among the descendants of Joseph a man who will be called the Lord's Messiah, and many people will assemble around him in Upper Galilee, and he will become their ruler.[10] Other people will continue gathering themselves to him, two or three coming from this province, and four or five from that one. Regarding this time[11] scripture states: "I will take you—one from a city, and two from a family" (Jer 3:14). However, most of Israel will remain in their places of exile, for they will not realize that the appointed time (הקץ) has come.

Then the Messiah of the lineage of Joseph will go up from Galilee to Jerusalem together with the people who had gathered themselves to him, and they will kill the official appointed by the ruler of Edom and the people associated with him. Regarding this time scripture states: "I will enact my vengeance against Edom by the agency of my people Israel" (Ezek 25:14). He will dwell in Jerusalem for a brief time.

When all the nations hear that a king for Israel has arisen in Jerusalem, they will rise up against them in the rest of the provinces and drive them out. They will say to them: "Up to now you dwelt loyally with us, since you had no ruler or prince of your own. But now that you have a ruler, you can no longer dwell in our land!" Many Israelites will go out into the wilderness regions adjacent to their (former) homelands—regarding this time scripture says: "I shall make you enter the wilderness of the peoples" (Ezek 20:35)—and they will dwell there in tents, as scripture says about this time: "I shall make you live in tents again" (Hos 12:10). Many of them will lack food and water, and they will experience suffering based on their (previous) deeds. Scripture states about this time: "I will make you pass beneath the rod, and I will bring you into the bond of the covenant" (Ezek 20:37). Many

[9] The requirement that Edom (i.e., Rome) must control Jerusalem before the redemption can begin is emphasized by Saadya, *K. al-Amānāt* (ed. Landauer), 239.11–13; 241.13–14.

[10] Compare the so-called *ʿAtidot R. Šimʿōn b. Yōḥai* (Even-Shmuel, *Midreshey Geʾullah*, 404): ואם זכו ישראל יצמח משיח בן יוסף בגליל העליון, "and if Israel is worthy, the Messiah of the lineage of Joseph will appear in Upper Galilee." See also *BHM* 3:141: ומחץ פאתי מואב אמר ר׳ הונא בשם ר׳ לוי מלמד שיהיו ישראל מקובצין בגליל העליון ויצפה עליהם שם משיח בן יוסף מתוך הגליל, "'and strike the corners of Moab' (Num 24:17). R. Huna said in the name of R. Levi: This teaches that Israel will gather in the Upper Galilee, and the Messiah of the lineage of Joseph will watch over them there within Galilee."

[11] ועל אותה שעה, literally "regarding this hour." Muslim eschatology envisions a series of catastrophic events that will occur immediately prior to the resurrection of the dead and the final judgment; these are mapped under the rubric "signs of the Hour" (*ashraṭ al-sāʿa*; cf. Q 47:18). It seems possible that Hai Gaon's apocalyptic lexicon mirrors this cultural environment.

will abandon the covenant with Israel, for they will be weary of their lives (as Jews), and about them scripture has stated: "I will purge from among you those who rebel and those who offend Me" (Ezek 20:38).

It will happen that when the Messiah of the lineage of Joseph and all the people who are with him have made their dwelling in Jerusalem, Armilos will hear the news about them. He will come and prepare charms and enticements so as to lead many astray by them. He will come up and do battle against Jerusalem, and he will defeat the Messiah of the lineage of Joseph and his people. Some of them he will kill, whereas others he will take captive, and he will divide their spoil. Regarding this time scripture states: "I will gather all the nations at Jerusalem to do battle" (Zech 14:2). Even the Messiah of the lineage of Joseph will be slain, and Israel will experience great distress. Scripture reveals about this time: "and they shall look to Me about the one whom they pierced, and they shall mourn for him as one would mourn an only child, and feel bitterness about him as one would feel bitterness about (the death of) a firstborn son. On that day the mourning will be great in Jerusalem" (Zech 12:10–11).[12]

Why will Armilos be granted the power to kill the Messiah of the lineage of Joseph? (This will occur) in order to break the heart(s) of the dissenters among Israel; that is, those who have no faith. They will say: "This is the man for whom we have been waiting? He has come and been slain! No more deliverance remains for [for Israel]!" They will abandon the covenant of Israel and cling to the gentile nations, but these latter will kill them, for scripture says about them: "all the sinners among My people will die by the sword" (Amos 9:10). Consequently those who remain in Jerusalem will be refined and purified, and also those who went out to the wilderness areas will be tested and refined; about two parts will be left over from these and about a third will be left of those. About them scripture testifies: "and it will come to pass in all the land—utterance of the Lord—that two portions in it will be cut off (and) will expire, and only a third will be left in it. And I will bring the third part into the fire, and I will refine them like one refines silver, and I will test them like one tests gold" (Zech 13:8–9). During that time all the "messianic birth-pangs"[13] will pass over them, those things that have been expounded in numerous places from scriptural verses and the teachings of our Sages, may their memory be blessed. Afterwards they will cry out, and the Holy One, blessed be He, will hearken to their cry, as scripture promises: "and he will call upon My name, and I will answer him" (Zech 13:9).

[12] See Ibn Ezra *ad loc.*

[13] חבלי משיח. Cf. "the tracks of the Messiah" (עקבות משיחא) in *m. Soṭah* 9.15.

At that time Elijah will appear in the desert among those who are located in the wilderness regions, and he will restore their hearts, as scripture says: "he shall turn the heart of the fathers to the children, and the heart of the children to their fathers" (Mal 3:24). The Messiah of the lineage of David will suddenly appear to those who are in the Land, for the Messiah of the lineage of Joseph had previously assembled the people before him, as scripture states: "behold, I am sending My messenger, and he will prepare the way before Me. Suddenly the Lord Whom you seek will enter His Temple" (Mal 3:1). The Israelites who are in the wilderness regions will follow Elijah until they meet the Israelites who are with the Messiah of the lineage of David in Judea. Scripture says about them: "in those days the house of Judah will come with the house of Israel,[14] and they will come together from a northern land unto the land that I bequeathed your ancestors" (Jer 3:18).

Most of those who were slain will lie dead in the Land for forty days, for when the Messiah of the lineage of Joseph is killed, his corpse will be cast aside for forty days. Nevertheless no impure thing will afflict it until the Messiah of the lineage of David comes and resurrects him at the command of the Lord. This will be the first of the signs that he will perform; namely, the resurrection of the dead, for he will regain life.

Then the Messiah of the lineage of David, Elijah, and the Israelites who came from the wilderness regions to Jerusalem will dwell securely (and) undisturbed for a long time. They will construct houses, plant vineyards, and enjoy prosperity in business and trade. (This situation will continue) until Gog hears news of them, as it is written: "I shall come up against a land of unwalled towns; I will come to those who are tranquil (and) who live unsuspectingly" (Ezek 38:11). The land of Gog is Magog, (a territory) in the land of Edom, for scripture has said about him: "[Gog of the land of Magog] is chief prince of Meshek and Tubal" (Ezek 38:2).[15] He will bring (with him) peoples from all of its surrounding areas and from Edom, as scripture attests: "the far reaches of the north and all his flanks—numerous peoples" (Ezek 38:6). These will, moreover, be augmented by masses (of people) drawn from every city and province through which they pass: (some will be) wicked and destructive men intending to mob them and annihilate them, but (also) others, some of the best of the gentiles, "who plan to gather beneath the wings of the Shekinah."[16] All of them will come

[14] See the Targum, Rashi, and Radaq *ad loc.*

[15] See Gen 10:2.

[16] For the import of this metaphor for divine protection and conversion to Judaism, see the remarks of Ephraim E. Urbach, *The Sages: Their Concepts and Beliefs* (2d enlarged ed.; 2 vols.; Jerusalem: Magnes, 1979), 1:47.

to do battle, and they will fight against Jerusalem with the Messiah of the lineage of David and those persons with him. Scripture says about this time: "behold I will make Jerusalem (to be) a cup of venom" (Zech 12:2), in addition to what is said in the passage about Gog (i.e., Ezekiel 38–39). At that time a mighty earthquake will also rock the Land of Israel.

"The Lord will come forth and wage battle against those nations"[17] with four types of catastrophic blows. Some of them will perish by fire, brimstone, and catapulted boulders—these latter are the "hailstones" (אבני אלגביש) mentioned in the scriptural verse: "torrential rain and hailstones, fire and brimstone" (Ezek 38:22). Some of them will perish by the sword being wielded by this one against that one, as scripture states: "I will summon for a sword to be used against him throughout all My hills—utterance of the Lord God—each one's sword will be against his brother" (Ezek 38:21). There are some whose flesh will rot away limb by limb. Regarding them scripture states: "this will be the plague with which the Lord will afflict all the peoples who unite together in battle against Jerusalem: their flesh will rot while they are still standing on their feet, their eyes will melt in their sockets, and their tongues will putrefy in their mouths" (Zech 14:12), and it will happen that when one (of these) grabs the hand of his colleague in order to gain support for himself, his hand will be pulled off, as scripture predicts: "each will grasp the hand of his colleague, and his hand will prevail over that of his colleague" (Zech 14:13). Others of them will fall casualty to blindness, an injured hand or foot, or a lacerated nose or ear. These will take flight and go to distant provinces, and there they will recount what they saw with their own eyes, as scripture says: "I will put a mark on them, and I will dispatch some of them as refugees to the nations, to Tarshish, Pul, and Lud, those who bend the bow, to Tubal and Ionia; distant coastlands that have not heard My news and have not seen My glory, and they shall recount My glory among the nations" (Isa 66:19).

At that time all the nations of the world will take thought and say, "What sort of gift might we bear to this king? Are not all kinds of money, clothing, or vessels reckoned as nothing before him? Let us bear to him the descendants of his people and his congregation as a gift!" For scripture states: "they will bring all your brethren as a gift for the Lord" (Isa 66:20). Each nation will transport them in accordance with its wealth. Some will ride on horses, in chariots, in wagons, on mules, and on dromedaries, whereas others will be carried by them on their shoulders, as scripture predicts: "They will bring your sons in their arms and will carry your daughters on (their) shoulder(s)" (Isa 49:22). Some will ride on ships from Tarshish, for scrip-

[17] Zech 14:3.

ture states: "ships from Tarshish will be among the first to bring your children from afar" (Isa 60:9). Others will be in reed vessels, as scripture says: "who sends emissaries by sea in reed vessels floating on the surface of the water" (Isa 18:2), and it also says: "from the other side of the rivers of Cush my suppliants, O daughter of Putzay, will bear my gift" (Zeph 3:10), and it also says: "O land of buzzing wings, which lies beyond the rivers of Cush" (Isa 18:1).[18] No wooden ships are able to travel there due to the rocks and shoals that lie concealed in the water. As for the remainder of Israel—those found in wilderness regions where there are no Gentiles to bring them—our God will lift them up as if by winds, for scripture states: "I will say to the north, 'Give!' and to the south, 'Do not hold back!'" (Isa 43:6), and they will likewise be borne upon clouds and fog, as scripture states: "Who are these floating like a cloud?" (Isa 60:8). At the approach of these exiles, the sea of Egypt will be divided for them at one spot, and the Euphrates river will be split at seven places. With regard to this time scripture states: "I will open rivers on the heights and fountains in the midst of plains; I will make the wilderness a pool of water, and the arid land a place where water gushes forth. I will place cedar, acacia, myrtle, and oil tree in the wilderness, and I will set out together in the barren plain cypress, elm, and box-tree" (Isa 41:18–19)—these latter will serve as shade for them. No single Israelite will be left alive in any (foreign) place when they come to Jerusalem, for scripture says: "I will not leave a single one of them there" (Ezek 39:28).

And after all who are alive have been gathered together (in Israel) and no Israelites remain (in the Diaspora) save for those who have died, a loud blast will be blown on the shofar, the earth will shake, and the Israelite dead will resurrect, as scripture says: "on that day a loud blast will be blown on the shofar" (Isa 27:13). They say that Zerubbabel will be the one who blows this shofar.[19] Why will there be a massive earthquake? This is to effect the release of the bones that have been crushed into powder and then incorporated into buildings and baked into bricks and upon which debris has collapsed, so that each bone can draw near to one another just as it is described in the scriptural portion about the valley (i.e., the "valley of dry bones," or Ezek 37:1–14). The Holy One, blessed be He, will stretch tendons among them, encase them in flesh, and cover them with skin, but they will be lacking an animating breath. Then the Holy One, blessed be He, will make a vivifying dew fall from heaven, a dew that contains within it a light that revives life, as scripture says: "Your dead will revivify; they will raise my corpse. Awake and

[18] See Radaq *ad* Zeph 3:10.

[19] Other sources identify Elijah or Michael as this trumpeter. Muslim tradition ascribes this task to the angel Isrāfīl; see Toufy Fahd, "Anges, demons et djinns en Islam," in *Génies, anges et demons* (Sources orientales 8; Paris: Éditions du Seuil, 1971), 168.

shout, O dwellers in dust, for your dew will be one containing light" (Isa 26:19). They will realize that they were formerly alive, then dead, and now revivified, for scripture says: "You will know that I am the Lord when I open your graves and conduct you out of your tombs, O My people!" (Ezek 37:13).[20] Everyone who had some sort of physical defect will initially arise with that defect: if one was elderly (at the moment of death), one will return in this elderly state and weakened condition. (This will be done) so that they [i.e., skeptics] might not say: "these are really different creatures (and not the resurrected dead)!"[21] Afterwards the Holy One, blessed be He, will heal them, as scripture states: "then the eyes of the blind will be opened, and the ears of the deaf will be cleared; the crippled one will leap like a gazelle, and the mute tongue will shout" (Isa 35:5–6), and scripture also says: "your youth will be renewed like the eagle's" (Ps 103:5).[22] [And from whence do we learn that the resurrection of the dead takes place during the time of the Messiah? Scripture says: "we shall raise for him] seven shepherds and eight human princes" (Mic 5:4). [Our Sages of blessed memory say that the seven shepherds] are Adam, Seth, Methuselah, Abraham, Jacob, Moses, and David; and the "eight human princes" (נסיכי אדם) are Jesse, Saul, Samuel, Amos, Zephaniah, Hezekiah, Elijah, and the Messiah.[23] Who will be resurrected? All those in Israel who were completely righteous and those who even though they committed sin made repentance (will be resurrected), but those whose iniquities are more numerous than their merits and did not make repentance will not arise during the time of the Messiah, for scripture states: "many of those who repose in the ground will awaken: some of them to life eternal, but others of them to derision (and) to eternal abhorrence" (Dan 12:2).[24] This is why our Sages have taught: "if someone is ill and approaching death, they say to him: 'Make confession!' Such is the way with all those who are about to die—they make confession. And if they do not know how to make confession, they tell them: 'Say—I have sinned, I have erred, and I have transgressed! May my death serve as atonement for my wickedness!'"[25] This ensures that all Israel will merit resurrection from the dead. Furthermore, the dead whom the Holy One, blessed be He, will resurrect will not return to dust, for scripture states: "these to eternal life" (Dan

[20] A similar exposition utilizing the same three biblical proof texts is found in Saadya, *K. al-Amānāt* (ed. Landauer), 215.1–13.

[21] Compare *2 Bar.* 50:2–4 for a similar justification; also *b. Pesaḥ* 68a bottom.

[22] Note *b. Sanh.* 91b: עומדין כמותן ואחר כך מתרפאין, "they will arise just as they died, but afterwards they will be healed," and compare Saadya, *K. al-Amānāt* (ed. Landauer), 227.14–19.

[23] See *b. Sukkah* 52b; also Radaq *ad* Mic 5:4. The Bavli's roster has "Zedekiah" in place of "Hezekiah," whereas Radaq's list substitutes "Enoch" (!) for "Adam."

[24] Compare Saadya, *K. al-Amānāt* (ed. Landauer), 216.3–12; 225.15–226.6.

[25] An amalgam of *b. Šabb.* 32a, *Sifra*, Aḥarey Mot §2 (Weiss, 81a), and *m. Sanh.* 6.2.

12:2),[26] and it also says: "all who are inscribed for life in Jerusalem will be called holy" (Isa 4:3).[27] Israel will marvel and ask: "From where have all these suddenly come?" This accords with scripture: "She [Zion] will say to herself: 'Who engendered these with me?'" (Isa 49:21). Even the gentile nations will be amazed, as scripture says: "Who has ever heard of anything like this? Who has ever seen anything like these things?" (Isa 66:8).

After the dead and the living have been assembled together, the form and feature(s) of the Temple will be revealed to us on its site: it will correspond to the vision that the priest (and) prophet Ezekiel the son of Buzi (upon him be peace!) saw. There are some who say that it will descend to its site from heaven, as scripture says: "Jerusalem already constructed like the city joined together with it" (Ps 122:3).[28]

Then all the children of Israel will become prophets, for scripture states: "it shall come to pass after this that I will pour out My spirit upon all flesh, and your sons and daughters will prophesy" (Joel 3:1). The same will happen to the male and female servants of Israel, as scripture says: "in those days I will pour out My spirit even upon slaves and maidservants" (Joel 3:2).

Those gentile nations who remain [alive] will become proselytes, as scripture says: "for then I will restore a pure speech to the nations so that all of them might invoke the name of the Lord" (Zeph 3:9), "and they will say: 'Come, let us ascend the mount of the Lord to the Temple of the God of Jacob, and He will teach us His ways so that we might walk in His paths. For Torah issues forth from Zion, and the word of the Lord (comes) from Jerusalem!' (Isa 2:3). And when they arrive in the presence of the King Messiah, he will command that they cease engaging in violence and wars, for scripture says: "they will beat their swords into ploughshares, and their spears into pruning hooks; one nation will no longer lift a sword against another, and no more will they learn the art of warfare" (Isa 2:4).

Then He will resettle Sodom and Gomorrah in their cities and the whole of the plain so that the Land of Israel will no longer be blemished by the devastation (that took place) within it, as it is written: "and your sisters—Sodom and her suburbs—will return to their former condition" (Ezek 16:55). All dangerous wild animals will cease to exist in the Land,[29] as scripture states: "the wolf will live with the lamb, and the panther will repose

[26] See *b. Sanh.* 92a; also quoted by Saadya, *K. al-Amānāt* (ed. Landauer), 223.17–19.

[27] Note that *Tg.* Isa 4:3 interprets the phrase כל הכתוב לחיים בירושלם as כל דכתיב לחיי עלמא, "all those recorded for eternal life"; i.e., the resurrected righteous ones of Israel.

[28] See the note to *Sefer Elijah* (p. 38 n. 59) that discusses the interpretation of this verse.

[29] Note *2 Bar.* 73:6: "and the wild beasts will come from the wood and serve men, and the asps and dragons will come out of their holes to subject themselves to a child." Translation cited from *OTP* 1:645.

with the goat-kid; the calf, the lion, and the fatling will be together, with a small child leading them. The cow and the bear will graze: their offspring will lie down together, and the lion will feed on straw like an ox. An infant will play over the hole of a serpent; a small child will stretch his hand over the lair of a snake. Nothing terrible or destructive will happen on the whole of My holy mountain, for the Land will be filled with knowledge of the Lord just like water covers the sea" (Isa 11:6–9).

The people whom the King Messiah found still alive will live long lives and then die, as scripture states: "they will not build and another live (there), nor will they plant and another consume (the fruits), for the days of My people will be as long as the days of a tree" (Isa 65:22). No one will die in the prime of life or as a child, for scripture says: "no longer will there be an infant or an elder who does not live out their full lifespan. A young boy will be one who dies at one hundred years of age, while the one who fails to attain one hundred years will be thought accursed" (Isa 65:20). It is doubtful that such a one would die; rather, this will be the way it is at the time of redemption. Whoever dies at the age of one hundred then will be comparable to one who dies at the age of twenty now, and should one who is one hundred years old wrong someone so that the latter curses him, they would not tolerate it, for he would not deserve toleration in their estimation, since he would be equivalent to our youth of about twenty years of age.[30] There are some who say that death will be uprooted from the world, for scripture says: "He will eradicate death forever" (Isa 25:8). Others say that they will be dead for only three days and then they will revivify, and about them scripture says: "He will invigorate us for two days, and on the third day He will raise us up, and we will live before Him" (Hos 6:2). The dead ones who resurrect during the time of the Messiah will live eternally in the World to Come, thanks to the merit of those who were completely righteous.

In those times when the Temple and Jerusalem are revealed, the Shekinah will descend from heaven and stand erect like a column of fire extending from the ground to the sky, as scripture foretells: "and the Lord will create upon all the locality of Mount Zion and its place of assembly a (canopy of) cloud and smoke by day, and a bright flame of fire by night" (Isa 4:5). All who seek to come to Jerusalem will see that column of fire on its eastern edge and will be guided by its light until they arrive in Jerusalem, as scripture states: "the nations will come to your light" (Isa 60:3).[31] That light consequently will be brighter than the light of the sun or moon, for it will darken them, as scripture says: "the moon will darken and the sun will

[30] Compare Saadya, *K. al-Amānāt* (ed. Landauer), 229.5–18.

[31] Cf. Saadya, *K. al-Amānāt* (ed. Landauer), 245.10–17; Naphtali Wieder, *The Judean Scrolls and Karaism* (London: East and West Library, 1962), 39–40 n. 4.

blush, for the Lord of Hosts will reign on Mount Zion and in Jerusalem" (Isa 24:23).

At that time they will notice that the heavens and earth will look as if they have been remade, as if the heavens and earth existing at the time when Israel was subjugated departed and were replaced, and a new set of heavens and earth put in their place. For scripture says: "behold, I am creating new heavens and a new earth" (Isa 65:17). Moreover, both Jerusalem and Israel will notice that they themselves have become as new, as if the Jerusalem and Israel existing at the time of their subjugation have passed away and been replaced, and others put in their place marked by joy and celebration, as scripture notes: "for behold, I am creating Jerusalem (as a place for) rejoicing, and her people (as a cause for) delight" (Isa 65:18).

They will dwell in their kingdom until the end of the world. There are some who say that this will be at the completion of seven thousand years counting from the era of Creation.[32] Others say that many thousands (of years) beyond reckoning will transpire, and that eventually the heavens and earth will perish, as scripture states: "for the heavens will dissipate like smoke, and the earth wear out like a cloth garment" (Isa 51:6). The dead who resurrected and witnessed the redemption will depart bodily for the World to Come (העולם הבא), as scripture says: "My redemption is eternal, and my victory will not break apart" (Isa 51:6). At that time the Holy One, blessed be He, will create another set of heavens and earth different from those (which deteriorated), and the righteous will make their dwelling among them for all eternity, as scripture envisions: "for just as the new heavens and the new earth which I made endure before Me, so will your offspring and your name endure!" (Isa 66:22).

[32] See *b. Sanh.* 97a–b and the discussions of Urbach, *Sages*, 1:676–82; Oded Irshai, "Dating the Eschaton: Jewish and Christian Apocalyptic Calculations in Late Antiquity," in *Apocalyptic Time* (ed. Albert I. Baumgarten; Leiden: Brill, 2000), 129–32. One might compare the *ḥadīth* stemming from Ibn ʿAbbās, which assigns a seven-thousand-year duration to life on earth; see Suliman Bashear, "Muslim Apocalypses and the Hour: A Case-Study in Traditional Reinterpretation," *IOS* 13 (1993): 95–96.

7

ʾ*Aggadat Ha-Mašiaḥ* (אגדת המשיח)

THIS POSTRABBINIC MIDRASH was first published separately by Adolph Jellinek,[1] who excerpted it from the *editio princeps* of the so-called *Midrash Leqaḥ Ṭov*, or *Pesiqta Zutarta*.[2] Within that larger collection it serves as an exegesis of Num 24:17–19. Yehudah Even-Shmuel provides an expanded text with a number of suggested emendations and an annotated commentary.[3] The present translation is based on Jellinek's edition.[4]

"A star steps forth from Jacob" (Num 24:17). It is taught in the name of our Sages:[5] the septennial cycle (שבוע) wherein the Son of David comes (will transpire as follows): (in) the first (year), there will not be food for all who need it;[6] (in) the second (year), the "arrows of famine" (cf. Ezek 5:16) will be unleashed; (in) the third (year), a severe famine; in the fourth (year), neither famine nor plenty;[7] in the fifth (year), great plenty, and a star will emerge in the east. This is the star of the Messiah, and it will be visible in the east for fifteen days. Should it linger, it will be to Israel's benefit.[8] (In) the

[1] Adolph Jellinek, ed., *Bet ha-Midrasch: Sammlung kleiner Midraschim und vermischter Abhandlungen aus der jüdischen Literatur* (6 vols.; Leipzig, 1853–77; repr., Jerusalem: Bamberger & Wahrmann, 1938), 3:141–43.

[2] Compiled from a variety of sources in the late eleventh century in Byzantium by R. Tobiah b. Eliezer. See especially Leopold Zunz and Ḥanokh Albeck, *Haderashot be-Yisrael* (2d ed.; Jerusalem: Mosad Bialik, 1954), 145–46.

[3] Yehudah Even-Shmuel, *Midreshey Ge'ullah* (2d ed.; Jerusalem: Mosad Bialik, 1954), 99–106.

[4] For another English translation, see David C. Mitchell, *The Message of the Psalter: An Eschatological Programme in the Book of Psalms* (JSOTSup 252; Sheffield: Sheffield Academic Press, 1997), 305–7; 335–36 (text). His suggestions about dating are best ignored.

[5] Based on *b. Sanh.* 97a, but with some alterations. See the following notes.

[6] Compare *b. Sanh.* 97a: "(in) the first year this verse will be fulfilled—'I will make it rain on one city, but on another city I will not allow it to rain' (Amos 4:7)."

[7] Compare *b. Sanh.* 97a: שובע ואינו שובע, "an alternation between plenty and poverty." Even-Shmuel suggests that the midrash is clarifying the talmudic source text.

[8] The information about the star is not in the talmudic source. Compare however the *Prayer of R.*

sixth (year), noises and sounds.[9] (In) the seventh (year), battles. And at the end of the seventh (year), one will behold the Messiah.

The "people of the west" (בני מערב)[10] will behave arrogantly, and they will maintain sovereignty without opposition.[11] They will come to Egypt and hold her entirely captive. In those days "the king strong of face" (מלך עז פנים)[12] will rise up against "the poor and impoverished nation" (Zeph 3:12), and he will "seize control of sovereignty by practicing deceptions" (cf. Dan 11:21). And about that time Isaiah has spoken: "Go, my people! Enter your rooms and lock your doors behind you! Hide for a short while until the danger is past!" (Isa 26:20).

The Sages have taught: R. Ḥiyya instructed those of his generation, "When you hear that 'the king strong of face' has arisen, do not remain there. For he will decree: 'Everyone who affirms that the God of the Hebrews is one will be put to death!' He will also say: 'Let all of us be of like expression and one people!' He will abolish (observance of) the holidays, festivals, sabbaths, and new moons, and he will suspend the Torah('s authority) over Israel, as scripture states: 'he will hope to change the appointed times and the religious law, and they will be given into his power for a time, two times, and half a time' (Dan 7:25). 'Time' (עידן) means a year; 'two times' (עידנין) means two (years), and 'half a time' (פלג עידן) means half a year."[13] They [his students] said to him, "Teacher, from where can we expect deliverance?" He answered them, "Upper Galilee,[14] for scripture states: 'a surviving remnant will be on Mount Zion and in Jerusalem' (Joel 3:5), and 'escape and holiness will be on Mount Zion' (Obad 1:17)."[15]

"... it will crush the corners of Moab" (Num 24:17). R. Huna repeated in the name of R. Levi: This verse teaches that Israel will assemble in Upper Galilee, and there within Galilee the Messiah of the lineage of Joseph will be

---

Shimʿōn b. Yōḥai (Jellinek, *BHM* 4.121): ובששית יצמח כוכב אחד ממזרח ובראשו שבט של אש כמו רומח ... ועושה ט"ו ימים ואם יתר הוא טוב לישראל, "And during the sixth (year) a star shall appear from the east and on top of it a rod of fire like a spear . . . and it will be visible for fifteen days. If it should be more, this is good for Israel."

[9] Only "noises" (קולות) are referred to in *b. Sanh.* 97a.

[10] I.e., Rome.

[11] בלא אפים. See Dan 11:20 and Rashi *ad loc.*

[12] Dan 8:23; cf. Deut 28:50; Prov 21:29.

[13] Compare the parallel but more extensive tradition found in *Prayer of R. Šimʿōn ben Yōḥai* (Jellinek, *BHM* 4:121.30–122.7).

[14] For the manifestation of the Messiah of the lineage of Joseph in Galilee, see *Sefer Zerubbabel*; also Saadya, *Kitâb al-Amânât waʾl-Iʿtiqâdât von Saʿadja b. Jûsuf al-Fajjûmî* (ed. S. Landauer; Leiden: Brill, 1880), 239.1–2. Note the remarks of Naphtali Wieder, *The Judean Scrolls and Karaism* (London: East and West Library, 1962), 21–22 n. 4, and his wider discussion (pp. 21–30).

[15] It is unclear how these two verses function as proof texts for the significance of Galilee. Even-Shmuel (*Midreshey Geʾullah*, 391) erases the crucial term שנאמר, "as it is said (i.e., in scripture)."

revealed to them. They will go up from there—he will be accompanied by all Israel—to Jerusalem in order to fulfill what scripture has stated: "and the forceful ones among your people will lift themselves up to fulfill the vision, but they will stumble" (Dan 11:14). He will go up and rebuild the Temple and offer sacrifices, and the fire (for kindling these offerings) will descend from heaven. He will crush all the nations of the world. He will come to Moab and slaughter half its population, whereas the remainder will endure captivity and bring him tax revenue. He will eventually establish an accord with Moab, as scripture says: "I shall restore the prosperity of Moab" (Jer 48:47), and they will dwell untroubled for forty years, eating and drinking, "and foreigners will serve as your farm-laborers and vineyard-tenders" (Isa 61:5).

". . . and it will demolish all the children of Seth" (Num 24:17). For he will destroy all the nations of the world who are named after Seth, as scripture states: "for God has established another seed for me" (Gen 4:25). And after all this, Gog and Magog will hear and come up against them, as scripture says: "the kings of the earth stand together, and rulers sit in council together against the Lord and His Messiah" (Ps 2:2).[16] He [i.e., Gog] will enter (the city) and kill him [i.e., the Messiah b. Joseph] in the streets of Jerusalem, as scripture predicts: "and it will be a time of trouble" (Dan 12:1).[17] Israel will see this and say, "the Messiah has perished from among us, and another Messiah will not return (for us)!" Four clans will mourn him, as scripture promises: "the land will mourn him individually by clans: the clan of the family of David individually, [the clan of the family of Nathan individually, the clan of the family of Levi individually, and the clan of Shimᶜi individually]" (Zech 12:12).

Then the Holy One, blessed be He, will go forth and do battle with them, as scripture says: "and the Lord will go forth and wage war against those nations" (Zech 14:3). The mountains will quake and the hills will shake, and the Mount of Olives will split across its middle[18] when the Holy One, blessed be He, descends upon it. Israel will run away and escape, as scripture says: "you will flee the valley of My mount . . . and this will be the plague" (Zech 14:5–12). And Israel will go into exile into the <"desert of the peoples">[19] to forage among the salt-plants and broom-sage roots for forty-

[16] For the eschatological application of this passage, see *Lev. Rab.* 27.11 (Margulies, 2:646–47); *Midr. Tanḥ.*, Noaḥ §18; *Midr. Tanḥ.* Buber, Noaḥ §24; *Midr. Teh.* 2 *passim*.

[17] According to the R. Šimᶜōn b. Yōḥai cycle of apocalypses (*Secrets*; *Prayer*) whose structural outline is here being mimicked, the Messiah of the lineage of Joseph will be slain by Armilos.

[18] והר הזתים יבקע מחציו; compare Zech 14:4: ונבקע הר הזיתים מחציו.

[19] *ʾAggadat ha-Mašiaḥ* has למדברי אגמות; *Secrets of R. Šimᶜōn b. Yōḥai* has למדברי אגמים. Neither is particularly meaningful ("uncleared wilderness"?). Instead, read with *Prayer of R. Šimᶜōn b. Yōḥai*

five days.[20] Clouds of glory will surround them, and there Israel will be concealed. If anyone should harbor a wavering thought in his mind about the Holy One, blessed be He, the clouds will cast him out and the nations of the world will kill him. Many from Israel will go out to the Gentile nations, and (as a result) they will have no portion with Israel in the World to Come.[21] Those, however, who [remain] must afflict themselves with salt-plant for forty-five days.

At the end of forty-five days, a heavenly voice (בת קול) will say to them: "Go down to Babylon," for scripture says: "and you shall come to Babylon; there you will be rescued" (Mic 4:10).[22] The heavenly voice will again thunder: "Proceed to Edom and wreak My vengeance!" This accords with the scriptural passage: "I will wreak My vengeance on Edom through the agency of My people Israel" (Ezek 25:14). So Israel will come to Rome.[23] The heavenly voice will come out a third time: "Treat it the same way that Joshua treated Jericho!"[24] So they will circumambulate the city, blowing on their shofars, and on the seventh circuit, they will let forth a shout, "Hear, O Israel: the Lord is our God; the Lord is One!" (Deut 6:4). Then the city wall will collapse. They will enter it (the city) and discover its young men sprawled dead in its plazas, for scripture says: "therefore her young men will collapse in her squares" (Jer 49:26; 50:30). Afterwards they will help themselves to all her spoils.

Then Israel will search for their God and for David their king,[25] and the King Messiah will forthwith be revealed to them. He will say to them, "I am the King Messiah for whom you have been waiting!" He will command them, "Lift up the silver and the gold," and they will carry it and go up [to Jerusalem], as scripture states: "a multitude of camels will cover you" (Isa 60:6).

A fourth heavenly voice will come forth and say, "(the) voice of one crying out: 'Prepare the way of the Lord in the desert!'" (Isa 40:3), and a fifth

---

(Jellinek, *BHM* 4:125): אל מדבר העמים, and see Ezek 20:35 and the note on this phrase in the commentary to *Prayer*.

[20] A slightly garbled quotation from the *Secrets of R. Šimʿōn b. Yōḥai* (see Jellinek, *BHM* 3:80).

[21] Apostasy before the final hour is a motif shared with the Christian *Apoc. Ps-Meth.* 12.1–8; 13:4–5, 15 (ed. Reinink). For an illuminating discussion of this concern, see especially G. J. Reinink, "Ps.-Methodius: A Concept of History in Response to the Rise of Islam," in *The Byzantine and Early Islamic Near East, I: Problems in the Literary Source Material* (ed. Averil Cameron and Lawrence I. Conrad; Studies in Late Antiquity and Early Islam 1; Princeton: Darwin Press, 1992), 152 n. 9, 159, 186ff.

[22] See *Sefer Elijah* (ed. Buttenwieser) 17–18, 36–37 n. 1.

[23] Note that the name Edom functions as a cipher for the city of Rome, here probably to be identified, as in Muslim texts, with Constantinople. See Buttenwieser, *Elias-Apokalypse*, 51.

[24] See Josh 6:1–20.

[25] This would seem to presume that the Davidic Messiah is sequestered in Rome.

heavenly voice will say, "no lion will be there" (Isa 35:9).[26] A sixth heavenly voice will say: "I will place in the desert cedar, acacia, and myrtle" (Isa 41:19), and a seventh heavenly voice will proclaim: "Console, console My people!" (Isa 40:1). Elijah will announce glad tidings to Israel: "your God has become sovereign!" (Isa 52:7).[27]

An eighth heavenly voice will announce and say: "Speak to the heart of Jerusalem" (Isa 40:2), (and) a ninth heavenly voice will say: "Open the gates and let the righteous people enter!" (Isa 26:2). A tenth heavenly voice will say: "Raise your heads, O gates!" (Ps 24:7, 9), and the dead will be resurrected, as scripture promised: "your dead will live again; they will raise up my body" (Isa 26:19). Then the exiles will be ingathered, as scripture says: "and it shall come to pass on that day that He will sound a great shofar [and those who were lost in the land of Assyria and those who were dispersed in the land of Egypt will come]" (Isa 27:13). Then will (the verse) "a star steps forth from Jacob . . ." (Num 24:17) be fulfilled, and thus may it be the will of our Heavenly Father to fulfill this verse during our lifetime and the lifetime of all Israel: "and He will hoist a banner to the nations, and He will collect the dispersed ones of Israel and re-gather the scattered ones of Judah from the four corners of the earth" (Isa 11:12).

'Aggadat ha-Mašiaḥ is finished.

[26] Note *Tg. Neb.* Isa 35:9, which interprets the "lion" as a "harsh ruler" (מלך מבאיש).

[27] For an analogous coordination of movements from Rome and the "wilderness," see *Tg. Tosefta* Exod 12:42 (Ms. T-S NS 182.69 *apud* Michael L. Klein, *Genizah Manuscripts of Palestinian Targum to the Pentateuch* [2 vols.; Cincinnati: Hebrew Union College Press, 1986], 1:221.11–12): משה ייסק מן גוא מדבר[א] <ומלכא משיחא מן גוא רומא>, "Moses will come up from the wilderness, <and the King Messiah (will come) from Rome>." The latter clause, although not present in the manuscript (pl. 161), is presupposed by the text's continuation and has been restored from the parallel rendition in *Maḥzor Vitry*. Note the cogent remarks of Klein, *Genizah Manuscripts*, 2:61. One wonders whether the curious mention of Moses in this role encodes a reference to the return of the *beney Mosheh*.

8

Pirqe Mašiaḥ

PIRQE MAŠIAḤ (alternatively *Pereq Mašiaḥ*) is a type of *Yalquṭ*, or loose anthology, of a number of traditional legends surrounding the events and personalities that were associated with the End of Days and the final vindication of Israel. Much of its content duplicates narrative episodes or exegetically based teachings that occur with greater literary integrity among earlier rabbinic sources or smaller, more cohesive collections of eschatological lore, such as *Pereq R. Yoshyahu*.[1] Of special interest are the sections dealing with the "wars" among the Persians, Arabs, and Romans at the time of the advent of the Messiah and the dispute between Israel and Ishmael for control of the Temple Mount, portions of which may be ultimately based on sources deriving from the seventh or eighth century.

The present translation follows the text published by Adolph Jellinek in his *Bet ha-Midrasch*.[2] Jellinek in turn simply reproduced a version that was first published in a collection of smaller midrashic texts at Salonika in 1743, the same early work from which Jellinek's editions of *Sefer Elijah* and the *Secrets of R. Šimᶜōn bar Yōḥai* were extracted. Even-Shmuel later prepared a heavily emended edition of Jellinek's text, which frequently incorporates the better readings found in the sources and parallel versions.[3] An early rendition of a small portion of this work is also extant among the Genizah fragments of Jewish messianic literature recovered from Cairo.[4] A partial English translation of Jellinek's text was supplied by David C. Mitchell.[5]

[1] Adolph Jellinek, ed., *Bet ha-Midrasch: Sammlung kleiner Midraschim und vermischter Abhandlungen aus der jüdischen Literatur* (6 vols.; Leipzig, 1853–77; repr., Jerusalem: Bamberger & Wahrmann, 1938), 6:112–16. The portion paralleling *Pirqe Mašiaḥ* begins at 6:113.26.

[2] Jellinek, *BHM* 3:68–78.

[3] Yehudah Even-Shmuel, *Midreshey Geʾullah* (2d ed.; Jerusalem: Mosad Bialik, 1954), 332–44.

[4] T-S A45.6, published with a transcription and brief textual notes by Simon Hopkins, *A Miscellany of Literary Pieces from the Cambridge Genizah Collections: A Catalogue and Selection of Texts in the Taylor-Schechter Collection, Old Series, Box A45* (Cambridge: Cambridge University Library, 1978), 11–14.

[5] David C. Mitchell, *The Message of the Psalter: An Eschatological Programme in the Book of Psalms* (JSOTSup 252; Sheffield: Sheffield Academic Press, 1997), 322–29; 344–47 (text).

Once the prophet Elijah (may his memory be for a blessing!) came to the academy of R. Yose. When R. Yose arrived, he discovered that Elijah was mournful. R. Yose said to him, "Why are you mournful?" He replied to him: "I have just come from the presence of the Holy One, blessed be He. He and the Messiah were occupied with (the study of) the consolations of the prophet Isaiah.[6] Then Samael, the prince of Rome,[7] came in and laid accusations of wrongdoing against Israel. I said to him, 'The Holy One, blessed be He, and His Messiah are occupied with the consolations of Isaiah, and you are denouncing them?' Thereupon he struck me, beat me, and expelled me, without saying anything to me!" (R. Yose) began (his lesson); he said: "'I will pronounce your righteousness' (Isa 57:12), and *all his* doings will gain *him nothing*."[8] (Interpreted, this means that) I will pronounce the righteousness of Israel, and all the doings of Samael will gain him nothing.

Another opinion:[9] After the Holy One, blessed be He, had delivered Samael over to Michael, he said before the Holy One, blessed be He: "Why have you put me under the authority of Michael? Let him come and judge my people before You." At once the Holy One, blessed be He, said to Michael: "Come and judge his people." Samael responded, saying: "If (you should convict) the gentiles of being criminals, (know that) Israel also engages in crimes. (Should you convict) the former of sexual immorality, (know that) the latter also practices sexual immorality. (Should you convict) the former of bloodshed, (know that) the latter is also guilty of bloodshed." So Michael remained silent. The Holy One, blessed be He, said to Michael: "You remain silent?!? Then I will speak up on behalf of My children so that all the doings of Samael may gain him nothing (לא יועילו). This is why scripture says: 'I will speak of righteousness, [mighty to deliver]' (Isa 63:1); that is, [I will speak of the righteousness of Israel] and I will deliver them on the Day of Judgment. What is this 'righteousness'? (It consists of) their acceptance of the Torah at Mount Sinai, for had they not accepted, the entire universe would have been destroyed." Immediately all the celestial groupings responded, saying: "'Mighty to deliver' (Isa 63:1)—this merit is mighty enough to deliver them from Gehinnom!" About this scripture

[6] This phrase is Aramaic: בנחמות דישעיה.

[7] For Samael's role as angelic patron of Rome, see the sources cited by Reuven Margaliot, *Malʾakey ʿelyon* (Jerusalem: Mosad ha-Rav Kook, 1945), 259–60; and especially Joseph Dan, "Samael and the Problem of Jewish Gnosticism," in idem, *Jewish Mysticism* (4 vols.; Northvale, N.J.: Jason Aronson, 1998–99), 3:374–77. Note also Ḥanokh Albeck, ed., *Midrash Bereshit Rabbati* (Jerusalem: Mekize Nirdamim, 1940), 166.4–167.8, a passage translated in the appendix below.

[8] A slightly distorted rendition of the Masoretic text of Isa 57:12, which reads: אני אגיד צדקתך ואת מעשיך ולא יועילוך. The changes in the text are italicized above.

[9] See *Midr. Teh.* 20.3 for a parallel version.

states: "and at that time your people—all those found inscribed in the book—will escape" (Dan 12:1). By what virtue do they escape? By virtue of the Torah, because they accepted everything that was written in the book (כל הכתוב בספר).[10] Consequently it states: "Israel, and I will bear witness for you" (Ps 50:7). (The spelling of "for you") *beth-kaph* (ב"ך) through gematria (is twenty-two, a sum equivalent to) the twenty-two letters used in the Torah: this teaches you that the Holy One, blessed be He, will testify to the merit of Israel because they accepted the Torah which was given using twenty-two letters.

Declare the greatness of the Sovereign King of Kings, the Holy One, blessed be He,[11] Who loves Israel more than (He loves) the ministering angels, and it is hardly necessary to say (that He loves Israel) more than the gentile nations! A mortal king has sons, servants, friends, each of whom is distinguishable from the other, but with regard to the sons you would be unable to rank them on the basis of his love for them. This is not the case with the Holy One, blessed be He, who has creations in the upper and lower levels of the universe, but none among all of them are as beloved to Him as is Israel! How is the status of "beloved" (made manifest) among the sons? The king clothes him with his garment, has him ride on his horse, seats him upon his throne, places a crown on his head, and has a herald announce before him: "this is the one beloved by the king!" Similarly the Holy One, blessed be He, as it were, clothed Israel with His garment, for scripture says: "for He has clothed me in garments of deliverance" (Isa 61:10). That was in the past, (but) for the future, what will attest it? Scripture promises: "glory and splendor will be his garment" (הוד והדר לבושו).[12] He, so to speak, mounted them on His horse, for scripture attests: "He made him ride over the heights of the earth" (Deut 32:13). That was in the past, (but) for the future, what will attest it? Scripture promises: "and I will make you ride over the heights of the earth" (Isa 58:14). He, so to speak, seated them on His throne, for scripture says: "and Solomon sat upon the throne of the Lord" (1 Chr 29:23). That was in the past, (but) for the future, what will attest it? Scripture promises: "They will call Jerusalem 'the throne of the Lord'" (Jer 3:17). He, so to speak, took His crown and set it on their head, as scripture says: "and eternal joy is upon their head" (Isa 35:10; 51:11),[13] and it also says "their king passed before them, and the Lord was at their head" (Mic 2:13).

[10] A periphrastic application of Dan 12:1.

[11] Cf. *m. Sanh.* 4.5; *b. Sanh.* 37a.

[12] *Sic.* This corresponds to no extant biblical verse. We should probably restore with Even-Shmuel (*Midreshey Ge'ullah*, 333) Ps 21:6: הוד והדר תשוה עליו, "you will place upon him glory and splendor."

[13] Based on the legend recounted in *b. Šabb.* 88a about Israel receiving crowns to wear when they first consented to accept and follow the Torah. Note also *Pirqe R. El.* §47 (Luria, 112a).

When the gentile nations behold all this praise and honor, immediately their eyes will bulge, their faces will turn pallid, their knees will knock against each other, and urine will stream down their thighs because the power of Israel will be like the power of the sun at which no one is able to gaze, as scripture states: "His friends are comparable to the rising of the sun with its full strength" (Judg 5:31).[14] Which intensity of the sun is meant? One would infer (it will be like) that of the summer solstice (בתקופת תמוז).

All of the nations of the world are destined to prostrate themselves before Israel and to lick the dust from their feet, as scripture states: "kings will serve as your tutors, [while their princesses will be your nursemaids; they will prostrate themselves facedown on the ground to you and lick off the dust from your feet]" (Isa 49:23). And should a gentile or a heretic ask you, saying, "Could this possibly happen?" say to him that it has already happened during the reign of Nebuchadnezzar, for scripture says: "he [i.e., the Babylonian king] bowed down to Daniel" (Dan 2:46).

We say in celebration of Jerusalem[15] that it is going to be rebuilt of precious stones and pearls, for scripture promises: "I will inlay your battlements with gemstones, etc." (Isa 54:12). Moreover, the borders of Israel will be inlaid with precious stones, for scripture says: "and all of your boundaries (I will set) with precious gems" (ibid.). And should a gentile or a heretic ask you, saying, "Is it possible that this thing could ever be?" say to him that it has already happened during the reign of Solomon, for scripture says: "and the king made silver in Jerusalem to be as abundant as stones" (1 Kgs 10:27). Behold, we have pronounced the praise(s) of Jerusalem.

Now we will speak in celebration of the Temple, which is destined to be rebuilt using twelve onyx-stones, for scripture states: "and Elijah took twelve stones corresponding to the number of the tribes of Israel" (1 Kgs 18:31). Does this not signal a *qal wa-ḥomer* argument? If the altar, which is only one of the ornaments of a temple, was fashioned using twelve stones, how much the more so should the (future) Temple (be so built), which will be the pride of Israel and the glory of the upper and lower beings and the adornment of the Holy One, blessed be He! The entire universe—all of it—will reflect the luminescence of the Temple, and (the glow) will encompass and rise up to the firmament, as far as ʿAraboth and the beasts and the chariot and the Throne of Glory. Consequently the altar is centered in relation to the Throne, and Jerusalem is directly beneath the Throne of Glory, and this is just what the prophet prophesied: "the Throne of Glory, exalted from the beginning, is the place for our sanctuary" (Jer 17:12).

[14] Note especially *Tg.* Judg 5:31, and cf. Isa 30:26.

[15] This expression is reminiscent of the extensive genre of Muslim literature termed *Faḍāʾil al-Bayt al-Maqdis*, or "Literature Celebrating Jerusalem."

In praise of the Omnipresent, blessed be He: who is able to articulate just one of the many thousands and myriads (of blessings) which He has brought upon Israel and with which He has delighted the upper and lower beings? A parable: it is like a king who bestowed a gift upon a province and caused joy among (His) courtiers. So too has the Holy One, blessed be He, produced joy; then the upper and lower beings (rejoiced), as scripture states: "Sing out, O heavens, for the Lord has acted; shout, O lower depths of the earth" (Isa 44:23).

And now we will celebrate the praise of the King Messiah. He is going to arrive "with the clouds of heaven" (עם ענני שמיא), and two seraphim will be on his right and on his left, as scripture says: "and behold, one like a human being came with the clouds of heaven" (Dan 7:13). Fiery seraphim will be sent into the palace, and stars will appear like fire in every place during the generation when the son of David comes.[16] There will be three consecutive years of plague, and this (calamity) is an agent of the Holy One, blessed be He, as scripture states: "plague advances before Him, and pestilence marches at His feet" (Hab 3:5). ["Pestilence" is actually "fire," as scripture attests]:[17] "its bolts are flames of fire" (Cant 8:6). And in the third year of the plague they will openly apostatize against Him. But at the end of the year the ruler will be slain, and they will flee into the deserts. The Land[18] will cry out from its place,[19] and the disciples of the Sages will perish. "Deceitful ones have deceived; very deceitfully have the deceitful ones deceived" (Isa 24:16). Another verse supports it: "and should a tenth part still remain, it will be burned again" (Isa 6:13). During the fifth year he [i.e., the King Messiah] will come and reveal himself among all the kingdoms. All of those rulers will fight with one another: the king of Persia (will fight) with the ruler of the Arabs and destroy it [i.e., their kingdom], for scripture states: "each will war with his brother and each with his neighbor, city against city, kingdom against kingdom" (Isa 19:2).[20] And when Edom falls, the heavens and the earth will shake from the noise of its collapse, since half of the world has been ensnared in its way [i.e., Christianity]. For scripture states: "the Lord will roar from the heavens, and He will sound His voice from His holy abode" (Jer 25:30). The Holy One, blessed be He, is going to collect them [i.e., Christians] into groups and deliver them into Israel's control, as scrip-

[16] For the periodization that follows, compare the sabbatical scheme of *b. Sanh.* 97a.

[17] Restore with Even-Shmuel.

[18] Or alternatively "the earth." Given the nationalist flavor of this composition, Eretz Israel may be the specific referent.

[19] Compare *1 En.* 7:6.

[20] Note *Gen. Rab.* 41(42).4 (Theodor-Albeck, 409): אמר ר' אלעזר בר' אבינא אם ראיתה מלכיות מתגרות אילו באילו צפה לרגליו שלמלך המשיח, "R. Eleazar taught in the name of Rav Avina: When you see the world empires warring with each other, look for the steps of King Messiah!"

ture promises: "I shall wreak My vengeance against Edom through the agency of My people Israel" (Ezek 25:14).

The Holy One, blessed be He, is going to bring the prince of Edom and flog him. The prince of Edom will say: "To where might I flee? I could go to Egypt, but God is present there,[21] for scripture says: 'behold, the Lord rode upon a swift cloud and came to Egypt' (Isa 19:1). I could flee to Edom, but God is present there, for scripture says: 'Who is This One coming from Edom' (Isa 63:1). I could flee to Babylon, but God is present there, for scripture says: 'for your sake *I was sent* to Babylon' (Isa 43:14).[22] I could flee to Elam, but God is present there, for scripture says: 'I placed My throne in Elam' (Jer 49:38)."

A parable. Once the lion said to the fox, "Pay me tax!" The latter arose and fled the distance of a three-day journey. The lion, however, still seized him and said to him, "Pay me the tax also in this place!" He [the fox] replied, "But I fled from you!" He [the lion] said: "You still remain in my place!" So too the Holy One, blessed be He, will say to the prince of Edom: "Can you possibly hide yourself from Me?" And the Holy One, blessed be He, will hand him over to Israel.

The Holy One, blessed be He, is going to put on garments of vengeance and avenge Himself on the seventy nations,[23] as scripture states: "vengeance and recompense are Mine" (Deut 32:35).[24] He will wear ten different garments to correspond to the ten times that Israel is termed God's "bride," and these are (those instances): "I have come to My garden, My beloved bride" (Cant 5:1); "come with Me from Lebanon, O bride" (Cant 4:8); "My beloved bride is a locked garden" (Cant 4:12); "how wonderful is your love, My beloved bride" (Cant 4:10); "your lips drip (like) a honeycomb, My beloved bride" (Cant 4:11); "you have enamored Me, My beloved bride" (Cant 4:9); "sound of the Groom and sound of the bride" (Jer 7:34; 16:9; 25:10; 33:11); "and you will tie them on like a bride" (Isa 49:18); "and the bridegroom delights over the bride" (Isa 62:5); and "like a bride puts on her jewelry" (Isa

[21] שכינה שם; i.e., "God's presence is there."

[22] Reading שולחתי in place of the text's שלחתי. See *y. Ta'an.* 1.1, 64a; *Mek.* Bo', Pisḥa §14 (Horovitz-Rabin, 52.3); *Sifre* Num §84 and §161 (Horovitz, 83, 223); *'Aggadat Berešit* (ed. Buber) §64; Ibn Ezra and Radaq *ad loc.* See also the discussion of Michael Fishbane, *Biblical Myth and Rabbinic Mythmaking* (Oxford: Oxford University Press, 2003), 139, 222–23, 352 n. 84.

[23] Beginning here, a parallel and textually smoother version of this set of traditions is provided in *Pereq R. Yoshyahu*. See Jellinek, *BHM* 6:113–16.

[24] *Pereq R. Yoshyahu* (Jellinek, *BHM* 6:113.26–27) begins this section as follows: ונתתי את נקמתי באדום א״ר שמואל בר נחמן עתיד הקב״ה ללבוש בגדי נקם להנקם משבעים אומות, "'And I shall wreak My vengeance against Edom' (Ezek 25:14). R. Samuel bar Nahman said: The Holy One, blessed be He, is going to put on garments of vengeance and avenge Himself on the seventy nations." Compare *Pesiq. Rab Kah.* 22.5 (Mandelbaum, 1:329–30); *Cant. Rab.* 4.1.

61:10). And these are the ten garments (which God wears): "The Lord is a king cloaked in majesty" (Ps 93:1)—during His creation of the universe; "the Lord is clothed; He has girded Himself with strength" (Ps 93:1)—on the day of the revelation of the Torah; "He has put on righteousness like armor" (Isa 59:17)—on the day when He hands the nations of the world over to Israel;[25] "He has put on garments of vengeance (as) clothing" (Isa 59:17)—on the day of the fall of Edom; "red of garment from Bosra" (Isa 63:1)—on the day He makes war against the nations of the world;[26] "this one majestic in His clothing" (Isa 63:1)—on the day of Gog and Magog; "their gore was splattered on My garments" (Isa 63:3)—with regard to the kingdom of Italy.[27] And these are the two garments (You will wear) on the day when the dead are resurrected: "Let my soul praise the Lord: You wear splendor and majesty" (Ps 104:1). "Why are Your garments red?" (Isa 63:2)—on the day that the Holy One, blessed be He, seizes His sword and wages war, for scripture states: "I will make My arrows drunk with blood, and My sword will eat flesh" (Deut 32:42). "And I shall wreak My vengeance against Edom through the agency of My people Israel" (Ezek 25:14).[28]

Before Edom falls,[29] they will devastate ten places, ten places will be overturned,[30] ten shofar-blasts will be blown, ten "sounds" (קולות) will be heard, fifteen provinces will be slaughtered, ten misfortunes[31] will transpire, and ten disasters will spring forth. A king "strong of face" (עז פנים) will arise and issue harsh decrees throughout his kingdom. A great king will go out to

[25] *Pereq R. Yoshyahu* (Jellinek, *BHM* 6:114.4): "on the day when the nations of the world are denouncing Israel."

[26] *Pereq R. Yoshyahu* (Jellinek, *BHM* 6:114.6): "on the day the Holy One, blessed be He, sends them (Israel) out against all the nations of the world."

[27] במלכות איטל׳. Even-Shmuel emends on the basis of *Pereq R. Yoshyahu* to read במלחמת איטליה, "regarding the battle of Italy."

[28] Instead of the proof text from Ezekiel, *Pereq R. Yoshyahu* (Jellinek, *BHM* 6:114.11–17) reads here as follows: "Another opinion. The Holy One, blessed be He, said: Woe to you, O wicked Esau! Two prophets have prophesied about you, Obadiah and Ezekiel. Obadiah said: 'Get up and let us rise up for battle against her' (1:1), and Ezekiel said: 'And I shall wreak My vengeance against Edom through the agency of My people Israel' (25:14). (As for) his collaboration with Ishmael, woe to you, O Esau and Ishmael! Just as the verse says: 'the tents of Edom and the Ishmaelites, of Moab and the Hagarenes' (Ps 83:7). (Whether) these be warriors of Tanis, terrifying mighty ones of Edom, great princes of Teman—all of them (will perish) by the sword or in captivity. For scripture states: 'your warriors, O Teman, will suffer annihilation' (Obad 1:9)."

[29] *Pereq R. Yoshyahu* (Jellinek, *BHM* 6:114.18): "Our Sages have taught (תנו רבנן): Before wicked Edom falls. . . ."

[30] This clause is lacking in *Pereq R. Yoshyahu*.

[31] רעות. *Pereq R. Yoshyahu* (Jellinek, *BHM* 6:114.20) reads: "earthquakes (זועות) will effect slaughter in fifteen regions, and ten horns of the kingdom will be toppled."

encamp against Alexandria,[32] and there will be horrible trouble in the world. He will rule for three and a half years, and then he will rebel (against the king "strong of face"?). The princes of Edom will fall:[33] ten battles will take place and then Israel will prevail over all the nations, "and I shall wreak My vengeance against Edom" (Ezek 25:14).[34]

Ships will embark for Edom from Eretz Israel, and Israel will announce: "Who is for us, and who is for Edom?" For scripture states: "Who will bring me to the fortified city? Who will lead me unto Edom?" (Ps 60:11).[35] Israel will go and encamp against "Tyre" (צור)[36] for forty days,[37] and at the end of forty days they will stand up at the time for the recitation of the *Shema* and say:[38] "Hear, O Israel! The Lord is our God; the Lord is One!" (Deut 6:4). Then the walls of the city will collapse, and the city will be conquered by them. They will leave within it all the gold, silver, and the rest who are despoiling it and (proceed) from there to Rome. They will procure the Temple vessels, and King Nehemiah the Messiah will come out with them, and they will come to Jerusalem.[39]

[32] *Pereq R. Yoshyahu* (Jellinek, *BHM* 6:114.22–23): "the king of Edom will go out against Alexandria."

[33] *Pereq R. Yoshyahu* (Jellinek, *BHM* 6:114.23–24): "for three years he will rebel, and the princes of Moab will fall."

[34] Even-Shmuel has rearranged the order of these sentences to read thus: "Ten battles will take place, and then Israel will prevail over all the nations. The princes of Edom will fall, as scripture announces: 'I shall wreak My vengeance against Edom through the agency of My people Israel'" (Ezek 25:14).

[35] Compare *Pereq R. Yoshyahu* (Jellinek, *BHM* 6:114.26–29): "Ninety ships will embark for Edom from Egypt, and every ship will carry ninety thousand Israelites. Once they are at sea, Israel will exclaim: 'What is there for us in Edom? Who will bring me to the fortified city? Etc.' (Ps 60:11)."

[36] Note *Tg.* Ps 60:11: מן הוא דיוביל יתי לקרתא חרובא דצור . . . According to an exegetical tradition cited in *Gen Rab.* 61.7 (Theodor-Albeck, 669), "every biblical verse which spells the place-name *Ṣor* (i.e., Tyre) fully refers to the city of Tyre; every verse which spells it defectively refers to Rome." Using the verse from Psalms, this apocalyptic fragment apparently envisions a two-stage campaign that begins with Tyre and ends in Rome.

[37] Is this a reminiscence of the alleged Jewish siege of Tyre which formed part of the Sasanian conquest of Palestine in 614 CE? See Robert Schick, *The Christian Communities of Palestine from Byzantine to Islamic Rule: A Historical and Archaeological Study* (Studies in Late Antiquity and Early Islam 2; Princeton: Darwin Press, 1995), 27–28.

[38] *Pereq R. Yoshyahu* (Jellinek, *BHM* 6:114.30): "they will say loudly (בקול רם)."

[39] *Pereq R. Yoshyahu* (Jellinek, *BHM* 6:114.31–115.1): "all the nations who are within it (Tyre) will be dead; none of them will retain any breath on account of (their) terror for Israel. Israel will enter the city and despoil it of all their silver and gold, and the rest they will make into a sword (?). From there they will proceed to Edom, and they will procure the Temple vessels. The King Messiah will come out with them, and they will come to Jerusalem."

Israel will say to the ruler of the Arabs:[40] "The Temple[41] is ours! Take (this) silver and gold and leave the Temple!"[42] The ruler of the Arabs will respond: "You have nothing to do with this sanctuary![43] However, if you choose, first (offer) for yourselves a sacrifice as you formerly used to do. We too will bring an offering, and (in accordance with) whoever's offering is accepted, we will all become one people (אומה)!"[44] Israel will present offerings, but they will not be accepted because Satan will be denouncing (them) before the Holy One, blessed be He. Then the sons of Qedar (i.e., the Muslims) will present offerings and they will be accepted, for scripture says: "every flock of Qedar will be collected for you" (Isa 60:7). At that time the Arabs will say to Israel: "Come and believe in our religion!"[45] But Israel will answer them: "Either we kill or wind up slain: we will never commit apostasy!"[46] Immediately swords will be drawn, bows stretched, and arrows sprayed, and corpses will be strewn "from the Gate of Ephraim unto the corner gate" (2 Kgs 14:13). Nehemiah will lie slain among them.[47] Those of

[40] The following intriguing dispute between Judaism and Islam over exclusive possession of the Temple Mount has a thematic parallel in the invaluable seventh-century Armenian history of Sebeos, wherein the initial Islamic conquest of Jerusalem, there portrayed as a joint Jewish-Muslim operation, is described. See Frédéric Macler, *Histoire d'Héraclius par l'évèque Sebéos* (Paris: E. Leroux, 1904), 102; Patricia Crone and Michael Cook, *Hagarism: The Making of the Islamic World* (Cambridge: Cambridge University Press, 1977), 10; Robert G. Hoyland, *Seeing Islam As Others Saw It: A Survey and Evaluation of Christian, Jewish and Zoroastrian Writings on Early Islam* (Studies in Late Antiquity and Early Islam 13; Princeton: Darwin Press, 1997), 127.

[41] בית המקדש. Since a common early Arabic designation for the city of Jerusalem is Bayt al-Maqdis (see Oleg Grabar, "al-Ḳuds," *EI*^{2} 5:323), a direct translation of the Hebrew term for the Temple, one could conceivably translate "Jerusalem is ours! Take (this) silver and gold and leave Jerusalem!"

[42] *Pereq R. Yoshyahu* (Jellinek, *BHM* 6:115.2–4): "The ruler of the Arabs will come out to meet Israel and say to them: 'Why are you in Jerusalem?' Israel will respond: 'The *ḥaram* (מקדש) is ours and the vessels are ours! Take silver and gold for yourselves and leave Bayt al-Maqdis (בית המקדש)!'"

[43] *Pereq R. Yoshyahu* (Jellinek, *BHM* 6:115.4): "The ruler of the Arabs said to Israel: 'You have no portion in this world!'" Cf. Neh 2:20.

[44] The use of Hebrew אומה permits a bilingual pun with Arabic *umma*, "people," a word that often bears the connotation of a "community of believers, i.e., Muslims." See Q 2:128; 3:110 and the recent extensive discussions by Frederick Mathewson Denny, "Community and Society in the Qurʾān," *EncQur* 1:367–86; idem, "Umma," *EI*^{2} 10:859–63. Curiously, according to the early Muslim document known as the "Constitution of Medina," the Jews are reckoned together with the Muslims as a single *umma*. See Crone and Cook, *Hagarism*, 7; Hoyland, *Seeing Islam*, 554–55; Uri Rubin, *Between Bible and Qurʾān: The Children of Israel and the Islamic Self-Image* (Studies in Late Antiquity and Early Islam 17; Princeton: Darwin Press, 1999), 48–49. A contrary opinion has been forcefully articulated by Moshe Gil, *Jews in Islamic Countries in the Middle Ages* (trans. David Strassler; Leiden: Brill, 2004), 21–45, esp. 35–41.

[45] *Pereq R. Yoshyahu* (Jellinek, *BHM* 6:115.9–10): "At that time the Ishmaelites will say to Israel: 'Come and do like us and we will be one community!'"

[46] *Pereq R. Yoshyahu* (Jellinek, *BHM* 6:115.10–11): "Israel will say to them: 'Even if we were to be put to death, we would never commit apostasy!'"

[47] This notice is lacking from this portion of *Pereq R. Yoshyahu*.

them who escape will flee to the wilderness of Moab and to the territory of the Ammonites, and there those refugees of Israel will wait, and there God will perform miracles for them: He will make a spring gush forth for them from the subterranean depths, for scripture says: "My scattered ones will sojourn with you, O Moab" (Isa 16:4). There they will eat broom-sage roots for forty-five days.[48]

At the end of forty-five days, Elijah will emerge there along with the King Messiah. There Elijah will announce to them and say: "Why are you here, O Israel?" Israel will respond and say: "We perish! We die!" Elijah will say to them: "Arise, for I am Elijah and this is the King Messiah!" But they will not believe him because Nehemiah had already come and was killed. He will say to them: "Perhaps you seek a sign like Moses?" They will respond: "Yes." At that time he will perform seven miracles.

The first miracle: he will bring Moses and his generation back from the wilderness, as scripture states: "Gather together My pious ones for Me" (Ps 50:5).[49] The second miracle: he will cause Qorah and all his congregation to ascend, for scripture says: "you will restore him to life again; you will bring him up again from the earth's abysses" (Ps 71:20).[50] The third miracle: he will raise up for them Nehemiah who had been slain.[51] The fourth miracle: he will disclose to them the hiding place of the Ark,[52] the jar of manna, and the anointing oil. The fifth miracle: the Holy One, blessed be He, will place a powerful staff (מטה עוז) in his hand, as scripture says: "the Lord will extend your mighty staff" (Ps 110:2).[53] The sixth (miracle): he will grind all the mountains of Israel as (one grinds) grain, as scripture states: "I will devastate mountains and hills" (Isa 42:15).[54] The seventh miracle: he will reveal "the mystery" (הסוד) to them, as scripture says: "this is the sign of the covenant" (Gen 9:12, 17).[55]

When they [i.e., Israel's enemies] behold these miracles, they will send to and inform all the princes despoiling Jerusalem, (saying) "Come and wage

[48] See *Secrets of R. Šimᶜōn bar Yoḥai* (Jellinek, *BHM* 3:80.14): ובשרשי רתמים מ"ה ימים. *Pereq R. Yoshyahu* (Jellinek, *BHM* 6:115.16–17) adds: "for the righteous among Israel, the broom-sage root will be as sweet as honey; but for the wicked among Israel, they will be bitter like wormwood."

[49] Compare *Sefer Zerubbabel* (Israel Lévi, "L'apocalypse de Zorobabel et le roi de Perse Siroès," *REJ* 68 [1914]: 139.2).

[50] Compare *Sefer Zerubbabel* (Lévi, "L'apocalypse de Zorobabel," 139.1–3).

[51] *Pereq R. Yoshyahu* (Jellinek, *BHM* 6:115.25–26): "he will raise up Nehemiah b. Ḥushiel who was slain at the gate of Jerusalem."

[52] Read הארון in place of the text's הארץ in accordance with *Pereq R. Yoshyahu* (Jellinek, *BHM* 6:115.27).

[53] A reference to the recovery of the miracle-working staff of Moses.

[54] *Pereq R. Yoshyahu* (Jellinek, *BHM* 6:115.31) adds: "He stood and measured the earth" (Hab 3:6).

[55] *Pereq R. Yoshyahu* (Jellinek, *BHM* 6:115.31–32) offers a different proof-text: "this is the covenant which I will make with the house of Israel" (Jer 31:32).

war on them!"[56] Those summoned will come out after Israel.[57] Israel will say to the King Messiah: "Was it not better for us to remain (here)? Why have you come to provoke war against us as before?"[58] But the King Messiah will answer them: "Stand fast and see the deliverance of the Lord!" He will blow with the breath of his mouth and all of them will fall down (as) corpses before him, as scripture promises: "he will slay the wicked with the breath of his lips" (Isa 11:4). Go and learn from (the example of) Sennacherib, as scripture says: "behold, all of them were dead bodies" (2 Kgs 19:35; Isa 37:36).[59]

At that time Elijah will fly throughout the whole world and proclaim a message to Israel, as scripture states: "Behold I will send Elijah the prophet to you" (Mal 3:23). That day will be a day of mercilessness and wrath, and that day will effect a separation between two worlds. The wicked will say: "Alas for the day! The day of the Lord is near!" (Joel 1:15). They will also say: "Woe to those who longed for the day of the Lord!" (Amos 5:18). Jerusalem will "expand and grow"[60] all that day, as scripture says: "and it will come to pass that one day will be known as 'the Lord's' . . . all the Land will become (יסוב) like the plain from Gevaʿ to Rimmon south of Jerusalem" (Zech 14:7–10).

Gog and Magog will come up on that day and encamp by Jerusalem for seven and a half days. He will capture Jerusalem! The people of Israel will say before the Holy One, blessed be He: "Master of the Universe! (With regard to) every nation that has despoiled me, I am ashamed to go and take back what is mine from their hand." The Holy One, blessed be He, will answer: "I shall assemble all of them to be among you, as scripture says: 'behold, the day of the Lord is coming when your spoil will be divided up in

[56] *Pereq R. Yoshyahu* (Jellinek, *BHM* 6:115.32–34): "When the Moabites see these miracles, they will send to and inform those who are looting and despoiling Jerusalem, (saying) 'Come and wage war on Israel!'"

[57] *Pereq R. Yoshyahu* (Jellinek, *BHM* 6:116.1–2) reads: "At that time the ruler of Ishmael and all the sons of Qedar will come forth armed with weapons to confront Israel."

[58] *Pereq R. Yoshyahu* (Jellinek, *BHM* 6:116.2–4): "At that time Israel will say to the King Messiah: 'Was it not better for us to live here (undisturbed)? Instead, you have come to incite the whole world against us!'"

[59] *Pereq R. Yoshyahu* (Jellinek, *BHM* 6:116.5–9) concludes: "The Messiah will stand before them and blow on them with the breath of his mouth, and consequently all of them will fall down (as) dead bodies. From whence do we know that they will die due to the breath of the mouth of the Messiah? It is written: 'he will strike the earth with the rod of his mouth, and he will slay the wicked with the breath of his lips' (Isa 11:4). At that time a great fear will grip the whole world, and a messenger (will come) to Israel. For scripture states: 'Behold I am sending Elijah the prophet to you before the advent of the great and terrible day of the Lord, etc.' (Mal 3:23–24)."

[60] An allusion to Ezek 41:7; thus read with Even-Shmuel נסבה in place of נסבה. See *Sifre* Deut §1 (Finkelstein, 7) and Radaq *ad* Zech 9:1. Note also Isa 54:2–3; Zech 1:17.

your midst, and I shall gather all the nations to Jerusalem for battle, [and the city will be captured]' (Zech 14:1–2). These will be those (nations): Gomer and his armies, Togarmah,[61] Africa, Garmit (?), Germamia, Cappadocia, Barbary, Italy, Kush, Spain,[62] Saba, Kirman,[63] Daylam,[64] Khurasan,[65] Sisunya, Galicia, Gotzia, Lombardy, Calabria, Pantopoli, Tripoli, Tyre, Macedonia, England, Munich (?), Sifri (?), Nero (?), Nuzan (Lausanne?), Drunia (?), Usia (?), Talki (?), Germany,[66] Tarsus, Elam, and all the rest.[67]

The inhabitants of those countries will issue forth with spears, swords, and bows, each of them reinforcing each other like a door that has been strengthened with nails, as scripture states: "each one helping his fellow" (Isa 41:6). They will be divided into three groups.[68] The first group will drink down all the waters of (the lake of) Tiberius, the second will drink up the dregs,[69] and the third will cross over (the lakebed) on foot. Each will say to his fellow: "Whose was this place?"[70] They will grind the stones of the mountains of Israel with their horses, and Jerusalem will be given over unto them. They will capture the city, but they will not kill anyone, for scripture says: "the city will be taken, the houses will be looted, and the women ravished" (Zech 14:2). They will abuse within it two women from two different families.

To what is this situation comparable? To that of a ruler who allowed thieves to enter his palace. The ruler thought: "If I arrest them while they are still in my house, they will think: 'The ruler only has power within his house!' Instead, I will be patient and wait for them to come outside." Thus did the Holy One, blessed be He, reason: "If I kill them while they are still in

[61] For these first three terms, see Ezek 38:6.

[62] אנדלוס.

[63] הרמן.

[64] דולים.

[65] אהרסן.

[66] אלמנייה.

[67] Lists of the various peoples or nations who make up the hordes of Gog and Magog are most frequently found in Christian and Muslim apocalypses, where their number is often standardized as 22 or 24. Compare, e.g., the Syriac *Apoc. Ps-Meth.* 8.10 (Reinink, 1:16), the Syriac *Apoc. Ps-Ephrem* (ed. Beck), 64.201–20, and the various traditions assembled by Nuʿaym b. Ḥammād, *Kitāb al-fitan* (ed. S. Zakkār; Beirut: Dār al-Fikr lil-Ṭibāʿah wa-al-Nashr wa-al-Tawzīʿ, 1993), 356–68. See also Paul J. Alexander, *The Byzantine Apocalyptic Tradition* (ed. Dorothy deF. Abrahamse; Berkeley: University of California Press, 1985), 185–92; David Cook, *Studies in Muslim Apocalyptic* (Studies in Late Antiquity and Early Islam 21; Princeton: Darwin Press, 2002), 182–88. Jewish sources usually enumerate them as "seventy nations" based on Genesis 10 and on the gematria value of גוג ומגוג. See, e.g., *Midr. Tanḥ*, Qoraḥ §12 end.

[68] Similarly Nuʿaym b. Ḥammād, *K. al-fitan* (ed. Zakkār), 358.

[69] An analogous thirst is displayed in Muslim traditions about these invaders; see Cook, *Studies*, 185; Keith Lewinstein, "Gog and Magog," *EncQur* 2:332.

[70] Even-Shmuel emends to read: 'Was there water in this place?'

Jerusalem, they will think 'He only has power in Jerusalem!' Instead, I will be patient and wait for them to come out to the Mount of Olives!" There the Holy One, blessed be He, will reveal Himself over them in His glory and wage war against them until not a single one of them remains, as scripture states: "and the Lord will go forth and wage war against those nations as at the time He fought on the day of battle" (Zech 14:3). Then the Holy One, blessed be He, will assemble all the wild animals and birds to feast on their flesh, as scripture says: "Say to every winged bird and every wild animal: Collect yourselves together and come; gather yourselves from all sides for My festival victim, for I have slaughtered for you a great meal upon the mountains of Israel, and you will eat flesh and drink blood" (Ezek 39:17). Israel will spend seven years burning the wooden components of their bows, shields, and spears.[71]

At that time the Holy One, blessed be He, will dress the Messiah with a diadem and place "the helmet of deliverance upon his head" (Isa 59:17). He will endow him with glory and splendor and enwrap him with rich garments, and He will station him upon the peak of a high mountain to make an announcement to Israel. Using his voice he will proclaim: "Deliverance has arrived!"[72] Israel will say: "Who are you?" He will respond, "I am Ephraim." Israel will ask: "Are you the one to whom the Holy One, blessed be He, referred when He said 'Ephraim, he is My firstborn' (Jer 31:8)? 'Could a child be more precious to Me than Ephraim' (Jer 31:19)?" He will answer them: "Yes!" Israel will say to him: "Go forth and impart the news to those who sleep at Machpelah,[73] for they must rise first." He will then go and impart the news to those sleeping at Machpelah, saying to them: "Abraham, Isaac, and Jacob! Arise, for you have slept long enough!" They will answer, saying: "Who is this who pulls the dust off of us?"[74] He will say to them: "I am the Lord's Messiah! Deliverance has come; the Hour has arrived!"[75] They will answer him: "If this is true, go and impart the news to Adam the Protoplast for he must rise first."[76] They [*sic*] will then say to Adam the Protoplast: "You have slept long enough!" He will answer: "Who

[71] See Ezek 39:9.

[72] Cf. Isa 56:1.

[73] I.e., the cave of Machpelah at Hebron where the patriarchs are buried. Mandelbaum (2:464–65) has published a manuscript supplement to *Pesiq. Rab Kah.* 5.9 which contains a passage that roughly parallels the Messiah's rousing of the patriarchs.

[74] Even-Shmuel reads: שמגלה עפר מעינינו, "who removes the dust from our eyes."

[75] A calque of Arabic *al-sāʿa* (Q 47:18)?

[76] The cave of Machpelah is also the burial place of Adam: see *b. ʿErub.* 53a; *Soṭah* 13a; *B. Bat.* 58a; *Pirqe R. El.* §20 (Luria, 47b-48a). Later mystical tradition views Machpelah as a portal to the Garden of Eden. Note Zohar 1.127a and the references given by J. H. Chajes, *Between Worlds: Dybbuks, Exorcists, and Early Modern Judaism* (Philadelphia: University of Pennsylvania Press, 2003), 196 nn. 10–11.

is this who wakes me from my sleep?" He will say: "I am the Lord's Messiah, one of your descendants!" Immediately Adam the Protoplast will arise, along with his entire generation, and Abraham, Isaac, and Jacob and all the righteous, and all the tribes and every generation from one end of the world to the other, and they will joyfully sing, as scripture states: "how wonderful on the mountains are the feet of the one who brings news!" (Isa 52:7).[77] Why (does the verse say) "on the mountains" (על ההרים)? Rather, "how wonderful" are Moses and his generation who are approaching from the desert! Another opinion: "how wonderful on the mountains" (Isa 52:7). It is comparable to a ruler who had two sons. One of them died, and so all the citizens of the country put on black garments. The ruler said, "You clothe yourselves in black now because of the death of my first son; I will clothe you in white (in the future) to celebrate my second son!" Similarly the Holy One, blessed be He, said to all the mountains: "Because you wept for My children when they were exiled from their land—as scripture attests, 'I took up weeping and wailing on the mountains' (Jer 9:9)—I will bring the joy of My children 'on the mountains,' as scripture states: 'how wonderful on the mountains' (Isa 52:7)."

It is fitting that the King Messiah imparts the news to Israel. The mountains will skip about like calves before him, and the trees of the field will applaud the deliverance of Israel, as scripture states: "for you will go forth rejoicing . . . mountains and hills will burst into song before you, and all the trees of the field will clap hands" (Isa 55:12). How fitting (too) that the mountains of Israel will flow with milk and honey like torrents of flooding waters and also with rivers of wine, as scripture says: "it will come to pass on that day that the mountains will drip new wine, and a fountain will flow forth from the Temple of the Lord and fill the Wadi Shittim" (Joel 4:18).

To what is the fountain comparable when it flows from the Holy of Holies to the threshold of the chamber?[78] At first it will resemble the thread of the warp until (it reaches) the sanctuary, where it will resemble the thread of the woof, until it reaches the court, where it will resemble bulls' horns or rams' horns. When it reaches the altar it will resemble the antennae of locusts, (and) when it reaches the outer courtyard it will resemble (the opening of) a small bottle, as scripture states: "flowing water" (Ezek 47:2). From there it will descend like a flooding torrent and purify (the Land) of iniquity, impurity, and sin. The Angel of Death will not be able to cross it, for scripture says: "[no 'swimming-boat' (אני שיט) can traverse it,] nor a mighty ship cross it" (Isa 33:21),[79] nor will a ship be able to cross it. It will

[77] For the messianic associations of this verse, see *Cant. Rab.* 2.4; *Pesiq. Rab Kah.* 5.9 (Mandelbaum, 1:97); also 11QMelch 2.15–22.

[78] See *y. Šeqal.* 6.2, 50a; *b. Yoma* 77b.

[79] Based on a *gezerah shavah* between שיט in Isa 33:21 and שוט in Job 1:7. See *b. Yoma* 77b.

descend to the Dead Sea and multiply fish for Israel, and they will acquire salt from that place, for scripture states about it: "its wetlands and swamps will not be fixed: they will produce salt" (Ezek 47:11). By it will grow all the pleasant trees of Lebanon, as scripture says: "and beside the river there will grow on either bank [trees] . . . which bear new fruit every month" (Ezek 47:12). This is the *ethrog* which is going to bear fruit monthly, and the tree will be edible like its fruit, for scripture says: "its fruit will serve as food and its foliage for medicine" (ibid.).[80] How wonderful is the Temple that will descend and be rebuilt upon its mound! For Scripture states: "and the city will be rebuilt on its ruins" (Jer 30:18).

The future Jerusalem that is built will have castles spread over an area a thousand times larger than Tefef, towers covering an area a thousand times larger than Qefel, gardens occupying an area a thousand times larger than Tefef, a thousand magnificent mansions, and each and every one (will be like those) in Sepphoris during her time of prosperity. R. Yose said: "I remember Sepphoris during her time of prosperity when her output was 180,000 puddings."[81] There are going to be three thousand towers in the midst of Jerusalem, and each tower will have a height of seven thousand (measures). She [Jerusalem] will sit on the peaks of three mountains: upon Sinai, Tabor, and Carmel. The rule for height will be set at seven thousand, and each unit of measure is equivalent to sixty-two cubits. She [Jerusalem] will be situated on the top of thirty-three side chambers (צלעות),[82] and the Temple will sit on top of all of them. How will they be able to go up to it? They will soar and fly like clouds and doves, as scripture states: "Who are these who fly like a cloud; like doves (returning) to their cotes" (Isa 60:8). The Temple will expand unto Damascus, for scripture says: "Burden of the word of the Lord: in the land of Hadrakh and Damascus will be His resting place" (Zech 9:1).[83] Seven walls will encompass Jerusalem which will be composed of silver, gold, jewels, bright stones, sapphire, carbuncle, and fire; and its brilliance will cast light from one end of the world to the other. The Temple will be built on four mountains (from) refined gold, purified gold, beaten gold, and the gold of Parvaim,[84] like gold that produces fruit,[85] set in

[80] See *Sifra*, Emor §16 (Weiss, 102d); *y. Sukkah* 3.5, 53d; *Lev. Rab.* 30.8 (Margulies, 2:706–707); *b. Sukkah* 35a.

[81] A somewhat garbled version of the tradition recounted by Resh Laqish in *b. B. Bat.* 75b. The meaning of the terms "Tefef" (טפף) and "Qefel" (קפל) is disputed; see Rashbam and Tosafot *ad loc.*

[82] Cf. Ezek 41:6–7.

[83] See *Sifre* Deut §1 (Finkelstein, 7–8).

[84] Cf. 2 Chr 3:6; 1QapGen^{ar} 2.23. Parvaim was apparently the name of a distant region renowned for the quality of its gold. According to *b. Yoma* 44b-45a, "gold of Parvaim" refers to a particular reddish-hued gold.

[85] A fanciful etymology for Parvaim (פרוים). See *Midr. Tanḥ.*, Naso §9.

sapphire (and) fixed in <bdellium>.[86] It will extend high into the heavens and reach up among the stars and to the spheres of the circuit of the Divine Chariot, as scripture says: "above the highest elevations of the city" (Prov 9:3). The Shekinah of God and His Glory will fill its sanctuary, and there He will appoint for each angel his particular service. Gabriel will be over His thousands, and Michael will be over His myriads. Vast hordes will enter one after another into its midst, and there He will set apart "these for eternal life and those for abuse and eternal disgrace" (Dan 12:2). The gates of the Garden of Eden will open from within it, as scripture says: "you were in Eden, the garden of God" (Ezek 28:13), and Gehinnom will (also) be open. There the Holy One, blessed be He, will descend with His throne and situate it in the Valley of Jehoshaphat,[87] and he will there make every nation and its idols pass (before Him). And after the nations of the world have passed by there, they will fall down within it, as scripture notes: "They are stationed like sheep for Sheol; Death will shepherd them" (Ps 49:15). And who brought about this (fate) for them? It is because they attacked "Zevul" [i.e., the Temple], as scripture states: "I have surely built a house for You (named) Zevul (זבול)" (1 Kgs 8:13). A person who commits a transgression against the Throne of Glory, if he is truly penitent then he will be pardoned, for scripture says: "Return, O Israel, unto the Lord" (Hos 14:2). But lo, the nations of the world will pass over into Gehinnom and fall down into it, and the apostates and rebels among Israel will cool Gehinnom with their tears, as scripture holds: "(They) pass through the valley weeping; they will make it (issue) from the eye" (Ps 84:7).[88] And when the apostates and rebels fall into Gehinnom, a fire from the Lord will burn through their body and their teeth will pop out from their mouths, for scripture says: "You have smashed the teeth of the wicked" (Ps 3:8). In place of reading "You have smashed" (שברת), read instead "You stretched, extended" (שירבבת).

R. Eliezer b. Jacob said: The academy of the Holy One, blessed be He, in the World to Come will be eighteen thousand myriad parasangs (in size), and the Holy One, blessed be He, will sit on a throne of judgment, and David will sit before him, as scripture says: "his throne is like the sun before Me" (Ps 89:37). All the learned[89] women who paid a wage for their sons so that they (i.e., the sons) might learn Torah, Bible, and Mishnah will be standing by a partition of reeds made like a wall[90] listening to the voice of

[86] Read with Even-Shmuel בבדלח in place of בגדולה.

[87] Cf. Joel 4:2, 12. A similar judgment scene takes place in *Secrets of R. Šimʿōn b. Yōḥai* and *Midrash Wa-yoshaʿ*. This particular location for God's judging activity is dictated, of course, by the proper name.

[88] A translation along these lines is required.

[89] See Isa 32:9 and *b. Ber.* 17a.

[90] See the remarks of Steven Fine, "'Chancel' Screens in Late Antique Palestinian Synagogues: A

Zerubbabel b. Shealtiel who will serve as *meturgeman* before the Holy One, blessed be He. They will chant responsively after he has finished: "May His Great Name be blessed and sanctified forever and ever!" The righteous will say "Amen," and the wicked who are in Gehinnom will say "Amen!" The Holy One, blessed be He, will ask the ministering angels: "Who are those who respond with 'Amen!' from the midst of Gehinnom?" The ministering angels will say before Him: "Master of the Universe! Those are the rebels and apostates from Israel who even though they are immersed in pain yet respond 'Amen!'" The Holy One, blessed be He, will say to them: "Bring them up from there!" When they bring them up, their faces will be black like the bottom of a cooking pot.[91] They will say before Him: "Master of the Universe! Well have You judged; well have You convicted; well have You made us a sign for all Israel!" At that time the Holy One, blessed be He, will open the gates of Paradise [lit., *Gan Eden*] and add them to the assembly of Israel, as scripture says: "Open the gates and let the righteous nation, the guardian of faithfulness, enter" (Isa 26:2).

Then Gabriel will enter *Gan Eden*, crying aloud and saying: "Take delight,[92] O righteous ones, in the work(s) of your hands!" They will say to him, "Who are you?" He will answer, "I am Gabriel!" Israel will say: "'Blessed be he who comes in the name of the Lord!'" (Ps 118:26), and Gabriel will say: "'We bless you in the name of the Lord!'"[93]

At that time the Holy One, blessed be He, will arrange tables, slaughter Behemoth, Leviathan, and the wild Ziz, and prepare a great banquet for the righteous.[94] Each one of them will be seated (at the table) in accordance with their honor. The Holy One, blessed be He, will say to them: "Do you wish to drink wine made from apples, pomegranates, or grapes?" The righteous will respond: "The authority is Yours to do whatever You decide!" The Holy One, blessed be He, will bring them wine made from grapes that has been reserved since the six days of the initial creation-week, as scripture states: "I will serve you spiced wine" (Cant 8:2).[95] The Holy One, blessed be

Source from the Cairo Genizah," in *Religious and Ethnic Communities in Later Roman Palestine* (ed. Hayim Lapin; Bethesda, Md.: University Press of Maryland, 1998), 67-85.

[91] Note *Pesiq. Rab.* §20 (Ish-Shalom, 95b): כיון שעלה מגיהנם פניו משחירים, "when he emerges from Gehinnom his face will be black." This change in facial hue reflects their shame or embarrassment and is not to be attributed to their exposure to the sooty fires of hell. See David M. Goldenberg, *The Curse of Ham: Race and Slavery in Early Judaism, Christianity, and Islam* (Princeton: Princeton University Press, 2003), 181. Note also the sources cited by Moritz Steinschneider, *Polemische und apologetische Literatur in arabischer Sprache zwischen Muslimen, Christen und Juden, nebst Anhängen verwandten Inhalts* (Leipzig, 1877; repr., Hildesheim: Georg Olms, 1966), 250–51 n. 18.

[92] Read התבסמו in place of the text's התבוססו?

[93] Ps 118:26b reads in its Masoretic version: ברכנוכם מבית י״י.

[94] A more expansive version of this same banquet scene can be found in Jellinek, *BHM* 5:45–46.

[95] Cf. *Seder Gan Eden* (Jellinek, *BHM* 2:52).

He, will satisfy the desire of the righteous when He places His Throne of Glory there and sits with them, as scripture says: "I have come to My garden, My sister, bride" (Cant 5:1). The Holy One, blessed be He, will produce every praiseworthy item belonging to *Gan Eden* and bring in each and every righteous person and (let them) see His Glory, and every one (of them) will point using (their) finger, saying, "'This is God, our God forever and ever!'" (Ps 48:15).

They will eat, drink, and rejoice until the Holy One, blessed be He, gives the command to lift the cup over which Grace is said. The righteous will say to Abraham, "Stand up and recite Grace," but Abraham will respond: "Ishmael casts blame upon me!" They will (next) address Isaac, but he will respond: "Esau casts blame upon me!" They will address Jacob, but he will respond: "(The matter of) two sisters casts blame upon me!" They will address the tribes, but they will respond: "The testimony of Joseph casts blame upon us!" They will continue thus until they reach David, and they will place in his hands four cups, which are "the Lord is a portion of my lot and my cup" (Ps 16:5), "my cup is full" (Ps 23:5), "I will raise the cup of deliverance" (Ps 116:13), and the cup over which Grace is said, which will have a capacity of two hundred and twenty *log*s, with each *log* equivalent to the size of one and a half eggs. David will reply: "It is fitting that I should offer blessing and praise!" He will stand and then offer blessings, glorifications, and praises using every type of melody, as scripture bears witness: "I will praise the Lord in accordance with His righteousness" (Ps 7:18). At that time the Holy One, blessed be He, will take His crown and place it on the head of David and on the head of the Messiah of the lineage of David, and He will reveal their praiseworthiness and their righteousness to all generations. Israel will live peacefully and tranquilly, and He will fashion a canopy for all the righteous—a dwelling place to match each one's honor[96]—and He will move about among the righteous, lifting His hand while each person claps hands in their joy. For thus did Isaiah say: "Lord, Your hand is raised; yet they do not see!" (Isa 26:11). The Holy One, blessed be He, will say: "I have previously said, 'They will see and be ashamed!' (ibid.)," and Israel will say: "O Master of the Universe! May 'they see and be ashamed,' just like You have said!" Then the Holy One, blessed be He, will raise the stature of the gentile nations to be higher than the walls surrounding *Gan Eden*, and they will look on the joy of Israel and be embarrassed. Fire will shoot forth from the mouths of the righteous and burn them up, as scripture states: "fire will consume those who are Your enemies" (ibid.).

[96] Compare *Pesiq. Rab.* §31 (Ish-Shalom, 145a): עתיד הקדוש ברוך הוא לעשות אהלי חופות של כבוד לצדיקים כל אחד ואחד לפי כבודו, "the Holy One, blessed be He, is going to fashion enveloping tents of glory for the righteous—each one befitting their honor." Note also the pericope below where God envelopes the righteous with seven distinct canopies.

The Holy One, blessed be He, is going to temper the brilliance of the sun and the moon,[97] and He will bring the skin of Leviathan and fashion tents (סוכות) from it for the righteous, as scripture says: "can you fill its skin with hooks (*śukkot*)" (Job 40:31).[98] They will make a tent for whoever deserves a tent, necklaces for whoever deserves necklaces, (and) a crown for whoever deserves a crown. That which is left over from it they will drape over the Temple, and its luster will radiate from one end of the world to the other. Israel will remain, eating and drinking, reproducing, and enjoying the glow of the Shekinah. The Holy One, blessed be He, will increase everyone's height to be two hundred cubits—so did R. Šimᶜōn teach. But R. Judah said (their height would be) one hundred cubits, like that of Adam the protoplast. This would, however, hold only for males: from where do we learn that females (also will be this tall)? Scripture states: "our daughters will be like corner-pillars" (Ps 144:12).[99] Every Israelite will engender progeny each day, as much as if not more than a hen bears! Do not be amazed at this (feat), but come and learn a lesson from the vine:[100] each and every vine during the messianic era will require no less than (the population of) one city for its harvesting, as scripture hints: "harness to each vine its city (עירה)" (Gen 49:11); and every barren tree[101] that has never previously borne fruit will become fruitful[102] to the extent that it becomes a burden for young asses to bear, as scripture promises: "for the barren one (ולשורקה), a young ass" (ibid.). And should you say "there will be no wine," scripture teaches: "he will wash his clothing in wine" (ibid.); should you say "it will not be red," scripture states: "his garment in the blood (דם) of grapes" (ibid.); should you say "it will not intoxicate," scripture notes: "its seduction (סותה)" (ibid.); should you say "it will have no taste," scripture uses the word חכלילי (Gen 49:12): every palate (כל חיך) that tastes it will think "it's mine, it's mine!" (לי לי). Should you say "it will be good for the young, but not good for the elderly," scripture teaches: "better than milk for the one who is old (בן שנים)" (ibid.).

R. Yohanan taught: Wine is better for the elderly than milk is for infants. If a gentile should question you, saying "this thing will never come to pass," reply to him: "O wicked one, go and learn from the example of Obed-Edom the Gittite (cf. 2 Sam 6:11), for whom his mother-in-law and eight daughters-in-law bore sixty-two children over the course of three months, with as

[97] להחפיר זיוה של חמה ושל לבנה. Cf. Isa 24:23.

[98] Cf. *b. B. Bat.* 75a.

[99] Cf. *b. B. Bat.* 75a; *Sanh.* 100a, where the first tradition is attributed to R. Meir. The variant ascription to R. Šimᶜōn b. Yōḥai probably derives from *Midr. Tanḥ.*, ᶜEqev §7.

[100] For the following series of questions, cf. *b. Ketub.* 111b; note also *Gen. Rab.* 98.10 (Theodor-Albeck, 1261).

[101] וכל אילן סרק.

[102] Cf. *b. Ketub.* 112b.

many as six (fetuses) in each womb.[103] And as for the vine, there is already the example of R. Aḥa bar Adda, who served as a teacher for the young children of R. Šimʿōn b. Leqish.[104] Once he left the children, and he (R. Šimʿōn) came to him. He said to him: "Why did you leave the children?" He [R. Aḥa] answered him: "My father left me one latticed grapevine. The first day I harvested from it three hundred bunches, each one of which filled a keg. The second day I harvested three hundred bunches, every two of which filled a keg. The third day I harvested three hundred bunches, every three of which filled a keg, and I left him more than half of it." But in the World to Come, it will not be so; instead, a person will bring his grapes in a wagon or on a boat and deposit them in a dark corner, and it [his deposit] will be like a large jar supplying (wine) for both that person and their household, as scripture forecasts: "you will drink (a *ḥomer*'s quantity) of the blood of grapes" (Deut 32:14). There in the future the vine will extend itself out straight like a staff and climb to the peaks of the mountains.[105] Should you say "it will surely prove irksome to harvest," scripture teaches: "it will shake (off) its fruit like Lebanon" (Ps 72:16). The Holy One, blessed be He, will cause the wind to blow on it, and it will blow down its fruits, and every Israelite will take up enough to sustain themselves and their households.

The Holy One, blessed be He, is going to erect seven canopies for every righteous person, canopies consisting of cloud, smoke, daylight, fire, brilliance, flame, and night.[106] Does scripture teach about the canopy of smoke? Only that everyone who envied the disciples of the Sages will have their eyes blinded by the smoke that emerges from the canopies of the righteous! Where do we find the canopy of daylight? Scripture states: "the <path>[107] of the righteous is like a brilliant light" (Prov 4:18). Where do we find the canopy of fire? Fire is going to shoot out from the canopies of the righteous and the wicked will be scorched by it, as scripture promises: "He will pour down coals on the wicked" (Ps 11:6). Where do we find the canopy of brilliance? Scripture states: "it will be bright like light" (Hab 3:4). Where do we find the canopy of flame that sets the wicked ablaze? Scripture says: "the voice of the Lord dividing flames of fire" (Ps 29:7). Where do we find the canopy of night? Scripture states: "and night will shine like day" (Ps 139:12). No single one of these canopies will come into contact with the canopy next to it.

[103] See *y. Yebam.* 4.6b; *b. Ber.* 63b; *Num. Rab.* 4.20.

[104] See *b. Ketub.* 111b.

[105] Compare *b. Ketub.* 111b: עתידה חטה שתתמר כדקל ועולה בראש הרים, "in the future wheat will grow tall like a palm-tree and ascend as high as mountain-tops."

[106] Based on the verbiage found in Isa 4:5. See *b. B. Bat.* 75a.

[107] Read וארח in place of ואור.

Jeremiah said: "I saw Him bringing out bridegrooms for the brides," for scripture notes: "the voice of the bridegroom and the voice of the bride" (Jer 7:34). Hosea said: "I saw Him multiplying Israel like (grains of) sand," for scripture states: "and the number of the descendants of Israel will be like the sand of the sea" (Hos 2:1). Joel said: "I saw Him exacting vengeance against His enemies," as scripture notes: "while I can hold blameless, I will not hold blameless (those who have shed) their blood" (Joel 4:21). The Holy One, blessed be He, has said: "Even were the gentile nations to hand over to Me all of their treasures, they would still fall short of compensating for the deaths of R. ʿAqiva and his companions."[108] Amos said: "I saw Him visiting upon the nations their transgressions," for scripture says: "for the three sins of Edom" (Amos 1:11). Obadiah said: "I saw Him assume the royal crown," for scripture says: "deliverers ascended Mount Zion [to judge the mount of Esau, and the kingdom became the Lord's]" (Obad 1:21). Jonah said: "I saw Him receive the prayers of His people with compassion," as scripture says: "and he prayed to the Lord" (Jonah 4:2). Micah[109] said: "I saw Him turning toward Jerusalem with compassion," as scripture states: "I will turn with compassion toward Jerusalem" (Zech 1:16). The rest of all the prophets, each and every one of them, will bring the consoling words which they uttered with them, and the Holy One, blessed be He, will station them in His Presence (arranged in order) from the first generation until the last, and He will say to them: "Come and see the reward which I have kept in store for you! Come, eat, and enjoy the blessing which I have saved for you, in accord with what Scripture promised: 'How magnificent is Your reward which You have preserved for those who revere You!' (Ps 31:20)."

APPENDIX
The Judgment of Samael, Prince of Rome[110]

"And Belaʿ died . . . from Bosra" (Gen 36:33). It is stated in scripture: "Who is this who comes from Edom, [red of garment from Bosra?]" (Isa 63:1). What is "who is this" (מי זה)? In the future the Holy One, blessed be He, will depart to exact vengeance against Edom. He will accomplish this

[108] Cf. *Cant. Rab.* 8.7: אם פותחין אוה״ע כל תיסבריות שלהן . . . ונותנין כל ממונם בדמיו של ר״ע וחביריו אין מתכפר להם לעולם, "(even) if the nations of the world were to open up all their treasuries . . . and hand over all their wealth for the blood of R. ʿAqiva and his companions, it would never compensate for them."

[109] Read "Zechariah"? So Even-Shmuel, *Midreshey Geʾullah*, 344.

[110] Translated from the edition found in Ḥanokh Albeck, ed., *Midrash Bereshit Rabbati* (Jerusalem: Mekize Nirdamim, 1940), 166.4–167.8. See also *S. Eli. Zut.* §19.

Himself and will not inform His ministering angels about His journey. Thus, when they seek to sing a song before the Holy One, blessed be He, they will not find Him. They will go to the sea and ask it, "Have you seen the Holy One, blessed be He? For scripture says: 'Who placed a highway in the sea'" (Isa 43:16). It will answer: "I have seen Him no more since the day He dried me so that His children could cross through me." They will go to Sinai and say, "Have you not seen the Holy One, blessed be He? For scripture states: 'the Lord has come from Sinai'" (Deut 33:2). It will answer them: "I have seen Him no more since the day He revealed Himself on me and gave Torah to His children." They will go to Zion (and) ask it, "Have you seen the Holy One, blessed be He? Scripture holds: 'for the Lord has chosen Zion'" (Ps 132:13). It will answer them: "I have seen Him no more since the day He left me, destroyed His Temple, and burned His sanctuary."

Isaiah encountered them (and) asked them: "What do you seek?" [They answered him: "The Holy One, blessed be He!"]. He said to them: "He is departing from Edom at this very moment, fulfilling the scripture that says, 'Who is this who comes from Edom, red (*ḥamūtz*) of garment etc.'" (Isa 63:1). The Holy One, blessed be He, will punish them because they plundered the wealth of Israel. The word *ḥamūtz* simply means "stolen," as scripture hints: "from the clutches of the crook and the robber (*ḥōmetz*)" (Ps 71:4). How then should the word *ḥamūtz* be understood? All who plunder Israel engage, so to speak, in the plundering of the Shekinah, for thus is it written: "I am with him in trouble" (Ps 91:15).

[Will the Holy One, blessed be He, thus come] from all the cities of Edom? Rather, at the time that the Holy One, blessed be He, judges Edom, there will come Samael, the prince of Rome, at the head of the Roman legation.[111] They will announce before the Holy One, blessed be He: "I should receive a reward alongside the righteous for the great benefactions I bestowed upon Israel." The Holy One, blessed be He, will respond to them: "What are the benefactions which you bestowed upon My children?!?" [They will say to Him:] "I built numerous highways for them; I established markets, bath-houses, and bridges for them!!" Then the Holy One, blessed be He, will say: "Fools! Everything you did was done only to corrupt them! Bath-houses wherein idols could be stationed, highways along which bandits could lie in wait, markets for the habitation of whores, bridges for the offices of the tax collectors—and not being content with this, you robbed them of everything which came into their possession each and every day!"[112] Samael said to the Holy One, blessed be He: "If we stole their

[111] סמאל שרה של רומי בראש פמליא של רומי.

[112] Cf. *b. Šabb.* 33b; ʿ*Abod. Zar.* 2b.

wealth, then it is incumbent upon us to furnish recompense, for scripture ordains 'he (i.e., the thief) will restore the stolen item, etc.'" (Lev 5:23).

The Holy One, blessed be He, said to him: "But how will you be able to make restitution for the Israelite blood which you have shed? Does not scripture state, 'Egypt will become a wasteland, and Edom will become a desolate wilderness on account of the violence expended upon the children of Judah, for they spilled innocent blood in their land'" (Joel 4:19)? Immediately Samael will be embarrassed and will flee in great anguish to Bosra.[113] Why would he flee to Bosra? Because he will be thinking that it is a city of refuge, on account of the scripture that says "Betzer (בצר) in the wilderness" (Deut 4:43). Then the Holy One, blessed be He, will follow him to Bosra and say to him: "Wicked One! You have confused Betzer with Bosra! Moreover, scripture states (that one will not be granted asylum in a city of refuge) 'if a person plots with premeditation against their fellow to murder them'" (Exod 21:14).[114] Immediately the Holy One, blessed be He, will hand him over to Michael, and he will bring him bound with iron chains and hand him over to Israel, and they will do with him whatever they want, as scripture states: "I shall wreak My vengeance against Edom [through the agency of My people Israel]" (Ezek 25:14). "... this one majestic in his clothing ..." (Isa 63:1): this refers to a garment of vengeance, for scripture says, "He will don garments of vengeance" (Isa 59:17). "... moving[115] with the greatness of His power ..." (Isa 63:1), for scripture says: "for the Lord has a sacrifice in Bosra" (Isa 34:6). "... I will speak of righteousness ..." (Isa 63:1), as scripture says: "I will pronounce your righteousness, etc." (Isa 57:12).[116]

[113] A pun in Hebrew: ובורח בצרה גדולה לבצרה.

[114] Cf. *b. Mak.* 12a, which mentions a third mistake to be made by the "prince of Rome": the laws of criminal asylum apply to humans, not angels.

[115] See Radaq *ad* Isa 51:14.

[116] See the opening paragraph of *Pirqe Mašiaḥ* above.

9

*Midrash Wa-Yosha*ᶜ (end)

*MIDRASH WA-YOSHA*ᶜ is an extended homiletic exposition of the biblical Song at the Sea (Exod 15:1–18), the final portion of which focuses on eschatological themes familiar from earlier apocalyptic works like *Sefer Zerubbabel* and the *Secrets of R. Šimᶜōn b. Yoḥai*. Its name derives from the narrative introduction to the biblical song contained in Exod 14:30: "on that day the Lord *rescued* (ויושע) Israel from the hand of Egypt . . . ," an act of national deliverance that R. Saadya Gaon labeled the "first redemption"[1] and which is paradigmatically destined to be repeated at the End of Days.[2]

In addition to the aforementioned apocalyptic sources, this work also depends on and develops pericopae found in *Pirqe de R. Eliezer*, *Pesiqta Rabbati*, and the *Chronicles of Moses*. It thus probably should be dated to the final half of the eleventh or beginning of the twelfth century. It was first published in Constantinople in 1519 within a collection of eighteen so-called "apocryphal texts."[3] The present translation relies upon the edition published by Adolph Jellinek.[4]

[1] S. Landauer, ed., *Kitâb al-Amânât wa'l-Iᶜtiqâdât von Saᶜadja b. Jûsuf al-Fajjûmî* (Leiden: Brill, 1880), 224.19; cf. also 225.1, 13–14. See Saadia Gaon, *The Book of Beliefs and Opinions* (trans. Samuel Rosenblatt; Yale Judaica Series 1; New Haven: Yale University Press, 1948), 282–83.

[2] Note Saadya's comparison of the chief features that will distinguish the "final" from the "first" redemption of Israel (ibid.). See Mic 7:15, the probable exegetical source for the conceptual paralleling of exodus and eschaton, and the examples cited by Louis Ginzberg, *An Unknown Jewish Sect* (New York: Jewish Theological Seminary of America, 1976), 234–38; Patricia Crone and Michael Cook, *Hagarism: The Making of the Islamic World* (Cambridge: Cambridge University Press, 1977), 158–59 nn. 44–46; Oded Irshai, "Dating the Eschaton: Jewish and Christian Apocalyptic Calculations in Late Antiquity," in *Apocalyptic Time* (ed. Albert I. Baumgarten; Leiden: Brill, 2000), 124–29. Christian exploitation of the same paradigm is visible in Lactantius, *Div. Inst.* 7.15 (cited in ibid., 140). For a fascinating chronomessianic connection of the emperor Julian's failed attempt to rebuild the Temple in 363 CE and the 430-year period of Egyptian servitude (cf. Exod 12:40–42), see ibid., 142–44.

[3] מעשיות (Constantinople: Astruq de Toulon, 1519), 76b–86a; the final eschatological portion translated here begins on 85b. For a listing of the contents of this work (which also includes an edition of *Sefer Zerubbabel* and an edition of *Ten Signs*), see M[oritz] Steinschneider, ed., *Catalogus librorum hebraeorum in bibliotheca Bodleiana* (Berlin: Ad. Friedlaender, 1852–60), 203.

[4] Adolph Jellinek, ed., *Bet ha-Midrasch: Sammlung kleiner Midraschim und vermischter Abhandlungen aus der jüdischen Literatur* (6 vols.; Leipzig, 1853–77; repr., Jerusalem: Bamberger & Wahrmann, 1938), 1:35–57; only 1:55–57 is translated here. An annotated edition is available in Yehudah

"The Lord will reign . . ." (Exod 15:18). Moses said to Israel: "You have seen all the miracles, mighty feats, and marvels that the Lord has done for you. Even more is he planning to do for you in the future age. The world to come will not be like the present world: the present world has wars and troubles, as well as the evil impulse, Satan, and the Angel of Death who have authority to rule in (this) world. But the World to Come will be free of troubles and hatred, Satan and the Angel of Death will be absent, there will be no lamentations or subjugation, and the evil impulse will exist no more, as scripture attests, 'He will destroy death forever, and the Lord will wipe the tears from every face' (Isa 25:8), and it is written 'on that day, behold, this is our God: we have waited for Him, and He will deliver us' (Isa 25:9)."

As the days of the Messiah draw near, Gog and Magog will come up against the land of Israel, for he will hear that Israel has no ruler and dwells unconcerned (about foreign attacks). Immediately he will take with him seventy-one nation(s) and come up to Jerusalem, thinking[5] "Pharaoh was a fool when he gave the command to kill (only the) males and leave the females.[6] Balaq was a simpleton, for he sought to curse them, but he did not realize that their God would (instead) bless them.[7] Haman was insane for he wanted to kill them, but he did not realize that their God would be able to deliver them.[8] However, I will not act thus; (instead), I will go up and do battle with their God first, and only after that will I kill them, for scripture says: 'the kings of the earth stand up together, and rulers take counsel together against the Lord and His anointed one' (Ps 2:2)."[9]

Even-Shmuel, *Midreshey Geʾullah* (2d ed.; Jerusalem: Mosad Bialik, 1954), 93–98. For further discussion of this midrash, see Leopold Zunz and Ḥanokh Albeck, *Haderashot be-Yisrael* (2d ed.; Jerusalem: Mosad Bialik, 1954), 141–42; Moshe D. Herr, "Midrashim, Smaller," *EncJud* 16:1517.

[5] A loose parallel to the remainder of this paragraph can be found in *Aggadat Bereshit* (see Jellinek, *BHM* 4:5); for an English translation, see Lieve M. Teugels, *Aggadat Bereshit* (Jewish and Christian Perspectives Series 4; Leiden: Brill, 2001), 8–9.

[6] Exod 1:15–16, 22.

[7] Num 22:1–24:25.

[8] Esth 3:5–15; 6:1–10:3.

[9] Apparently the order in which the adversaries are listed (". . . against the Lord [first] and [then] His anointed one") is the pertinent clue for Gog and Magog. For the strategy criticized by Gog and Magog, see *Midr. Tanḥ.*, Pequdey §4: אמר רבי חייא למה אומות העולם דומין לאדם שהיה שונא את המלך והיה מבקש להתגרות בו ולא היה יכול מה עשה הלך אצל אדריונטוס שלו ומבקש להפילו . . . כך אומות העולם הם מבקשים להתגרות בהקב׳ה ואינן יכולין ובאין להתגרות בישראל אמר דוד יתיצבו מלכי ארץ וגו׳ משל מי שאינו יכול להכות לחמור מכה את האוכף, "R. Hiyya said, To what might we compare the Gentile nations? They are like a man who detests the king and who seeks to incite revolt against him but who is unable (to attract attention). What does he do? He goes to his (the king's) statue and seeks to topple it . . . similarly the Gentile nations seek to incite rebellion against the Holy One, blessed be He, but they are unable (to wage war directly against Him). Instead, they come and fight against Israel, (as) David

The Holy One, blessed be He, will say to him: "Wicked one! You wish to do battle with Me? By your life, I will indeed do battle with you!" Immediately the Holy One, blessed be He, will rain down on him stones of hail which are stored in the heavens and strike them a crushing blow, as scripture states: "and this will be the blow that the Lord will strike the Gentiles when they amass armies against Jerusalem—his flesh will rot where he is standing, his eyes will decay in their sockets, and each one's tongue will rot in their mouths" (Zech 14:12).

After that another king will arise, a wicked one and "strong of face" (עז פנים),[10] and he will wage war with Israel for three months. His name is Armilos, and these are his signs:[11] he will be bald, with one of his eyes small and the other large. His right arm is short, and his left arm is two and a half cubits long. His forehead will be leprous, and his right ear will be closed up and the (other) one open. Whenever a person comes to tell him good things, he turns his closed up ear toward him, but if a person wants to speak wickedly, he turns his open ear toward him.[12] He will come up to Jerusalem and kill the Messiah of the lineage of Joseph, as scripture attests: "and they shall look to Me about the one whom they pierced, and they shall mourn for him like one who mourns an only child" (Zech 12:10). After that the Messiah of the lineage of David will come, regarding which scripture affirms: "and behold with the clouds of heaven one like a mortal man" (Dan 7:13), and it is written afterwards: "he will have authority and royal dignity" (Dan 7:14). He will kill Armilos the wicked, as scripture attests: "he will slay the wicked one with the breath of his lips" (Isa 11:4).

Then the Holy One, blessed be He, will gather Israel—those who have been dispersed here and there—as scripture says: "Let Me whistle for them and I will gather them, when I have redeemed them, and they will be as numerous as they formerly were" (Zech 10:8). In Jerusalem will be suspended seventy-two precious stones that will shine from one end of the world to the other, and the nations of the world will come to that light, as it

mentioned: 'the kings of the earth stand up together, etc.' (Ps 2:2). An aphorism: (it is like) one who cannot beat the donkey so he beats the saddle instead!"

[10] See Dan 8:23.

[11] Interestingly the peculiar legend about the unnatural birth of Armilos is missing. See also Samuel Krauss, *Das Leben Jesu nach jüdischen Quellen* (Berlin: S. Calvary & Co., 1902; repr., Hildesheim: Georg Olms Verlag, 1994), 216. Note that unlike the "dynastic" apocalypses associated with the name of R. Šimʿōn ben Yoḥai, this interpretive tradition equates "the king strong of face" with Armilos.

[12] Salo W. Baron states that this particular motif makes its first appearance here, and that it is indebted to the "pre-Islamic ethical biases" of Zoroastrianism and Judaism; cf. his *A Social and Religious History of the Jews* (18 vols.; 2d ed.; Philadelphia: Jewish Publication Society; New York: Columbia University Press, 1952–84), 5:358–59 n. 10.

is written: "the nations will come to your light, and rulers (will come) to the luster of your shine" (Isa 60:3). The Holy One, blessed be He, will lower the Temple from heaven—the same one that the Holy One, blessed be He, showed to Moses, as scripture states: "You will bring them and plant them upon the mount of Your territory; a place for Your dwelling have You made, O Lord; a Temple, my Lord, Your hands have established" (Exod 15:17). Israel shall dwell there for two thousand years,[13] and they will feast (upon the flesh of) Leviathan.[14]

At the end of the two thousand years, the Holy One, blessed be He, will seat Himself upon a throne of judgment in the Valley of Jehoshaphat.[15] Immediately the heavens and the earth will be displaced and the sun and the moon embarrassed, as scripture states: "the moon will be ashamed, and the sun embarrassed" (Isa 24:23). From whence do we learn that (final) judgment will be pronounced on the third day? Scripture attests: "He will revitalize us for two days; on the third day He will stand us up and we will live before Him" (Hos 6:2)—this (verse) refers to the (final) judgment. The Holy One, blessed be He, will bring (before Him) every nation and language group and say: "What did you serve in the world that has departed, and whom did you worship?" They will respond: "Idols of silver and gold." The Holy One, blessed be He, will say to them: "Pass through the fire there, and should your god(s) be able to rescue you, he will rescue!" Immediately they will pass through and be immolated, as scripture says: "the wicked will return to Sheol, all the nations who have forgotten God" (Ps 9:18). Then Israel shall come, and the Holy One, blessed be He, will say to them: "Whom have you worshiped?" Immediately they will respond: "Indeed, You, our Father! For Abraham did not know us, nor did Israel recognize us, but You, O Lord, are our Father; our Eternal Deliverer is Your name!" (Isa 63:16). Immediately the Holy One, blessed be He, will rescue them from the sentence of Gehinnom, and they will dwell in the Garden of Eden and enjoy its fruits, as scripture states: "and the poor will inherit the earth and enjoy abundant prosperity" (Ps 37:11). Then the Holy One, blessed be He, will

[13] A reflection of the *baraita* attributed to the "school of Elijah" (תנא דבי אליהו) in *b. Sanh.* 97a: שני אלפים ימות המשיח, "the messianic era will last two thousand years." See also *b.* ᶜ*Abod. Zar.* 9a; *Pesiq. Rab.* §1 (Ish-Shalom, 4b) and *Midr. Teh.* 90.17, where the notion of a two-thousand–year messianic era is attributed to R. Joshua. Note especially the discussions of Ephraim E. Urbach, *The Sages: Their Concepts and Beliefs* (2 vols.; Jerusalem: Magnes, 1979), 1:677–78, 2:1000–1001; Irshai, "Dating the Eschaton," 130–32.

[14] Compare *1 En.* 60:24; *4 Ezra* 6:49–52; *2 Bar.* 29:4; and, in general, the remarks and references supplied by Louis Ginzberg, *The Legends of the Jews* (7 vols.; Philadelphia: Jewish Publication Society of America, 1909–38), 5:43–46.

[15] See Joel 4:2, 12. This section is heavily indebted to the *Secrets of R. Šim*ᶜ*ōn b. Yōḥai.*

renovate the heavens and the earth for them, as scripture says: "for behold, I create new heavens and a new earth" (Isa 25:17).

When the Holy One, blessed be He, renews the world, He will arrange the orders of the righteous and the orders of the pious, and He will do similarly for every generation, created entity, and breathing organism. The earth that He is destined to renew will bring forth trees and all types of choice fruits, and everything will live forever and ever. The One who has performed miracles and marvels during these (present) days and at this (present) time—He is the One who will perform miracles and marvels for us during these (future) days and at this (future) time! He will gather us from the four ends of the earth and lead us to Jerusalem, where He will gladden us within it and we will say "Amen, Selah!"

Thematic Excursuses

1

Metatron as Apocalyptic Persona

THE REVELATORY ROLE granted in several of these apocalypses to Metatron, a supernal entity aptly designated by Steven Wasserstrom as "the most important of postbiblical Jewish angels,"[1] would appear to supply some potentially crucial evidence for the commonly posited conceptual linkage of late antique Jewish apocalyptic with posttalmudic Hekhalot and other cognate genres of Jewish esotericism.[2] Despite a number of assumptions and claims regarding the antiquity of this supernal entity, there is no unambiguous evidence that a figure bearing the name Metatron played any role whatsoever in Jewish angelology prior to the redaction of the Babylonian Talmud.[3] Even there he is mentioned only three times. One passage (*b. Ḥag.* 15a) relates the infamous visionary experience of the heretic Sage Elisha b. ʾAvuya, who "espied Metatron (מיטטרון) to whom had been granted the authority to sit (and) record the merits of Israel." As a result he lapsed into dualism, mistakenly concluding that there were actually "two powers" (שתי רשויות) who ruled the universe, and hence Metatron was punished with "sixty strokes of fire" (פולסי דנורא) for failing to stand while the human visitor was present. Another instance (*b. Sanh.* 38b) records R. ʾIdit's reply to a rhetorical query from an anonymous sectarian (*min*) challenger regarding the theological import

[1] Steven M. Wasserstrom, *Between Muslim and Jew: The Problem of Symbiosis under Early Islam* (Princeton: Princeton University Press, 1995), 190.

[2] Apart from the Sabbatian expansions of *Sefer Zerubbabel* found in some editions of *Hekhalot Rabbati* (see the introduction to *Sefer Zerubbabel* above), note especially the apocalyptic materials incorporated into New York Ms. 8128 of *Hekhalot Rabbati* (§§122–26, 130–38, 140–45) as signaled by Peter Schäfer, ed., *Synopse zur Hekhalot-Literatur* (TSAJ 2; Tübingen: J. C. B. Mohr, 1981), xi. Important studies that highlight the continuities between Jewish apocalyptic and mystical literature include Ithamar Gruenwald, *Apocalyptic and Merkavah Mysticism* (AGJU 14; Leiden: Brill, 1980); Martha Himmelfarb, "Heavenly Ascent and the Relationship of the Apocalypses and the *Hekhalot* Literature," *HUCA* 59 (1988): 73–100.

[3] Scholem (see n. 9 below) correctly dismisses *Sifre* Deut §338 (Finkelstein, 388), and it is very doubtful whether the cosmological treatise *Reʾuyot Yeḥezqʾel* predates the geonic era. The occasional appearance of Metatron among the supernatural *dramatis personae* of the Babylonian magical bowl corpus does not alter this temporal assessment. For an extensive collection of Metatron testimonia, see Reuven Margaliot, *Malʾakey ʿelyon* (Jerusalem: Mosad ha-Rav Kook, 1945), 73–108, 199–200.

of the puzzling third-person reference to the deity in the direct discourse of Exod 24:1,[4] where the unidentified scriptural speaker is presumably this same entity. R. ʾIdit explains that the speaker of the command "Ascend to the Lord!" is in fact the supernal being "Metatron (מטטרון),[5] whose name is like the Name of His Lord," and he connects this latter qualifying clause with Exod 23:21 ("for My Name is within him"). The third talmudic reference portrays Metatron as the angelic pedagogue of children who tragically die prematurely during infancy (*b. ʿAbod. Zar.* 3b).[6]

These talmudic passages presage several of the variegated functions accorded the angel Metatron in posttalmudic literature. Interestingly, two of the passages embed the name within broader discussions about or involving "heretics," an association perhaps suggestive of the typical ideological context wherein Metatron and kindred divine "vice-regent"[7] figures were customarily invoked.[8] Scholem has persuasively argued that the posttalmudic portraiture of Metatron exhibits an uneasy fusion of what were once at least two separate streams of older theosophical lore.[9] One of these streams constructs Metatron as the heavenly avatar of the seventh antediluvian human forefather Enoch (Gen 5:21–24), a stunning metamorphosis securely rooted in some of the more loquacious traditions about the fate of Enoch contained in earlier Jewish and Christian parascriptural lore.[10] The other rivulet concentrates a variety of themes and mythic motifs that originally pertained to separate heavenly entities like the mysterious "prince of the world" (שר העולם),[11] the demiurgic "creator of the world" (יוצר העולם or

[4] ואל משה אמר עלה אל י״י אתה ואהרן נדב ואביהוא ושבעים מזקני ישראל והשתחויתם מרחק.

[5] Compare *Tg. Ps.-J.* Exod 24:1: . . . ולות משה אמר מיכאל סרכן חכמתא, "and Michael, the prince of wisdom, said to Moses. . . ."

[6] Metatron's role as primary school tutor for those who die prematurely is echoed in the so-called *3 Enoch*; note Vatican Ms. 228 and Munich Ms. 22 as reproduced by Schäfer, *Synopse*, 37 (§75).

[7] I have borrowed this taxon from the recent comparative study of Nathaniel Deutsch, *Guardians of the Gate: Angelic Vice Regency in Late Antiquity* (Brill's Series in Jewish Studies 22; Leiden: Brill, 1999).

[8] The Syriac *Gannat Bussame* (quoted below) pregnantly contextualizes such entities alongside its dismissal of the followers of Marcion, Bardaisan, and Mani. Note also the still pertinent remarks of Adolph Jellinek about the relevance of Metatron for the elucidation of the angelology of a prominent Islamicate Jewish sect in his *Beiträge zur Geschichte der Kabbala: Erstes Heft* (Leipzig: C. L. Fritzsche, 1852), 54–56.

[9] Gershom G. Scholem, *Jewish Gnosticism, Merkabah Mysticism, and Talmudic Tradition* (2d ed.; New York: Jewish Theological Seminary of America, 1965), 43–55, esp. 49–51. Note also Philip S. Alexander, "The Historical Setting of the Hebrew Book of Enoch," *JJS* 28 (1977): 159–67.

[10] See *Tg. Ps.-J.* Gen 5:24; *3 Enoch* §§4–5 (Vatican Ms. 228 *apud* Schäfer, *Synopse*, 5); *ʾOtiyyot de R. ʿAqiva* (Jellinek, *BHM* 3:114–15); *Berešit Rabbati* 26.25–27.7 (cf. Ḥanokh Albeck, ed., *Midrash Bereshit Rabbati* [Jerusalem: Mekitze Nirdamim, 1940]); *Pseudo-Ben Sira* A §22 (*apud* Eli Yassif, *The Tales of Ben Sira in the Middle-Ages: A Critical Text and Literary Studies* [Jerusalem: Magnes, 1984], 253–54). For a pre-geonic "angelification" of Enoch, compare *1 En.* 70:1–71:17; *2 En.* 22:1–11, neither of which however mentions the name Metatron.

[11] See *b. Sanh.* 94a and Rashi *ad loc.*; Scholem, *Jewish Gnosticism*, 131. Note too the excellent study

יוצר בראשית),[12] the so-called lesser YHWH, the angel Yahoel,[13] the archangel Michael, and even God Himself,[14] eventually combining and fusing these diverse attributes under the new rubric. The resultant figure of Metatron is thus a volatile amalgam of originally distinct personalities, character traits, and bureaucratic responsibilities. He radiates and accentuates different aspects of his hybrid parentage throughout a broad range of textual production and commerce among the Abrahamic religious communities of the Islamicate and Byzantine worlds.

There is no need in this study to detour through the immense secondary literature devoted to the origin and evolution of the figure of Metatron.[15] Instead the present excursus will highlight the novel role played by Metatron as an other-worldly mediator of eschatological mysteries in certain literary works produced by Jewish authors during the latter half of the first millennium CE. The motif of an angelic teacher or instructor imparting secret knowledge to a human initiate who then transmits this valuable information in written form to the larger society is well attested among the various religious groups inhabiting the Near East during late antiquity.[16] Such apocalyptic compositions can feature a bewildering variety of heavenly or quasi-divine revealers, some of whom remain anonymous but many of whom bear names, such as Gabriel, Michael, Uriel, the resurrected Jesus, or Elijah/al-Khidr. One of the first texts which casts Metatron in this signal role is

by Alan F. Segal, "The Ruler of This World," in idem, *The Other Judaisms of Late Antiquity* (BJS 127; Atlanta: Scholars Press, 1987), 41–77.

[12] See Ithamar Gruenwald, "Re'uyyot Yeḥezq'el," in *Temirin I: Texts and Studies in Kabbala and Hasidism* (ed. Israel Weinstock; Jerusalem: Mosad ha-Rav Kook, 1972), 131.

[13] Gershom G. Scholem, *Major Trends in Jewish Mysticism* (3d ed.; New York: Schocken, 1961), 68–69; idem, *Jewish Gnosticism*, 41–42. For further discussion of the seeming synonymity of the names Metatron, Yahoel, and Michael, see Alexander, "Historical Setting," 156–80, esp. 161–67; John C. Reeves, *Heralds of That Good Realm: Syro-Mesopotamian Gnosis and Jewish Traditions* (NHMS 41; Leiden: Brill, 1996), 71–74.

[14] Daniel Abrams has called attention to Munich Ms. 22 of *Hekhalot Rabbati* in Schäfer, *Synopse* §279: וזהו מטטרון י״י אלהי ישראל אלהי השמים וארץ, "and this is Metatron, the Lord God of Israel, the God of Heaven and Earth." See his "The Boundaries of Divine Ontology: The Inclusion and Exclusion of Meṭaṭron in the Godhead," *HTR* 87 (1994): 296 n. 17, as well as his citations from kabbalistic sources throughout the remainder of the article. Note also the Aramaic incantation bowl text cited and analyzed by Alexander, "Historical Setting," 166–67.

[15] Much of this can be accessed in the studies of Hans Bietenhard, *Die himmlische Welt im Urchristentum und Spätjudentum* (WUNT 2; Tübingen: J. C. B. Mohr, 1951), 143–60; Gedaliahu G. Stroumsa, "Form(s) of God: Some Notes on Meṭaṭron and Christ," *HTR* 76 (1983): 269–88; P[hilip S.] Alexander, "3 (Hebrew Apocalypse of) Enoch," *OTP* 1:242–44; Abrams, "Boundaries," 291–321; Deutsch, *Guardians*, 27–77. Of signal but still under-appreciated importance for the appropriation of Metatron by non-Jewish groups is Wasserstrom, *Between Muslim and Jew*, 181–205.

[16] To the useful roster of names and sources supplied by Bietenhard (*Die himmlische Welt*, 249), one can add figures like that of Poimandres in *Corpus Hermeticum* I, the "Twin" from hagiographical accounts of the early life of Mani, and Jibrīl (i.e., Gabriel) in the traditions surrounding the revelation of the Qur'ān to Muhammad.

the Hebrew Book of Enoch, or so-called *3 Enoch*, a clearly composite work of allegedly celestial lore whose time of composition roughly coincides with the waves of messianic excitement surging out of the social and cultural upheavals in the Near East during the seventh and eighth centuries.[17]

The extant versions[18] of *3 Enoch* recount a legendary journey to heaven undertaken by R. Ishmael, an early-second-century tannaitic Sage who figures as a prominent character in Hekhalot literature. Upon his arrival at the gate of the seventh and final "palace," he is met by Metatron, "the angelic Prince of the Presence," the escort who subsequently serves as R. Ishmael's host and guide for the duration of his visit. Largely unprompted by his guest, Metatron reveals to him a number of cosmological and supernal marvels, typically prefacing a description of the sights he shows him with the formulaic phrase "Come and I will show you . . ." (בא . . . ואראך). Interestingly Metatron also provides the awestruck sage with an account of his own metamorphosis from mortal to angel,[19] a circumstance strongly suggestive of the novelty of the figure in this narrative context.

Yet Metatron is also privy to esoteric information that pertains to the dolorous march of history, including traditional actors and events associated with the redemption and restoration of Israel and the retributive punishment of her oppressors, and it is this particular aspect of his revelatory profile that presages and parallels those found in the "later" apocalypses. We read: "Metatron said to me: 'Come and I will show you the Curtain of the Omnipresent (פרגוד של מקום) which is hung before the Holy One, blessed be He, (and) upon which is engraved all the generations of the world and all the deeds of the world's generations, whether already accomplished or still to be performed up to the end of all generations.' So I went and he pointed for me with his fingers the way a father teaches his children the letters of the Torah. I saw each generation and their rulers, etc."[20]

[17] The "core" of *3 Enoch*, usually defined as the materials contained in chaps. 3–15, probably emerged during the fifth or sixth century. See Scholem, *Jewish Gnosticism*, 7 n. 19; Alexander, *OTP* 1:227–28.

[18] Schäfer, *Synopse*, 4–39 (§§1–80). See the discussions of Gruenwald, *Apocalyptic*, 191–208; Alexander, *OTP* 1:223–53.

[19] "I am (actually) Enoch b. Yared. When the Flood-generation acted sinfully and committed corrupt deeds and said to God, 'Depart from us!,' as scripture attests, 'They say to God, "Leave us alone! We do not want to learn Your ways!"' (Job 21:14), the Holy One, blessed be He, took me from among them to be a witness against them in the high heavens for (the sake of) all the future inhabitants of the world." Translated from Vatican Ms. 228 as published by Schäfer, *Synopse*, 5 (§5).

[20] Schäfer, *Synopse*, 31 (§64). For the notion of the "heavenly curtain" and its functions, see especially Alexander, *OTP* 1:296 n. 45a. Compare Ms. T-S K 21.95.J fol. 2b lines 2–4, part of a *Shiʿur Qomah* type text: וכל מעשה בני אדם חקוקין בפרגד שלו בין שלעבר ובין שלעתיד בין גמור ובין שאינו גמור, "and every deed of humanity is inscribed on his curtain, whether past or future, whether accomplished or not yet completed." Text cited from Peter Schäfer, ed., *Geniza-Fragmente zur Hekhalot-Literatur* (TSAJ 6; Tübingen: J. C. B. Mohr, 1984), 133.

After perusing a lengthy roster of "historical" figures and events, and perhaps triggered by a juxtaposed contrapuntal rehearsal of the activities of the "(gentile) nations of the world," we eventually reach the following items:

> (and I saw) every military campaign which the nations of the world would wage against Israel during their (i.e., the nations') period of sovereignty. Then I saw the Messiah of the lineage of Joseph and his generation and all the things which the nations of the world would do there.[21] And I saw the Messiah of the lineage of David and his generation and all the battles and wars and their actions and deeds with which they would engage Israel, both good and bad. And I saw all the battles and wars with which Gog and Magog would engage Israel during the messianic era, and everything which the Holy One, blessed be He, would do to them in the future age.[22]

Here Metatron's profile as angelic initiate into and exponent of the esoteric secrets underlying the structures of the divine pleroma and its inhabitants is enriched by the crucial components of national memory and eschatological certainty. Metatron can provide details not only about matters of cosmological or ritual import: he also mediates between the earthly and heavenly realms, and is fully capable of disclosing trustworthy information pertaining to world history and the end of the present age. In this respect the angel Metatron essentially perpetuates the liminal and oracular vocations of his mortal "ancestor" Enoch. Enoch functions as an oral and scribal conduit for the delivery of messages from earth to heaven and vice versa. Earlier Jewish and Christian Enochic writings repeatedly credit their antediluvian hero with an encyclopedic range of knowledge that was largely gained during a lengthy period of angelic tutelage.[23] Greco-Egyptian and Syro-Mesopotamian hermetic currents, the latter type of which explicitly assimilates scriptural Enoch/Idrīs with the mythical character Hermes Trismegistos, also underscore this alchemical wedding of diplomatic, scientific, and prophetic talents. Given these considerations, it seems very likely that the impetus for the late antique thematic association of an announcement of end-time events with Metatron springs from an intellectual familiarity with his genetic code.

Metatron is explicitly introduced as the revealing angel in *Sefer Zerubbabel*, the *Secrets of R. Šimᶜōn b. Yoḥai*, and the *Prayer of R. Šimᶜōn b. Yoḥai*. The *Prayer*, which in most respects is textually linked to and largely derivative from the chronologically prior *Secrets*, supplies no explanatory information about the identity or attributes of this angel in the two places where the name is expressly mentioned.[24] Metatron as apocalyptic revealer for the author(s) of the *Prayer*

[21] Reading with Munich Ms. 40 (*apud* Schäfer, *Synopse*, 32).

[22] Schäfer, *Synopse*, 33 (§65).

[23] E.g., *1 En.* 1:2; 12:1–2; 17:1–36:4; 72:1; 80:1–81:10; 93:2; 103:1–2; 106:7; 106:19–107:1.

[24] Jellinek, *BHM* 4:119.9: והנה מלאך אחד ששמו מטטרון, where he is simply distinguished from a previously unnamed angel modeled on the divine messenger of Judges 13; and ibid. 4:119.22.

would thus seem to be unremarkable. The *Secrets* has but a single reference to an *angelus interpres*, where he is designated as "Metatron, the prince of the Presence" (מטטרון שר הפנים),[25] one of the standard epithets borne by this figure in Jewish theosophical literature. It is *Sefer Zerubbabel* that contains the lion's share of references to this name and which therefore merits serious consideration as the work primarily responsible for the popularization of Metatron's role as a reliable channel of knowledge about the impending time of redemption. The name of Metatron occurs nine times in the *Yeraḥmeʾel* manuscript version of *Sefer Zerubbabel* that was published in a critical edition by Israel Lévi almost a century ago,[26] and then again with lesser attention to versional variants recently by Eli Yassif.[27] A Genizah fragment of the work that was unknown to Lévi adds still another instance to this roster of occurrences.[28]

References to Metatron in extant accessible versions of *Sefer Zerubbabel* can be catalogued as follows:

a. "Michael answered Metatron and said to me . . ."[29]
b. "Metatron in *gematria* equals Shadday."[30]
c. "Metatron, the leader of the host of the Lord (שר צבא י״י)."[31]
d. "to Metatron and to Michael the prince (השר)."[32]
e. "Metatron . . . my lord Metatron (אדוני מיטטרון)."[33]
f. "Michael who is Metatron (מיכאל והוא מיטטרון)."[34]
g. "Metatron, the leader of the host of the Lord."[35]
h. "Metatron, the leader of the host of the Lord."[36]
i. "the words which Metatron spoke."[37]
j. "I am Metatron-Michael (מיטטרון מיכאל), the leader of the host of the Lord."[38]

[25] Jellinek, *BHM* 3:78.21. On this epithet, see especially Deutsch, *Guardians*, 43.

[26] Israel Lévi, "L'apocalypse de Zorobabel et le roi de Perse Siroès," *REJ* 68 (1914): 129–60.

[27] Eli Yassif, ed., *Sefer ha-Zikronot huʾ Divrey ha-Yamim le-Yeraḥmeʾel* (Tel Aviv: Tel Aviv University, 2001), 427–35.

[28] T-S A45.19 line 17, published in Simon Hopkins, *A Miscellany of Literary Pieces from the Cambridge Genizah Collections: A Catalogue and Selection of Texts in the Taylor-Schechter Collection, Old Series, Box A45* (Cambridge: Cambridge University Library, 1978), 64.

[29] Yassif, *Sefer ha-Zikronot*, 428.19.

[30] Yassif, *Sefer ha-Zikronot*, 428.23–429.1.

[31] Yassif, *Sefer ha-Zikronot*, 429.5.

[32] Yassif, *Sefer ha-Zikronot*, 429.23.

[33] Yassif, *Sefer ha-Zikronot*, 431.11–12.

[34] Yassif, *Sefer ha-Zikronot*, 431.14–15.

[35] Yassif, *Sefer ha-Zikronot*, 431.23.

[36] Yassif, *Sefer ha-Zikronot*, 433.18.

[37] Yassif, *Sefer ha-Zikronot*, 435.5. This is from the colophon.

[38] T-S A45.19 line 17, published in Hopkins, *Miscellany*, 64. This particular passage would correspond in placement to Yassif, *Sefer ha-Zikronot*, 428.13.

Two things stand out in this litany of citations. First, the sole descriptive epithet borne by the angelic revealer in *Sefer Zerubbabel* is "the leader of the host of the Lord," a designation modeled in turn upon the biblical description of Joshua's startling encounter with a menacing figure at Jericho (Josh 5:13–15). No proper name is given to the mysterious entity by the biblical passage, which simply depicts him as "a man standing opposite him with a drawn sword in his hand." Initially unrecognized and so challenged by Joshua to reveal his intentions, the strange warrior pronounces himself "the leader of the host of the Lord" (שר צבא י״י), and commands the suddenly cowed Israelite leader ("Joshua fell face-down on the ground and prostrated himself") to remove his shoes in deference to the sanctity of the site where the interview takes place. Although he remains anonymous in the biblical text, his militant posture and claim to divine honors invites comparison with the later figure of Michael,[39] the prominent angel whom Dan 12:1 describes as "the great prince (השר הגדול) who stands over the members of your people," and even the potential object, in one rabbinic tradition, of a heterodox sacrificial devotion.[40] Moreover, eschatological lore roughly contemporary with the *Sefer Zerubbabel* cycle of traditions, and ultimately indebted to exegeses of Daniel 10–12, anticipates the reappearance of Michael in his guise as military commander for the reconquest of Eretz Israel.[41]

Second, the cited texts accentuate this referential ambiguity by engaging in an almost farcical interchange of names when disclosing the actual identity of Zerubbabel's angelic interlocutor. Both the name Michael and the name Metatron appear in discourse surrounding the identity of the revealing angel: both can be represented as present and can even relay messages through the other ("Michael answered Metatron and said to me"), but the direction of the general movement of the tradition seems to find expression in the important declarative statement that Michael is in fact identical with Metatron ("Michael who is Metatron").

[39] Note Rashi *ad* Josh 5:15. The Old Greek rendering of his title (ὁ ἀρχιστράτηγος) is reprised in the later *Testament of Abraham*, recension A, as the primary epithet for the archangel Michael.

[40] See *t. Ḥul.* 2.18 (Zuckermandel, 503): "Should one slaughter in the name of the sun or moon or stars or planets or Michael the great prince of the host (מיכאל שר צבא הגדול) or even a tiny snail, this meat is considered to be like offerings made to the dead." Cf. *b. Ḥul.* 40a. Note also the tenth-century Nestorian text *Gannat Bussame*, wherein we read: ܟܠܗܘܢ ܕܝܢ ܫܪܟܐ ܡܚܘܐ ܐܢܐ ܠܡܫܡܘܕܥܘ ܐܚܕ ܡܠܟ ܕܡܫܠܛܘܗܝ ܕܐܕܘܢܝ ܠܪܒܐ ܒܥܘܢܝ ܣܓܝܕܬܐ ܕܐܣܛܠܝܐ ܕܒܢܝ ܐܝܣܪܝܠ, "I bring attention to only one (false deity): the lesser *Adonai*, the leader of the host of the greater *Adonai*, a foul error accorded worship by the Israelites." Text cited from Joseph Bidez and Franz Cumont, *Les mages hellénisés: Zoroastre, Ostanès et Hystaspe d'après la tradition grecque* (2 vols.; Paris: Société d'éditions "Les belles lettres," 1938; repr., New York: Arno Press, 1975), 2:115. For the magical adjuration of "Michael the great prince," see, e.g., Dan Levene, *A Corpus of Magic Bowls: Incantation Texts in Jewish Aramaic from Late Antiquity* (London and New York: Kegan Paul, 2003), 44–49.

[41] See especially *Tg. Ps.-J.* Deut 34:3, and also the seventh and eighth "signs" recounted in *ʾOtot ha-Mašiaḥ* (Jellinek, *BHM* 2:58–63). Note too the references supplied by Margaliot, *Malʾakey ʿelyon*, 133–35.

Given the recognizable antiquity of Michael's status as angelic leader in the heavenly hierarchy and his well-attested position as principal revealing angel in comparable contemporary apocalyptic compositions,[42] it seems possible that *Sefer Zerubbabel* provides an important window for viewing the infiltration of speculative theosophical currents as expressed in Hekhalot and other esoteric cosmological texts into the literary development of Jewish apocalyptic.

[42] Michael is the revealing angel, for example, in the roughly contemporary *Sefer Elijah* and the Christian *Gospel of the Twelve Apostles.*

2

The Eschatological Appearance of the Staff of Moses

As a potent artifact of hierohistory, the mytheme of the miracle-working "staff of Moses" is interwoven throughout the parascriptural eschatological lore of late antique Judaism and early Islam. Now in occlusion, it is destined to reappear during the tumultuous events marking the final days of the present age. Post-talmudic midrashim envision the royal Messiah engaged in a triumphal march to Jerusalem, endowed with the staff of Moses,[1] and the Qurʾān affirms that divine approval of royal leadership will be expressed in the miraculous manifestation of the "ark (of the covenant) … and the relics (*baqīyya*)of Moses and the family of Aaron" (Q 2:247–48), among which is numbered the marvelous staff (see Ṭabarī's commentary *ad loc.*).[2] According to *Sefer Zerubbabel*, God would reveal the staff to Hephṣibah, the mother of the Davidic Messiah: it would be recovered from its place of concealment in the city of Tiberias in Galilee,[3] and she would efficaciously wield it in the course of her subsequently depicted military triumphs. Islamic tradition similarly held that the "staff of Moses" would be one of the sacred relics recovered when the Muslim armies finally conquered Constantinople;[4] interestingly, there is extant a Byzantine tradition that indeed

[1] *Num. Rab.* 18.23; *Yal. Šim.* Psalms, §869.

[2] One Muslim tradition states that the staff of Moses was preserved at Mecca, but was lost during the Qarmaṭī sack of the city in 930. See Ignác Goldziher, *Muslim Studies* (ed. S. M. Stern; trans. C. R. Barber and S. M. Stern; 2 vols.; Chicago: Aldine, 1966–71), 2:326–27.

[3] Israel Lévi, "L'apocalypse de Zorobabel et le roi de Perse Siroès," *REJ* 68 (1914): 135.3–6: והמטה אשר יתן ייי לחפצי בה אם מנחם [בן] עמיאל מן שקד הוא גנוז ברקת עיר נפתלי הוא המטה אשר נתן ייי לאדם ולמשה ולאהרן וליהושע ולדוד המלך והוא המטה אשר פרח והציץ באהל על יד אהרן ואליהו בן אלעזר גנז אותו ברקת עיר נפתלי והוא טברייא, "The rod which the Lord will give to Hephṣibah, the mother of Menahem [ben] ʿAmiel, is made of almond-wood; it is hidden in Raqqat, a city in (the territory of) Naphtali. It is the same rod which the Lord previously gave to Adam, Moses, Aaron, Joshua, and King David. It is the same rod which sprouted buds and flowered in the Tent (of Meeting) for the sake of Aaron. Elijah ben Eleazar (i.e., the priest Phineas) concealed it in Raqqat, a city of Naphtali, which is Tiberias." See ibid. 134.5–6 for the initial appearance of the staff: מטה ישועות האלה יתן ייי לחפצי בה אם מנחם בן עמיאל וכוכב גדול יגיח לפניה, "The Lord will give a rod (for accomplishing) these salvific acts to Hephṣibah, the mother of Menahem ben ʿAmiel. A great star will shine (read נוגה) before her."

[4] Saïd Amir Arjomand, "Islamic Apocalypticism in the Classic Period," in *The Encyclopedia of*

affirmed that a ceremonial "staff of Moses" was associated with the imperial court of that city.[5] Expanded descriptions of the mysterious qur᾽ānic apocalyptic "beast" (*dābba*) invariably depict it carrying the staff of Moses and using it to differentiate the saved from the damned.[6]

The "history" of the staff is not a topic for discussion in either the Bible or the Qur᾽ān: therein it is simply a tool that Moses employs in his guise as herdsman, subsequently revealing itself as a physical channel through which God can produce signs and wonders.[7] Nothing is said in the canonical scriptures about its ownership or even its existence prior to the dialogue between Moses and God at the burning bush, nor do they provide information about the staff's fate after the death of the lawgiver. It seems likely that the biblical narrator's reluctance to identify the burial site of Moses (Deut 34:5–6) cast a concomitant aura of mystery around the final disposition of his personal effects. A number of Jewish and Muslim sources display an understandable tendency to conflate the staff of Moses with the flowering "rod of Aaron,"[8] in which case the post-Mosaic location of the staff

---

Apocalypticism (ed. Bernard McGinn et al.; 3 vols.; New York and London: Continuum, 1998), 2:255. Other treasures to be recovered on that occasion include the Temple vessels and the ark of the covenant. Note also the so-called Apocalypse of Nāth(ā) contained in Nuʿaym b. Ḥammād, *Kitāb al-fitan* (ed. Suhayl Zakkār; Beirut: Dār al-Fikr lil-Ṭibāʿah wa-al-Nashr wa-al-Tawzīʿ, 1993), 429–32, wherein it states that after the fall of Constantinople, there will be recovered "the gate of Zion, the Ark (with its) stave(s) in place, the earring of Eve, the *kitōn* of Adam; i.e., his clothing or cloak, and the (priestly) finery of Aaron" (432.4–5). For further discussion of this intriguing "apocalypse," see Michael Cook, "An Early Islamic Apocalyptic Chronicle," *JNES* 52 (1993): 25–29; Uri Rubin, *Between Bible and Qur᾽ān: The Children of Israel and the Islamic Self-Image* (Studies in Late Antiquity and Early Islam 17; Princeton: Darwin Press, 1999), 259–61; a full translation is now available in David Cook, *Studies in Muslim Apocalyptic* (Studies in Late Antiquity and Early Islam 21; Princeton: Darwin Press, 2002), 344–50. Might Nāth be a corruption of T(h)āt(h), which was in turn a hermetic designation for Enoch?

5 Constantine VII Porphyrogenitus, *Book of Ceremonies* 1.6.24; cited by Samuel Krauss, *Studien zur byzantinisch-jüdischen Geschichte* (Leipzig: Buchhandlung Gustav Fock, 1914), 107; also Heinrich Speyer, *Die biblischen Erzählungen im Qoran* (repr. Hildesheim: Georg Olms, 1988), 255 n. 2.

6 Q 27:82 speaks of the emergence of a "beast" from the earth who will verbally admonish humankind for their unbelief. For its endowment with the staff of Moses, see Nuʿaym b. Ḥammād, *K. al-fitan* (ed. Zakkār), 403: "the beast will emerge, having with it the staff of Moses and the seal of Solomon (upon whom be peace!), and the face(s) of the believers will be revealed by the staff." See also Arjomand, "Islamic Apocalypticism," 268; Arthur Jeffery, "ʿAṣā," *EI*^{2} 1:680; Armand Abel, "Dābba," *EI*^{2} 2:71; Jaroslav Stetkevych, *Muhammad and the Golden Bough: Reconstructing Arabian Myth* (Bloomington and Indianapolis: Indiana University Press, 1996), 142–43 n. 32.

7 Exod 4:2–5, 17, 20; 7:9–12, 15–21; 8:1, 12–13; 9:23; 10:13; 14:16; 17:5–13; Num 17:16–26; 20:7–12; Q 20:17–21; cf. 2:60; 7:107, 117, 160; 27:10; 28:31. Exod 4:20; 17:9 term it "the staff of God" (מטה האלהים). For a fascinating intercultural discussion on the motif of magic staffs or rods, see Stetkevych, *Muhammad and the Golden Bough*, 83–89.

8 Note the remark of Ibn Ezra on Exod 4:20: ומטה האלהים הוא מטה משה והוא מטה אהרן, "the staff of God is the same as the staff of Moses and the staff of Aaron," as well as the excerpt of *Sefer Zerubbabel* cited above. This confusion is discussed further by Louis Ginzberg, *The Legends of the Jews* (7 vols.;

should coincide with that of the lost "ark of the covenant," since that staff is described in the Bible as being deposited for safekeeping in the ark (Num 17:25–26).[9] The effect of this textual linkage of staff and ark is to subsume the fate of the staff among the numerous legends found among Jews, Christians, and Muslims which voice their anticipation of the reappearance of the ark and the lost Temple vessels at the End of Days.[10]

Parascriptural legends supply several explanations for the origin of the staff. One early stream of interpretation simply lists the staff among the ten items that God supposedly created *ex nihilo* on the eve of Sabbath during the initial week of creation.[11] Nothing is said in these traditions regarding the staff's physical properties, such as its appearance, size, shape, or composition, nor is anything explicitly communicated regarding the marvelous powers with which it was supposedly endowed. However, its very inclusion in a list of future "wonders" or "anomalies of nature" hints at the latent possibilities awaiting a creative narrative development.[12]

One interpretive trajectory utilized within Jewish literature supplements the meager scriptural information about the staff by exploiting the surrounding narrative characters and context wherein both Moses and the staff first appear; namely, the refugee sojourn of Moses among the family of the Midianite priest

---

Philadelphia: Jewish Publication Society, 1909–38), 6:106–7 n. 600; Jeffery, *EI*^{2} 1:680; note also A. Fodor, "The Rod of Moses in Arabic Magic," *Acta Orientalia Academiae Scientiarum Hungaricae* 32 (1978): 2; Christine Meilicke, "Moses' Staff and the Return of the Dead," *JSQ* 6 (1999): 347.

[9] See *y. Šeqal.* 6.1, 49c: "when the ark was hidden, there were hidden with it the jar of manna, the bottle of oil for anointing, the staff of Aaron with its blooms and almonds, and the box wherein the Philistines returned a guilt-offering to the God of Israel. Who hid it? Josiah hid it." See also Heb 9:4; *y. Soṭah* 8.3, 22c; *t. Yoma* 2.15; *t. Soṭah* 13.1; *b. Yoma* 52b; and Q 2:247–48 above. Note also *Massekhet Kelim* 1 (*apud* Jellinek, *BHM* 2:88).

[10] See especially Rivka Nir, *The Destruction of Jerusalem and the Idea of Redemption in the Syriac Apocalypse of Baruch* (SBLEJL 20: Atlanta: Society of Biblical Literature, 2003), 43–77. For Islamic traditions regarding the recovery of the ark, see Wilferd Madelung, "Apocalyptic Prophecies in Ḥimṣ in the Umayyad Age," *JSS* 31 (1986): 149; idem, "The Sufyānī Between Tradition and History," *Studia Islamica* 63 (1986): 30; Arjomand, "Islamic Apocalypticism," 255. One early tradition reported by Nuʿaym b. Ḥammād (*K. al-fitan*, 223) states that the Mahdī will recover the ark from the bottom of the "sea of Tiberias," a location that should be compared with that of the hiding place of the staff of Moses in *Sefer Zerubbabel*. Note too the curious tradition found in *Reʾuyot Yeḥezqʾel*: הראהו הר מתחתיו שלנהר שבו עתידין כלי בית המקדש לחזור, "He [God] showed him [Ezekiel] the mountain at whose base is a river (?) by which the Temple vessels are destined to be restored." Text cited from the edition of Ithamar Gruenwald, "Reʾuyot Yeḥezqʾel," in *Temirin: Texts and Studies in Kabbala and Hasidism, Volume I* (ed. I. Weinstock; Jerusalem: Mosad ha-Rav Kook, 1972), 110.

[11] See *m. ʾAbot* 5.6; *ʾAbot R. Nat.* B §37 (Schechter, 48a); *Mek.* Beshalaḥ, Va-yassaʿ §5 (Horovitz-Rabin, 171); *Sifre* Deut §355 (Finkelstein, 418); *Tg. Ps-J.* Exod 2:21: חוטרא דאיתבריאת ביני שימשתא, "the staff which had been created at twilight (of the sixth day of the creation-week)." Note also *Midrash Wa-yoshaʿ* (Jellinek, *BHM* 1:42).

[12] These possibilities are succinctly summarized by Isaak Heinemann, *Darkey ha-Aggadah* (2d ed.; Jerusalem: Magnes; Ramat-Gan: Masadah, 1954), 30–31.

Jethro, herein depicted as a former advisor and court magician to Pharaoh. This is the way the story appears in one recension of the medieval aggadah entitled *Chronicles of Moses*:

> Now during that time Jethro had issued a decree and circulated an announcement among all his lands that the person who could come and uproot the staff which was planted in his garden would be given his daughter Zipporah to wed. Kings, mighty princes, and warriors had been coming, but none (of them) had been able to pull up the staff. After Moses was released from prison,[13] he was walking around in the garden, and he noticed the staff "stuck in the ground":[14] it was made of sapphire, and the Ineffable Name (of God) was engraved upon it. Moses put his hand on the staff and pulled it up from its place with ease, and the staff was in his hand. He returned to the house with the staff in his hand. When Jethro saw the staff in the hand of Moses, he was utterly amazed, and he gave him Zipporah his daughter to be his wife.[15]

In this trajectory the staff is described as composed of "sapphire" (ספיר);[16] some sources equate this material with the same precious stone of which the heavenly throne of God is composed.[17] This detail does not necessarily conflict with the notion of the staff's Sabbath eve creation found in earlier rabbinic sources. The staff also bears the imprint of the Ineffable Name of God.[18] Other allied sources multiply descriptive details: it was also engraved with the names of the ten Egyptian plagues, and it supposedly weighed the equivalent of forty *seah*s of grain.[19] A variant version of the *Chronicles of Moses* contained within the so-called *Yeraḥmeel* Manuscript (Oxford Ms. Heb. d. 11 [2797]) interjects the following "historical" data:

[13] Recognizing Moses as a fugitive from Pharaoh's court, Jethro at first imprisoned Moses upon his arrival in Midian. See *Tg. Ps-J.* Exod 2:21.

[14] Gen 28:12.

[15] Translated from the version printed in Jellinek, *BHM* 2:7. Variant versions of Moses' imprisonment by Jethro and the trial with the magic staff are found in *Midrash Wa-yoshaᶜ* (Jellinek, *BHM* 1:42–43), *Yal. Šim.* Torah, §168, and in Oxford Bodleian Ms. Heb. d. 11 (2797) as published by Avigdor Shinan, "Divrey ha-yamim shel Mosheh rabbenu," *Hasifrut* 24 (1977): 111–12, and Eli Yassif, ed., *Sefer ha-Zikronot huʾ Divrey ha-Yamim le-Yeraḥmeʾel* (Tel Aviv: Tel Aviv University, 2001), 166–67.

[16] The tradition that the staff was made of sapphire (סנפירינון) occurs already in *Mek.* Beshalaḥ, Vayassᶜa §6 (Horovitz-Rabin, 175.3). Note Rashi *ad* Exod 17:6.

[17] *Tg. Ps-J.* Exod 4:20: ונסיב משה ית חוטרא דנסב מן גינוניתא דחמוי והוא מספיר כורסי יקרא מתקליה ארבעין סאין ועילוי חקיק ומפרש שמא רבא ויקירא. Text cited from David Rieder, ed., *Targum Jonathan ben Uziel on the Pentateuch* (Jerusalem: Salomon, 1974), 86. The throne's appearance is compared to that of sapphire in Ezek 1:26 and 10:1; "sapphire brickwork" lies beneath God's feet in Exod 24:10. Note also *1 En.* 18:8.

[18] For the magical importance of the inscriptions borne by the staff, see Fodor, "Rod of Moses," 6–15.

[19] *Midr. Tanḥ.*, Wa-ʾera §9; Tazriᶜa §8; *Exod. Rab.* 5.6; *Midrash Wa-Yoshaᶜ* (Jellinek, *BHM* 1:42). According to *Tg. Ps.-J.* Exod 31:18, the original set of engraved tablets given to Moses by God on Sinai were hewn from "sapphire-stone taken from the Throne of Glory weighing forty *seahs*."

> This is the staff which was created by God . . .[20] among the divine works after He finished creating the heavens and the earth and all their hosts (and) the seas, rivers, and all their fish. And when Adam was driven out of the Garden of Eden, he took the staff along with him and used it to work the soil from which he had been taken. The staff eventually came to Noah, and he gave it to Shem and his descendants, and it eventually came into the possession of Abraham the Hebrew. Since Abraham bequeathed all that he owned to Isaac, he also inherited the miracle-working staff (מטה האותות).[21] Moreover, when Jacob fled to Paddan Aram, he took it along with him,[22] and when he returned to his father at Beersheva, he certainly did not leave it behind. When he went down to Egypt, he took it with him and presented it to Joseph, "a portion more than his brothers" (שכם על אחיו).[23] It came to pass that after Joseph died certain Egyptian officials lived in Joseph's house, and the staff came into the possession of Re^cuel the Midianite. At the time when he left Egypt, he took it with him and planted it in the middle of his garden.[24]

This narrative expansion, which ties the staff's creation-week point of origin to the expulsion from Eden, Adam the protoplast, and a named chain of custodians, first appears in Jewish literary sources in the eighth-century *Pirqe de R. Eliezer*:[25]

> That staff was created at twilight (of the sixth day of the creation-week). It was given to Adam the protoplast in the Garden of Eden. Adam gave it to Enoch, Enoch gave it to Noah, Noah gave it to Shem, Shem gave it to Abraham, Abraham gave it to Isaac, Isaac gave it to Jacob, and Jacob brought it down to Egypt and gave it to Joseph his son. After Joseph died, everything in his house was taken and placed in the palace of Pharaoh. Now one of Pharaoh's Egyptian magicians noticed the staff and the lettering which was on it, and he formed a secret desire to own it. He took it away,

[20] The manuscript contains the unintelligible character string בתבל; similarly, *Yal. Šim.* Torah, §168.

[21] The same sobriquet occurs in *Yal. Šim.* Ezekiel, §375: "during the forty years when Moses shepherded the flock of Jethro with the 'miracle-working staff,' no wild beast successfully preyed on them; instead, they [the flock] greatly multiplied and increased." *Yal. Šim.* Torah, §168 refers to it as the מטה האותיות or "belettered staff."

An Aramaic rendering of the same epithet appears twice in the early liturgical acrostic *ʾEzel Mosheh* as חוטר נסייה, "staff of miracles." See Joseph Yahalom, "ʾEzel Moshe—According to the Berlin Papyrus," *Tarbiz* 47 (1978): 173–84; Klaus Beyer, *Die aramäischen Texte vom Toten Meer* (Göttingen: Vandenhoeck & Ruprecht, 1984), 331–34; also Michael L. Klein, *Genizah Manuscripts of Palestinian Targum to the Pentateuch* (2 vols.; Cincinnati: Hebrew Union College Press, 1986), 1:236–39, where we find the spellings [חוט]ר ניסייא and חוטר ניסיה.

[22] According to *Yal. Šim.* Torah, §168, Jacob forcibly took the staff away from his brother Esau.

[23] See Gen 48:22 as interpreted in *b. B. Bat.* 123a. Since Joseph (and his descendants) displace Reuben as "firstborn" (see 1 Chr 5:1–2), they merit a "double portion" (see Deut 21:17) as their inheritance.

[24] Shinan, "Divrey ha-yamim," 112; Yassif, *Sefer ha-Zikronot*, 166–67.

[25] See, however, the so-called *Visions of ʿAmram* in 4Q546 11 3: עתיד חטרא דן לא[הרון], "this staff is destined for A[aron (?)]," perhaps the remnant of an early roster of the worthies who have custody of the wonder-working staff. See Émile Puech, "Visions de ʿAmram^{d}," in *Qumrân Grotte 4, XXII: Textes araméens, première partie, 4Q529–49* (DJD 31; Oxford: Clarendon, 2001), 363–64.

> brought it, and planted it in the garden of Jethro's house. He could observe the staff, but no one could approach it at all. When Moses came to his house, he went into the garden of Jethro's house, saw the staff, and read the letters which were on it. He extended his hand and took it. When Jethro saw what Moses had done, he exclaimed: "This one is destined to redeem Israel from Egypt!" Therefore he gave him his daughter Zipporah as a wife.[26]

One might compare the more elaborate first-person rendition of this legend found in the *Midrash Wa-Yosha*ᶜ, a homiletic exposition keyed to Exod 14:30–15:18 that dates from the eleventh or twelfth century:

> I told her [i.e., Zipporah] that I wanted to make her my wife, but Zipporah told me that every man who sought to marry one of her father's daughters faced an ordeal by means of a tree that was in his garden. Whenever one approached it, it would immediately swallow him! I asked her from where he had gotten this tree. She said to <me>:[27] "This is the staff which the Holy One, blessed be He, created on the eve of the Sabbath when He created His world. The Holy One, blessed be He, entrusted it to Adam the protoplast, and Adam entrusted it to Enoch, Enoch entrusted it to Noah, Noah entrusted it to Shem, Shem entrusted it to Abraham, Abraham entrusted it to Isaac, and Isaac entrusted it to Jacob. Jacob took it back (?!) to Egypt[28] and entrusted his son Joseph with it. When Joseph died, the Egyptians looted his house and brought that staff into Pharaoh's palace. My father Jethro was one of the chief magicians of Pharaoh: he saw that staff, secretly coveted it, stole it, and brought it to his own house. On that staff is engraved the Ineffable Name and the ten plagues which the Holy One, blessed be He, is going to bring upon the inhabitants of Egypt. . . ."[29]

It is of interest here that a named succession of owners or trustees of the staff plays a prominent role in some Christian and Muslim versions of this legend. One might compare, for example, the narration of the staff's "history" which we have read above with the form of the legend as it appears in the *Qiṣaṣ al-anbiyā*ᵓ collection of al-Kisāᵓī, an anthology of popular prophetic legends of uncertain date,[30] where the staff also is associated with the Garden of Eden:

> Shuᶜayb [i.e., Jethro][31] said: "O Moses, this staff derives from one of the trees of the Garden. It was presented to Adam the day he departed from the Garden, and he

[26] *Pirqe R. El.* §40 (Luria, 94a).

[27] Read לי instead of the text's לו.

[28] This verb would seem to presuppose reliance upon a fuller narrative wherein the staff enjoyed an earlier sojourn in Egypt, perhaps in conjunction with Abraham's visit there (Gen 12:10–20). See the excerpt from the *Book of the Bee* below.

[29] *Midrash Wa-Yosha*ᶜ (Jellinek, *BHM* 1:42).

[30] See Tilman Nagel, "Kisāᵓī, Ṣāḥib Ḳiṣaṣ al-Anbiyāᵓ," *EI*^{2} 5:176. According to Nagel, the earliest manuscript of this work dates from the thirteenth century.

[31] For the common identification of the qurᵓānic prophet Shuᶜayb as biblical Jethro, see Abraham Geiger, *Judaism and Islam* (trans. F. M. Young; 1898; repr., New York: Ktav, 1970), 137–42; Brannon

leaned upon it. Afterwards Abel leaned upon it, then Seth, Idrīs [i.e., Enoch], Noah, Hūd, Ṣāliḥ, Abraham, Ishmael, Isaac, and Jacob. Do not let it depart from your hand; each one of the prophets who handled it was granted victory by God over his adversaries."[32]

Al-Kisāʾī provides, of course, an "islamicized" version of the staff's career, supplementing and/or replacing a biblical chain of ancestral worthies with a qurʾānic list of early prophets. Its potency is subtly underscored: those who wield the staff will triumph over their foes. Unlike the Jewish renditions, this version of the story does not explicitly inform us how the chronological and generational gap from Jacob to Shuʿayb was bridged. The "bridegroom ordeal" motif is also lacking from this version; instead, Moses selects the staff from a shed storing similar implements and is initially unaware of its wonder-working prowess. Shuʿayb, however, immediately recognizes it and attempts to maintain possession to no avail by repeatedly sending Moses back into the shed to select another tool: no matter where he hides it, though, the staff reverts to the hand of Moses.[33]

One should also note that al-Kisāʾī's version features an important transitional development in the continuing evolution of the legend. Adam receives the staff from God, as in the *Midrash Wa-Yoshaʿ* version above.[34] The material composition of the staff, however, is no longer that of stone quarried from the Divine Throne, but wood; and not just any wood, but wood procured from "one of the trees of the Garden." One could explain this change as due to the rationalizing imagination of the storytellers, since a wooden shepherd's staff is a more plausible and comfortable accessory than one of stone. It seems likely too that a growing contextual association of the marvelous staff with the primal inhabitants of the Garden, coupled with their infamous engagement with similarly endowed "trees" (and a serpent!) in that Garden, influenced a critical transmutation in the staff's origin. The culmination of this trend emerges in Zoharic legendry, wherein the staff of Moses is explicitly traced to the Edenic Tree of Knowledge, and the angels Metatron and Samael are deemed responsible for governing its beneficent and

---

M. Wheeler, *Prophets in the Quran: An Introduction to the Quran and Muslim Exegesis* (London and New York: Continuum, 2002), 154–56; Moshe Gil, *Jews in Islamic Countries in the Middle Ages* (trans. David Strassler; Leiden: Brill, 2004), 14–15. Gil suggests that Shuʿayb might be better explained as Balaam.

[32] Muhammad Ibn ʿAbd Allāh al-Kisāʾī, *Qiṣaṣ al-anbiyāʾ* (ed. I. Eisenberg; 2 vols.; Leiden: Brill, 1922–23), 2:208.12–16. See also Bernard Heller, "Mūsā," *EI*[2] 7:639.

[33] Ṭabarī (*Taʾrīkh*, 1:460–61) recounts another tradition wherein Moses and his father-in-law argue over possession of the staff. An angel is forced to intervene in Moses' favor.

[34] Another tradition has the angel Gabriel take the staff from Adam after the latter's death and then later present it to Moses, a mode of deliverance that bypasses the putative human chain of trustees. See Ṭabarī, *Taʾrīkh*, 1:460–61; Max Grünbaum, *Neue Beiträge zur semitischen Sagenkunde* (Leiden: E. J. Brill, 1893), 162.

maleficent aspects, respectively.[35] Yet in contrast to the Jewish versions of this story examined above, wherein God is represented as the creator of the staff, many of these latter traditions take a further step in identifying Adam as the one who first made the staff.

According to the qurʾānic commentators Zamakhsharī and Bayḍāwī, Adam detached a branch from a myrtle tree in the Garden and fashioned the wonder-working staff from it.[36] The choice of this particular species is not accidental: the magical properties of myrtle are renowned in Near Eastern folklore.[37] Perhaps even more importantly, the Jewish messianic imposter Abū ʿĪsā al-Iṣfahānī is depicted in one Muslim source wielding a "myrtle rod" which he uses to protect his followers from the military attacks of their persecutors:[38] given the close linkages discernible between the recovery of Moses' staff and the advent of the "True Messiah," it seems possible that Abū ʿĪsā's "myrtle rod" was intended to represent this powerful token. Other traditions connect the staff with the thornbush from which God addresses Moses in Exod 3:1–5 and its qurʾānic parallels.[39] This latter identification may also be ultimately linked (at least thematically) with the myrtle.[40] Adam's staff is subsequently handed down through the successive generations until it comes into the possession of Jethro, from whom, as in certain streams of the Jewish and Muslim traditions surveyed above, Moses manages to acquire it. These later traditions also elaborate and enhance the miraculous powers associated with the staff. In the collection of prophetic legends attributed to Thaʿlabī, we find an extensive catalogue of the staff's endowments: it illuminates darkness, bears fruit when planted into the soil, exudes milk and honey, obliterates mountain and rock, warns of danger, protects both Moses and his flock from predators and assassins while they sleep, and transforms itself into a dragon in

[35] A convenient anthology of these passages is provided by Reuven Margaliot, *Malʾakey ʿelyon* (Jerusalem: Mosad Harav Kook, 1945), 97.

[36] *Ad* Q 2:60. See Grünbaum, *Neue Beiträge*, 161.

[37] See Jacob Z. Lauterbach, "The Origin and Development of Two Sabbath Ceremonies," *HUCA* 15 (1940): 367–424, esp. 392ff.; Ludwig Blau, "Salamander," *JE* 10:646; Fodor, "Rod of Moses," 3 n. 10; A. Dietrich, "Ās," *EI²*, *Supplement 1–2* (Leiden: Brill, 1980), 87. When Maimonides draws a portrait of a necromancer engaged in his nefarious craft, he depicts him as follows: "He stands and burns a certain incense, holding and waving a myrtle wand (שרביט של הדס) in his hand, and whispering certain incantations . . ." (*Mishneh Torah, Hilkhot ʿAvodat Kokhavim* 6.1).

[38] Shahrastānī, *Kitāb al-milal waʾl-niḥal* (ed. M. b. Fath Allāh Badrān; 2 vols.; [Cairo]: Matbaʿat al-Azhar, [1951–55]), 1.506–7; Steven M. Wasserstrom, *Between Muslim and Jew: The Problem of Symbiosis under Early Islam* (Princeton: Princeton University Press, 1995), 76.

[39] See Q 20:10–16; 28:29–30; and Grünbaum, *Neue Beiträge*, 162; Fodor, "Rod of Moses," 3 n. 11.

[40] *Gen. Rab.* 63.9 (Theodor-Albeck, 692): ר׳ פינחס בשם ר׳ לוי משל להדס ועצבונית שהיו גדילים זה על גבי זה כיון שהגדילו הפריחו זה ריחו וזה חוחיו, "R. Pinhas said in the name of R. Levi, (Jacob and Esau) can be compared to the myrtle and the thornbush: while they were growing up, they were interchangeable, but after they matured (and bore fruit), this one was fragrant, but that one had thorns."

order to combat enemies.[41] One can also discern a tendency to depict the inert form or shape of the staff as that of a living serpent. Some sources mention that the top of the staff was forked and crested, and when the staff became a snake, the prongs transformed into a mouth with a forked tongue. When relating the contest between Moses and Pharaoh's court magicians, al-Kisāʾī states that the staff of Moses shifted into the shape of a seven-headed serpent.[42] The ninth-century historian Yaʿqūbī recounts how the Egyptian magicians attempted to render their own staffs "serpentlike" by hollowing wooden rods and leather ropes and filling them with mercury; when exposed to heat, these props would wriggle and writhe as if they were living beings.[43]

The thirteenth-century Christian *Book of the Bee* is perhaps the crowning representative of all these trends: it even devotes a specially subtitled section to the "history" (ܫܪܒܐ) of the staff, developing and expanding the tradition in the following way:

> When Adam and Eve departed from Paradise, Adam—as if knowing he would never again return there—cut off a branch from the Tree of Good and Evil,[44] which was the fig tree,[45] took it with him and left. That (branch) served him as a staff all the days of his life. After the death of Adam, his son Seth took it because at that time weapons did not yet exist.[46] That staff was transferred from hand to hand until it reached Noah. Shem received it from Noah, and from Shem it was handed down to Abraham as a gift from the Paradise of God. Abraham used it to shatter the images, carvings, and idols which his father had made.[47] It was on account of this that God said to him: "Leave the house of your father, etc." (Gen 12:1ff.). The staff remained in his possession every place he dwelt, including Egypt and in Palestine after returning from Egypt. Afterwards Isaac received it, and Jacob received it from Isaac, and Jacob used it while shepherding the flocks of Laban the Aramaean in Paddan-Aram. From Jacob it was received by Judah, the fourth of his sons, and this was the staff which Judah gave to his daughter-in-law Tamar along with his seal and his robe as

[41] Heller, "Mūsā," 7:639; Fodor, "Rod of Moses," 5–6. See now Thaʿlabī, *ʿArāʾis al-majālis fī qiṣaṣ al-anbiyāʾ or "Lives of the Prophets"* (trans. William M. Brinner; Leiden: Brill, 2002), 294–95.

[42] Kisāʾī, *Qiṣaṣ al-anbiyāʾ*, 2:216; Fodor, "Rod of Moses," 15.

[43] Yaʿqūbī, *Taʾrīkh* (2 vols.; Beirut: Dār Sādir, 1960), 1.35.6–16; Fodor, "Rod of Moses," 15 n. 89.

[44] As noted above, the Zohar, a product of late-thirteenth-century Spanish Jewish circles but rooted in older migratory sources, *also* connects the staff of Moses with the Tree of Knowledge. The mutual attestation of such a distinct mytheme within these two widely disparate cultural contexts suggests an earlier, wider, and perhaps even common currency for this motif.

[45] This is a popular interpretation based on the fig's cooperative behavior in Gen 3:7. See *b. Sanh.* 70b and Ginzberg, *Legends* 5:97–98 n. 70.

[46] Does this laconic comment presume a dependence on the Enochic myth embedded in *1 En.* 8:1 (cf. 69:6) that the forging of weapons was a technology first acquired from the "fallen angels"? Or does it simply express the well-attested protective powers of the wonder-working staff?

[47] Abraham's smashing of the idols (*sans* staff) is a widespread tale also found in both Jewish and Muslim contexts. See *Jub.* 12:1–14; *Apoc. Abr.* 1:1–8:6; *Gen. Rab.* 38.13; *b. Pesaḥ.* 118a; *b. ʿErub.* 53a; *Pirqe R. El.* §26; Q 6:74–84; 19:41–50; 21:53–73; 26:69–86; 29:16–27; 37:83–98; 43:26–27; 60:4.

payment for what he had done.[48] From him it came to Peretz. Then wars broke out in every land, and an angel took the staff and put it in the Cave of Treasures in the hill country of Moab[49] until Midian was built. Now there was a certain man in Midian who was just and righteous before God whose name was Jethro. While this one was shepherding his flocks in the hill country, he discovered the Cave and at divine instigation removed the staff.[50] He used it to shepherd his flocks until he grew old, and after he gave his daughter to Moses, Jethro said to Moses: "Come, my son, take the staff and shepherd your flocks!" As Moses stepped on the threshold of the door, an angel caused the staff to fly out by itself toward Moses.[51] Moses took that staff, and it was with him until the time when God spoke with him on Mount Sinai. When he told him to cast the staff on the ground and he accordingly threw it down, it became a large serpent; and when the Lord said for him to pick it up, he grasped it and it became a staff as before.[52] This is the staff which God gave him as an assistant and as an agent of deliverance and to be a marvelous wonder: using it he rescued Israel from the oppression of the Egyptians. By the will of the living God it became a large serpent in Egypt. God addressed Moses by means of it, and it swallowed the staff of Pūsdī (ܦܘܣܕܝ) the Egyptian witch. He struck the Sea of Reeds with it along its length and its width, and "the depths were congealed in the midst of the sea" (Exod 15:8b). This same staff was in the possession of Moses in the wilderness of Ašīmōn,[53] and he used it to strike the solid rock to make water flow copiously (from it).[54] God then gave serpents the power to destroy them due to His anger over the "waters of controversy" (Num 20:13). Moses prayed to the Lord, and God told him: "Make a bronze serpent and raise it on top of the staff, and have the children of Israel look at it so that they might be cured."[55] Moses acted as the Lord had commanded him, and he set up a bronze serpent in the wilderness in the sight of all the children of Israel: they looked at it and they were cured.[56] After the death of all the

[48] See Gen 38:18, 25. Judah's staff is equated with those of Moses and Aaron in *Num. Rab.* 18.23; *Yal. Šim.* Torah, §763, paralleled in *Yal. Šim.* Psalms, §869; and *Baʿal ha-Ṭūrim* to Gen 38:18. Ps 110:2 is the crucial linchpin in this equation.

[49] This location seems to presuppose a tradition that links the hiding place of the staff with the future grave of Moses (Deut 34:5–6). See also 2 Macc 2:4–8 and the remarks of Andreas Su-Min Ri, *Commentaire de la Caverne des Trésors: Étude sur l'histoire du texte et de ses sources* (CSCO 581; Louvain: Peeters, 2000), 76 n. 81.

[50] Note that this explanation of how Jethro comes to possess the staff differs from that provided in Jewish sources. According to the latter tradition, Jethro acquires the staff in Egypt thanks to his status as an advisor to Pharaoh.

[51] Similar powers of levitation are exhibited in some of the Jewish and Muslim traditions surrounding Moses' initial acquisition of the staff.

[52] Cf. Exod 4:3–4.

[53] That is, Hebrew ישימון. See Num 21:20; Deut 32:10; Ps 78:40–41; 106:14; 107:4.

[54] Cf. Num 20:11.

[55] Cf. Num 21:8. The Masoretic text is silent about the material from which Moses should fashion the image of the serpent; note Rashi *ad* Num 21:9: "He (God) did not tell him to make it of bronze." Note however the Peshitta: ܥܒܕ ܠܟ ܚܘܝܐ ܚܪܡܢܐ ܕܢܚܫܐ, "Make *a deadly serpent of bronze* . . . ," and compare *Tg. Ps-J.* Num 21:8: ואמר יי למשה עיבד לך חיויא דנחשא, "God said to Moses: Make a *bronze serpent*," a textual detail which mirrors the identical rendering in the Syriac legend.

[56] As might be expected, the apotropaic and therapeutic powers of the staff are also exploited in

children of Israel—except for Joshua bar Nun and Caleb bar Yofanʾa—they entered the Promised Land, taking the staff along with them due to wars with the Philistines and the Amalekites. Phineas[57] hid the staff in the desert, beneath the dirt at the gate of Jerusalem (ܬܪܥܐ ܕܐܘܪܫܠܡ),[58] and it remained there until Our Lord the Messiah was born. By the will of the Deity He showed the staff to Joseph, the husband of Miriam,[59] and that staff was in his possession when he fled to Egypt with Our Lord and Miriam, (and) until he returned to Nazareth. After Joseph, his son James—the one called the brother of Our Lord—took it, and Judas Iscariot stole it from James, for he was a thief. When the Jews crucified Our Lord, they lacked sufficient wood for the arms of Our Lord, and Judas due to his wickedness gave them the staff.[60] This became a judgment and a calamity for them, but a covenant for many (others).[61]

Despite its extensive elaboration, one should note that this Syriac narrative shares one interesting motif with the Jewish *Sefer Zerubbabel* account: both stories credit the priest Phineas with concealing the staff until its timely reemergence in the messianic age. This common assignment is undoubtedly due to the early Jewish assimilation of the character Phineas to the prophet Elijah[62] and that latter

magical texts. A seventh-century silver amulet from Arbela begins: "*By the staff of Moses* (ובחטרה דמשה) and the head-plate of Aaron the high priest and the signet ring of Solomon and [...] of David and the horns of the altar and the name of the living and enduring God, may you be expelled." This text was first published by James A. Montgomery, "Some Early Amulets from Palestine," *JAOS* 31 (1911): 272–81, at pp. 273–79, and reprinted with some revised readings by Beyer, *Die aramäischen Texte*, 374–75. It was republished with much improved readings by Joseph Naveh and Shaul Shaked, *Magic Spells and Formulae: Aramaic Incantations of Late Antiquity* (Jerusalem: Magnes, 1993), 91–95; note also idem, *Amulets and Magic Bowls: Aramaic Incantations of Late Antiquity* (Jerusalem/Leiden: Magnes/Brill, 1985), 22 n. 23. Naveh and Shaked also refer to an unpublished Genizah fragment (ENA 3513.11a) which similarly begins with the invocation: . . . בחוטרא דמשה נבייא.

[57] That is, the son of Eleazar the priest and grandson of Aaron. See Num 25:7–13; 31:6; Josh 22:13–32; 24:33; Judg 20:28; Ps 106:30.

[58] Is this syntagm a reflex of the "gate of Zion" in the "Apocalypse of Nāth(ā)" cited above?

[59] For a typological association of Joseph's "rod" with the wonder-working staff, cf. *Prot. Jas.* 8:3–9:1. This apocryphal episode undoubtedly underlies the curious legend alluded to in Q 3:44.

[60] Compare the tradition found in the earlier *Cave of Treasures* that the cross was fashioned from wood that came from the Tree of Life. There is also extant a Jewish tradition that Moses made his staff from a branch that he took from the Tree of Life. See *ʾAbot R. Natan* A, *hosaphah* 2 §4 (Schechter, 157); Ginzberg, *Legends* 6:165 n. 958.

[61] Ernest A. Wallis Budge, ed., *The Book of the Bee* (Anecdota Oxoniensia Semitic Series 1.2; Oxford: Clarendon Press, 1886), 50.4–52.18 (text). Note also Grünbaum, *Neue Beiträge*, 162–63; Speyer, *Erzählungen*, 255; Louis Ginzberg, "Aaron's Rod," *JE* 1:5–6; Meilicke, "Moses' Staff," 359–60. This legend plays no role in the Syriac *Cave of Treasures*, but a cognate version of the story is contained in the Ethiopic book of *Qalēmenṭos* (i.e., Clement), a work in the *Cave* cycle that was apparently translated from an Arabic *Vorlage*. See Ri, *Commentaire*, 67 and 88.

[62] *L.A.B.* 48:1; *Tg. Ps-J.* Num 25:12; *Pirqe R. El.* §§8 and 47; Ginzberg, *Legends* 6:316–17 n. 3; Robert Hayward, "Phineas—the Same is Elijah: The Origins of a Rabbinic Tradition," *JJS* 29 (1978): 22–34.

figure's well-attested role in the recovery of the hidden Temple vessels at the time of redemption.

Why should the staff of Moses be connected with the events surrounding the End of Days? Why do so many biblically grounded religious traditions underscore the recovery or remanifestation of this staff as an essential sign or token signaling the time of redemption? The "messianic" associations of the staff are by no means limited to "orthodox" expressions of late antique prophetism as articulated in Judaism, Christianity, and Islam. Samaritan eschatology, for example, likewise views possession of the "staff of miracles" as a sign of messianic authenticity.[63] And it is surely significant that the earliest literary portrait we possess of Mani, the third-century self-styled "messenger of the God of truth to Babylonia"[64] and the founder of what can arguably be termed the first "world religion," a religion thoroughly imbued with biblical modes of discourse, depicts him clad in Persian garments "*carrying a strong ebony-wood staff* in his right hand."[65] Apart from the important typological alignment of the events and themes of what Saadya Gaon termed the "first redemption" (i.e., the exodus from Egypt) alongside those slated to transpire at the "final redemption," it would appear that the crucial reason is an exegetical one.

Several biblical texts that are traditionally passed through an eschatological filter feature lexemes that suggest a return of the staff. According to Num 24:17, "a star will stride forth from Jacob, and *a staff will rise from Israel*." Interpretative currents extending back into the Second Temple period already decipher the "star" (כוכב) and/or the "staff" (שבט) of this verse as end-time designations for one or more messianic figures.[66] Ps 110:2, nominally addressed to the newly enthroned ruler in Jerusalem, reinforces this association: "the Lord will extend *your mighty staff* (מטה עזך) out from Zion—dominate your enemies!" Similarly the Masoretic text of Isa 11:4b also mentions a "staff" (שבט) which the anticipated scion from

---

[63] See, for example, the medieval hagiograph *Sefer ʾAsaṭīr* 12.24: וקדקד יקום בקשט יכתב ארהותה ואטר פליאתה באדה אור ולא יהי חשך מרן יזרז בכן, "a prince will arise: he will inscribe the true Torah and bear the wonder-working staff in his hand. There will be light and no more darkness. May our Lord hasten this!" Text cited from the edition published by Zeʾev Ben-Hayyim, "Sefer ʾAsaṭir," *Tarbiz* 14 (1943): 125. Note also the traditions cited by Jarl E. Fossum, *The Name of God and the Angel of the Lord* (WUNT 36; Tübingen: J. C. B. Mohr, 1985), 117–19.

[64] Bīrūnī, *Athār al-bāqiya ʿan-il-qurūn al-khāliya: Chronologie orientalischer Völker von Albêrûnî* (ed. C. E. Sachau; Leipzig, 1878; repr., Leipzig: Otto Harrassowitz, 1923), 207.13.

[65] *Acta Archelai* 14.3: *in manu vero validissimum baculum tenebat ex lingo ebelino*. The complete text is available in Hegemonius, *Acta Archelai* (ed. C. H. Beeson; GCS 16; Leipzig: J. C. Hinrichs, 1906), 22.24–23.1.

[66] See CD 7:18–20 (= 4Q266 3 III 20–21), where the "staff" of Num 24:17 is explicitly identified as "the Prince of the whole Congregation" (השבט הוא נשיא כל העדה). Note too the LXX translation of שבט by ἄνθρωπος, as well as *T. Levi* 18:3; *T. Jud.* 24:1.

[67] Note especially 1QSb 5:24, 27–28 for an application of this biblical verse to the eschatological "Prince of the Congregation" (נשיא העדה).

"the stem of Jesse" (11:1) will use to smite the earth and to slay the wicked.[67] The textual evocation in these particular passages of imagery conjoining messianic deliverance with a "staff" readily encourages the ancillary idea that the future agent of deliverance, mirroring his ancient Mosaic prototype, will come equipped with a wonder-working "staff," perhaps even the very effective one previously wielded by Moses.

3

The "People of Moses" (בני משה)

Beney Mosheh or "people of Moses" is the appellation used by the elusive Eldad ha-Dani, a traveling messianic agitator of the eighth or ninth century,[1] for the Jewish inhabitants of a distant land located east of Eretz Israel beyond the legendary Sambatyon or "sand" river. Renowned for their exemplary piety and extraordinary righteousness, they dwelt (according to Eldad) adjacent to those regions where various descendants of the infamous "lost tribes" of Israel were likewise situated, but who were lacking the special protection afforded by the marvelous river. A careful examination of the traditions surrounding the *beney Mosheh* and their role in end-time events reveals that this group is not simply the product of Eldad's fertile imagination, but is instead textually grounded in a complex weave of exegetical speculation that transcends even confessional boundaries.

The forced expulsion and expatriate settlement of ethnic communities who associated themselves with biblical Israel by repeated waves of Assyrian and Babylonian invaders must have had a devastating effect on political attempts to forge a stable social entity in Eretz Israel. The narratological movement of the primary nationalist myths hints at the disruptive impact of these traumas. The developing epic cycles of Abraham and Jacob, rooted in tales originally featuring largely regional heroes and local foundation-legends, each incorporate a series of episodes underscoring the importance of "return" to "the land of promise," and

[1] For general bibliographic information, see Leopold Zunz and Ḥanokh Albeck, *Haderashot be-Yisrael* (2d ed.; Jerusalem: Mosad Bialik, 1954), 65; 310–11 nn. 83–88. The most comprehensive treatment of the Eldad ha-Dani texts and traditions remains the 1891 study of Abraham Epstein, "Sefer Eldad ha-Dani," reprinted in A. M. Habermann, ed., *Kitvey Avraham Epstein* (2 vols.; Jerusalem: Mosad ha-Rav Kook, 1949–56), 1:1–211, see also 1:357–90. See also D. H. Müller, "Die Recensionen und Versionen des Eldad Had-Dani . . . veröffentlicht und kritisch untersucht," *Denkschriften der kaiserlichen Akademie der Wissenschaften in Wien, philosophisch-historische Klasse* 41 (1892): 1–80; Max Schloessinger, *The Ritual of Eldad ha-Dani* (Leipzig and New York: Rudolf Haupt, 1908); and Joseph Dan, *Ha-Sippur ha-ʿivri be-yemey ha-beyanim: ʿIyyunim be-toldotav* (Jerusalem: Keter, 1974), 47–61. A recent useful summary of the primary traditions about this figure is provided by David J. Wasserstein, "Eldad ha-Dani and Prester John," in *Prester John, the Mongols and the Ten Lost Tribes* (ed. Charles F. Beckingham and Bernard Hamilton; Aldershot: Variorum, 1996), 213–36.

significantly both Abraham and Jacob are represented as effecting migrations from both Mesopotamia and Egypt to Canaan. The subtlety of the message communicated by this narrative skeleton was reinforced by the Judean scribal schools responsible for the literary redaction of the Israelite prophetic corpus. Therein we discern that an "ingathering of the exiles," including a return to the homeland for the "lost" northern and trans-Jordanian tribes, forms an essential component of prophetic eschatology (see Isa 11:11–15; Jer 31:6–13; Ezek 37:19–24).

The legends surrounding the "people of Moses" are intimately bound with memories and tales depicting the fate of those tribes who suffered exile at the hands of foreign invaders from the East. Two early Jewish parascriptural sources contain the nucleus of what will eventually emerge as the full-fledged version of the tale narrated by Eldad ha-Dani and other tradents. The first is found in *4 Ezra* 13:39–47, a passage that provides its eponymous seer with an authoritative interpretation of a portion of the enigmatic and frightening dream previously described in 13:1–13. In this dream Ezra observed a human figure emerge from a storm-tossed sea, fly through the air, and then erect a mountain that would become the staging ground of a battle with an immense horde of warring peoples. When the battle began, the mysterious figure obliterated the attacking army by shooting fire and flames from its mouth. Once the smoke had cleared, the human figure descended the mountain and summoned another group of people who, in pointed contrast to the first horde, remained serenely pacific. "The figures of a large group of human beings approached him: some of them were rejoicing, but some were mournful; some of them were prisoners, and some were bringing those things which could serve as offerings" (13:13).[2] It is this final scene that prompts the following explanation:

> And as for when you saw him summon and gather to himself another large multitude who were peaceful, these are the nine and one-half tribes who were led away captive from their land in the days of King Josiah [*sic*], those whom Shalmaneser, king of the Assyrians, took captive.[3] He took them to the other side of the Euphrates river,[4] and they dwelt as captives in another land. However, they formed a plan among themselves and reached this counsel; namely, that they would depart from

[2] Translated from the Syriac version of *4 Ezra* as edited by R. J. Bidawid and published in *The Old Testament in Syriac According to the Peshitta Version*, Part IV, Fascicle 3: *Apocalypse of Baruch, 4 Esdras* (Leiden: Brill, 1973). Syriac ܕܡܘ̈ܬܐ here means "forms, figures, images"; compare the Arabic versions and Syriac 13:3 at the beginning of the chapter: ܐܝܟ ܕܡܘܬܐ ܕܒܪܢܫܐ, "something like a human figure." For the Arabic versions of *4 Ezra*, I have consulted the texts accumulated in Adriana Drint, ed., *The Mount Sinai Arabic Version of IV Ezra* (2 vols.; CSCO 563–64, scrip. arabici 48–49; Louvain: Peeters, 1997).

[3] Compare 2 Kgs 17:1–6. "Josiah" is an error for "Hoshea."

[4] The name Euphrates is a gloss in the Syriac and Arabic versions of *4 Ezra* 13:40 that probably originates from Josephus, *Ant.* 11.133. The Latin version reads simply "he took them across the river" (*et transtulit eos trans flumen*). Note also *2 Bar.* 78:1, which appears to echo the same episode.

> the multitude of nations and travel to a remote country where none of the human race had lived since time began, for there they might even observe their laws which they neglected to observe in their homeland. They began (their journey) by the narrow entrances of the Euphrates, for then the Most High performed wonders for them (and) blocked the passages of the river until all of them had crossed over, so that they traveled on dry ground.[5] It was a long journey to travel, a journey which lasted one and one-half years. That place (where they dwell) is called Arzaf (ܐܪܙܦ),[6] (at) the edge of the world. They live there until the final age, and then they are destined to come (here) again. The Most High will again block the passages of the Euphrates river so they will be able to cross (it). This is why you saw the gathered multitude who assembled peacefully.[7]

In other words, the "peaceful group" whom Ezra witnessed gathering at the base of the mountain around the salvific figure are the reassembled descendants of the "lost tribes" of Israel who were taken into exile by Shalmaneser when he conquered Samaria. One notes in this remarkable passage a number of motifs that reappear, as we shall see, in later versions of the legend of the "lost tribes" and the "people of Moses." First, a conscious resistance to the corruptive mores and customs of the dominant society or the surrounding environment shows itself in the exiles' steely determination to remove themselves from the "multitude of nations" and to reconstruct their native culture in a distant land. Second, God effects a miracle to assist the exiles in making their escape from Assyria. Third, the route that leads to the new domicile of the exiles involves the fording of a "river," an action effected through the agency of the captor (13:40; *2 Bar.* 78:1) or God Himself (13:44). Fourth, at least one of the rivers (usually the one marking the boundary between the exiles and the rest of the inhabited world) exhibits unusual disruptions in its flow. Fifth, the descendants of these exiles are slated to return to Israel during the messianic era. One should also note that the description of the

[5] This last clause represents another gloss in the Syriac version that is not present in the Latin and is misunderstood in the Arabic. The Syriac manuscript reads: ܕܢܐܙܠܘܢ ܗܘܘ ܕܝܢ ܒܫܝܢܐ, whose final word was plausibly emended by Adolf Hilgenfeld (*Messias Judaeorum* [Leipzig: Sumptu Fuesiano (R. Reisland), 1869], 256) to read ܒܝܒܫܐ, "dry ground." This gloss was intended to establish a typological connection with Exod 14:29; 15:19; and especially Josh 3:17: וכל ישראל עברים בחרבה עד אשר תמו כל הגוי לעבור את הירדן, "and all Israel crossed on dry ground until the whole nation had finished crossing over the Jordan."

[6] Same orthography in the Arabic versions of this verse. The Latin has *Arzaret*, long recognized as a corrupt transliteration of Hebrew ארץ אחרת, "another land" based on Deut 29:27; note also *m. Sanh.* 10.3. According to the early qurʾānic commentator Muqātil b. Sulaymān (*ad* Q 17:104), there are seventy thousand Israelites dwelling in China on the far side of a "river of sand" named Ardaf, presumably a reflex of this nomenclature. See Uri Rubin, *Between Bible and Qurʾān: The Children of Israel and the Islamic Self-Image* (Studies in Late Antiquity and Early Islam 17; Princeton: Darwin Press, 1999), 27.

[7] Translated from the Syriac version of *4 Ezra* (ed. Bidawid) and compared with the Arabic versions published by Drint.

returned exiles as provided in *4 Ezra* 13:13 (see above) exhibits some intriguing linkages with earlier prophetic passages that pertain to this group.[8]

A second early Jewish parascriptural source occurs in *y. Sanh.* 10.6, 29c, and it reappears in subtly variant guises in contemporary and subsequent rabbinic literature. That talmudic passage reads:

> R. Berakhiah and R. Ḥelbo in the name of R. Samuel b. Naḥman taught about three exiles which Israel experienced. One was to the east side of the River Sanbatyon (סנבטיון), one was to Daphne of Antioch (דפני של אנטוכיא),[9] and one was when the cloud descended upon them and concealed them, which was the same as going into exile. What is the reason for the three exiles? "You have traveled the same path as your sister, hence I will put her cup in your hand" (Ezek 23:31). When they repent, they will return from the three exiles. What is the meaning of "Say to the prisoners, Depart!" (Isa 49:9)? These (prisoners) are those who were exiled beyond the River Sanbatyon. ". . . to those in darkness, Become visible!" (ibid.). These are those upon whom the cloud descended and concealed them. ". . . they will graze on the ways, and their pasturage will be on all the high places" (ibid.). These are those who were exiled to Daphne of Antioch.

A later version of this tradition effects some subtle but influential modifications: "R. Berakhiah and R. Ḥelbo in the name of R. Samuel b. Naḥman taught that Israel suffered exile *to three places*: one was *within* (לפנים מן) the River Sambatyon (סמבטיון), as scripture states . . . (Isa 49:9), one was *without* (חוץ מן) the River Sambatyon . . . , and (one was) to Daphne of Antioch" (*Lam. Rab.* 2.9 [13]). What were originally three separate *occasions* of exile have here been transmuted into three specific *locations* where exiled Israelites could be found. Moreover, the group whom the Yerushalmi characterizes as being hidden by a cloud is situated by this later midrash on the near side of the Sambatyon, thus establishing a symmetrical balance of protected societies: the miraculous river (although no wonders are here explicitly associated with the river) surrounds and isolates one community of exiles, and the dense cloud conceals and protects those tribes who do not dwell on the opposite side of the river. The seventh-century apocalypse *Sefer Elijah* does not seem cognizant of these narrative adjustments since it still appears to operate with the older understanding of three distinct exiles, only one of which it associates with the Sambatyon legend: "On the twenty-fifth (day) of Tishri, the second group of exiles will depart from the region of the River Sa(m)batyon."[10]

[8] The reference to the "prisoners" (ܐܣܝܪ̈ܐ) in 13:13 is meant to invoke Isa 49:9: לאמר לאסורים צאו, "Say to the prisoners, 'Depart!'" This biblical text plays a central role in marking textual complexes whose primary referent is the return of the "lost tribes." As for those who bring offerings, see Isa 66:20.

[9] According to 2 Macc 4:33, this was the place where the deposed high priest Onias III took refuge from his persecutor Menelaus.

[10] בכ״ה לתשרי גלות שנייה שבנהר סבטיון יוצאה. Text cited from the edition of Moses Buttenwieser, *Die hebräische Elias-Apokalypse und ihre Stellung in der apokalyptischen Litteratur des rabbinischen Schrifttums und der Kirche* (Leipzig: Eduard Pfeiffer, 1897), 17.7.

The relatively late midrash *Pesiqta Rabbati* contains a homily that weds the notion of the three locales for exile with the missing Ten Tribes and their inclusion in the eschatological drama. After an extended citation of Isa 49:8–13 and a justification of its contextual placement within the biblical oracle, the homilist asks:

> To what does (the verse) "Say to the prisoners, Depart!" (Isa 49:9) refer? The Ten Tribes underwent three exiles. One exile was to the Sambatyon (לסמבטיון), one exile was beyond the Sambatyon (לפנים מסמבטיון), and one was to Daphne of Riblah (לדפנו של רבלתה),[11] where it was swallowed up (ונבלעה שם)—"Israel was swallowed up" (Hos 8:8). "Say to the prisoners, Depart!" (Isa 49:9) refers to those situated by the Sambatyon. "(Say) to those in darkness, Become visible!" (ibid.) refers to those situated beyond the Sambatyon. And as for those swallowed up in Riblah, the Holy One, blessed be He, will make subterranean tunnels for them, and they will burrow through them until they arrive beneath the Mount of Olives in Jerusalem.[12] Then the Holy One, blessed be He, will stand upon it, and it will split open for them, and they will climb out from within it, as Zechariah says: "His feet will stand that day on the Mount of Olives east of Jerusalem, and the Mount of Olives will split apart, half of it eastward and westward, etc." (Zech 14:4). This is what has been written: "and you will think, 'Who has engendered these for me? I was bereaved and solitary, exiled and turned away. Who has raised these? Behold, I was left by myself. Where did these come from?'" (Isa 49:21). And those three exiled communities do not return alone; rather, in every place where Israel is, they will be gathered and come (to the Land). "Behold, these come from a distant locale, and these are from the north and the west" (Isa 49:12)—this refers to those situated in the distant regions of Spain. "And these are from the land of Sinim" (ibid.)—this refers to the people of Jonadab ben Rechab.[13]

It is particularly interesting to note the contextual juxtaposition in this source of the exiled tribes dwelling in the vicinity of the Sambatyon and the infamous descendants of Jonadab ben Rechab or the biblical "Rechabites" (Jer 35:1–19).

---

[11] See *b. Sanh.* 96b, where Riblah (1 Kgs 25:6) is identified as "Antioch" (אנטוכיא).

[12] Similar tunneling operations to effect the return of all the Israelite dead who were buried outside of Eretz Israel are described in *Gen. Rab.* 96.5 (ed. Vilna; but also reproduced in the textual apparatus of Theodor-Albeck, 1199); *Midr. Tanḥ.*, Vayeḥi §3; *Pesiq. Rab.* §1 (Ish-Shalom, 3b). Interestingly, there are several *ḥadīth* which recount that in order to escape their sinful compatriots, one or more "tribes" of the "people of Moses" (cf. Q 7:159) passed through a tunnel from the Temple Mount to China where they now live as paragons of virtue and piety. Muhammad visited them during the course of his so-called "night journey" (see Q 17:1 and its commentaries) and introduced them to Islam. These cognate traditions are summarized in Rubin, *Between Bible and Qur'ān*, 27–28, 46–48.

[13] *Pesiq. Rab.* §31 (Ish-Shalom, 146b-147a). See also Hezekiah (Chiskia) ben Abraham, מלביאל (Vilna and Grodno: [Romm?], 1819), 29a-b. The "land of Sinim" (ארץ סינים) in medieval Hebrew refers to China; one should note the identical Muslim mapping of the "people of Moses" referred to in the previous note, as well as the testimony of Muqātil b. Sulaymān cited below.

According to this biblical text, the Rechabites (בית הרכבים) constituted a clan particularly renowned for its fidelity to the eccentric precepts of its "founder," having vowed to abstain from the drinking of wine, the construction of fixed settlements or housing, and the practice of agriculture. They instead lived in tents on the fringes of civilization, there cultivating a pastoral lifestyle whereby they could presumably escape the material temptations posed by sedentary urban life. While the "lost tribes" and the Rechabites are exegetically distinguished in the present midrash, a number of medieval Jewish sources forge a physical linkage between them, placing the Ten Tribes, the Rechabites, and the *beney Mosheh* together within an "inaccessible utopia" beyond the mythical Sambatyon.[14] There are also some tantalizing traditions similar to those associated with the *beney Mosheh* that prescribe a definite role for the Rechabites in the messianic drama.[15] An intriguing teaching preserved in some manuscripts of *Pesiqta de-Rav Kahana* constructs an end-time scenario that has the Rechabites announcing the arrival of the age of redemption to the patriarchs buried in Hebron; they also take the lead in restoring sacrificial worship to the Temple Mount.[16] One might also add that the Christian legend of the "Rechabites," who according to the monk Zosimus inhabit a "blessed land" situated at the ends of the earth, are nothing more than a relatively late Christian adaptation of this medieval Jewish motif.[17]

The traditional name accorded the liminal river—the Sambatyon—apparently puns on a peculiar behavioral pattern it allegedly displays; namely, it ceases to flow on and hence "observes the Sabbath."[18] The form "Sam/nbatyon" seems to result from a geminate dissimilation of the labial consonant in a prior Greek form Σαββάτιον.[19] Both Pliny and Josephus make reference to a "sabbatical river"

[14] See the sources assembled by Israel Friedlaender, "The Jews of Arabia and the Rechabites," *JQR* n.s. 1 (1910–11): 252–57. Note also Louis Ginzberg, *The Legends of the Jews* (7 vols.; Philadelphia: Jewish Publication Society, 1909–38), 6:407–9; Eli Yassif, *The Tales of Ben Sira in the Middle Ages: A Critical Text and Literary Studies* (Jerusalem: Magnes, 1984), 109–10 (Hebrew). For possible "Rechabite" influence upon at least one messianic agenda, see the testimony of the Karaite scholar Yehudah Hadassi cited by Aaron Zeʾev Aescoly, *Messianic Movements in Israel,* Volume 1, *From the Bar-Kokhba Revolt until the Expulsion of the Jews from Spain* (ed. Yehudah Even-Shmuel; 2d ed.; Jerusalem: Mosad Bialik, 1987), 142.

[15] Note the references in the preceding note, as well as Patricia Crone and Michael Cook, *Hagarism: The Making of the Islamic World* (Cambridge: Cambridge University Press, 1977), 36–37; Zeʾev Safrai, "The Sons of Yehonadav ben Rekhav and the Essenes," *Bar-Ilan Annual* 16–17 (1979): 53–55 (Hebrew).

[16] *Pesiq. Rab Kah., nispaḥ* §5 (Mandelbaum, 2:464, also 466).

[17] See *The History of the Rechabites,* Volume 1, *The Greek Recension* (ed. James H. Charlesworth; Chico, Calif.: Scholars Press, 1982); also *OTP* 2:443–61.

[18] Note that R. ʿAkiba's explanation in *b. Sanh.* 65b, derived in turn from *Gen. Rab.* 11.5, already presumes a connection between the name of this river and the Sabbath day. A more creative etymology is supplied by some of the later medieval legends; see below.

[19] Presumably after the word had reentered a Semitic language environment, since almost all vari-

(Σαββατικόν) in Syria,[20] a purportedly natural marvel that regularly synchronized its flow with the passage of the days of a planetary week, although the precise operation of this phenomenon is explained differently by the first-century writers.[21] It is this same river, on the basis of living folk traditions associated with its character, that the *Alexander Romance* of Pseudo-Callisthenes transforms into a "river of sand,"[22] which manifests in later Arabic language sources as the "sand river." By the fourth or fifth century, early rabbinic literature already associates this same peculiar "desiccation-motif" with the sabbatically observant Sambatyon: "the Sabtinos river furnishes proof (for the special status of the Sabbath), because it flows (with) rocks all week long, but it ceases (flowing) on the Sabbath."[23]

Early Muslim traditions, almost all of which predate the journey and narrative accounts of Eldad ha-Dani, exploit the same complex of motifs and provide further nuances to the eschatological mission of a sequestered "people of Moses," a group usually conflated with the "lost tribes." Two passages in the Qurʾān (7:159; 17:104) are commonly interpreted as making reference to an end-time role for these groups. The former verse features the phrase "people of Moses" (*qawm Mūsā*), an in itself unremarkable qurʾānic locution for a prophet's particular generation,[24] but it goes on to mention a subgroup among them who are especially celebrated for their piety and righteousness. Early commentaries to Q 7:159 explicitly equate this pious faction of the people of Moses with the lost tribes, situating them at the edge of the inhabitable world where they presently live a life of ease and bounty, but who will in the future ally themselves with the Muslims in their struggle against Rome.[25] The latter qurʾānic verse (17:104) also attracts eschatological interpretation and is taken to refer to a future, divinely supervised reunion of the tribes of Israel, including those who were carried off into exile. Significantly the early traditionist Muqātil b. Sulaymān (d. 767 CE) locates these lost tribes in China on the far side of a "river of sand" bearing the name Ardaf/q. This "river" flows with sand during the first six days of the week, but it solidly congeals on the Sabbath.[26] One easily recognizes in Muqātil's commentary the primary

ant Hebrew forms of the name for this river render the initial sibilant as ס and Greek τ (originally ת) with the emphatic ט. Note also Ramban *ad* Deut 32:26.

[20] Pliny, *Naturalis historia* 31.11; Josephus, *B.J.* 7.96–99.

[21] It is likely that both Josephus and Pliny are here reliant upon a common written source.

[22] Pseudo-Callisthenes, *Alexander Romance* 2.30. See B. P. Reardon, ed., *Collected Ancient Greek Novels* (Berkeley: University of California Press, 1989), 705.

[23] *Gen. Rab.* 11.5 (Theodor-Albeck, 93): נהר סבטיינוס יוכיח שמושך אבנים כל השבוע ובשבת מניח. See also Rashi to *b. Sanh.* 65b.

[24] Compare the analogous qurʾānic designations "people of Noah," "people of Abraham," "people of Lot," etc.

[25] Rubin, *Between Bible and Qurʾān*, 24–29.

[26] See Rubin, *Between Bible and Qurʾān*, 27–28.

mythemes found in the parallel Jewish tales that surround the existence of a "people of Moses" and the fate of the lost tribes.

A ratcheting upward of eschatological excitement is discernible in the apocalyptically charged atmosphere of the initial decades of ʿAbbāsid rule. According to a reliable source, the Jewish messianic activist Abū ʿĪsā al-Iṣfahānī "undertook a journey to the people[27] of Moses b. ʿImrān, those who were beyond the river of sand, in order to announce the word of God to them."[28] Presumably Abū ʿĪsā made this pilgrimage to inform the "people of Moses" of his advent and to remind them of their ancillary role in the dramatic social and political cataclysms marking the end of days. Maimonides in his *Iggeret Teiman* also apparently refers to this same legendary mission, although there he depicts the charlatan as initially successful in convincing the "people of Moses" to become his allies: the Mosaic tribes reluctantly return to their "exile" once his deception has been exposed.[29] It should be recalled that some Muslim traditions report that Muhammad made the same journey during his own lifetime.[30] This report, certainly apocryphal, serves nevertheless to solidify the "Jewish" credentials of the Prophet as a harbinger of the messianic age.[31] Scarcely a generation after Abū ʿĪsā, the proto-Karaite Jewish heresiarch ʿAnan b. David reportedly based his teachings on what were supposedly superior "manuscripts of the Mishnah [*sic!*] written in the handwriting copied from the prophet Moses," copies of which ʿAnan allegedly brought with him to Baghdad "from the East."[32] Given the oft-repeated testimony in the later

[27] Arabic *aṣḥāb*; many manuscripts read here *banū* and thus provide a direct parallel to Hebrew בני משה.

[28] Shahrastānī, *Kitāb al-milal wa-al-niḥal* (2 vols.; ed. M. b. Fath Allāh Badrān; [Cairo]: Matbaʿat al-Azhar, [1951–55]) 1.507; compare the version of the text published in William Cureton, ed., *Kitāb al-milal wa-al-niḥal: Book of Religious and Philosophical Sects, by Muhammad al-Shahrastáni* (2 vols.: London: Society for the Publication of Oriental Texts, 1842–46), 2:168.8–9. See also Jellinek, *BHM* 2:xxviii n. 2; Daniel Gimaret and Guy Monnot, *Shahrastani: Livre des religions et des sectes* (2 vols.; Paris: Peeters, 1986–93), 1:604; Steven M. Wasserstrom, *Between Muslim and Jew: The Problem of Symbiosis under Early Islam* (Princeton: Princeton University Press, 1995), 76; idem, "Šahrastānī on the Maġāriyya," *IOS* 17 (1998): 139.

[29] *A Maimonides Reader* (ed. Isadore Twersky; West Orange, N.J.: Behrman House, 1972), 458–59.

[30] Rubin plausibly suggests that the seventh-century Armenian chronicler Sebeos was already familiar with legends recounting a meeting between the Arabian Prophet and "exiled" Israelite tribes (*Between Bible and Qurʾān*, 49–52). For more on Sebeos and his distinctive account of the rise of Islam, see Crone and Cook, *Hagarism*, 6–8; Robert G. Hoyland, *Seeing Islam As Others Saw It: A Survey and Evaluation of Christian, Jewish and Zoroastrian Writings on Early Islam* (Studies in Late Antiquity and Early Islam 13; Princeton: Darwin Press, 1997), 124–32.

[31] See the almost contemporary *Doctrina Jacobi nuper baptizati* 5.16 (quoted in English translation by Hoyland, *Seeing Islam*, 57) wherein Muhammad is presented as a prophet proclaiming "the advent of the anointed one, the Christ who was to come" and as the custodian of "the keys of Paradise." Note also Harry Turtledove, *The Chronicle of Theophanes* (Philadelphia: University of Pennsylvania Press, 1982), 34.

[32] Text cited from Maqrīzī, *Khiṭaṭ*, as published in A. I. Silvestre de Sacy, *Chrestomathie arabe* (3

Hebrew accounts that the "people of Moses" were the custodians of the most authentic versions of the scriptures revealed to Moses on Sinai (see below),[33] it seems clear that ʿAnan's scripturalist claim was purposely designed to undermine Rabbanite arguments about the antiquity of the Oral Torah and to exploit the messianic overtones of his suggested alliance with the "people of Moses."[34]

Since the theme of the "people of Moses" became such a prominent part of the medieval apocalyptic *mentalité*, and because the testimonies still remain largely unknown among Anglophone readers, I have decided to incorporate here a selection of annotated English translations of the most important texts.[35]

1. *Chronicles of Yeraḥmeʾel* (ed. Yassif):[36]

The levitical people of Moses (הלוים בני משה): they are encamped east of the River Sa(m)batyon.[37] Our Sages say that at the time when Israel went into exile to Babylon, they brought them to the Euphrates river, as scripture says: "we sat down <there> by the rivers of Babylon, etc." (Ps 137:1). Their captors said to them; that is, to the Levites: "Serve before the idol and sing a song the same way which you sang in the Temple." They answered them: "You fools! Had we sung (only) one song to celebrate all the miracles which the Holy One, blessed be He, has performed for us, we would not have been exiled from our land. Instead, He would have augmented our honor with yet more honors! And we should sing before an idol?!?" They [the Babylonians] immediately arose and killed great heaps (תילי תילים) of them. Even

---

vols.; Paris: Imprimerie imperiale, 1806), 1:161.6–8. See Steven M. Wasserstrom, "Species of Misbelief: A History of Muslim Heresiography of the Jews" (Ph.D. diss., University of Toronto, 1985), 436.

[33] Belonging to this same stream of tradition may be the interesting remark attributed to R. Saadya Gaon toward the end of Abraham Ibn Ezra's introduction to his commentary on Song of Songs concerning a performance of Psalm 90 by the *beney Mosheh*.

[34] Due in part to this intriguing scripturalist overlap between the arguments of early Karaism and the alleged possession by the *beney Mosheh* of a more authentic Torah, Eldad is sometimes branded a Karaite propagandist spinning tall tales in the service of a more insidious cause. See, e.g., Heinrich Graetz, *Geschichte der Juden von den ältesten Zeiten bis auf die Gegenwart* (3d ed.; 11 vols. in 13; Leipzig: Oskar Leiner, 1890–1908), 5:452.

[35] A conflate paraphrase featuring many of the most important themes associated with the "people of Moses" is available in Ginzberg, *Legends*, 4:316–18. A more comprehensive version is Micha Joseph bin Gorion, *Mimekor Yisrael: Selected Classical Jewish Folktales* (ed. Emanuel bin Gorion; trans. I. M. Lask; Bloomington and Indianapolis: Indiana University Press, 1990), 126–31.

[36] Oxford Ms. Heb. d. 11 (2797). See Eli Yassif, ed., *Sefer ha-Zikronot huʾ Divrey ha-Yamim le-Yeraḥmeʾel* (Tel Aviv: Tel Aviv University, 2001), 220–21. Note also Epstein, "Sefer Eldad ha-Dani," 1:88–94.

[37] For this particular location, see *Gen. Rab.* 73.6 (Theodor-Albeck, 850).

though they slew a large number of them, (their?) joy was great,[38] for they [the Levites] would not worship an idol. Therefore scripture says: "*our heaps* (produced) joy" (Ps 137:3).[39]

What did the remaining Levites do? They severed the fingers of their hands so that they could not play the harps, and when they commanded them to play the harps and sing the same way that they did in the Temple, they showed them their severed fingers.[40] At nightfall a cloud covered them: it concealed them, their wives, their sons, and their daughters. The Holy One, blessed be He, shone over them in a column of fire, and He led them throughout the night until daybreak, and He brought them to the shore of the sea. When the sun rose, the cloud lifted, and (also) the column of fire (departed). The Holy One, blessed be He, stretched out the river[41] before them—the Sabbatyinos (סבטיינוס)—and it closed around them so that no one would be able to cross over to them. It surrounds them for a distance of a three-month journey by a three-month journey on every side, and the back side is surrounded by the sea in every direction. The Holy One, blessed be He, stretched out that river and it closed before them. The depth of that river is three hundred cubits. The river is full of sand and rocks, and it flows (like) an earthquake, its sound (carrying) at night a distance of half a day's journey. It drags sand and rocks all during the six days on which one is permitted to labor, but on the Sabbath it rests. Then a fire emerges from the western side of the valley, burning from the eve of Sabbath until its end, and no one is able to approach closer than about a mile while the fire is burning (and) shooting out in all directions around the river.

No unclean animal or bird or reptile can be found among them; they have with them (only) their flocks and cattle. Six springs are there whose waters they have collected into a pool that they constructed, and they irrigate their land from the pool. All types of pure fish flourish in it (the pool), and by the springs and the pool flourish all kinds of pure waterfowl. They enjoy all kinds of fruits: (the fertility of the land is such that) whoever plants one seed harvests a hundredfold.

They are religiously observant, each of them learned in Torah, Bible, Mishnah, and Aggadah. They are "pure pietists" (טהורים חסידים). None of them ever swears a false oath. They live to be 120 years old, and a son or daughter never dies during the life span of their father: they (usually) wit-

[38] Following Yassif's suggestion to emend the manuscript's וכלה השמחה to גדולה השמחה on the basis of the version in *Bereshit Rabbati*.

[39] It is necessary to translate the problematic ותוללינו (see the commentaries and lexicons) along these lines.

[40] This legend was already known to Rashi; see his commentary to *b. Qidd.* 69b *s.v.* ואבינה בעם.

[41] Read הנהר in place of the manuscript's ונהל.

ness the succession of three or four generations. They construct their own houses and do their own sowing and harvesting because they have no slaves or maidservants. They never lock their doors at night. A very small child might go and tend their cattle for a number of days, and no one will be in the least bit anxious, for there are no thieves or dangerous wild animals or pests, and there are no demons or anything that might cause harm.[42] Because they are holy and persist in the sanctity revealed by our teacher Moses, He [God] has granted all this to them and chosen them. They never interact with other human beings, nor do other humans interact with them, save for only four (Israelite) tribes: (those of) Dan, Naphtali, Gad, and Asher, who live "on the other side of the rivers of Cush" (Isa 18:1; Zeph 3:10),[43] with the River Sa(m)batyon separating them. They will remain there until the time of the eschaton,[44] and scripture says about them: "Say to the captive ones, 'Depart!'" (Isa 49:9); i.e., (to) those in the direction of the River Sa(m)batyon.[45]

2. *Chronicles of Yeraḥmeʾel* (ed. Yassif):[46]

The exile of Titus, Vespasian, and Hadrian took place on the eve of the ninth of Av, at the end of Sabbath, and during the final period of a sabbatical year. The Levites remained in their places with their harps in their hands and continued singing their songs. What verse were they reciting? "He turns upon them their wickedness and annihilates them with their evil" (Ps 94:23). They had not finished saying "He annihilates them" before the enemy came upon them, killed some of them, and exiled the rest. When Nebuchadnezzar exiled them, it was also on the eve of the ninth of Av, at the end of the Sabbath day, and during the final period of a sabbatical year. The Levites remained in their places, sixty myriads of them, and they moreover were descended from the lineage of our teacher Moses. They were reciting

[42] For the close association of wild animals and demons, see Isa 13:21; 34:13–15; perhaps also Job 5:21–23; and the remarks of William Robertson Smith, *Lectures on the Religion of the Semites* (2d ed.; Edinburgh: A. & C. Black, 1894), 119–32.

[43] Cush as a geographic designation generally refers to the lands south and/or east of Egypt; that is, east Africa and southwest Arabia. For a comprehensive discussion of the term, see David M. Goldenberg, *The Curse of Ham: Race and Slavery in Early Judaism, Christianity, and Islam* (Princeton: Princeton University Press, 2003), 17–45.

[44] עד עת קץ. Cf. Dan 12:4, 9.

[45] See also Moses Gaster, *The Chronicles of Jerahmeel; or, the Hebrew Bible Historiale* (London, 1899; repr., New York: Ktav, 1971), 188–89.

[46] Yassif, ed., *Sefer ha-Zikronot*, 219–20; Epstein, "Sefer Eldad ha-Dani," 1:87. For a variant version of this text, see Jellinek, *BHM* 2:111–12.

this verse with their harps in their hands, saying: "He turns upon them their wickedness and annihilates them with their evil" (ibid.). They had not finished saying "He annihilates them" before the enemy came upon them and exiled them to Babylon.

When they arrived in Babylon, their enemies and captors said to them: "Sing us one of the songs of Zion!" (Ps 137:3). They responded: "How can we sing a song of Zion in a foreign land?"[47] Their captors said to them: "You will nevertheless be compelled to sing now!" Immediately they bit off their fingers with their teeth and threw them down before them, saying: "How can we strum in a foreign land with fingers we used to play with in the Temple?!? The Holy One, blessed be He, has said: 'I will forget My right hand before I forget you, O Jerusalem!' (Ps 137:5)."

A cloud came and lifted up all the *beney Mosheh*—they only with their flocks and cattle—and brought them to Havilah in the east and set them down there at night.[48] That night they heard there a heavy rumbling, for He was changing the location of the river.[49] There was no spray from water: (they heard only) the rolling of stones and sand from a place where no great river had previously been. The river rolled stones and sand—not a drop of water—with a loud rumbling. If one were to encounter the great river it would crush him until the end of the Sabbath.[50] This is the River Sa(m)batyon, and they named it Sabbatyinos (סבטיינוס). There were places at that river which were no wider than sixty cubits, and they would stand on one bank of the river and speak from there. On the Sabbath it would stop (flowing), but on the eve of the Sabbath a cloud would descend over it and it [the valley] would be filled with fog, and no one was able to approach nearer to it, neither we to them or they to us.

No harmful animal or unclean beast or vermin or insects live among them: (they live alone) with just their flocks and cattle. They plow and they sow. These once made inquiry of those (on the opposite side of the river), and they recounted to them (the news) about the destruction of the Second Temple.

[47] Compare Ps 137:4.

[48] Cf. Jellinek, *BHM* 2:111 bottom: ובא הענן ונשאום עם אהליהם וצאנם ובקרם והוליכם לחוילה והורידום שם בלילה, "A cloud came and lifted them up with their tents, flocks, and cattle and brought them to Havilah and set them down there at night."

[49] Cf. Jellinek, *BHM* 2:111: והסיעם להם את הנהר.

[50] The text has suffered corruption here; compare the renderings found in Yassif, ed., *Sefer ha-Zikronot*, 219 n. 32; Jellinek, *BHM* 2:112: שאלמלא היה פוגע בהר של ברזל היה נפצו והנהר גולל כל ששת ימי השבוע אבנים וחול בלי שום טיפת מים ובשבת נח ובשעה שיעריב יום הששי בה"ש תרד עליו ענן ואין אדם יכול ליגש עליו עד מוצאי שבת, "if one encountered a mountain of iron it would crush him. The river flowed with rocks and sand, without a drop of water, all six days of the week and rested on the Sabbath. When the evening of the sixth day arrived, at nightfall, a cloud would descend over it; and no one was able to approach it until the end of the Sabbath."

We do not know what there is beyond the people of Moses, but Naphtali, Gad, and Asher came to Dan after the destruction of the Second Temple. (Initially) they were with Issachar in the mountains of Tehom (בהררי תהום),[51] but they would quarrel with them, for they would call them "descendants of the maidservants." Fearing hostilities would break out between them, they journeyed until they reached Dan, and (now) four tribes remain in one place.

3. *Bereshit Rabbati* (ed. Albeck):[52]

Some say that the levitical people of Moses (הלוים בני משה) are encamped east of the River Sa(m)batyon. Our Sages say that at the time when Israel went into exile to Babylon, they brought them to the Euphrates River, as scripture says: "we sat down <there> by the rivers of Babylon, etc." (Ps 137:1). The nations of the world said to the Levites: "Serve before the idol and sing a song the same way which you sang in the Temple." The Levites answered them: "You fools! Had we sung (only) one song to celebrate all the miracles which the Holy One, blessed be He, has performed for us, we would not have been exiled from our land. Instead, He would have augmented our honor with yet more honors and our greatness with yet more greatness! And we should sing before an idol?!?" They (the Babylonians) immediately arose against them and killed great heaps (תילי תילים) of them. Even though they slew a large number of them, (their?) joy was great, for they [the Levites] would not worship an idol. Therefore scripture says: "*our heaps* (produced) joy" (Ps 137:3).

What did the remaining Levites do? They severed their fingers so that they could not play the harps, and when they commanded them to sing, they displayed their severed fingers and said to them: "How can we sing? Our fingers are severed!" When nightfall came, a cloud descended and covered them, their wives, their daughters, and their sons. The Holy One, blessed be He, shone for them in a column of fire, and He led them throughout the night until daybreak, and He left them on the shore of the sea. When the sun rose, the cloud lifted, and (also) the column of fire

[51] Note Ḥanokh Albeck , ed., *Midrash Bereshit Rabbati* (Jerusalem: Mekize Nirdamim, 1940), 126.9: ושבט יששכר היו שרויים בהרי תהום. For the location of this mountain range, see *Bereshit Rabbati* below.

[52] Albeck, *Bereshit Rabbati*, 124.3–127.8. See also Epstein, "Sefer Eldad ha-Dani," 1:64–67; Jellinek, *BHM* 6:15–18. This version of the legend is closely related to the first account translated above from the *Chronicles of Yeraḥme'el*, which suggests that they both stem from a common source. See the discussion of Adolf Neubauer, "Where Are the Ten Tribes?" *JQR* o.s. 1 (1888–89): 113–14, who opines that this may be the oldest form of the text.

(departed). The Holy One, blessed be He, stretched out a river before them named the Sa(m)batyon (סבטיון), and it closed around them so that no one would be able to cross over to them. It[53] surrounds them for a distance of a three-month journey by a three-month journey on every side, and (since) the back[54] side was not surrounded in every direction, the Holy One, blessed be He, stretched out that river, and it closed before them. The depth of that river is two hundred cubits. The river is full of sand and rocks, and it drags sand and rocks and makes a loud rumbling at night (whose noise carries) a distance of half a day's journey. It drags sand and rocks all during the six days on which one is permitted to labor, but on the Sabbath it rests. Then a fire emerges from the side of the valley, and the fire burns from the eve of Sabbath until its end, and no one is able to approach it; that is, the valley any closer than about a mile. The fire burns away all the vegetation surrounding the valley until the ground is swept clean. These are the levitical people of Moses, and they remain on the east side of the valley.

No unclean domestic beast or wild animal or any type of pest can be found among them; they have with them (only) their flocks and cattle. They have, moreover, six springs whose waters they have collected into a pool, and they irrigate their land from them. In that pool all types of fish flourish, and by the springs and the pool fly all kinds of pure waterfowl. They enjoy all kinds of fruits: they sow and they harvest, and (the fertility of the land is such that) whoever plants one seed harvests a hundredfold.

They are religiously observant, each of them learned in Torah, Mishnah, and Aggadah. They are pious sages and saints (חכמים חסידים וקדושים). None of them ever swears a false oath. They live to be 120 years old, and a son or daughter never dies during the life span of their father: they (usually) witness the succession of three or four generations. They construct their own houses and do their own plowing and sowing because they have no slaves or maidservants. They never lock their doors at night. A very small child might go and tend their cattle for a number of days, and no one will be anxious, for there are no thieves or dangerous wild animals or pests, and there are no demons or anything that might cause harm. Because they are holy and still persist in the sanctity revealed by our teacher Moses, He [God] has granted all this to them and chosen them. They never interact with any other human beings, nor do any other humans interact with them, save for only four (Israelite) tribes: (those of) Dan, Naphtali, Gad, and Asher, who live "on the other side of the rivers of Cush" (Isa 18:1; Zeph 3:10).

How did they (i.e., the aforementioned four tribes) arrive there? Our

[53] Read with Albeck והיה in place of והים; cf. Yassif, ed., *Sefer ha-Zikronot*, 221.

[54] Read with Albeck האחר in place of האחד; cf. Yassif, ed., *Sefer ha-Zikronot*, 221.

Sages say[55] that when Jeroboam b. Nebat arose and made two golden calves and made Israel err by seceding from the kingdom of the House of David, he assembled the Ten Tribes of Israel and ordered them: "Go forth and make war against Rehoboam and the inhabitants of Jerusalem!" They said to him: "Why should we fight with our kinsmen, the citizens of our lord David, the king of Israel and Judah?" The elders of Israel came up to him and said to him: "In all Israel there is not among us warriors and soldiers as mighty and skilled as the tribe of Dan. Command them to make war on Judah!" Immediately Jeroboam said to the Danites: "Go forth and fight against Judah!" They answered him: "We swear by the life of our ancestor Dan that we will not make war against our kinsman and that we will not shed blood without cause!" Then the Danites took up their swords, bows, arrows, and spears, and resigned themselves[56] to doing battle with Jeroboam until the Lord delivered them from having to shed the blood of their kinsmen. They made proclamation throughout the entire tribe of Dan, saying: "(Let us) flee, O Danites, and leave the Land of Israel! We will go to Egypt!" They were planning to destroy and kill all the inhabitants of the land of Egypt, (but) their leaders said to them: "Is this where we should go? Is it not already written in the Torah: 'you will not see them (i.e., the Egyptians) again forever' (Exod 14:13)?" They continued to discuss (the possibility of invading) Egypt or Ammon,[57] but when they saw that it was written in the Torah that the Holy One, blessed be He, would prevent Israel from taking possession of their territory(s), [they withdrew until][58] the Holy One, blessed be He, could give them good direction.

The Danites went up opposite the River Pishon[59] and journeyed on camels, setting up encampments, until they arrived among the rivers of Cush. They found the land to be rich, desirable, and broad, consisting of fields, vineyards, gardens, and parks. The inhabitants of the land did not prevent the Danites from dwelling (there) with them, and they formed an alliance with them. The Cushites paid them tribute, and they dwelt with them for many years until they had grown very populous and numerous.

After the death of Sennacherib, three tribes from Israel made the journey to them; namely, Naphtali, Gad, and Asher. They journeyed, setting up encampments, until they arrived next to the territory of the Danites. Each tribe spends three months a year killing the Cushites. . . .[60] Members of the

[55] Regarding this particular legend, see especially Dan, *Sippur*, 55–57.

[56] Read ומסרו עצמם in place of ומהרו עצמם.

[57] There are a number of textual variants to this list of countries; see the critical apparatus compiled by Albeck, *Bereshit Rabbati*, 125.

[58] פירשו עד, restored on the basis of Yassif, ed., *Sefer ha-Zikronot*, 222.

[59] See Gen 2:11. The Pishon is traditionally identified with the Nile.

[60] The text is corrupt; compare Yassif, ed., *Sefer ha-Zikronot*, 222.

tribe of Simeon are with the Danites, [and the Levites are][61] with these three tribes camped in Havilah "where there is gold" (Gen 2:11). They possess gold, for it is as common as stones, and very many flocks, herds, camels, and horses. They sow and reap; they dwell in tents made of hair; and they migrate and encamp from border to border over an area two hundred days' journey by two hundred days' journey in size. The place where they pitch their tents is not a place where one should enter, and they only set up camp in fields and vineyards. They adjudicate in accordance with the four types of capital punishment.[62] Scripture says about them: "on the other side of the rivers of Cush are My worshipers, the progeny of My dispersed ones: they will bring My offering" (Zeph 3:10).

The tribe of Issachar dwell among the mountains of Tehom. These are located in the lower part of the land of the Medes and Persians. They are fulfilling (the scriptural verse) "the book of the Torah will not depart [from your mouths]" (Josh 1:8); consequently, no yoke of sovereignty achieves dominance over them except for the yoke of the Torah. They enjoy security and tranquility, "untroubled by any adversary or misfortune" (1 Kgs 5:18).[63] They encamp (over an area the size of) a ten-day journey in circumference. They possess numerous herds, camels, and slaves. However, they do not raise horses, nor do they own any weapons except for the knife which they use for slaughtering (animals). They are religiously observant and never experience robbery or theft. Should they chance to find some money in the road, even their slaves will not extend their hands to take it. (By contrast), their neighbors are wicked: they worship fire (and) contract marriages with their mothers and their sisters.[64] They do not engage in the tilling of the soil or in labor on vineyards, but purchase everything (produced agriculturally) with money. They have a judge and a prince who adjudicate with the four types of capital punishment. They speak Hebrew, Persian, and Arabic.

The descendants of Zebulon encamp in the hill country of Paran, pitching tents of hair. They come from Armenia and extend up to the Euphrates River. The tribe of Reuben is opposite them on the back side of the mountains of Paran. They enjoy peace and friendship between themselves, fighting their wars in common and cutting the roads which they make . . .[65] and

[61] Read והלוים היו.

[62] See *m. Sanh.* 7.1; *t. Sanh.* 9.10; *Midr. Tanḥ.*, Vayera §9; Maimonides, *Mishneh Torah*, *Hilkhot Sanhedrin* 14.1.

[63] אין שטן ואין פגע רע. Cf. *Jub.* 23:29; 50:5; also 4Q504 1–2 iv 13.

[64] That is, they are Zoroastrian.

[65] The text is corrupt; see the long list of variants supplied by Albeck, *Bereshit Rabbati*, 126. As he states, highway robbery rather than road construction would seem to be the intended topic of the clause.

together they divide all their spoil. They acquire a camel's load of a kind of food for two pieces of silver. They speak Arabic and possess the Bible, Mishnah, Talmud, and Haggadah. Every Sabbath they expound (the scripture portions) in Hebrew and translate (them) into the Arabic language. The tribe of Simeon and the half-tribe of Manasseh are in the land of the Chaldeans, a six-month journey's distance from the Temple.[66] They are too numerous to be counted. They receive tribute from twenty-five kingdoms, and some of the Ishmaelites even pay them a tax. The tribe of Ephraim and the other half of the tribe of Manasseh are there opposite the city of Mecca (מדינת מאקה).[67] They are ill-tempered and dull-minded, skilled horsemen. They show mercy to no one and will cut out their heart. They possess no wealth except for the spoil taken from their enemies. They are professional warriors: one of them (can prevail) over a thousand (adversaries). However, the tribes of Judah and Benjamin are dispersed among all lands. Woe to the "other son" (Gen 30:24): "another" (אחר) for exile! Another opinion: he will do the work of others (אחרים).[68]

4. *BHM* 2.103–105 (ed. Jellinek):[69]

And also (there) are members of the "people of Moses" our teacher (upon whom be peace!) making their encampment next to the river which is named Sa(m)batyon. It is so called because they fled from Eretz Israel[70] and the river surrounds them. The gentile nations call that river Σαββάτιον (סבטיון). The river surrounds them for a distance of a three-month journey on every side. They dwell in houses, courtyards, and towers, and there is no impure thing among them. There are no impure birds or animals, no dogs or wolves, no dangerous wild animals, no flies, no fleas, no lice, no swarms,[71] no scorpions, no snakes, no foxes, no lions, and no panthers—only flocks and cattle. Their flocks give birth twice a year, and they sow and reap. They possess all the kinds of fruit there are in the world and all kinds of legumes, cucumbers, melons, onions, and garlic.[72]

[66] See the remarks of Epstein, "Sefer Eldad ha-Dani," 1.68 n. 6.

[67] Compare the parallel tradition about the tribes of Ephraim and Manasseh that is cited in Graetz, *Geschichte*, 5:453: ושבט אפרים וחצי שבט מנשה הם בהרים נגד מדינת נביא הישמעאלי שנקרא מיכה, "the tribe of Ephraim and the half-tribe of Manasseh are located in the hill country near the city of the Ishmaelite prophet [i.e., Muhammad] that is named Mecca."

[68] For these final statements regarding Judah and Benjamin, see *Gen. Rab.* 73.6 (Theodor-Albeck, 850).

[69] See also Epstein, "Sefer Eldad ha-Dani," 1:37 note, 76–77; Neubauer, "Ten Tribes," 110–12.

[70] Epstein, "Sefer Eldad ha-Dani," 1:76 reads: שנסו מעבודה זרה, "they fled from idolatry."

[71] The text reads עורבים, "crows," but the pest of Exod 8:17–27 is surely the intended reference.

[72] Cf. Num 11:5.

They are religiously observant, being learned in Torah, Mishnah, and Talmud. When they teach, they say: "(Thus did) Joshua b. Nun say, who received it orally from God." They never mention the name of a (rabbinic) Sage, for they do not know them. They do not know how to speak except in Hebrew. Their *halakhot* pertaining to libation wine, ritual slaughter, and declaring animals ritually unfit for food are stricter than those of the scribes, because Moses our teacher (upon whom be peace!) made them more stringent than the rulings of the scribes.[73] They maintain purity, they are pious, they are righteous, and they never swear oaths using the Name (of God). And if they hear that someone has sworn by the Name, they say to him: "Wretch! Why did you swear with the Ineffable Name? How can you bear the Name in your mouth? Is it a morsel of bread that you can eat it, or water that you can drink it? You will realize no benefit from mentioning the Name in vain. Come and see, for it is on account of swearing oaths that children die while they are still young!" They are religiously observant and pious, and they live long lives, almost 120 years, and no child dies during the life span of their father. They behold (their) children and grandchildren up to the third and fourth generations.

They sow and they harvest. A small child accompanies their herds on a journey lasting a number of days, but they do not worry about anything: there are no dangerous animals, no demons, or anything extant that might cause harm. It is on account of their holiness, purity, righteousness, and piety that the Holy One, blessed be He, has granted them all these good things, for they still persist in maintaining the sanctity associated with Moses our teacher (upon whom be peace!). They dwell alone: they never see (other) human beings, nor do (other) human beings ever see them, save for the four tribes who dwell adjacent to them on the other side of the River Cush [*sic*]. The River Sa(m)batyon effects a division between them. They are the ones of whom the verse speaks: "Say to the prisoners, 'Depart,' and to those in darkness, 'Become visible!'" (Isa 49:9). They have vast quantities of gold. They sow flax and raise the worm that yields scarlet coloring and manufacture beautiful garments from them. They are very soft, more than twice as soft as those produced by Egypt. Of those four tribes scripture states: "O land of buzzing wings, which lies beyond the rivers of Cush" (Isa 18:1).

The width of the River Sa(m)batyon is two hundred and twenty cubits, "about a bowshot's distance" (Gen 21:16). The river is full of sand and rocks. It all flows for a great distance, and the noise of the rocks is similar to

[73] For the "scribes" (סופרים) and their role in the evolution of halakhah, see especially Ephraim E. Urbach, *The Halakhah: Its Sources and Development* (trans. Raphael Posner; Yad ha-Talmud; [Ramat Gan]: Masada Ltd., 1986), 95–105.

a great rumbling like that of the waves of the sea or like a storm wind, and at night its noise is audible a distance of a half-day's journey. They possess a number of springs from which they collect the waters into one pool and from which they irrigate their land. In that pool swarm all kinds of fish, and all kinds of pure waterfowl flourish around it. The river and the sand and the rocks flow all the days of the week, but they cease (flowing) on the Sabbath. It remains stationary from Sabbath eve until the end of the Sabbath. On the other side of the river is a fire (whose nature is) that no one is able to approach the river closer than about a mile. The fire burns everything surrounding the river which the ground has produced. Those four tribes come with their herds to the bank of the river in order to shear their flocks, for the ground is flat and clear: no thorns or briars or vegetation or grass takes root there. When the people of Moses our teacher (upon whom be peace!) see them, they assemble and stand on the (opposite) bank of the river. They call out to them, saying: "By the life of the One Who is![74] O Danites, show us <your>[75] horses, camels, and asses!" They discuss how long this one is, how long its neck is, how small its ear appears, (and) how much it has straightened. They are righteous and pious, and they dwell securely, peacefully, and complacently.

5. *BHM* 3.9–11 (ed. Jellinek):[76]

And also (there) is the tribe of Moses our teacher (upon whom be peace!), the righteous one (and) servant of the Lord. The tribe's name is called by us "Yanūs" (ינוס), for it fled (נס) from idolatry and adhered to reverence for the Lord. The sea surrounds them for a distance of a three-month journey by a three-month journey. They live in magnificent houses and in splendid structures and in towers which they erected for themselves at the time they celebrated (victory?) over the elephant (?).[77] No impure thing troubles them: there are no impure birds, wild beasts, or cattle, and there are no flies, fleas, lice, foxes, scorpions, snakes, or dogs, for all these are the result of idolatrous worship practiced in a land. (No animals live there) except for flocks, herds, and game fowl. Their flocks give birth twice a year,

[74] The text reads: חי היה חי היה.

[75] Read שלכם in place of the text's שלהם.

[76] See also Epstein, "Sefer Eldad ha-Dani," 1:54–55; Neubauer, "Ten Tribes," 112. This version derives from the printed edition of the narrative pertaining to Eldad ha-Dani published in Constantinople in 1519.

[77] See Neubauer, "Ten Tribes," 112; Epstein, "Sefer Eldad ha-Dani," 1:62 n. 25, where the Hebrew הלפנט is identified as Italian *liofante*.

and they also plant their seed twice a year, sowing and harvesting. They have gardens, parks, olive groves, pomegranates, figs, and all kinds of legumes, melons, vegetables, onions, garlic, barley, and wheat. Each crop yields a hundredfold.

They are religiously observant, learned in Mishnah, Talmud, and Aggadah. Their Talmud is entirely in Hebrew, and this is what they say: "Our Sages learned it this way orally from Joshua b. Nun, who received it orally from our ancestor Moses, who received it orally from God."[78] They have no knowledge of the Sages who were active during the Second Temple period, nor do they engage in argument with them. The only language which they can speak is Hebrew.

All of them observe (the rules of) purity, engaging in ritual immersion. They never swear oaths. Should someone ever trivially invoke the Name, they cry out against that person saying, "Because of (your) sinful oath, your children may prematurely die!" They have prolonged life spans, living to an age of 100 or 120, and no child dies during the lifetime of its parent; instead their life spans overlap those of the third or fourth succeeding generations. They do their planting and harvesting [themselves], for they have no bondsmen or maidservants. All of them are equal (in social status). They never lock their houses at night: (such a habit) would cause them shame. A small child might accompany the herd for a distance of a ten-day journey, and there is no anxiety about thieves or demons. All of them are Levites; no priests or laity are present among them. They still maintain the sanctity associated with Moses our Teacher, the servant of the Lord.

They never see other human beings, nor do other humans see them except for those four tribes who inhabit "the opposite side of the rivers of Cush" (Isa 18:1; Zeph 3:10). There is a spot where they can see and converse with one another by each shouting (to the other), with the River Sa(m)batyon separating them. They (the people of Moses) will say, "Something like this happened to us in battle," and they (the four tribes) will communicate to all Israel what happened to them. And when they wish to relate an important message or matter, they possess among them a certain type of pigeon: they write down their messages and tie them to the wings or the feet of the pigeons, and the pigeons then fly over the River Sa(m)batyon and come to their (i.e., the four tribes') rulers and princes.[79]

They, moreover, possess a vast quantity of precious stones, silver, and gold. They sow flax and raise the worm that yields scarlet coloring and

[78] Cf. *m. ʾAbot* 1.1.

[79] Regarding these carrier pigeons, see especially Edward Ullendorff and C. F. Beckingham, *The Hebrew Letters of Prester John* (Oxford: Oxford University Press, 1982), 155.

manufacture countless beautiful garments. They are more than five times as numerous as those produced by Egypt.

The width of that spot by the river is two hundred cubits, "about a bow-shot's distance" (Gen 21:16). The river is full of stones, both large and small, and their noise thunders like a massive earthquake, like a storm wind during the day, and at night its noise is audible a distance of a day's journey. They have among them six springs, and they collect all of them into a single pool from which they irrigate their land. Pure fish swarm in it. The river flows and the rocks and the sand thunder during the six days when one labors, but on the seventh day it ceases and rests until the end of the Sabbath. On the opposite side of the river at the side of those three [*sic*!] tribes, there is a fire burning in the place, and no one is able to approach the side of the land of the *princep[e]* (פרינסי"ף)[80] closer than about the distance of a mile.

6. *BHM* 5.18–20 (ed. Jellinek):[81]

And also (there) is the tribe of Moses our teacher, the righteous one (and) servant of the Lord. Its name is called "tribe that flees" (שבטינוס), for it "fled" (נס) from idolatry and adhered to reverence for the Lord.[82] The river surrounds them for a distance of a three-month journey by a three-month journey on every side. They live in magnificent houses and in splendid structures and in towers which they erected for themselves. No impure thing is among them: there are no impure fowl, animals, or cattle. There are no dangerous wild animals, flies, foxes, fleas, lice, serpents, scorpions, dogs, or any thing that might cause harm. They have only their flocks and herds, and their flocks bear young twice a year. They sow and reap, and they have gardens and parks and all kinds of fruits and all kinds of legumes, melons, vegetables, onions, garlic, wheat, and barley, and each (seed) yields a hundredfold.

They are religiously observant, learned in Torah, Mishnah, Talmud, and Aggadah. Their Talmud is in Hebrew, and this is how they teach: "Thus did

[80] This *princeps*, or "ruler," is "Prince John," that is, Prester John, the legendary oriental Christian prince whose story is intimately bound with that of the "people of Moses" and Eldad ha-Dani. See Epstein, "Sefer Eldad ha-Dani," 1:63 n. 29; Ullendorff and Beckingham, *Hebrew Letters*, 70 n. 1, 153–59; Wasserstein, "Eldad ha-Dani," 213–36.

[81] See also Epstein, "Sefer Eldad ha-Dani," 1:69–74; Neubauer, "Ten Tribes," 113. Both Epstein and Neubauer consider this to be the best text of the legend. It is based on the edition published in Venice in 1544, which is probably a reprint of the 1516 Constantinople edition. It is also allegedly identical with Oxford Ms. Heb. 2585.

[82] This is actually an attempt to explain the name of the river rather than that of the tribe.

our ancestors learn it, and thus did our Sages learn it orally from Joshua b. Nun, (who learned it) orally from Moses, (who received it) orally from God." They know nothing about the tannaim or amoraim (whose *floruit* was) during the period of the Second Temple because they [i.e., their teachings] did not reach them and they have no knowledge of them. They only know how to speak Hebrew. They are stringent regarding the use of libation wine, and whereas the Rabbis were strict in the *halakhot* pertaining to slaughter and the fitness of animals for sacrifice in accordance with the opinions of the scribes, Moses our Teacher was more stringent than the opinions of the scribes. They never swear oaths using the Name, and they become vocally angry[83] with anyone who so swears in their presence. They upbraid them and say to them: "O wretches! How can you bear to mention the Name with your mouth? (Think of) all that has been on your mouth! Is it bread that you can eat it, or water that you can drink it? Do you not know that your children will die while they are young for the sin of swearing?" Thus do they warn everyone to serve the Lord with awe and reverence and complete integrity. The "people of Moses, servant of the Lord" have prolonged life spans, living for 100 or 120 years. No daughter or son dies during the lifetime of their parent, and they attain (an age) reaching to the third or fourth generation (after them), personally seeing their children, grandchildren, and their descendants.

They (themselves) do their plowing and harvesting because they have no slaves or maidservants. They are store-owners (?).[84] While their houses have locks, they never shut them at night because there are no thieves or criminals among them, nothing that would cause damage. There is also this: a small child will go with the cattle a distance of many days, and no one worries at all about brigands or demons or dangerous animals or anything else in the world that is harmful, for they maintain sanctity and purity. They are Levites who exert themselves for the Torah and the commandments, and they still maintain the level of sanctity associated with Moses our Teacher. For this reason the Holy One, blessed be He, has given them all this. They, moreover, never see other human beings, nor do other humans see them except for those four tribes who inhabit "the opposite side of the rivers of Cush" (Isa 18:1; Zeph 3:10). They can see each other and they can converse together, with the River Sa(m)batyon between them. Scripture says about them: "[Say] to the prisoners, Depart!" (Isa 49:9).

They possess, moreover, large quantities of silver and gold. They sow flax and raise the worm that yields scarlet coloring and manufacture beautiful garments and cloaks. Their population is twice or four times that (of Israel)

[83] ועל פיהם יחרה אפם.

[84] Jellinek: בעלי דנויות; Epstein: בעלי חנויות.

at the time of the exodus, so many the number cannot be determined. The width of the River Sa(m)batyon is two hundred cubits, "about a bowshot's distance" (Gen 21:16). The river is full of sand and rocks, but no water, and the noise of those rocks rumbles like the loud sound of thunder, or like (the sound of) the waves of the sea, or like that of a windstorm, and its noise is audible at night up to a distance of half a day's journey. They possess springs there, and they collect all of them into a single pool which they use to irrigate their land. Fish swarm in that pool, and all kinds of pure waterfowl fly around it on every side. That river rumbles on account of the rocks and the sand during the six days when one labors, but on the Sabbath it ceases and rests, and immediately a fire ascends on the banks of the river from Sabbath eve until the end of the Sabbath, and the fire blazes with flame, and no one is able to approach the river or either shore of the river closer than half a mile. The fire consumes everything that grows on the banks of the river until the ground is bare. Those four tribes—Dan, Naphtali, Gad, and Asher—stand with their cattle next to the bank of the river in order to shear their flocks, for the ground is smooth, level, and bare with no thorns or vegetation growing. When the tribe of Moses sees (them), they come together and stand on the (opposite) bank of the river. They shout (to them) and say: "Tribes of Jeshurun,[85] our brethren! Show us camels, dogs, and asses!" They ask: "How long is this camel? How long is its neck? How short is its tail?" They exchange greetings with one another.

7. Cambridge Genizah Fragment:[86]

. . . concerning them and concerning the Levites which were among them. They said to them: "Sing us one of the songs of Zion!" (Ps 137:3). The Levites arose and focused their thoughts upon God, and then their group collectively sought to sever their fingers with their teeth, for they said: "We once used our fingers to play song(s) in the Temple! How can we use them for music in an impure land?!" They assembled themselves and sought to move, and the Holy One, blessed be He, performed a miracle for them and assisted their departure. While they journeyed, a cloud surrounded them so that they, their children, and their herds effected a departure to the ancient land of Havilah. They arrived at that place where the cloud stopped during the night—thus their ancestors recounted to them. That night there was a

[85] A poetic designation for Israel; see Deut 32:15; 33:5; Isa 44:2. According to *Exod. Rab.* 38.11, the phrase "tribes of Jeshurun" concludes the inscription of tribal names on the twelve stones of the priestly breastplate. Note also *b. Yoma* 73b.

[86] See Epstein, "Sefer Eldad ha-Dani," 1:85. Ellipses mark lacunae in the manuscript.

mighty thundering and quaking, and when it was morning they saw a great and resplendent light, for there were among them righteous ones, pious ones, perfect ones, fearers of God, and His servants.[87] At that time a river which rolled stones and sand surrounded them, having burst forth where no river had previously been located. It rolled many rocks and (a quantity of) sand that defied measurement, making a loud noise which was audible to a great distance. On the Sabbath it would be filled with smoke, and the areas around it would be encompassed by fog and darkness. No one was able to approach it, nor could anyone discern the road or its [i.e., the river's] location until the end of the Sabbath when it would return (to flowing) as it previously did. They call it the River Sanbatyon (סנבטיון), but in their language they call it "Sabbatyinos." By this river are places where the width (of it) is sixty cubits.

These are tribes who have no knowledge about the destruction of the Second Temple, for they went into exile at the time of the first destruction, but Naphtali, Gad, and Asher were exiled <before>[88] the destruction of the First Temple. They gathered together adjacent to the Danites, and they were with. . . .

The Sages of Eretz Israel and the Sages of Babylonia have one Mishnah expressed in one language, with no (textual) deficiencies or additions except for the matter of Talmud. There are differences between them, for these will have a reason for this (practice or interpretation), but those will substitute another reason. So too for this (group) scriptural verses appear with one intonation, and for that (group) they appear with a different intonation: even when the consonantal spelling has been fixed, they retain between them differences in pronunciation. The Babylonians have arranged, added, opened, closed, punctuated, supplied Masorah, and demarcated the verses. This is all the more so with regard to Mishnah, which is an opaque subject "and very deep—who can find it out?" (Qoh 7:24), where one does not find differences between the (two schools of Sages), but is not so with regard to Talmud, for the Babylonians learn it in Aramaic, but those of Eretz Israel use their own rendition. And what you have said is that the (lost) tribes have their own Talmud, for the Sages who went into exile to Cush with the tribes arranged for them a Talmud in Hebrew, and their Mishnah does not record the name of a Sage, for before. . . .[89]

[87] This latter clause seems misplaced.

[88] This is surely what is intended.

[89] This is a version of the responsum of R. Ṣemaḥ Gaon to the sages of Kairowan regarding their inquiries about the traveler Eldad ha-Dani and his tales. See Epstein, "Sefer Eldad ha-Dani," 1.37–41; Jellinek, *BHM* 2:102–13.

8. Cambridge Genizah Fragment:[90]

And he (i.e., Eldad) recounted the excellence of the tribes, they being Dan, Asher, and Naphtali, who dwell on "the opposite side of the rivers of Cush" (Isa 18:1; Zeph 3:10) in the ancient land of Havilah,[91] where they inhabit a territory measuring forty days' journey square in size. He testified that his custom was to go out (sailing) upon the Great Sea, to procure garments and iron, and then to return to his home. But this time the Holy One, blessed be He, decided to reveal His power to him. A great windstorm blew up over them at midnight and cast them in the land of their enemies, where they were captured by Cushites who were cannibals. One who was with them (i.e., the shipwrecked merchants) from the tribe of Naphtali was fat, and they ate him. The Holy One, blessed be He, worked a miracle for me: a raiding party attacked them and took me along with them as spoil. I remained with them for four years, being passed (as a slave) from the possession of one to another in the land of Cush until they brought me near the border of Ishmael, and Isr[ael] ransomed me. I came among the tribe of Issachar, who lived among the mountains of Tehom in the land of the Medes and Persians.

He said: They are pious, learned sages, and fearers of Heaven. I went up from there to the mountains of Paran, wherein is <Mecca>[92] about which the Ishmaelites get excited. There I saw the descendants of Zebulun, who are tent-dwellers, and behind them the tribe of Reuben, and behind them the tribes of Manasseh and Ephraim.

He moreover said: These tribes possess among them Torah and abundant wisdom, for they were exiled from Sa[maria] before the destruction of the First Temple, and they retain their wisdom . . . narrative. And when we heard this message . . . Elijah to instruct us (about) this matter, and by the taking of this R. Eldad ha-Dani to inform us.[93] May He gather our dispersed ones soon, Amen!

[90] See Epstein, "Sefer Eldad ha-Dani," 1:86. Ellipses mark lacunae in the manuscript.

[91] בארץ החוילה הקדומה.

[92] Epstein suggests reading מכה in place of the text's מכות.

[93] Note the possible correlation of the missions of Elijah (Mal 3:22–24) and Eldad ha-Dani.

Bibliography

Abel, Armand. "Boṣrā." Pages 1275-77 in vol. 1 of the *Encyclopaedia of Islam*. New ed. Leiden: Brill, 1954-2002.

———. "Dābba." Page 71 in vol. 2 of the *Encyclopaedia of Islam*. New ed. Leiden: Brill, 1954-2002.

———. "al-Dadjdjāl." Pages 76-77 in vol. 2 of the *Encyclopaedia of Islam*. New ed. Leiden: Brill, 1954-2002.

Abraham ben Azriel. *Sefer ʿArugat ha-Bosem*. Edited by Ephraim E. Urbach. 4 vols. Jerusalem: Mekitze Nirdamim, 1939.

Abrams, Daniel. "The Boundaries of Divine Ontology: The Inclusion and Exclusion of Meṭaṭron in the Godhead." *Harvard Theological Review* 87 (1994): 291-321.

Adang, Camilla. *Muslim Writers on Judaism and the Hebrew Bible: From Ibn Rabban to Ibn Hazm*. Leiden: Brill, 1996.

Adler, Elkan Nathan, ed. *Jewish Travellers in the Middle Ages: 19 Firsthand Accounts*. London: Routledge, 1930. Repr., New York: Dover, 1987.

Aescoly, Aaron Zeʾev. *Messianic Movements in Israel, Volume One: From the Bar-Kokhba Revolt until the Expulsion of the Jews from Spain*. Edited by Yehudah Even-Shmuel. 2d ed. Jerusalem: Mosad Bialik, 1987.

Albeck, Ḥanokh. "Agadot im Lichte der Pseudepigraphen." *Monatschrift für Geschichte und Wissenschaft des Judentums* 83 (1939): 162-69.

———, ed. *Midrash Bereshit Rabbati*. Jerusalem: Mekize Nirdamim, 1940.

———, ed. *Shishah sidrei Mishnah*. 6 vols. Jerusalem and Tel Aviv: Mosad Bialik and Devir, 1957-59.

Alexander, Paul J. *The Byzantine Apocalyptic Tradition*. Edited by Dorothy deF. Abrahamse. Berkeley: University of California Press, 1985.

———. "The Medieval Legend of the Last Roman Emperor and its Messianic Origin." *Journal of the Warburg and Courtauld Institutes* 41 (1978): 1-15.

Alexander, Philip S. "The Historical Setting of the Hebrew Book of Enoch." *Journal of Jewish Studies* 28 (1977): 156-80.

———. "Jewish Aramaic Translations of Hebrew Scriptures." Pp. 217-53 in *Mikra: Text, Translation, Reading and Interpretation of the Hebrew Bible in Ancient Judaism and Early Christianity*. Edited by Martin Jan Mulder. Compendia rerum iudaicarum ad Novum Testamentum 2.1. Assen & Philadelphia: Van Gorcum & Fortress, 1988.

———. "3 (Hebrew Apocalypse of) Enoch." Pp. 223-315 in vol. 1 of *Old Testament Pseudepigrapha*. Edited by James H. Charlesworth. 2 vols. New York: Doubleday, 1983-85.

[Anonymous]. מעשיות. Constantinople: Astruq de Toulon, 1519.

Arjomand, Saïd Amir. "Islamic Apocalypticism in the Classical Period." Pp. 238-83 in vol. 2 of *The Encyclopedia of Apocalypticism*. Edited by Bernard McGinn et al. 3 vols. New York and London: Continuum, 1998.

Ashkenazi, R. Eliezer. טעם זקנים. Frankfurt am Main: I. Kauffman, 1854.

Assemani, J. S., ed. *Sancti patris nostri Ephraem Syri opera omnia*. 6 vols. Rome: Typographia Vaticana, 1737-43.

Avi-Yonah, Michael. *The Jews of Palestine: A Political History from the Bar Kokhba War to the Arab Conquest*. New York: Schocken Books, 1976.

Baron, Salo W. *A Social and Religious History of the Jews*. 2d ed. 18 vols. Philadelphia and New York: Jewish Publication Society and Columbia University Press, 1952-83.

Barth, Lewis. "Is Every Medieval Hebrew Manuscript a New Composition? The Case of *Pirqé Rabbi Eliezer*." Pp. 43-62 in *Agendas for the Study of Midrash in the Twenty-first Century*. Edited by Marc Lee Raphael. Williamsburg, Va.: College of William and Mary, 1999.

Bashear, Suliman. "Muslim Apocalypses and the Hour: A Case-Study in Traditional Reinterpretation." *Israel Oriental Studies* 13 (1993): 75-99.

———. "Riding Beasts on Divine Missions: An Examination of the Ass and Camel Traditions." *Journal of Semitic Studies* 37 (1991): 37-75.

———. "The Title «*Fārūq*» and its Association with 'Umar I." *Studia Islamica* 72 (1990): 47-70.

Bauckham, Richard. "Early Jewish Visions of Hell." *Journal of Theological Studies* 41 (1990): 355-85.

Beck, Edmund, ed. *Des heiligen Ephraem des Syrers Sermones III*. Corpus scriptorum christianorum orientalium 320. Louvain: Secrétariat du Corpus SCO, 1972.

Beit-Arié, Malachi. *Catalogue of the Hebrew Manuscripts in the Bodleian Library: Supplement of Addenda and Corrigenda to Volume I (A. Neubauer's Catalogue)*. Oxford: Clarendon, 1994.

Ben-Hayyim, Ze'ev. "Sefer ʾAsaṭīr." *Tarbiz* 14 (1943): 104-25; 175-90; 15 (1944): 71-87; 128.

Berger, Abraham. "Captive at the Gate of Rome: The Story of a Messianic Motif." *Proceedings of the American Academy for Jewish Research* 44 (1977): 1-17.

Berger, David. "Three Typological Themes in Early Jewish Messianism: Messiah son of Joseph, Rabbinic Calculations, and the Figure of Armilus." *Association for Jewish Studies Review* 10 (1985): 141-64.

Beyer, Klaus. *Die aramäischen Texte vom Toten Meer*. Göttingen: Vandenhoeck & Ruprecht, 1984.

Biale, David. "Counter-History and Jewish Polemics Against Christianity: The *Sefer toldot yeshu* and the *Sefer zerubavel*." *Jewish Social Studies* n.s. 6 (1999): 130-45.

Bidawid, R. J., ed. "4 Esdras." Pages [1]-[47] in *The Old Testament in Syriac According to the Peshitta Version, Part IV, fascicle 3: Apocalypse of Baruch, 4 Esdras*. Leiden: Brill, 1973.

Bidez, Joseph and Franz Cumont. *Les mages hellénisés: Zoroastre, Ostanès et Hystaspe d'après la tradition grecque*. 2 vols. Paris: Société d'éditions "Les belles lettres", 1938. Repr., New York: Arno Press, 1975.

Bietenhard, Hans. *Die himmlische Welt im Urchristentum und Spätjudentum*. Wissenschaftliche Untersuchungen zum Neuen Testament 2. Tübingen: J. C. B. Mohr, 1951.

Bin Gorion, Micha Joseph. *Mimekor Yisrael: Selected Classical Jewish Folktales*. Edited by Emanuel bin Gorion. Translated by I. M. Lask. Bloomington and Indianapolis: Indiana University Press, 1990.

Bīrūnī, *Athār al-bāqiya ʿan-il-qurūn al-khāliya: Chronologie orientalischer Völker von Albêrûnî*. Edited by C. E. Sachau. Leipzig: Brockhaus, 1878. Repr., Leipzig: Otto Harrassowitz, 1923.

Blau, Ludwig. "Salamander." Pages 646-47 in vol. 10 of *The Jewish Encyclopedia*. Edited by Cyrus Adler, et al. 12 vols. New York: Funk & Wagnalls, 1901-6.

Bonwetsch, [G.] N., ed. *Doctrina Iacobi nuper baptizati*. Abhandlungen der königlichen Gesellschaft der Wissenschaften zu Göttingen, phil.-hist. klass., n.f., bd. 12, nr. 3. Berlin: Weidmannsche Buchhandlung, 1910.

Bousset, Wilhelm. *The Antichrist Legend: A Chapter in Christian and Jewish Folklore*. Translated by A. H. Keane. London: Hutchinson, 1896. Repr., Atlanta: Scholars Press, 1999.

Bowley, James E. and John C. Reeves. "Rethinking the Concept of 'Bible': Some Theses and Proposals." *Henoch* 25 (2003): 3-18.

Boyarin, Daniel. *Dying for God: Martyrdom and the Making of Christianity and Judaism*. Stanford: Stanford University Press, 1999.

Brandes, Wolfram. "Heraclius Between Restoration and Reform: Some Remarks on Recent Research." Pp. 17-40 in *The Reign of Heraclius (610-641): Crisis and Confrontation*. Edited by Gerrit J. Reinink and Bernard H. Stolte. Leuven: Peeters, 2002.

Brock, Sebastian. "Syriac Views of Emergent Islam." Pp. 9-21 in *Studies on the First Century of Islamic Society*. Edited by G. H. A. Juynboll. Carbondale, Ill.: Southern Illinois University Press, 1982.

Brody, Robert. *The Geonim of Babylonia and the Shaping of Medieval Jewish Culture*. New Haven and London: Yale University Press, 1998.

Budge, Ernest A. Wallis, ed. *The Book of the Bee*. Anecdota Oxoniensia Semitic Series 1.2. Oxford: Clarendon Press, 1886.

Busse, Heribert. "Jerusalem in the Story of Muhammad's Night Journey and Ascension." *Jerusalem Studies in Arabic and Islam* 14 (1991): 1-40.

———. "ʿOmar b. al-Ḫaṭṭāb in Jerusalem." *Jerusalem Studies in Arabic and Islam* 5 (1984): 73-119.

———. "ʿOmar's Image as the Conqueror of Jerusalem." *Jerusalem Studies in Arabic and Islam* 8 (1986): 149-68.

———. Review of Andreas Kaplony, *The Ḥaram of Jerusalem 324-1099. Jerusalem Studies in Arabic and Islam* 29 (2004): 431-40.

Buttenwieser, Moses. *Die hebräische Elias-Apokalypse und ihre Stellung in der apokalyptischen Litteratur des rabbinischen Schrifttums und der Kirche.* Leipzig: Eduard Pfeiffer, 1897.

———. *Outline of the Neo-Hebraic Apocalyptic Literature.* Cincinnati: Jennings & Pye, 1901.

Cameron, Averil. "Byzantines and Jews: Some Recent Work on Early Byzantium." *Byzantine and Modern Greek Studies* 20 (1996): 249-74.

———. "The Jews in Seventh-Century Palestine." *Scripta Classica Israelica* 13 (1994): 75-93.

Cameron, Averil and Lawrence I. Conrad, eds. *The Byzantine and Early Islamic Near East, I: Problems in the Literary Source Material.* Princeton, N.J.: The Darwin Press, 1992.

Chajes, J. H. *Between Worlds: Dybbuks, Exorcists, and Early Modern Judaism.* Philadelphia: University of Pennsylvania Press, 2003.

Charlesworth, James H., ed. *The History of the Rechabites, Volume I: The Greek Recension.* Chico, Calif.: Scholars Press, 1982.

Chwolsohn, D. *Die Ssabier und der Ssabismus.* 2 vols. St. Petersburg: Kaiserlichen Akademie der Wissenschaften, 1856.

Cohen, Gerson D. *A Critical Edition with a Translation and Notes of the Book of Tradition (Sefer Ha-Qabbalah) by Abraham ibn Daud.* Philadelphia: Jewish Publication Society, 1967.

———. "Esau as Symbol in Early Medieval Thought." Pp. 19-48 in *Jewish Medieval and Renaissance Studies.* Edited by Alexander Altmann. Cambridge: Harvard University Press, 1967.

Collins, John J. *The Apocalyptic Imagination: An Introduction to Jewish Apocalyptic Literature.* 2d ed. Grand Rapids: William B. Eerdmans, 1998.

———. *The Apocalyptic Vision of the Book of Daniel.* Harvard Semitic Monographs 16. Missoula, Mont.: Scholars Press, 1977.

Cook, David. "An Early Muslim Daniel Apocalypse." *Arabica* 49 (2002): 55-96.

———. *Studies in Muslim Apocalyptic.* Studies in Late Antiquity and Early Islam 21. Princeton, N.J.: Darwin Press, 2002.

Cook, Michael. "An Early Islamic Apocalyptic Chronicle." *Journal of Near Eastern Studies* 52 (1993): 25-29.

Crone, Patricia and Michael Cook. *Hagarism: The Making of the Islamic World.* Cambridge: Cambridge University Press, 1977.

Cureton, William, ed. *Kitāb al-milal wa-al-niḥal: Book of Religious and Philosophical Sects, by Muhammad al-Shahrastáni*. 2 vols. London, 1842-46. Repr., Leipzig: O. Harrassowitz, 1923.

Dagron, Gilbert. "Introduction historique: Entre histoire et apocalypse." *Travaux et mémoires* 11 (1991): 17-46.

Dalman, Gustav. *Aramäische Dialektproben*. 2d ed. Leipzig: J. C. Hinrichs, 1927. Repr., Darmstadt: Wissenschaftliche Buchgesellschaft, 1960.

Dan, Joseph. "Armilus: The Jewish Antichrist and the Origins and Dating of the *Sefer Zerubbavel*." Pp. 73-104 in *Toward the Millennium: Messianic Expectations from the Bible to Waco*. Edited by Peter Schäfer and Mark Cohen. Leiden: Brill, 1998.

———. "The Memory of the Future and the Utopia of the Past." Pp. 109-28 in vol. 1 of idem, *Jewish Mysticism*. 4 vols. Northvale, N.J.: Jason Aronson, 1998-99.

———. "Samael and the Problem of Jewish Gnosticism." Pp. 367-90 in vol. 3 of idem, *Jewish Mysticism*. 4 vols. Northvale, N.J.: Jason Aronson, 1998-99.

———. *Ha-Sippur ha-ʿivri be-yemey ha-beyanim: ʿIyyunim be-toldotav*. Jerusalem: Keter, 1974.

Denny, Frederick Mathewson. "Community and Society in the Qurʾān." Pages 367-86 in vol. 1 of the *Encyclopaedia of the Qurʾān*. Edited by Jane Dammen McAuliffe. Leiden: Brill, 2001- .

———. "Umma." Pages 859-63 in vol. 10 of the *Encyclopaedia of Islam*. New ed. Leiden: Brill, 1954-2002.

Deutsch, Nathaniel. *Guardians of the Gate: Angelic Vice Regency in Late Antiquity*. Brill's Series in Jewish Studies 22. Leiden: Brill, 1999.

Dietrich, A. "Ās." Page 87 in the *Encyclopaedia of Islam, New Edition, Supplement 1-2*. Leiden: Brill, 1980.

Donner, Fred M. *The Early Islamic Conquests*. Princeton: Princeton University Press, 1981.

Drijvers, Han J. W. "The Gospel of the Twelve Apostles: A Syriac Apocalypse from the Early Islamic Period." Pp. 189-213 in *The Byzantine and Early Islamic Near East, I: Problems in the Literary Source Material*. Edited by Averil Cameron and Lawrence I. Conrad. Studies in Late Antiquity and Early Islam 1. Princeton, N.J.: Darwin Press, 1992.

Drijvers, Jan Willem. "Heraclius and the *Restitutio Crucis*: Notes on Symbolism and Ideology." Pp. 175-90 in *The Reign of Heraclius (610-641): Crisis and Confrontation*. Edited by Gerrit J. Reinink and Bernard H. Stolte. Leuven: Peeters, 2002.

Drint, Adriana, ed. *The Mount Sinai Arabic Version of IV Ezra*. 2 vols. Corpus scriptorum christianorum orientalium 563-564, scrip. arabici 48-49. Louvain: Peeters, 1997.

Ebied, R. Y. and L. R. Wickham. "Al-Yaḳūbī's Account of the Israelite Prophets and Kings." *Journal of Near Eastern Studies* 29 (1970): 80-98.

Elad, Amikam. *Medieval Jerusalem and Islamic Worship: Holy Places, Ceremonies, Pilgrimages.* 2d ed. Leiden: Brill, 1999.

Epstein, Abraham. *Sefer Eldad ha-Dani.* [Pressburg], 1891. Reprinted as pages 1-211 of vol. 1 of *Kitvey Avraham Epstein* . Edited by A. M. Habermann. 2 vols. Jerusalem: Mosad ha-Rav Kook, 1949-56.

Epstein, J. N. *Diqduq Aramit Bavlit.* Edited by E. Z. Melamed. Jerusalem and Tel Aviv: Magnes and Devir, 1960.

Erder, Yoram. "The Doctrine of Abū ʿĪsā al-Iṣfahānī and its Sources." *Jerusalem Studies in Arabic and Islam* 20 (1996): 162-99.

Ess, Josef van. "'Abd al-Malik and the Dome of the Rock: An Analysis of Some Texts." Pp. 89-103 in vol. 1 of *Bayt al-Maqdis: ʿAbd al-Malik's Jerusalem.* Edited by Julian Raby and Jeremy Johns. 2 vols. Oxford: Oxford University Press, 1992.

Even-Shmuel, Yehudah. *Midreshey Geʾullah.* 2d ed. Jerusalem: Mosad Bialik, 1954.

Even-Shoshan, Avraham. *Millon ḥadash.* 5 vols. Jerusalem: Qiryat Sefer, 1964.

Fahd, Toufy. "Anges, demons et djinns en Islam." Pp. 155-214 in *Génies, anges et demons.* Sources orientales 8. Paris: Éditions du Seuil, 1971.

Fakhry, Majid, trans. *An Interpretation of the Qur'an: English Translation of the Meanings, A Bilingual Edition.* New York: New York University Press, 2002.

Fine, Steven. "'Chancel' Screens in Late Antique Palestinian Synagogues: A Source from the Cairo Genizah." Pp. 67-85 in *Religious and Ethnic Communities in Later Roman Palestine.* Edited by Hayim Lapin. Bethesda, Md.: University Press of Maryland, 1998.

Firestone, Reuven. "Jewish Culture in the Formative Period of Islam." Pp. 267-302 in *Cultures of the Jews: A New History.* Edited by David Biale. New York: Schocken, 2002.

Fishbane, Michael. *Biblical Myth and Rabbinic Mythmaking.* Oxford: Oxford University Press, 2003.

Fodor, A. "The Rod of Moses in Arabic Magic." *Acta Orientalia Academiae Scientiarum Hungaricae* 32 (1978): 1-21.

Fossum, Jarl E. *The Name of God and the Angel of the Lord.* Wissenschaftliche Untersuchungen zum Neuen Testament 36. Tübingen: J.C.B. Mohr, 1985.

Fowden, Garth. *Quṣayr ʿAmra: Art and the Umayyad Elite in Late Antique Syria.* Berkeley: University of California Press, 2004.

Frankfurter, David. *Elijah in Upper Egypt: The Apocalypse of Elijah and Early Egyptian Christianity.* Studies in Antiquity and Christianity. Minneapolis: Fortress Press, 1993.

———. "The Legacy of Jewish Apocalypses in Early Christianity: Regional Trajectories." Pp. 129-200 in *The Jewish Apocalyptic Heritage in Early Christianity.* Edited by James C. VanderKam and William Adler. Compendia rerum iudaicarum ad Novum Testamentum 3.4. Assen/Minneapolis: Van Gorcum/Fortress, 1996.

Friedlaender, Israel. "The Jews of Arabia and the Rechabites." *Jewish Quarterly Review* n.s. 1 (1910-11): 252-57.

Friedlander, Gerald, trans. *Pirke De Rabbi Eliezer*. London, 1916. Repr., New York: Sepher-Hermon Press, 1981.

Friedmann, Meir. *Pseudo-Seder Eliahu Zuta*. Wien: [s.n.], 1904.

Gardet, L[ouis]. "Ḳiyāma." Pages 235-38 in vol. 5 of the *Encyclopaedia of Islam*. New ed. Leiden: Brill, 1954-2002.

Gaster, Moses. *The Chronicles of Jerahmeel; or, the Hebrew Bible Historiale*. London, 1899. Repr., New York: Ktav, 1971.

Gaudeul, Jean-Marie. "The Correspondence Between Leo and 'Umar: 'Umar's Letter Rediscovered?" *Islamochristiana* 10 (1984): 109-57.

Geiger, Abraham. *Judaism and Islam*. Translated by F. M. Young. 1898. Repr., New York: Ktav, 1970.

Gerö, Stephen. "Ophite Gnosticism According to Theodore bar Koni's Liber Scholiorum." Pp. 265-74 in *IV Symposium Syriacum 1984: Literary Genres in Syriac Literature (Groningen-Oosterhesselen 10-12 September)*. Edited by H. J. W. Drijvers et al. Orientalia christiana analecta 229. Rome: Pont. Institutum Studiorum Orientalium, 1987.

Gil, Moshe. "The Exilarchate." Pp. 33-65 in *The Jews of Medieval Islam: Community, Society, and Identity*. Edited by Daniel Frank. Études sur le judaïsme medieval 16. Leiden: Brill, 1995.

———. *A History of Palestine, 634-1099*. Translated by Ethel Broido. Cambridge: Cambridge University Press, 1992.

———. "The Jewish Community." Pp. 163-200 in *The History of Jerusalem: The Early Muslim Period, 638-1099*. Edited by Joshua Prawer and Haggai Ben-Shammai. Jerusalem and New York: Yad Izhak Ben-Zvi and New York University Press, 1996.

———. *Jews in Islamic Countries in the Middle Ages*. Translated by David Strassler. Leiden: Brill, 2004.

———. "The Political History of Jerusalem During the Early Muslim Period." Pp. 1-37 in *The History of Jerusalem: The Early Muslim Period, 638-1099*. Edited by Joshua Prawer and Haggai Ben-Shammai. New York: New York University Press, 1996.

Gimaret, Daniel and Guy Monnot. *Shahrastani: Livre des religions et des sectes*. 2 vols. Paris: Peeters, 1986-93.

Ginzberg, Louis. "Aaron's Rod." Pages 5-6 in vol. 1 of *The Jewish Encyclopedia*. Edited by Cyrus Adler, et al. 12 vols. New York: Funk & Wagnalls, 1901-6.

———. *The Legends of the Jews*. 7 vols. Philadelphia: The Jewish Publication Society, 1909-38.

———. *An Unknown Jewish Sect*. New York: The Jewish Theological Seminary of America, 1976.

Goitein, S. D. *Jews and Arabs: Their Contacts Through the Ages*. Rev. ed. New York: Schocken, 1974.

Goldenberg, David M. *The Curse of Ham: Race and Slavery in Early Judaism, Christianity, and Islam*. Princeton: Princeton University Press, 2003.

Goldish, Matt. *The Sabbatean Prophets*. Cambridge, Mass.: Harvard University Press, 2004.

Goldziher, Ignác. *Muslim Studies*. Edited by S. M. Stern. Translated by C. R. Barber and S. M. Stern. 2 vols. Chicago: Aldine, 1966-71.

———. "Ueber muhammedanische Polemik gegen Ahl al-kitāb." *Zeitschrift der deutschen morgenländischen Gesellschaft* 32 (1878): 341-87.

Gottheil, Richard [J. H.]. "A Christian Bahira Legend." *Zeitschrift für Assyriologie* 13 (1898): 189-242.

Grabar, Oleg. "al-Ḳuds." Pages 322-44 in vol. 5 of the *Encyclopaedia of Islam*. New ed. Leiden: Brill, 1954-2002.

———. *The Shape of the Holy: Early Islamic Jerusalem*. Princeton: Princeton University Press, 1996.

Graetz, Heinrich. *Geschichte der Juden von den ältesten Zeiten bis auf die Gegenwart*. 3d ed. 11 vols. in 13. Leipzig: Oskar Leiner, 1890-1908.

Griffith, Sidney H. "Theodore bar Kônî's *Scholion*: A Nestorian *Summa contra Gentiles* from the First Abbasid Century." Pp. 53-72 in *East of Byzantium: Syria and Armenia in the Formative Period*. Edited by Nina G. Garsoïan et al. Washington, D.C.: Dumbarton Oaks, 1982.

Grossman, Avraham. "Jerusalem in Jewish Apocalyptic Literature." Pp. 295-310 in *The History of Jerusalem: The Early Muslim Period, 638-1099*. Edited by Joshua Prawer and Haggai Ben-Shammai. Jerusalem and New York: Yad Izhak Ben-Zvi and New York University Press, 1996.

Grünbaum, Max. *Neue Beiträge zur semitischen Sagenkunde*. Leiden: E. J. Brill, 1893.

Gruenwald, Ithamar. *Apocalyptic and Merkavah Mysticism*. Arbeiten zur Geschichte des antiken Judentums und des Urchristentums 14. Leiden: Brill, 1980.

———. "Re'uyyot Yeḥezq'el." Pp. 101-39 in *Temirin I: Texts and Studies in Kabbala and Hasidism*. Edited by Israel Weinstock. Jerusalem: Mosad ha-Rav Kook, 1972.

Grunebaum, Gustave E. von. *Medieval Islam: A Study in Cultural Orientation*. 2d ed. Chicago: University of Chicago Press, 1953.

Habermann, A. M., ed. *Kitvey Avraham Epstein*. 2 vols. Jerusalem: Mosad ha-Rav Kook, 1949-56.

Harris, J. Rendel, ed. *The Gospel of the Twelve Apostles: Together with the Apocalypses of Each One of Them*. Cambridge: The University Press, 1900.

Hasson, Isaac. "Last Judgment." Pages 136-45 in vol. 3 of the *Encyclopaedia of the Qur'ān*. Edited by Jane Dammen McAuliffe. Leiden: Brill, 2001- .

———. "The Muslim View of Jerusalem: The Qur'ān and Ḥadīth." Pp. 349-85 in *The History of Jerusalem: The Early Muslim Period, 638-1099*. Edited by Joshua Prawer and Haggai Ben-Shammai. Jerusalem and New York: Yad Izhak Ben-Zvi and New York University Press, 1996.

Hayward, Robert. "The Date of Targum Pseudo-Jonathan: Some Comments." *Journal of Jewish Studies* 40 (1989): 7-30.

———. "Phineas—the Same is Elijah: The Origins of a Rabbinic Tradition." *Journal of Jewish Studies* 29 (1978): 22-34.

———. "Pirqe de Rabbi Eliezer and Targum Pseudo-Jonathan." *Journal of Jewish Studies* 42 (1991): 215-46.

———. "Targum Pseudo-Jonathan and Anti-Islamic Polemic." *Journal of Semitic Studies* 34 (1989): 77-93.

Hegemonius. *Acta Archelai.* Edited by Charles Henry Beeson. Die griechische christliche Schriftsteller der ersten [drei] Jahrhunderte 16. Leipzig: J. C. Hinrichs, 1906.

Heinemann, Isaak. *Darkey ha-Aggadah.* 2d ed. Jerusalem/Ramat Gan: Magnes/Masadah, 1954.

Heller, Bern(h)ard. "Agadische Literatur." Pages 979-1036 in vol. 1 of *Encyclopaedia Judaica.* 10 vols. Berlin: Verlag Eschkol A.-G., 1928-34.

———. "Muhammedanisches und Antimuhammedanisches in den Pirke R. Eliezer." *Monatschrift für Geschichte und Wissenschaft des Judentums* 69 (1925): 47-54.

———. "Mūsā." Pages 638-40 in vol. 7 of the *Encyclopaedia of Islam.* New ed. Leiden: Brill, 1954-2002.

Henze, Matthias. *The Syriac Apocalypse of Daniel: Introduction, Text, and Commentary.* Studien und Texte zu Antike und Christentum 11. Tübingen: Mohr Siebeck, 2001.

Herr, Moshe David. "Midrashim, Smaller." Pages 1515-18 in vol. 16 of *Encyclopaedia Judaica.* 16 vols. Jerusalem: Keter, 1972.

———. "Pirkei de-Rabbi Eliezer." Pages 558-60 in vol. 13 of *Encyclopaedia Judaica.* 16 vols. Jerusalem: Keter, 1972.

Hezekiah (Chiskia) ben Abraham. מלביאל. Vilna and Grodno: [Romm?], 1819.

Higger, Michael. *Halakhot va-aggadot.* New York: The Jewish Theological Seminary, 1933.

Hildesheimer, Ezriel, ed. *Halakhot Gedolot ʿal pi ketav yad Romi.* Berlin: Hevrat Meqitze Nirdamim, 1888-92.

Hilgenfeld, Adolf. *Messias Judaeorum.* Leipzig: Sumptu Fuesiano (R. Reisland), 1869.

Himmelfarb, Martha. "Heavenly Ascent and the Relationship of the Apocalypses and the *Hekhalot* Literature." *Hebrew Union College Annual* 59 (1988): 73-100.

———. "The Mother of the Messiah in the Talmud Yerushalmi and Sefer Zerubbabel." Pp. 369-89 in *The Talmud Yerushalmi and Graeco-Roman Culture, III.* Edited by Peter Schäfer. Texte und Studien zum antiken Judentum 93. Tübingen: Mohr Siebeck, 2002.

———. "Sefer Zerubbabel." Pp. 67-90 in *Rabbinic Fantasies: Imaginative Narratives from Classical Hebrew Literature.* Edited by David Stern and Mark Jay Mirsky. Philadelphia: Jewish Publication Society, 1990.

———. *Tours of Hell: An Apocalyptic Form in Jewish and Christian Literature.* Philadelphia: University of Pennsylvania Press, 1983. Repr., Philadelphia: Fortress Press, 1985.

Hopkins, Simon. *A Miscellany of Literary Pieces from the Cambridge Genizah Collections: A Catalogue and Selection of Texts in the Taylor-Schechter Collection, Old Series, Box A45.* Cambridge: Cambridge University Library, 1978.

Houtsma, M. T., ed. *Ibn Wadih qui dicitur al-Ja'qubi historiae* . . . . 2 vols. Leiden: Brill, 1883.

Hoyland, Robert G. *Seeing Islam As Others Saw It: A Survey and Evaluation of Christian, Jewish and Zoroastrian Writings on Early Islam.* Studies in Late Antiquity and Early Islam 13. Princeton, N.J.: Darwin Press, 1997.

Ibn Qutayba. *Kitāb al-maᶜārif.* 2d ed. Edited by Tharwat ᶜUkkāsha. Cairo: Dār al-Maᶜārif, 1969.

Idel, Moshe. *Messianic Mystics.* New Haven and London: Yale University Press, 1998.

Irshai, Oded. "Dating the Eschaton: Jewish and Christian Apocalyptic Calculations in Late Antiquity." Pp. 113-53 in *Apocalyptic Time.* Edited by Albert I. Baumgarten. Leiden: Brill, 2000.

Jeffery, Arthur. "'Aṣā." Page 680 in vol. 1 of the *Encyclopaedia of Islam.* New ed. Leiden: Brill, 1954-2002.

———. "Ghevond's Text of the Correspondence between Umar II and Leo III." *Harvard Theological Review* 37 (1944): 269-332.

Jellinek, Adolph. *Beiträge zur Geschichte der Kabbala: Erstes Heft.* Leipzig: C. L. Fritzsche, 1852.

———, ed. *Bet ha-Midrasch: Sammlung kleiner Midraschim und vermischter Abhandlungen aus der jüdischen Literatur.* 6 vols. Leipzig, 1853-77. Repr., Jerusalem: Bamberger & Wahrmann, 1938.

Jenks, Gregory C. *The Origins and Early Development of the Antichrist Myth.* Berlin and New York: Walter de Gruyter, 1991.

Kaegi, Walter E. *Byzantium and the Early Islamic Conquests.* Cambridge: Cambridge University Press, 1992.

———. *Heraclius: Emperor of Byzantium.* Cambridge: Cambridge University Press, 2003.

———. "Initial Byzantine Reactions to the Arab Conquest." *Church History* 38 (1969): 139-49.

Kalmin, Richard. "Rabbinic Traditions about Roman Persecutions of the Jews: A Reconsideration." *Journal of Jewish Studies* 54 (2003): 21-50.

Khoury, Raif Georges. *Les legends prophétiques dans l'Islam: Depuis le Ier jusqu'au IIIe siècle de l'Hégire = Kitāb bad' al-ḫalq wa-qiṣaṣ al-anbiyāʾ.* Wiesbaden: Otto Harrassowitz, 1978.

———. "Wahb b. Munabbih, Abū ᶜAbd Allāh." Pages 34-36 in vol. 11 of the *Encyclopaedia of Islam.* New ed. Leiden: Brill, 1954-2002.

al-Kisāʾī, Muhammad Ibn ʿAbd Allāh. *Qiṣaṣ al-anbiyāʾ*. Edited by Isaac Eisenberg. 2 vols. Leiden: Brill, 1922-23.

Klausner, Joseph. *The Messianic Idea in Israel: From its Beginning to the Completion of the Mishnah.* New York: Macmillan, 1955.

Klein, Michael L. *Genizah Manuscripts of Palestinian Targum to the Pentateuch.* 2 vols. Cincinnati: Hebrew Union College Press, 1986.

Koenen, Ludwig. "Manichaean Apocalypticism at the Crossroads of Iranian, Egyptian, Jewish and Christian Thought." Pp. 285-332 in *Codex Manichaicus Coloniensis: Atti del Simposio Internazionale (Rende-Amantea 3-7 settembre 1984)*. Edited by Luigi Cirillo and Amneris Roselli. Cosenza: Marra Editore, 1986.

Kraus, Paul. "Hebräische und syrische Zitate in ismāʿīlitischen Schriften." *Der Islam* 19 (1930): 243-63.

Krauss, Samuel. *Das Leben Jesu nach jüdischen Quellen.* Berlin: S. Calvary & Co., 1902. Repr., Hildesheim: Georg Olms Verlag, 1994.

———. "Der römisch-persische Krieg in der jüdischen Elia-Apocalypse." *Jewish Quarterly Review* o.s. 14 (1902): 359-72.

———. *Studien zur byzantinisch-jüdischen Geschichte.* Leipzig: Buchhandlung Gustav Fock, 1914.

Lactantius. *L. Caeli Firmiani Lactanti Opera omnia.* Corpus scriptorum ecclesiasticorum latinorum 19. Edited by Samuel Brandt. Prague: F. Tempsky, 1890.

Lange, N. R. M. de. "Jewish Attitudes to the Roman Empire." Pp. 255-81 in *Imperialism in the Ancient World: The Cambridge University Research Seminar in Ancient History.* Edited by P. D. A. Garnsey and C. R. Whittaker. Cambridge: Cambridge University Press, 1978.

Lauterbach, Jacob Z. "The Origin and Development of Two Sabbath Ceremonies." *Hebrew Union College Annual* 15 (1940): 367-424.

Leemhuis, Frederik. "Apocalypse." Pages 111-14 in vol. 1 of the *Encyclopaedia of the Qur'ān.* Edited by Jane Dammen McAuliffe. Leiden: Brill, 2001- .

Levene, Dan. *A Corpus of Magic Bowls: Incantation Texts in Jewish Aramaic from Late Antiquity.* London and New York: Kegan Paul, 2003.

Lévi, Israel. "L'apocalypse de Zorobabel et le roi de Perse Siroès." *Revue des études juives* 68 (1914): 129-60; 69 (1914): 108-21; 71 (1920): 57-65.

———. "Une apocalypse judéo-arabe." *Revue des études juives* 67 (1914): 178-82.

Levy, Jacob. *Chaldäisches Wörterbuch über die Targumim und einen grossen Theil des rabbinischen Schrifttums.* 2 vols. Leipzig: Baumgärtner, 1867-68.

Lewinstein, Keith. "Gog and Magog." Pages 331-33 in vol. 2 of the *Encyclopaedia of the Qur'ān.* Edited by Jane Dammen McAuliffe. Leiden: Brill, 2001- .

Lewis, Bernard. "An Apocalyptic Vision of Islamic History." *Bulletin of the School of Oriental and African Studies* 13 (1949-51): 308-38.

———. "On That Day: A Jewish Apocalyptic Poem on the Arab Conquests." Pp. 197-200 in *Mélanges d'Islamologie: Volume dédié à la mémoire de Armand Abel.* Edited by Pierre Salmon. Leiden: Brill, 1974.

Lidzbarski, Mark. *De propheticis, quae dicuntur, legendis arabicis: Prolegomena.* Lipsiae: Guilelmi Drugulini, 1893.

———. *Das Johannesbuch der Mandäer.* 2 vols. Giessen: Alfred Töpelmann, 1905-15.

Liebes, Yehuda. "The Messiah of the Zohar: On R. Simeon bar Yohai as a Messianic Figure." Pp. 1-84 in idem, *Studies in the Zohar.* Albany: State University of New York Press, 1993.

Luria, R. David. *Pirqe de-Rabbi Eliezer ha-Gadol.* Warsaw: T. Y. Bamberg, 1852.

Macler, Frédéric. *Histoire d'Héraclius par l'évèque Sebéos.* Paris: E. Leroux, 1904.

Madelung, Wilferd. "Apocalyptic Prophecies in Ḥimṣ in the Umayyad Age." *Journal of Semitic Studies* 31 (1986): 141-85.

———. "Ḳarmaṭī." Pages 660-65 in vol. 4 of the *Encyclopaedia of Islam.* New ed. Leiden: Brill, 1954-2002.

———. "The Sufyānī Between Tradition and History." *Studia Islamica* 63 (1986): 5-48.

Magdalino, Paul. "The History of the Future and its Uses: Prophecy, Policy and Propaganda." Pp. 3-34 in *The Making of Byzantine History: Studies Dedicated to Donald M. Nicol.* Edited by Roderick Beaton and Charlotte Roueché. Aldershot: Variorum, 1993.

Makhir, R. ספר אבקת רוכל. Amsterdam: Nehemiah b. Abraham, 1716.

Mann, Jacob. *The Bible as Read and Preached in the Old Synagogue, Volume 1: The Palestinian Triennial Cycle: Genesis and Exodus.* Cincinnati, 1940. Repr., New York: Ktav, 1971.

———. "Proceedings of the American Oriental Society at the Meeting in Cincinnati, Ohio, 1927." *Journal of the American Oriental Society* 47 (1927): 364.

Margaliot, Reuven. *Malʾakey ʿelyon.* Jerusalem: Mosad ha-Rav Kook, 1945.

Marmorstein, Arthur. "Les signes du Messie." *Revue des études juives* 52 (1906): 176-86.

Marx, Alexander. "Additions et rectifications." *Revue des études juives* 71 (1920): 222.

———. "Studies in Gaonic History and Literature." *Jewish Quarterly Review* n.s. 1 (1910-11): 61-104.

McGinn, Bernard. *Antichrist: Two Thousand Years of the Human Fascination with Evil.* San Francisco: HarperSanFrancisco, 1994. Repr., New York: Columbia University Press, 2000.

———. *Visions of the End: Apocalyptic Traditions in the Middle Ages.* Rev. ed. New York: Columbia University Press, 1998.

Meilicke, Christine. "Moses' Staff and the Return of the Dead." *Jewish Studies Quarterly* 6 (1999): 345-72.

Mitchell, David C. *The Message of the Psalter: An Eschatological Programme in the Book of Psalms.* Journal for the Study of the Old Testament: Supplement Series 252. Sheffield: Sheffield Academic Press, 1997.

Momigliano, Arnaldo. "The Origins of Universal History." Pp. 31-57 in his *On Pagans, Jews, and Christians*. Middletown, Conn.: Wesleyan University Press, 1987.

Montgomery, James A. "Some Early Amulets from Palestine." *Journal of the American Oriental Society* 31 (1911): 272-81.

Moscati, Sabatino. "Abū Muslim." Page 141 in vol. 1 of the *Encyclopaedia of Islam*. New ed. Leiden: Brill, 1954-2002.

Müller, D. H. "Die Recensionen und Versionen des Eldad Had-Dani ... veröffentlicht und kritisch untersucht." *Denkschriften der kaiserlichen Akademie der Wissenschaften in Wien, philosophisch-historische Klasse* 41 (1892): 1-80.

Nagel, Tilman. "Kisāʾī, Ṣāḥib Ḳiṣaṣ al-Anbiyāʾ." Page 176 in vol. 5 of the *Encyclopaedia of Islam*. New ed. Leiden: Brill, 1954-2002.

Naveh, Joseph and Shaul Shaked. *Amulets and Magic Bowls: Aramaic Incantations of Late Antiquity*. Jerusalem/Leiden: Magnes/Brill, 1985.

———. *Magic Spells and Formulae: Aramaic Incantations of Late Antiquity*. Jerusalem: The Magnes Press, 1993.

Neubauer, Adolf. *Catalogue of the Hebrew Manuscripts in the Bodleian Library ....* Oxford: Clarendon, 1886.

———. "Egyptian Fragments, C." *Jewish Quarterly Review* o.s. 9 (1897): 29-36.

———. *Mediaeval Jewish Chronicles and Chronological Notes*. 2 vols. Oxford, 1887-95. Repr., Amsterdam: Philo Press, 1970.

———. "Where Are the Ten Tribes?" *Jewish Quarterly Review* o.s. 1 (1888-89): 14-28; 95-114; 185-201; 408-23.

Neubauer, Adolf and A. E. Cowley. *Catalogue of the Hebrew Manuscripts in the Bodleian Library Volume Two*. Oxford: Clarendon, 1906.

Newby, Gordon D. "Text and Territory: Jewish-Muslim Relations 632-750 CE." Pp. 83-96 in *Judaism and Islam: Boundaries, Communication and Interaction: Essays in Honor of William M. Brinner*. Edited by Benjamin H. Hary, John L. Hayes, and Fred Astren. Leiden: Brill, 2000.

Nir, Rivka. *The Destruction of Jerusalem and the Idea of Redemption in the Syriac Apocalypse of Baruch*. Society of Biblical Literature Early Judaism and Its Literature 20. Atlanta: Society of Biblical Literature, 2003.

Nöldeke, Theodor. *Geschichte der Perser und Araber zur Zeit der Sasaniden*. Leiden, 1879. Repr., Leiden: Brill, 1973.

Nuʿaym b. Ḥammād. *Kitāb al-fitan*. Edited by S. Zakkār. Beirut: Dār al-Fikr lil-Ṭibāʿah wa-al-Nashr wa-al-Tawzīʿ, 1993.

Ohana, M. "La polémique judéo-islamique d'Ismaël dans Targum Pseudo-Jonathan et dans Pirke de Rabbi Eliezer." *Augustinianum* 15 (1975): 367-87.

Olster, David M. "Byzantine Apocalypses." Pp. 48-73 in vol. 2 of *The Encyclopedia of Apocalypticism*. Edited by Bernard McGinn et al. 3 vols. New York and London: Continuum, 1998.

———. *Roman Defeat, Christian Response, and the Literary Construction of the Jew*. Philadelphia: University of Pennsylvania Press, 1994.

Peters, F. E. *Jerusalem: The Holy City in the Eyes of Chroniclers, Visitors, Pilgrims, and Prophets from the Days of Abraham to the Beginnings of Modern Times.* Princeton: Princeton University Press, 1985.

Puech, Émile, ed. *Qumrân Grotte 4, XXII: Textes araméens, première partie, 4Q529-49.* Discoveries in the Judaean Desert 31. Oxford: Clarendon, 2001.

Pulcini, Theodore. *Exegesis as Polemical Discourse: Ibn Ḥazm on Jewish and Christian Scriptures.* Atlanta: Scholars Press, 1998.

Rabin, Chaim. *Qumran Studies.* Oxford: Oxford University Press, 1957. Repr., New York: Schocken Books, 1975.

Ratzaby, Yehuda. *Saadya's Translation and Commentary on Isaiah.* Qiryat Ono: Makhon Mishnat ha-Rambam, 1993.

Reardon, B. P., ed. *Collected Ancient Greek Novels.* Berkeley: University of California Press, 1989.

Reeves, John C. "Exploring the Afterlife of Jewish Pseudepigrapha in Medieval Near Eastern Religious Traditions: Some Initial Soundings." *Journal for the Study of Judaism in the Persian, Hellenistic, and Roman Periods* 30 (1999): 148-77.

———. *Heralds of That Good Realm: Syro-Mesopotamian Gnosis and Jewish Traditions.* Nag Hammadi and Manichaean Studies 41. Leiden: Brill, 1996.

———. "Scriptural Authority in Early Judaism." Pp. 63-84 in *Living Traditions of the Bible: Scripture in Jewish, Christian, and Muslim Practice.* Edited by James E. Bowley. St. Louis: Chalice Press, 1999.

Reinink, Gerrit J. "Heraclius, The New Alexander: Apocalyptic Prophecies during the Reign of Heraclius." Pp. 81-94 in *The Reign of Heraclius (610-641): Crisis and Confrontation.* Edited by Gerrit J. Reinink and Bernard H. Stolte. Leuven: Peeters, 2002.

———. "Pseudo-Ephraems 'Rede über das Ende' und die syrische eschatologische Literatur des siebenten Jahrhunderts." *ARAM* 5 (1993): 437-63.

———. "Ps.-Methodius: A Concept of History in Response to the Rise of Islam." Pp. 149-87 in *The Byzantine and Early Islamic Near East, I: Problems in the Literary Source Material.* Edited by Averil Cameron and Lawrence I. Conrad. Studies in Late Antiquity and Early Islam 1. Princeton, N.J.: Darwin Press, 1992.

———. *Die syrische Apokalypse des Pseudo-Methodius.* 2 vols. Corpus scriptorum christianorum orientalium 540-541, scrip. syri 220-221. Louvain: E. Peeters, 1993.

Ri, [Andreas] Su-Min, ed. *La Caverne des Trésors: Les deux recensions syriaques.* Corpus scriptorum christianorum orientalium 486, scrip. syri 207. Louvain: E. Peeters, 1987.

———. *Commentaire de la Caverne des Trésors: Étude sur l'histoire du texte et de ses sources.* Corpus scriptorum christianorum orientalium 581. Louvain: Peeters, 2000.

Rieder, David, ed. *Targum Yonatan ben 'Uziel on the Pentateuch*. Jerusalem: Salomon, 1974.

Robinson, Neal. "Antichrist." Pages 107-11 in vol. 1 of the *Encyclopaedia of the Qur'ān*. Edited by Jane Dammen McAuliffe. Leiden: Brill, 2001- .

Rosenfeld, Ben-Zion. "R. Simeon b. Yohai: Wonder Worker and Magician Scholar, *Saddiq* and *Hasid*." *Revue des etudes juives* 158 (1999): 349-84.

Rubenstein, Jeffrey L. *Talmudic Stories: Narrative Art, Composition, and Culture*. Baltimore and London: The Johns Hopkins University Press, 1999.

Rubin, Uri. *Between Bible and Qur'ān: The Children of Israel and the Islamic Self-Image*. Studies in Late Antiquity and Early Islam 17. Princeton, N.J.: Darwin Press, 1999.

———. *The Eye of the Beholder: The Life of Muhammad as Viewed by the Early Muslims*. Studies in Late Antiquity and Early Islam 5. Princeton, N.J.: Darwin Press, 1995.

———. "Sāʿa." Pages 655-57 in vol. 8 of the *Encyclopaedia of Islam*. New ed. Leiden: Brill, 1954-2002.

Runciman, Steven. *A History of the Crusades*. 3 vols. Cambridge: The University Press, 1951-54.

Russell, D. S. *The Method & Message of Jewish Apocalyptic: 200 BC — AD 100*. Philadelphia: Westminster, 1964.

Saadya Gaon. *The Book of Beliefs and Opinions*. Translated by Samuel Rosenblatt. Yale Judaica Series 1. New Haven: Yale University Press, 1948.

———. *Kitâb al-Amânât wa'l-I'tiqâdât von Sa'adja b. Jûsuf al-Fajjûmî*. Edited by S. Landauer. Leiden: Brill, 1880.

Safrai, Ze'ev. "The Sons of Yehonadav ben Rekhav and the Essenes." *Bar-Ilan Annual* 16-17 (1979): 37-58.

Schäfer, Peter, ed. *Geniza-Fragmente zur Hekhalot-Literatur*. Texte und Studien zum antiken Judentum 6. Tübingen: J. C. B. Mohr, 1984.

———. *The History of the Jews in Antiquity: The Jews of Palestine from Alexander the Great to the Arab Conquest*. N.p.: Harwood Academic Publishers, 1995.

———. *Mirror of His Beauty: Feminine Images of God from the Bible to the Early Kabbalah*. Princeton: Princeton University Press, 2002.

———, ed. *Synopse zur Hekhalot-Literatur*. Texte und Studien zum antiken Judentum 2. Tübingen: J. C. B. Mohr, 1981.

Schäfer, Peter and Shaul Shaked, eds. *Magische Texte aus der Kairoer Geniza, Band I*. Texte und Studien zum antiken Judentum 42. Tübingen: J. C. B. Mohr, 1994.

Schick, Robert. *The Christian Communities of Palestine From Byzantine to Islamic Rule: A Historical and Archaeological Study*. Studies in Late Antiquity and Early Islam 2. Princeton, N.J.: The Darwin Press, 1995.

Schloessinger, Max. *The Ritual of Eldad ha-Dani*. Leipzig and New York: Rudolf Haupt, 1908.

Scholem, Gershom G. *Jewish Gnosticism, Merkabah Mysticism, and Talmudic Tradition*. 2d ed. New York: The Jewish Theological Seminary of America, 1965.

———. *Major Trends in Jewish Mysticism*. 3d ed. New York: Schocken Books, 1961.

———. *Sabbatai Ṣevi: The Mystical Messiah, 1626-1676*. Princeton: Princeton University Press, 1973.

Schreiner, Martin. "Beiträge zur Geschichte der Bibel in der arabischen Literatur." Pp. 495-513 in *Semitic Studies in Memory of Rev. Dr. Alexander-Kohut*. Edited by George Alexander Kohut. Berlin: Calvary, 1897.

———. "Zur Geschichte der Polemik zwischen Juden und Muhammedanern." *Zeitschrift der deutschen morgenländischen Gesellschaft* 42 (1888): 591-675.

Segal, Alan F. "The Ruler of This World." Pp. 41-77 in idem, *The Other Judaisms of Late Antiquity*. Brown Judaic Studies 127. Atlanta: Scholars Press, 1987.

Shahrastānī, *Kitāb al-milal waʾl-niḥal*. Edited by Muhammad b. Fath Allāh Badrān. 2 vols. [Cairo]: Matbaʿat al-Azhar, [1951-55].

Sharf, Andrew. *Byzantine Jewry from Justinian to the Fourth Crusade*. New York: Schocken Books, 1971.

Sharon, Moshe. "An Arabic Inscription from the Time of the Caliph ʿAbd al-Malik." *Bulletin of the School of Oriental and African Studies* 29 (1966): 367-72.

Shinan, Avigdor. "Divrey ha-yamim shel Mosheh rabbenu." *Hasifrut* 24 (1977): 100-16.

Silver, Abba Hillel. *A History of Messianic Speculation in Israel*. New York, 1927. Repr., Boston: Beacon, 1959.

Silvestre de Sacy, A. I. *Chrestomathie arabe*. 3 vols. Paris: Imprimerie impériale, 1806.

Sivan, Hagith. "From Byzantine to Persian Jerusalem: Jewish Perspectives and Jewish/Christian Polemics." *Greek, Roman, and Byzantine Studies* 41 (2000): 277-306.

Smith, Jane I. "Eschatology." Pages 44-54 in vol. 2 of the *Encyclopaedia of the Qur'ān*. Edited by Jane Dammen McAuliffe. Leiden: Brill, 2001- .

Smith, William Robertson. *Lectures on the Religion of the Semites*. 2d ed. Edinburgh: A. & C. Black, 1894.

Speck, Paul. "The Apocalypse of Zerubbabel and Christian Icons." *Jewish Studies Quarterly* 4 (1997): 183-90.

Sperber, Alexander, ed. *The Bible in Aramaic: Based on Old Manuscripts and Printed Texts*. 5 vols. Leiden, 1959-73. Repr., Leiden: Brill, 1992.

Speyer, Heinrich. *Die biblischen Erzählungen im Qoran*. Repr., Hildesheim: Georg Olms, 1988.

Starr, Joshua. *The Jews in the Byzantine Empire, 641-1204*. Athens: Verlag der byzantinisch-neugriechischen Jahrbücher, 1939.

Steinschneider, Moritz. "Apokalypsen mit polemischer Tendenz." *Zeitschrift der deutschen morgenländischen Gesellschaft* 28 (1874): 627-59; 29 (1875): 162-66.

———. *Catalogus librorum hebraeorum in bibliotheca Bodleiana*. Berlin: Ad. Friedlaender, 1852-60.

———. *Polemische und apologetische Literatur in arabischer Sprache zwischen Muslimen, Christen und Juden, nebst Anhängen verwandten Inhalts*. Leipzig, 1877. Repr., Hildesheim: Georg Olms, 1966.

Stetkevych, Jaroslav. *Muhammad and the Golden Bough: Reconstructing Arabian Myth*. Bloomington and Indianapolis: Indiana University Press, 1996.

Stone, Michael E. "Apocalyptic Literature." Pp. 383-441 in *Jewish Writings of the Second Temple Period: Apocrypha, Pseudepigrapha, Qumran Sectarian Writings, Philo, Josephus*. Compendia rerum iudaicarum ad Novum Testamentum 2.2 Edited by Michael E. Stone. Assen/Philadelphia: Van Gorcum/Fortress, 1984.

———. *Fourth Ezra: A Commentary on the Book of Fourth Ezra*. Minneapolis: Fortress Press, 1990.

———. "The Metamorphosis of Ezra: Jewish Apocalypse and Medieval Vision." *Journal of Theological Studies* n.s. 33 (1982): 1-18.

Stone, Michael E. and John Strugnell. *The Books of Elijah: Parts 1-2*. Society of Biblical Literature Texts and Translations 18. Missoula, Mont.: Scholars Press, 1979.

Strack, H. L. and G. Stemberger. *Introduction to the Talmud and Midrash*. Minneapolis: Fortress Press, 1992.

Stroumsa, Gedaliahu G. "Form(s) of God: Some Notes on Meṭaṭron and Christ." *Harvard Theological Review* 76 (1983): 269-88.

Swain, J. W. "The Theory of the Four Monarchies: Opposition History under the Roman Empire." *Classical Philology* 35 (1940): 1-21.

Swartz, Michael D. "Hekhalot Rabbati ##297-306: A Ritual for the Cultivation of the Prince of the Torah." Pp. 227-34 in *Ascetic Behavior in Greco-Roman Antiquity: A Sourcebook*. Edited by Vincent L. Wimbush. Studies in Antiquity and Christianity. Minneapolis: Fortress Press, 1990.

———. *Scholastic Magic: Ritual and Revelation in Early Jewish Mysticism*. Princeton: Princeton University Press, 1996.

al-Ṭabarī, Abū Ja'far Muḥammad b. Jarīr. *The History of al-Ṭabarī, Volume V: The Sāsānids, the Byzantines, the Lakmids, and Yemen*. Translated by C. E. Bosworth. Albany: State University of New York Press, 1999.

Talmon, Shemaryahu. "The Presentation of Synchroneity and Simultaneity in Biblical Narrative." Pp. 9-26 in *Studies in Hebrew Narrative Art Throughout the Ages*. Edited by Joseph Heinemann and Shmuel Werses. Scripta hierosolymitana 28. Jerusalem: Magnes Press, 1978.

Teugels, Lieve M. *Aggadat Bereshit*. Jewish and Christian Perspectives Series 4. Leiden: Brill, 2001.

Thaʿlabī, *ʿArāʾis al-majālis fī qiṣaṣ al-anbiyāʾ or "Lives of the Prophets"*. Translated by William M. Brinner. Leiden: Brill, 2002.

Theodore bar Konai. *Liber Scholiorum*. Edited by Addai Scher. 2 vols. Corpus scriptorum christianorum orientalium, scrip. syri series II, t. 65-66. Paris: Carolus Poussielgue, 1910-12.

Theophanes, *Chronographia*. Edited by Carl de Boor. 2 vols. Leipzig: B. G. Teubner, 1883-85.

Turtledove, Harry. *The Chronicle of Theophanes*. Philadelphia: University of Pennsylvania Press, 1982.

Twersky, Isadore, ed. *A Maimonides Reader*. West Orange, N.J.: Behrman House, 1972.

Ullendorff, Edward and C. F. Beckingham. *The Hebrew Letters of Prester John*. Oxford: Oxford University Press, 1982.

Urbach, Ephraim E. *The Halakhah: Its Sources and Development*. Translated by Raphael Posner. Yad ha-Talmud. [Ramat Gan]: Masada Ltd., 1986.

———. *The Sages: Their Concepts and Beliefs*. 2 vols. Jerusalem: Magnes Press, 1979.

VanderKam, James C. and William Adler. *The Jewish Apocalyptic Heritage in Early Christianity*. Compendia rerum iudaicarum ad Novum Testamentum 3.4. Assen/Minneapolis: Van Gorcum/Fortress, 1996.

Waddell, W. G. *Manetho with an English Translation*. Loeb Classical Library. Cambridge, Mass.: Harvard University Press, 1940.

Wansbrough, John. *The Sectarian Milieu: Content and Composition of Islamic Salvation History*. Oxford: Oxford University Press, 1978.

Wasserstein, David J. "Eldad ha-Dani and Prester John." Pp. 213-36 in *Prester John, the Mongols and the Ten Lost Tribes*. Edited by Charles F. Beckingham and Bernard Hamilton. Aldershot: Variorum, 1996.

Wasserstrom, Steven M. *Between Muslim and Jew: The Problem of Symbiosis Under Early Islam*. Princeton: Princeton University Press, 1995.

———. "The ʿĪsāwiyya Revisited." *Studia Islamica* 75 (1992): 57-80.

———. "Šahrastānī on the Maġāriyya." *Israel Oriental Studies* 17 (1998): 127-54.

———. *Species of Misbelief: A History of Muslim Heresiography of the Jews*. Ph.D. diss., University of Toronto, 1985.

Weiser, Asher, ed. *Perushey ha-Torah le-Rabbenu Abraham Ibn Ezra*. 3 vols. Jerusalem: Mosad Harav Kook, 1977.

Wertheimer, S. A. *Batey Midrashot*. 4 vols. in 3. Jerusalem: M. Lilyanthal, 1893-97.

———. *Batey Midrashot*. Edited by A. J. Wertheimer. 2d ed. 2 vols. Jerusalem, 1948-53. Repr., Jerusalem: Ktav wa-Sefer, 1980.

Wheeler, Brannon M. "Imagining the Sasanian Capture of Jerusalem: The 'Prophecy and Dream of Zerubbabel' and Antiochus Strategos' 'Capture of Jerusalem.'" *Orientalia christiana periodica* 57 (1991): 69-85.

———. *Prophets in the Quran: An Introduction to the Quran and Muslim Exegesis.* London and New York: Continuum, 2002.

Wieder, Naphtali. *The Judean Scrolls and Karaism.* London: East and West Library, 1962.

Wilken, Robert L. *The Land Called Holy: Palestine in Christian History and Thought.* New Haven and London: Yale University Press, 1992.

Yadin, Yigael. *The Temple Scroll.* 3 vols. Jerusalem: Israel Exploration Society, 1983.

Yahalom, Joseph. "ʿAl toqpan shel yetsirot sifrut ke-maqor le-berur she'elot historiyot." *Cathedra* 11 (1979): 125-33.

———. "'Ezel Moshe — According to the Berlin Papyrus." *Tarbiz* 47 (1978): 173-84.

———. "The Temple and the City in Liturgical Hebrew Poetry." Pp. 270-94 in *The History of Jerusalem: The Early Muslim Period, 638-1099.* Edited by Joshua Prawer and Haggai Ben-Shammai. Jerusalem and New York: Yad Izhak Ben-Zvi and New York University Press, 1996.

Yaʿqūbī. *Tarīkh.* 2 vols. Beirut: Dār Sādir, 1960.

Yassif, Eli. *The Hebrew Folktale: History, Genre, Meaning.* Bloomington and Indianapolis: Indiana University Press, 1999.

———, ed. *Sefer ha-Zikronot hu' Divrey ha-Yamim le-Yeraḥme'el.* Tel Aviv: Tel Aviv University, 2001.

———. *The Tales of Ben Sira in the Middle-Ages: A Critical Text and Literary Studies.* Jerusalem: Magnes Press, 1984.

Yuval, Israel J. "Jewish Messianic Expectations Towards 1240 and Christian Reactions." Pp. 105-21 in *Toward the Millennium: Messianic Expectations from the Bible to Waco.* Edited by Peter Schäfer and Martin Cohen. Leiden: Brill, 1998.

Zunz, Leopold and Ḥanokh Albeck. *Haderashot be-Yisrael.* 2d ed. Jerusalem: Mosad Bialik, 1954.

Indexes

Bible, Jewish and Christian Parascriptural Sources, and Qur'ān

1. Hebrew Bible

Genesis
2:7 — 37
2:11 — 214, 215
3:7 — 195
4:25 — 146
5:21-24 — 180
9:12 — 158
9:17 — 158
10 — 160
10:2 — 137
10:12 — 52
10:26 — 82
12:1 — 195
12:10-20 — 192
15:7 — 14
15:7-21 — 14, 92
15:9 — 15
15:10 — 15
15:11 — 16
18:10 — 54
21:16 — 217, 220, 222
22:11-13 — 54
22:13 — 104
25:26 — 13
28:12 — 190
29:1 — 65
30:24 — 216
32:25-31 — 54
36:32 — 21
36:33 — 169
38:18 — 195
38:25 — 195
48:22 — 191
49:11 — 167

Exodus
1:10 — 132
1:15-16 — 173
1:22 — 173
2:10 — 43
2:22 — 48
2:25 — 93
3:1-5 — 194
4:2-5 — 188
4:3-4 — 196
4:17 — 188
4:20 — 188
7:9-12 — 188
7:15-21 — 188
8:1 — 188
8:12-13 — 188
8:17-27 — 216
9:23 — 188
10:13 — 188
12:38 — 111
12:40-42 — 172
13:21 — 101
14:13 — 105, 128, 214
14:16 — 188
14:29 — 202
14:30 — 172
14:30-15:18 — 192
15:1-18 — 49, 172
15:8 — 196
15:17 — 86, 175
15:18 — 173
15:19 — 202
17:5-13 — 188
17:6 — 190
17:9 — 188
20:2-3 — 103, 125
20:3 — 118, 120
21:14 — 171
23:21 — 55, 180
24:1 — 180
24:10 — 190
33:7 — 131
33:11 — 52

Leviticus
5:23 — 171
16:8 — 67
20:26 — 116

Numbers
10:29 — 81
11:4 — 111
11:5 — 216
14:20 — 115-16
14:35 — 62
15:37-41 — 111
16:1-11 — 61
16:16-24 — 61
16:26-33 — 61
17:16-26 — 57, 188
17:23 — 57
17:25-26 — 189
20:7-12 — 188
20:11 — 196
20:13 — 196

Numbers (*cont.*)
21:8 — 196
21:9 — 196
21:20 — 196
22-24 — 20, 173
23:1 — 65
24:17 — 44, 89, 97, 135, 144, 145, 146, 148, 198
24:17-19 — 144
24:18-19 — 134
24:21 — 72, 77, 78, 81, 82, 93, 94
24:22 — 99, 100, 134
24:23 — 117, 123
24:24 — 134
25:7 — 57
25:7-13 — 197
31:6 — 197

Deuteronomy
4:43 — 171
6:4 — 100, 147, 156
7:6 — 56
8:3 — 34
9:18 — 92
11:24 — 64
12:5 — 129
14:2 — 56
14:21 — 56
21:17 — 191
28:1 — 36
28:50 — 54, 84, 98, 145
29:27 — 202
32:10 — 196
32:13 — 151
32:14 — 168
32:15 — 222
32:26 — 34, 206
32:35 — 154
32:39 — 37
32:42 — 155
33:2 — 98, 170
33:3 — 58
33:5 — 222
33:17 — 11
34:1-3 — 49
34:5-6 — 188, 196

Joshua
1:4 — 64
1:8 — 215
3:17 — 202
5:13-15 — 54, 185
5:14-15 — 54
5:15 — 185
6:1-20 — 147
9:23-27 — 111
15:37 — 37
18:28 — 63
19:35 — 57
22:13-32 — 197
24:33 — 197

Judges
4:11 — 81
5:1-31 — 49
5:31 — 131, 152
6:3 — 65
13 — 183
13:18 — 93
20:28 — 197

1 Samuel
2:4 — 112
2:6 — 61
3:14 — 122
4:19 — 93

2 Samuel
6:11 — 167
11:25 — 34
21:2 — 111
21:17 — 54
22:40 — 112

1 Kings
5:11 — 81
5:18 — 215
8:9 — 100
8:13 — 164
10:27 — 152
18:31 — 152
19:1-8 — 29
19:5 — 31
25:6 — 204

2 Kings
2:12 — 80
14:13 — 157
17:1-6 — 201
17:6 — 34, 128
19:35 — 159
19:35-36 — 54
21:1 — 55

Isaiah
1:18 — 71
2:2 — 64
2:3 — 141
2:4 — 141
2:18 — 117
2:19 — 117
4:3 — 141
4:5 — 142, 168
6:13 — 153
7:18 — 95
7:19 — 98
11:1 — 46, 113, 199
11:4 — 19, 49, 62, 66, 86, 116, 119, 121, 159, 174, 198
11:5 — 36
11:6-9 — 141-42
11:10 — 64
11:11 — 103, 128
11:11-15 — 201
11:12 — 148
11:13 — 61
13:10 — 108
13:13 — 108
13:15 — 98
13:21 — 210
14:5 — 84, 95
16:4 — 115, 158
18:1 — 139, 210, 213, 217, 219, 221, 224
18:2 — 139
18:6 — 37

Isaiah (*cont.*)
19:1 — 154
19:2 — 153
19:14 — 58
21:3 — 93
21:6-7 — 7, 8, 9, 10, 12
21:6-9 — 8, 9
21:7 — 9, 10, 11, 12, 15, 80, 94
21:12 — 64
21:13 — 73, 82
21:15 — 73
24:16 — 153
24:18-20 — 108
24:22 — 123
24:23 — 86, 143, 166, 175
25:8 — 132, 142, 173
25:9 — 173
25:17 — 176
26:2 — 148, 165
26:11 — 166
26:19 — 139-40, 148
26:20 — 98, 145
26:21 — 37
27:10 — 58
27:13 — 62, 104, 105, 127, 139, 148
29:4 — 36
30:26 — 130, 152
32:9 — 164
33:9 — 71
33:21 — 162
33:24 — 132
34:1-17 — 73
34:6 — 113, 171
34:13-15 — 210
35:3-4 — 105
35:5-6 — 140
35:6 — 131
35:9 — 148
35:10 — 131, 151
37:36 — 159
37:36-37 — 54
40:1 — 148
40:2 — 148
40:3 — 147
40:5 — 86, 132
41:2 — 94
41:6 — 160
41:18 — 129
41:18-19 — 139
41:19 — 148
42:13 — 62
42:15 — 158
43:2 — 87
43:6 — 139
43:14 — 154
43:16 — 170
44:2 — 222
44:23 — 153
44:28 — 33
45 — 96
45:1 — 33
45:3 — 88, 96
49:7 — 87, 95
49:8-13 — 204
49:9 — 203, 204, 210, 217, 221
49:10 — 129
49:12 — 119, 204
49:18 — 154
49:21 — 64, 141, 204
49:22 — 128, 138
49:23 — 36, 152
51:6 — 143
51:11 — 131, 151
51:14 — 171
52:1 — 101
52:7 — 148, 162
52:12 — 101
53:3 — 53, 86
53:5 — 23
54:2-3 — 159
54:9 — 112
54:10 — 87
54:12 — 39, 130, 152
54:13 — 39
55:12 — 162
56:1 — 161
57:12 — 150, 171
58:14 — 151
59:15 — 121
59:16 — 124
59:17 — 61, 62, 155, 161, 171
60:2 — 112
60:3 — 86, 142, 175
60:6 — 147
60:7 — 157
60:8 — 102, 129, 139, 163
60:9 — 139
60:21 — 87
60:22 — 85
61:5 — 146
61:10 — 151, 154-55
62:4 — 55
62:5 — 154
63:1 — 73, 150, 154, 155, 169, 170, 171
63:2 — 155
63:3 — 155
63:16 — 87, 175
65:17 — 143
65:18 — 143
65:20 — 132, 142
65:22 — 132, 142
66:8 — 141
66:17 — 113
66:19 — 138
66:20 — 138, 203
66:22 — 143
66:24 — 38

Jeremiah
3:14 — 124, 135
3:17 — 151
3:18 — 137
4:23 — 108
4:24 — 108
4:28 — 108
7:1 — 51
7:34 — 154, 169
9:9 — 162
11:1 — 51
12:9 — 16
16:9 — 154

Jeremiah (*cont.*)
17:12 — 152
18:1 — 51
21:1 — 51
23:5 — 46, 55
25:10 — 154
25:30 — 153
30:1 — 51
30:18 — 129, 163
31:3 — 131
31:6-13 — 201
31:7 — 131
31:8 — 128, 161
31:11 — 105
31:19 — 161
31:32 — 158
32:1 — 51
33:11 — 154
33:15 — 46, 55
34:1 — 51
34:8 — 51
35:1 — 51
35:1-19 — 204
40:1 — 51
44:1 — 51
48:47 — 146
49:9 — 99
49:26 — 147
49:28 — 65
49:38 — 154
50:11 — 14
50:20 — 115, 116
50:30 — 101, 147

Ezekiel
1:1 — 92
1:26 — 190
3:23 — 51
4:13 — 71, 81
5:16 — 97, 108, 144
7:19 — 98
8:3 — 52
10:1 — 190
10:22 — 51
12:14 — 36
16:20 — 64
16:55 — 141
17:23 — 96
20:35 — 104, 135, 147
20:37 — 135
20:38 — 126, 136
20:40 — 96
20:41 — 63
22:2 — 52
23:31 — 203
24:6 — 52
24:9 — 52
25:5 — 70
25:14 — 13, 100, 132, 135, 147, 154, 155, 156, 171
28:13 — 164
34:14 — 96
36:8 — 36
36:26 — 132
36:33-38 — 71
36:35 — 129
37:1-14 — 139
37:8 — 37
37:13 — 140
37:19-24 — 128, 201
38-39 — 119, 138
38:2 — 137
38:6 — 137, 159
38:11 — 137
38:19-20 — 108
38:20 — 62
38:21 — 62, 138
38:22 — 128, 138
39:9 — 37, 161
39:10 — 63
39:10-14 — 63
39:12 — 37
39:17 — 161
39:28 — 139
40:4 — 53
41:6-7 — 163
41:7 — 159
43:3 — 51
44:9 — 118
47:1-12 — 65
47:2 — 162
47:10 — 38
47:11 — 163
47:12 — 38, 163

Hosea
2:1 — 169
2:16 — 104, 126
3:4 — 122
6:2 — 87, 142, 175
8:8 — 204
9:6-7 — 94
10:2 — 52
10:11 — 14
12:1 — 33
12:10 — 135
14:2 — 164
14:6 — 117, 123
14:6-8 — 112

Joel
1:15 — 159
2:3 — 129
2:10 — 108
3:1 — 132, 141
3:2 — 141
3:3 — 111, 117, 123
3:4 — 103, 123
3:5 — 98, 145
4:2 — 61, 81, 86, 164, 175
4:12 — 61, 86, 164, 175
4:14 — 126
4:16 — 34
4:17 — 118
4:18 — 61, 65, 162
4:19 — 97, 171
4:21 — 169

Amos
1:11 — 169
4:7 — 108, 144
5:18 — 159
8:9 — 104
9:10 — 120, 136
9:11 — 82

Obadiah
1:1 — 155
1:3-4 — 93

Obadiah (*cont.*)
1:5 — 99
1:9 — 155
1:16 — 38
1:17 — 145
1:18 — 13, 128
1:21 — 135, 169

Jonah
1:2 — 52
2:9 — 124
3:2 — 52
4:2 — 169
4:11 — 52

Micah
2:13 — 87, 129, 151
4:8 — 53
4:10 — 34, 147
5:2 — 85, 122
5:4 — 100, 140
5:8 — 69
7:15 — 102, 172

Nahum
3:1 — 52
3:3 — 96

Habakkuk
1:6 — 88, 96
3:4 — 168
3:5 — 153
3:6 — 158

Zephaniah
1:17 — 99
2:13 — 118
3:9 — 132, 141
3:10 — 139, 210, 213, 215, 219, 221, 224
3:12 — 145
3:20 — 105, 129

Haggai
1:1 — 43
1:8 — 130
1:12 — 43
1:14 — 42, 43
2:2 — 43
2:4 — 43
2:21 — 43
2:23 — 43

Zechariah
1:7 — 51
1:16 — 51, 169
1:17 — 159
2:9 — 37
3:1-2 — 22
3:2 — 114
3:8 — 43, 46, 55
4:1 — 93
4:1-6 — 45
4:6-7 — 43
4:7 — 22, 115
4:9 — 42, 51
6:12 — 46, 55
6:13 — 61
7:2 — 52
8:10 — 65
8:21-22 — 52
8:23 — 111, 113
9:1 — 159, 163
9:9 — 8, 11, 64, 80, 94, 131
9:14 — 62, 127
10:8 — 86, 174
12:2 — 138
12:10 — 50, 85, 174
12:10-11 — 136
12:12 — 114, 146
13:8-9 — 136
13:9 — 85, 111, 126, 136
14:1-2 — 160
14:2 — 59, 136, 160
14:3 — 36, 105, 128, 138, 146, 160-61
14:4 — 62, 146, 204
14:4-5 — 108
14:5-12 — 146
14:7 — 16
14:7-10 — 159
14:8 — 65
14:12 — 36, 138, 174
14:13 — 138
14:15 — 36
14:18 — 36

Malachi
3:1 — 60, 114, 137
3:4 — 57, 63
3:19 — 117
3:20 — 117, 123
3:22-24 — 224
3:23 — 159
3:23-24 — 159
3:24 — 119, 121, 137

Psalms
2:2 — 116, 146, 173, 174
3:8 — 164
7:18 — 166
9:18 — 87, 175
11:6 — 38, 168
16:5 — 166
19:5 — 117
21:6 — 151
23:5 — 166
24:7 — 148
24:9 — 148
29:6 — 108
29:7 — 168
31:20 — 39, 169
33:6 — 52
34:10 — 56
37:11 — 89, 175
46:3-4 — 108
46:7 — 108
48:15 — 166
49:15 — 164
50:5 — 158
50:7 — 151
50:11 — 86
60:11 — 156
71:4 — 170
71:20 — 61, 158
72:16 — 102, 168
72:17 — 35

Psalms (*cont.*)
78:40-41 — 196
80:5 — 78
80:14 — 86
83:7 — 155
84:7 — 164
89:1 — 81, 94
89:37 — 164
89:52 — 106
90 — 208
90:4 — 87
91:15 — 170
93:1 — 155
94:23 — 210
103:5 — 140
104:1 — 155
104:35 — 35
106:2 — 67
106:14 — 196
106:30 — 197
107:4 — 196
110:1 — 105, 127
110:2 — 158, 195, 198
116:13 — 166
118:26 — 165
119:165 — 39
122:3 — 38, 141
132:13 — 170
137:1 — 208, 212
137:3 — 209, 211, 212, 222
137:4 — 211
137:5 — 211
139:12 — 168
144:12 — 167

Proverbs
4:18 — 168
9:3 — 164
21:13 — 132
21:29 — 145

Job
1:3 — 65
1:7 — 162
5:21-23 — 210
21:14 — 182
30:4 — 65, 115, 126
32:18 — 60
40:31 — 167

Song of Songs
2:14 — 14, 15
4:8 — 154
4:9 — 154
4:10 — 154
4:11 — 154
4:12 — 154
5:1 — 154, 166
5:16 — 124
6:10 — 60
7:11 — 102
7:13-8:14 — 49
8:2 — 165
8:6 — 153

Lamentations
1:16 — 55

Qohelet
1:9 — 100
2:5 — 71
4:14 — 116
7:24 — 223
8:1 — 54

Esther
3:5-15 — 173
6:1-10:3 — 173

Daniel
2 — 12, 107
2:31-45 — 99
2:39 — 93
2:44 — 72, 96
2:46 — 152
6:29 — 43
7 — 12
7:7 — 14
7:8 — 19, 33, 35
7:13 — 86, 116, 153, 174
7:14 — 86, 116, 174
7:18 — 56, 66
7:21-22 — 56
7:23 — 14
7:25 — 56, 98, 99, 145
7:27 — 56
7:28 — 101
8 — 12
8:6 — 14
8:8 — 14
8:17 — 53
8:23 — 54, 84, 98, 145, 174
8:24 — 56, 62
10-12 — 185
10:1 — 56
10:16 — 93
11:2 — 15
11:4 — 14, 15
11:5 — 50
11:14 — 85, 146
11:16 — 97
11:19 — 118
11:20 — 145
11:21 — 145
11:25 — 53
11:31 — 83, 99
11:34 — 56
11:39 — 70, 81
11:40 — 53, 98
11:42 — 104, 127
11:44 — 35
11:45 — 35, 104, 118, 120, 127
12:1 — 31, 101-2, 115, 119, 120, 126, 146, 151, 185
12:2 — 131, 140-41, 164
12:3 — 123
12:4 — 2, 29, 53, 210
12:7 — 56
12:9 — 53, 210
12:9-13 — 2
12:10 — 126
12:11 — 99, 127
12:11-12 — 104
12:12 — 127

Ezra
1:8 — 43
2:1-2 — 42
3:2 — 42, 43
3:8 — 42, 43
4:2-3 — 42
4:2-5 — 42
4:7 — 33
4:8 — 33
4:11 — 33
4:23 — 33
5:1-2 — 43
5:2 — 42, 43
6:14 — 33
7:1 — 33
7:5 — 115
7:11 — 33
7:12 — 33
7:21 — 33
7:23 — 33
8:1 — 33

Nehemiah
2:1 — 33
2:20 — 157
5:14 — 33
7:6-7 — 42
8:14 — 51
9:1 — 51
11:1 — 101
11:24 — 118
12:1 — 42, 43
12:47 — 42
13:6 — 33

1 Chronicles
1:43 — 21
2:6 — 94
2:55 — 81
3:17-19 — 43
3:19 — 43
5:1-2 — 191
5:26 — 128
29:23 — 151

2 Chronicles
3:1 — 82
3:6 — 163
9:5 — 56
10:19 — 100
28:8-15 — 50
32:21-22 — 54

2. New Testament

Matthew
24:3-44 — 107
24:8 — 107

Mark
13:3-36 — 107
13:8 — 107

2 Thessalonians
2:1-12 — 103
2:8 — 62

Hebrews
9:4 — 189
11:16 — 38

1 John
2:22 — 109

Revelation
13:11 — 108
21:9-27 — 63
21:18-20 — 130
22:2 — 38
22:8-10 — 29

3. Jewish Apocrypha and Pseudepigrapha

Apocalypse of Abraham
1:1-8:6 — 195
29:15-30:8 — 107

Apocalypse of Elijah (Coptic)
3:15 — 33

Assumption of Moses
1:16-18 — 29

1 Enoch
1:2 — 183
7:6 — 153
8:1 — 195
12:1-2 — 183
17:1-36:4 — 183
18:6 — 32
18:8 — 190
21:7 — 32
22:11 — 32
24:2-25:7 — 38
60:24 — 175
69:6 — 195
70:1-71:17 — 180
72:1 — 183
80:1-81:10 — 183
82:1 — 29
90:29 — 63
91:12-17 — 107
93:1-10 — 107
93:2 — 183
103:1-2 — 183
106:7 — 183
106:19-107:1 — 183

2 Enoch
22:1-11 — 180

1 Esdras
3:1-4:63 — 42
5:5 — 43
5:7-8 — 42
5:47-73 — 42
6:1-2 — 42
6:2 — 42
6:17 — 43

4 Ezra
3:1 — 43
3:14 — 92
4:52-5:13 — 107
5:48-56 — 107
6:20-24 — 107

4 Ezra (cont.)
6:49-52 — 175
8:63-9:6 — 107
10:27 — 38
12:36-38 — 2, 29
13:1-13 — 201
13:9-11 — 62
13:13 — 201, 203
13:34-45 — 128
13:39-47 — 201
13:40 — 201, 202
13:44 — 202
14:10 — 107
14:44-48 — 2
14:45-48 — 29

Jubilees
12:1-14 — 195
23:11-25 — 107
23:29 — 215
50:5 — 215

Liber antiquitatum biblicarum (Pseudo-Philo)
48:1 — 57, 197

Lives of the Prophets
15.3 — 43

1 Maccabees
7:31 — 37
7:40 — 37
7:45 — 37
12:49 — 35

2 Maccabees
1:18-36 — 42
2:4-8 — 196
4:33 — 203

Psalms of Solomon
17:11 — 104
17:17 — 104
17:24 — 116
17:28 — 118

Sibylline Oracles
2.154-213 — 107
3.796-808 — 107

Sirach
49:11-12 — 42

Syriac Apocalypse of Baruch (2 Baruch)
4:2-6 — 38
24:3-30:5 — 107
26-29 — 97
29:4 — 175
48:30-41 — 107
50:2-4 — 140
70:1-71:2 — 107
73:6 — 141
78:1 — 201, 202
85:10 — 107

Testament of Levi
18:3 — 198

Testament of Judah
24:1 — 198

4. Qumran Literature

Damascus Document
2.20-21 — 38
7.18-20 — 198

Genesis Apocryphon
2.23 — 163

Rule of the Blessings (1QSb)
5.24 — 199
5.24-25 — 62, 116
5.27-28 — 199

War Scroll (1QM)
1.3 — 104
10.10 — 56

4Q266
3 iii 20-21 — 198

4Q504
1-2 iv 13 — 215

4Q546
ii 3 — 191

11Q13 (*Melchizedek*)
2.15-22 — 162

5. Graeco-Jewish Authors

Josephus, *Antiquitates judaicae*
11.13-14 — 42
11.31-67 — 42
11.73 — 43
11.92 — 42
11.116-19 — 42
11.133 — 201

Josephus, *Bellum judaicum*
7.96-99 — 206

6. Rabbinic Literature

Mishnah
Ma'aśer Šeni
5.12 — 129
Yoma
5.2 — 82, 113
6.4 — 39
Soṭah
3.4 — 125
9.12 — 131
9.15 — 106, 121, 136
Sanhedrin
4.5 — 151
6.2 — 140
7.1 — 215

Sanhedrin (*cont.*)
10.3 — 61, 62, 202
ʿEduyyot
2.10 — 87
ʾAbot
1.1 — 219
5.6 — 48, 189

Tosefta
Peʾah
4.7 — 129
Yoma
2.14 — 82, 113
2.15 — 189
Soṭah
13.1 — 189
Sanhedrin
4.5 — 129
9.10 — 215
13.4 — 87
Zebaḥim
13.6-8 — 51
Menaḥot
7.8 — 129
Ḥullin
2.18 — 185

Babylonian Talmud (Bavli)
Berakot
17a — 164
63b — 167
Šabbat
32a — 140
33b — 170
33b-34a — 78
88a — 131, 151
118a — 107
ʿErubin
21b — 124
53a — 161, 195
Pesaḥim
54a — 35
68a — 140
118a — 107, 195
Yoma
9a — 56
10a — 13, 52, 134
21b — 130
44b-45a — 163
52b — 189
57a — 124
73b — 222
77b — 162
Sukkah
35a — 163
52a — 85
52b — 140
Roš Haššanah
17a — 87
Taʿanit
5a — 38
Megillah
5b-6a — 57
12a — 33
Ḥagigah
12b — 86
15a — 179
Ketubbot
106a — 50
111b — 167, 168
112b — 167
Nedarim
39a — 35
Nazir
25a-b –129
Soṭah
13a — 161
13b — 122
Qiddušin
69b — 209
Baba Qamma
97a — 71
Baba Meṣiʿa
86b — 54
Baba Batra
15a — 81
58a — 161
73b — 86
75a — 167, 168
75b — 163
123a — 191
Sanhedrin
37a — 151
37b-38a — 43
38a — 42, 46
38b — 37, 179
65b — 34, 205, 206
70b — 195
91b — 140
92a — 141
94a — 51, 180
96b — 65, 204
97a — 97, 106, 107-8, 121, 122, 134, 144, 145, 153, 175
97a-b — 143
98a — 53, 84, 85
98b — 35, 53, 107, 134
99a — 36
100a — 167
105a — 20, 59
108b — 110
Makkot
12a — 171
ʿAbodah Zarah
2b — 170
3b — 180
9a — 175
9b — 86
Ḥullin
24a — 51
40a — 185
Meʿilah
17a-b — 90
17b — 124

Palestinian Talmud (Yerushalmi)
Berakot
1.1, 2c — 60
2.4, 5a — 55, 113
4.5, 8c — 82
Šebiʿit
9.1, 38d — 78
Šeqalim
6.1, 49c — 189

Šeqalim (cont.)
6.2, 50a — 162
Yoma
3.2, 40b — 60
Sukkah
3.5, 53d — 163
Ta^canit
1.1, 64a — 154
Megillah
1.1, 70a — 57
Yebamot
4.6b — 167
Soṭah
8.3, 22c — 189
Sanhedrin
10.3, 29b — 87
10.6, 29c — 34, 203

Midrashim
Canticles Rabbah
2.4 — 121, 134, 162
4.1 — 154
6.16 — 60
8.7 — 169

Exodus Rabbah
5.6 — 190
18.5 — 54
38.11 — 222

Genesis Rabbah
6.6 — 117
11.5 — 34, 205, 206
38.13 — 195
41(42).4 — 153
44.15 — 14
44.17 — 14
61.7 — 156
63.9 — 194
73.6 — 34, 208, 216
75.6 — 11
79.6 — 78
96.5 — 204
98.10 — 167

Lamentations Rabbah
1.51 — 55
2.9(13) — 34, 203

Leviticus Rabbah
9.1 — 81
10.5 — 43
27.11 — 146
30.8 — 163

Mekhilta de R. Ishmael
Boʾ, Pisḥa
§1 — 51
§14 — 154
Beshalaḥ, Va-yassaʿ
§4 — 107
§5 — 107, 189
§6 — 190
Yitro, Baḥodesh
§9 — 14, 92

Midrash Tehillim
2 — 146
20.3 — 150
21.1 — 53
60.3 — 102
68.9 — 64
90.17 — 36, 175

Numbers Rabbah
4.20 — 167
18.23 — 187, 195

Pesiqta de Rav Kahana
5.9 — 107, 121, 134, 161, 162
7.11 — 111
11.16 — 78
21.4 — 64
22.5 — 154
23.1 — 37
nispaḥ §5 — 205

Pesiqta Rabbati
§1 — 36, 175, 204
§15 — 121
§17 — 111
§20 — 165
§31 — 34, 166, 204
§35 — 129

Qohelet Rabbah
1.28 — 102
10.8 — 78

Sifra
Aḥarey Mot
§2 — 140
ʾEmor
§16 — 163

Sifre Deut
§1 — 64, 159, 163
§62 — 82
§338 — 179
§355 — 189

Sifre Num
§84 — 154
§161 — 154

Tanḥuma
Noaḥ
§3 — 34
§18 — 146
Vayera
§9 — 215
§3 — 204
Boʾ
§4 — 111
Wa-ʾera
§9 — 190
Teṣawweh
§8 — 117
Pequdey
§1 — 38
§4 — 173
Tazriʿa
§8 — 190
Naso
§9 — 163

Qoraḥ
§12 — 55, 160
ʿEqev
§7 — 36, 167

Tanḥuma Buber
Noaḥ
§24 — 146
Wayeṣe
§24 — 129
Wayishlaḥ
§8 — 84

Targumim
Fragment Targum
Exod 12:42 — 61

Targum Ketuvim
Ps 60:11 — 156
Ps 89:1 — 81
Ps 89:52 — 106
Ps 122:3 — 38
Cant 7:13-8:14 — 48
Qoh 8:1 — 54, 84, 98
1 Chr 1:43 — 21

Targum Neviʾim
Judg 5:31 — 152
Isa 4:3 — 141
Isa 11:4 — 49
Isa 21:17 — 82
Isa 30:26 — 130
Isa 35:9 — 148
Jer 2:10 — 82
Jer 3:18 — 137
Hos 2:16 — 126
Mic 4:8 — 53

Targum Onkelos
Num 24:21 — 81
Num 33:52 — 62
Deut 33:3 — 58

Targum Pseudo-Jonathan
Gen 5:24 — 180
Gen 25:13 — 82
Gen 25:14 — 68
Gen 36:32 — 21
Exod 2:21 — 189, 190
Exod 4:20 — 190
Exod 24:1 — 180
Exod 31:18 — 190
Exod 34:10 — 34
Num 21:8 — 196
Num 25:12 — 57, 197
Deut 34:1-3 — 49-50
Deut 34:3 — 185

Targum Tosefta
Exod 12:42 — 148
Zech 12:10 — 50

Miscellaneous Rabbinic Texts
ʾAbot de Rabbi Natan
A §41 — 124
A, hosaphah 2 §4 — 197
B §37 — 189

Pirqe Rabbi Eliezer
§§1-2 — 67
§3 — 67
§8 — 57, 197
§14 — 67
§18 — 55
§19 — 55
§20 — 161
§24 — 67
§25 — 67
§26 — 195
§27 — 67
§28 — 14, 92, 93
§30 — 67-75, 77, 81
§31 — 104
§32 — 35
§39 — 67
§40 — 67, 192
§41 — 67
§46 — 67
§47 — 57, 151, 197
§48 — 55, 69
§54 — 67

Seder ʿOlam Rabbah
§3 — 87

Yalqut Shimoni
Torah
§76 — 17, 92
§168 — 190, 191
§763 — 195
Ezekiel
§375 — 191
Micah
§552 — 134
Psalms
§869 — 187, 195

7. Qurʾān

2:60 — 188, 194
2:124 — 81
2:128 — 157
2:247-48 — 187, 189
3:44 — 197
3:110 — 157
6:74-84 — 195
7:107 — 188
7:117 — 188
7:157 — 80
7:159 — 204, 206
7:160 — 188
7:187 — 108
15:6 — 94
17:1 — 38, 204
17:47 — 94
17:104 — 202, 206
18:93-99 — 108
18:98 — 23
18:99 — 108
19:41-50 — 195
20:10-16 — 194
20:17-21 — 188
21:53-73 — 195
21:96 — 108

Qur'ān (*cont.*)
21:104 — 108
22:78 — 81
25:25 — 108
26:69-86 — 195
27:10 — 188
27:82 — 108, 188
28:29-30 — 194
28:31 — 188
29:16-27 — 195
33:63 — 108
37:83-98 — 195
38:4 — 94
39:68 — 108
43:26-27 — 195
43:28 — 81
43:61 — 23
44:10 — 108
47:18 — 108, 135, 161
50:20 — 108
50:41-42 — 108
55:37 — 108
60:4 — 195
69:16 — 108
73:14 — 108
73:18 — 108
75:8 — 108
79:42-46 — 108
81:3 — 108
82:1 — 108
82:4 — 108
84:1 — 108
99:1-3 — 108
100:9 — 108

8. Other Late Antique and Medieval Literary Sources

Acta Archelai — 198
'Aggadat Bereshit — 154, 173
'Aggadat ha-Mašiaḥ — 97, 99, 144-48
'Aggadat R. Ishmael — 14, 56, 92
Alexander Romance — 206
Apocalypse of Nāth(?) — 188, 197
Apocalypse of Paul — 29
Apocalypse of Pseudo-Ephrem — 71, 72, 103, 160
Apocalypse of Pseudo-Methodius — 13, 19, 70, 111, 147, 160
'Atidot R. Šim'ōn b. Yoḥai — 11, 77, 135
Bereshit Rabbati — 180, 209, 212-16
Book of the Bee — 57, 192, 195
Cave of Treasures — 42, 68, 97, 197
Chronicles of Moses — 172, 190
Cologne Mani Codex — 29
Corpus Hermeticum — 181
Doctrina Jacobi nuper baptizati — 19, 59, 79, 207
Eldad ha-Dani — 41, 128-29, 200, 201, 206, 208, 218, 220, 223, 224
3 Enoch — 180, 182
'Ezel Mosheh — 191
Gannat Bussame — 180, 185
Gospel of the Twelve Apostles — 13, 88, 186
Halakhot Gedolot — 45
Hekhalot Rabbati — 40, 45, 48, 122, 179, 181
Ma'aseh Daniel — 45
Maḥzor Vitry — 48, 117, 148
Massekhet Kelim — 29, 189
Megillat Aḥima'aṣ — 91
Midrash 'Aseret ha-Dibbarot — 63
Midrash Konen — 23, 61
Midrash Leqaḥ Tov (Pesiqta Zutarta) — 144
Midrash Wa-yosha' — 19, 54, 85, 86, 164, 172-76, 189, 190, 192, 193
'Otiyyot de R. 'Aqiva — 35, 37-38, 44, 180
'Otot R. Šim'ōn b. Yoḥai — 22, 111-16
Pereq R. Yoshyahu — 149, 154, 155, 156, 157, 158, 159
Prayer (Tefillat) of R. Šim'ōn b. Yoḥai — 11, 19, 76, 77, 78, 79, 80, 83, 84, 87, 88, 89-105, 124, 144-45, 146-47, 183
Protevangelium James — 197
Pseudo-Ben Sira — 180
Pseudo-Seder Eliyahu Zuta — 44
Qalēmenṭos — 197
Re'uyot Yeḥezq'el — 179, 189
Secrets (Nistarot) of R. Šim'ōn b. Yoḥai — 10, 11, 12, 15, 16, 19, 25, 31, 54, 69, 70-71, 76-89, 92, 93, 94, 95, 96, 99, 104, 134, 146, 147, 149, 158, 164, 172, 175, 183, 184
Seder Eliyahu Zuta — 169
Seder Gan Eden — 165

Seder ʿOlam Zuta — 43, 60, 133
Seder Rav ʿAmram — 117
Sefer ʾAsaṭīr — 198
Sefer Elijah — 29-39, 77, 78, 141, 147, 149, 186, 203
Sefer Zerubbabel — 19, 20, 25, 29, 33, 40-66, 73, 85, 104, 116, 122, 145, 158, 172, 179, 183, 184, 185, 186, 187, 188, 189, 197
Shiʿur Qomah — 182
Testament of Abraham — 185
Yeraḥmeʾel — 20, 41, 121, 184, 190, 208-212
Zohar — 48, 76, 171

9. Hebrew and Aramaic Manuscripts

Berlin Ms. Sachau
10 — 109

Cambridge T-S
A45.3 — 94
A45.5 — 41
A45.6 — 149
A45.7 — 41
A45.8 — 116, 119
A45.19 — 41, 52, 53, 54, 55, 56, 57, 184
A45.22 — 41
K 21.95.J — 182
NS 182.69 — 148

Cincinnati HUC
Ms. 75 — 14, 15, 55, 69, 70, 71, 72, 73, 75, 81, 92, 93
Ms. 2043 — 70, 71, 72, 73, 75

Codex Reuchlinianus — 50

Munich Ms. Hebr.
22 — 180, 181
40 — 183
222 — 31, 78, 79, 83, 84

New York JTS
Ms. 8128 — 32, 179
ENA 3513.11a — 197
ENA 3635.17 — 32

Oxford Ms.
Heb. d. 11 (2797) — 41, 121, 130, 190, 208
Heb. d. 46 (2643) — 78
Heb. f. 27 (2642) — 40, 51, 58, 59, 78
Heb. 2585 — 220
Opp. 236a — 41, 50, 51, 59, 63, 64, 65, 66
Opp. 603 — 41, 51

Paris Ms. B.N.
326 — 41

Vatican Ms.
228 — 45, 180, 182

Ancient and Medieval Authors, Tradents, and Commentators

ʿAbd Allāh b. Salām — 42
Abraham ben Azriel — 134
Abraham Ibn Daud — 133
Abraham Ibn Ezra — 21, 35, 43, 48, 55, 56, 73, 80, 85, 93, 102, 111, 114, 136, 154, 188, 208
ʿAlī Ibn Rabban al-Ṭabarī — 9
ʿAnan b. David — 79, 207, 208
Arculfus — 82
Arṭāt b. al-Mundhir — 84
Baʿal ha-Ṭūrim — 195
Bayḍāwī — 194
Bīrūnī — 9, 80, 198
Clement of Alexandria — 42
Constantine VII Porphyrogenitus — 188
R. Eleazar b. Judah of Worms — 48
Eleazar ha-Qallir — 44, 48
Ephrem Syrus — 44
Epiphanius — 46
R. Hai b. Sherira Gaon — 19, 45, 47, 48, 63, 79, 131, 133-43
Ḥanbal b. Isḥāq — 110
Hippolytus — 46
Ibn ʿAbbās — 143
Ibn al-Layth — 9
Ibn Isḥāq — 7
Ibn Qutayba — 8
Irenaeus — 46
Jacob ben Reuben — 81
Jerome — 36
Judah ha-Levi — 68
Kaʿb al-Aḥbār — 6, 22, 42, 70, 109, 110

Kirmānī — 9, 80
Kisāʿī — 192, 193, 195
Lactantius — 35, 172
Maʿmar b. Rāshid — 110
Maimonides — 10, 18, 68, 194, 207, 215
Manetho — 56
Maqdisī — 72
Maqrīzī — 79, 207-8
Māwardī — 45
Muqātil b. Sulaymān — 202, 204, 206
Nathan of Gaza — 58
Nuʿaym b. Ḥammād — 20, 22, 23, 70, 110, 160, 188, 189
Pirkoi ben Baboi — 68
Pliny — 205, 206
Radaq — 43, 61, 63, 73, 81, 82, 111, 126, 129, 132, 137, 139, 140, 154, 159, 171
Ramban — 34, 67, 206
Rashbam — 163
Rashi — 38, 48, 50, 51, 56, 61, 62, 65, 68, 81, 84, 86, 102, 111, 124, 130, 137, 145, 180, 185, 190, 196, 206, 209
R. Saadya Gaon — 12, 19, 48, 61, 63, 85, 131, 133, 135, 140, 141, 142, 145, 172, 198, 208
Sebeos — 13, 156, 207
Shahrastānī — 129, 194, 207
R. Simeon Qayyara — 45
Socrates Scholasticus — 61-62
Ṭabarī — 8, 58, 83, 187, 193
Thaʿlabī — 8, 194, 195
Theodore bar Konai — 46
Theophanes — 35, 59
Timothy I — 9
R. Tobiah b. Eliezer — 144
ʿUmāra b. Wathīma — 7
Wahb b. Munabbih — 6, 42, 110
Yaḥyā b. ʿAbd al-Hamid al-Hamani — 110
Yaʿqūbī — 42, 43, 195
Yehudah Hadassi — 205
Zamakhsharī — 194
Zosimus — 205

Modern Authors

Abel, Armand — 22, 24, 113, 188
Abrahamse, Dorothy deF. — 72, 113, 160
Abrams, Daniel — 181
Adang, Camilla — 8, 9, 43
Adler, Elkan Nathan — 129
Adler, William — 2, 3, 5
Aescoly, A. Z. — 77, 78, 81, 83, 102, 205
Albeck, Ḥanokh — 11, 14, 34, 40, 48, 49, 67, 68, 70, 71, 72, 74, 85, 106, 117, 144, 150, 153, 156, 167, 169, 173, 180, 194, 200, 204, 206, 208, 212, 213, 214, 215, 216
Alexander, Paul J. — 72, 113, 160
Alexander, Philip S. — 49, 68, 180, 181, 182
Altmann, Alexander — 69
Arjomand, Saïd Amir — 110, 187-88, 189
Ashkenazi, R. Eliezer — 134
Assemani, J. S. — 44
Astren, Fred — 72
Avi-Yonah, Michael — 33

Badrān, Muhammad b. Fath Allāh — 194, 207
Barber, C. R. — 187
Baron, Salo W. — 47, 49, 77, 86, 89, 174
Barth, Lewis — 68
Bashear, Suliman — 7, 80, 81, 143
Bauckham, Richard — 32
Baumgarten, Albert I. — 32, 102, 143, 175
Beaton, Roderick — 93
Beck, Edmund — 71, 103, 160
Beckingham, Charles F. — 200, 219, 220
Beeson, Charles Henry — 198
Beit-Arié, Malachi — 41
Ben-Hayyim, Zeʾev — 198
Ben-Shammai, Haggai — 38, 39, 49, 82, 86, 98, 134
Berger, Abraham — 53, 73
Berger, David — 20, 59, 65
Beyer, Klaus — 191, 197

Biale, David — 21, 47, 48, 52, 53, 55, 62, 110
Bidawid, R. J. — 201, 202
Bidez, Joseph — 185
Bietenhard, Hans — 181
Bin-Gorion, Emanuel — 129, 208
Bin-Gorion, Micha Joseph — 129, 208
Blau, Ludwig — 194
Bonwetsch, G. N. — 59, 79
Boor, Carl de — 59
Bosworth, C. E. — 58
Bousset, Wilhelm — 17, 19, 72
Bowley, James E. — 6, 92
Boyarin, Daniel — 76
Brandes, Wolfram — 20
Brandt, Samuel — 35
Brinner, William M. — 195
Brock, Sebastian — 72
Brody, Robert — 45, 133
Broido, Ethel — 56, 71, 79, 94, 113
Buber, Salomon — 154
Budge, Ernest A. Wallis — 57, 197
Busse, Heribert — 38, 80-81, 82
Buttenwieser, Moses — 31, 32, 33, 34, 35, 36, 37, 38, 40, 78, 85, 87, 89, 147

Cameron, Averil — 3, 57, 82, 88, 147
Chajes, J. H. — 92, 161
Charlesworth, James H. — 205
Chwolsohn, Daniel — 81
Cirillo, Luigi — 56
Cohen, Gerson D. — 69, 133
Cohen, Mark [R.] — 47, 101
Collins, John J. — 1, 107
Conrad, Lawrence I. — 3, 88, 147
Cook, David — 22, 24, 109, 110, 113, 160, 188
Cook, Michael — 16, 62, 78-79, 80, 81, 83, 93, 102, 156, 157, 172, 188, 205, 207
Cowley, A. E. — 51, 78
Crone, Patricia — 16, 62, 78-79, 80, 81, 83, 93, 102, 156, 157, 172, 205, 207
Cumont, Franz — 185
Cureton, William — 129, 207

Dagron, Gilbert — 3, 57, 77
Dalman, Gustav — 49, 50
Dan, Joseph — 20, 40, 45, 47, 52, 55, 68, 150, 200, 214
Denny, Frederick Mathewson — 157
Deutsch, Nathaniel — 180, 181, 184
Dietrich, Albert — 194
Donner, Fred M. — 113
Drijvers, H. J. W. — 46, 88
Drijvers, Jan Willem — 20
Drint, Adriana — 42, 201, 202

Ebied, Rifaat Y. — 43
Eisenberg, Isaac — 193
Elad, Amikam — 72, 82
Epstein, Abraham — 200, 208, 210, 212, 216, 218, 220, 221, 222, 223, 224
Epstein, J. N. — 47
Erder, Yoram — 79
Ess, Josef van — 72, 95
Even-Shmuel, Yehudah — 14, 19, 22, 31, 33, 34, 35, 40, 41, 44, 45, 48, 49, 50, 51, 54, 56, 57, 60, 77, 78, 84, 89, 92, 93, 95, 96, 98, 102, 103, 104, 105, 111, 113, 116, 121, 122, 124, 125, 128, 130, 134, 135, 144, 145, 149, 151, 153, 155, 156, 160, 161, 163, 169, 172-73, 205
Even-Shoshan, Avraham — 36

Fahd, Toufy — 139
Fakhry, Majid — 108
Fine, Steven — 164
Finkelstein, Louis — 64, 82, 159, 163, 179, 189
Firestone, Reuven — 110
Fishbane, Michael — 33, 113, 154
Fleischer, Ezra — 59
Fodor, A. — 189, 190, 194, 195
Fossum, Jarl E. — 198
Fowden, Garth — 83
Frank, Daniel — 44
Frankfurter, David — 2, 29, 30, 32, 33, 106
Friedlaender, Israel — 34, 129, 205
Friedlander, Gerald — 70
Friedmann (Ish-Shalom), Meir — 34, 36, 44, 111, 121, 129, 165, 166, 175, 204

Gardet, Louis — 108

Garnsey, P. D. A. — 13, 69
Garsoïan, Nina G. — 46
Gaster, Moses — 210
Gaudeul, Jean-Marie — 8, 9
Geiger, Abraham — 192
Gerö, Stephen — 46
Gil, Moshe — 44, 56, 57, 71, 79, 80, 81-82, 83, 94, 98, 113, 114, 133, 157, 193
Gimaret, Daniel — 207
Ginzberg, Louis — 34, 44, 50, 64, 102, 172, 175, 188-89, 195, 197, 205, 208
Goitein, Shlomo Dov — 79
Goldenberg, David M. — 165, 210
Goldish, Matt — 58
Goldziher, Ignaz/Ignác — 9, 187
Gottheil, Richard J. H. — 109
Grabar, Oleg — 52, 157
Graetz, Heinrich — 20, 35, 47, 49, 69, 70, 76, 77, 80, 81, 83, 84, 85, 87, 89, 208, 216
Griffith, Sidney H. — 46
Grossman, Avraham — 38, 64, 86, 134
Grünbaum, Max — 193, 194, 197
Gruenwald, Ithamar — 48, 179, 181, 182, 189
Grunebaum, Gustave E. von — 80

Habermann, A. M. — 200
Hamilton, Bernard — 200
Harris, J. Rendel — 88
Hary, Benjamin H. — 72
Hasson, Isaac/Izhak — 39, 108
Hayes, John L. — 72
Hayward, Robert — 57, 68, 198
Heinemann, Isaak — 104, 189
Heinemann, Joseph — 33
Heller, Bern(h)ard — 67, 68, 193, 195
Henze, Matthias — 24
Herr, Moshe David — 67, 173
Hezekiah ben Abraham — 40, 204
Higger, Michael — 70, 71, 72, 73, 74, 111, 116
Hildesheimer, Ezriel — 45
Hilgenfeld, Adolf — 202
Himmelfarb, Martha — 21, 32, 48, 51, 53, 55, 58, 64, 179
Hopkins, Simon — 41, 50, 52, 53, 54, 55, 56, 57, 94, 116, 119, 149, 184
Horovitz, H. S. — 14, 51, 92, 107, 154, 189, 190
Horowitz, Ḥ. M. — 70, 77
Houtsma, M. T. — 43
Hoyland, Robert G. — 49, 70, 71, 79, 82, 157, 207

Idel, Moshe — 52, 55
Irshai, Oded — 32, 102, 143, 172, 175

Jeffery, Arthur — 9, 188, 189
Jellinek, Adolph — 11, 23, 29, 31, 32, 33, 34, 35, 36, 37, 38, 40, 41, 44, 45, 47, 48, 50, 51, 52, 57, 61, 63, 69, 71, 77, 80, 85, 87, 88, 89, 91, 96, 97, 99, 100, 102, 103, 105, 121, 125, 128, 129, 130, 131, 132, 134, 135, 144, 145, 147, 149, 154, 155, 156, 157, 158, 159, 165, 172, 173, 180, 183, 184, 185, 189, 190, 192, 207, 210, 211, 212, 216, 218, 220, 221, 223
Jenks, Gregory C. — 17
Johns, Jeremy — 72, 95
Juynboll, G. H. A. — 72

Kaegi, Walter Emil — 13, 47, 63, 113
Kalmin, Richard — 91
Keane, A. H. — 17, 72
Khoury, Raif Georges — 7, 110
Klausner, Joseph — 53
Klein, Michael L. — 148, 191
Klein, Samuel — 60
Koenen, Ludwig — 56
Kohut, George Alexander — 8, 45
Kraus, Paul — 9, 80
Krauss, Samuel — 21, 33, 70, 71, 92, 124, 174, 188

Landauer, S. — 19, 63, 85, 133, 135, 140, 141, 142, 145, 172
Lange, Nicholas R. M. de — 13, 69
Lapin, Hayim — 164

Lask, I. M. — 129, 208
Lauterbach, Jacob Z. — 194
Leemhuis, Frederik — 108
Levene, Dan — 185
Lévi, Israel — 21, 40, 41, 45, 47, 50, 51, 52, 53, 54, 56, 57, 58, 59, 65, 72, 158, 184, 187
Levy, Jacob — 20
Lewin, B. M. — 134
Lewinstein, Keith — 160
Lewis, Bernard — 49, 72, 79, 80, 81, 82, 83, 84, 88, 89, 93, 95, 97, 98, 99, 100, 102
Lidzbarski, Mark — 46, 110
Lieberman, Saul — 82, 113
Liebes, Yehuda — 76-77
Luria, R. David — 35, 55, 67, 69, 104, 151, 161, 192

McGinn, Bernard — 17, 72, 110, 112, 188
Macler, Frédéric — 156
Madelung, Wilferd — 84, 98, 109, 189
Magdalino, Paul — 93
Makhir, R. — 121
Mandelbaum, Bernard — 37, 64, 78, 107, 111, 121, 134, 154, 161, 162, 205
Mann, Jacob — 73, 84
Margaliot, Reuven — 150, 179, 185, 194
Margulies, Mordecai — 43, 81, 146, 163
Marmorstein, Arthur — 22, 111, 113
Marx, Alexander — 41, 48
Meilicke, Christine — 189, 197
Melamed, E. Z. — 47
Mirsky, Mark Jay — 21, 51
Mitchell, David C. — 51, 78, 121, 144, 149
Momigliano, Arnaldo — 107
Monnot, Guy — 207
Montgomery, James A. — 197
Moscati, Sabatino — 96
Müller, D. H. — 200
Mulder, Martin Jan — 68

Nagel, Tilman — 192
Naveh, Joseph — 197
Neubauer, Adolf — 41, 44, 51, 73, 78, 92, 133, 212, 216, 218, 220
Newby, Gordon D. — 72, 73
Nir, Rivka — 38, 106-7, 189
Nöldeke, Theodor — 58

Ohana, M. — 68
Olster, David M. — 59, 79, 111-12, 113

Peters, F. E. — 52, 57, 82
Posner, Raphael — 217
Prawer, Joshua — 38, 39, 49, 82, 86, 98, 134
Puech, Émile — 191
Pulcini, Theodore — 9

Rabin, Chaim — 79, 109
Rabin, I. A. — 14, 51, 92, 107, 154, 189, 190
Raby, Julian — 72, 95
Raphael, Marc Lee — 68
Ratzaby, Yehuda — 12
Reardon, B. P. — 206
Reeves, John C. — 6, 68, 92, 181
Reinink, Gerrit J. — 13, 20, 70, 111, 147, 160
Ri, Andreas Su-Min — 42, 196, 197
Rieder, David — 50, 190
Robinson, Neal — 22, 110
Roselli, Amneris — 56
Rosenblatt, Samuel — 85, 133, 172
Rosenfeld, Ben-Zion — 76
Roueché, Charlotte — 93
Rubenstein, Jeffrey L. — 78
Rubin, Uri — 6, 16, 70, 79, 108, 109, 110, 157, 188, 202, 204, 206, 207
Runciman, Steven — 94
Russell, D. S. — 107

Sachau, C. E. — 9, 80, 198
Safrai, Ze᾽ev — 205
Salmon, Pierre — 49
Schäfer, Peter — 21, 32, 45, 47, 48, 55, 58, 101, 179, 180, 181, 182, 183
Schechter, Solomon — 124, 189, 197
Scher, Addai — 46
Schick, Robert — 71, 156
Schloessinger, Max — 200
Scholem, Gershom G. — 48, 179, 180, 181, 182
Schreiner, Martin — 8, 45
Segal, Alan F. — 181
Shaked, Shaul — 32, 197
Sharf, Andrew — 92
Sharon, Moshe — 71

Shinan, Avigdor — 190, 191
Silver, Abba Hillel — 72, 73
Silvestre de Sacy, A. I. — 79, 208
Sivan, Hagith — 58, 59
Smith, Jane I. — 108
Smith, William Robertson — 210
Speck, Paul — 21
Sperber, Alexander — 49, 50
Speyer, Heinrich — 188, 197
Starr, Joshua — 73, 92
Steinschneider, Moritz — 12, 24, 56, 68, 69, 74, 78, 79, 82, 83, 84, 89, 95, 103, 109, 110, 121, 134, 165, 172
Stemberger, Günter — 67
Stern, David — 21, 51
Stern, S. M. — 187
Stetkevych, Jaroslav — 82, 188
Stolte, Bernard H. — 20, 71
Stone, Michael E. — 5, 19, 32, 33, 43
Strack, H. L. — 67
Strassler, David — 81, 133, 157, 193
Stroumsa, Gedaliahu G. — 181
Strugnell, John — 19, 32, 33
Swain, J. W. — 12
Swartz, Michael D. — 45

Talmon, Shemaryahu — 33
Teugels, Lieve M. — 173
Theodor, Julius — 11, 14, 34, 117, 153, 156, 167, 194, 204, 206, 208, 216
Turtledove, Harry — 35, 59, 83, 207
Twersky, Isadore — 207

ᶜUkkāsha, Tharwat — 8
Ullendorff, Edward — 219, 220
Urbach, Ephraim E. — 97, 106, 134, 137, 143, 175, 217

VanderKam, James C. — 2
Vielhauer, Philip — 3

Waddell, W. G. — 56
Wansbrough, John — 3, 6
Wasserstein, David J. — 200, 220
Wasserstrom, Steven M. — 72, 79, 179, 181, 194, 207, 208
Weinstock, Israel — 181
Weiser, Asher — 21, 48
Weiss, I. H. — 140, 163
Werses, Shmuel — 33
Wertheimer, A. J. — 40
Wertheimer, S. A. — 40, 50, 55, 57, 58, 62, 78
Wheeler, Brannon M. — 42, 47, 193
Whittaker, C. R. — 13, 69
Wickham, Lionel R. — 43
Wieder, Naphtali — 62, 84, 99, 101, 129, 142, 145
Wilken, Robert L. — 29, 33, 36, 55, 57
Wimbush, Vincent L. — 45

Yadin, Yigael — 39
Yahalom, Joseph — 49, 191
Yassif, Eli — 41, 44, 50, 52, 55, 62, 68, 90, 121, 122, 130, 133, 180, 184, 190, 191, 205, 208, 209, 210, 211, 213, 214
Young, F. M. — 192
Yuval, Israel J. — 101

Zakkār, Suhayl — 20, 22, 23, 70, 110, 160, 188
Zuckermandel, M. S. — 87, 185
Zunz, Leopold — 40, 48, 49, 67, 68, 70, 71, 72, 74, 85, 144, 173, 200

www.ingramcontent.com/pod-product-compliance
Lightning Source LLC
Chambersburg PA
CBHW021805220426
43662CB00006B/186
9781589831025